Ford Cortina Mk II Owners Workshop Manual

by J H Haynes
Associate Member of the Guild of Motoring Writers

Models covered

1297 cc	Saloon, DeLuxe, Estate Car
1498 cc	Super, DeLuxe
1498 cc	GT
1598 cc	Super, DeLuxe, Estate Car
1598 cc	GT, 1600E

Including automatic transmission

ISBN 0 900550 14 7

© J H Haynes and Company Limited 1974   1607/014

Printed in England

J H HAYNES AND COMPANY LIMITED
SPARKFORD YEOVIL SOMERSET ENGLAND

distributed in the USA by
HAYNES PUBLICATIONS INC.
9421 WINNETAKA AVENUE
CHATSWORTH
CALIFORNIA 91311 USA

ACKNOWLEDGEMENTS

My thanks are due to the Ford Motor Company for the generous assistance given in the supply of technical material and illustrations; to Castrol Ltd., for supplying the lubrication chart. Special thanks are due to Mr. R. T. Grainger, Mr. J. R. S. Hall and Mr. L. Tooze whose experience and practical help were of great assistance in the compilation of photographs for this manual.

Champion Sparking Plug Company Limited for the provision of spark plug photographs. The bodywork repair photographs used in this manual were provided by Lloyds Industries Limited, who supply 'Turtle Wax', Holts 'Dupli Color' and a range of other Holts products.

Although every care has been taken to ensure that all the data in this manual is correct, bearing in mind that the manufacturers' current practice is to make small alterations and design changes without reclassifying the model, no liability can be accepted for damage, loss or injury caused by any errors or omissions in the information given.

PHOTOGRAPHIC CAPTIONS

& CROSS REFERENCES

For the ease of reference this book is divided into numbered chapters, sections and paragraphs. The title of each chapter is self explanatory. The sections comprise the main headings within the chapter. The paragraphs appear within each section.

The captions to the majority of photographs are given within the paragraphs of the relevant section to avoid repetition. These photographs bear the same number as the sections and paragraphs to which they refer. The photograph always appears in the same chapter as its paragraph. For example if looking through chapter ten it is wished to find the caption for photograph 9:4 refer to section 9 and then read paragraph 4.

To avoid repetition once a procedure has been described it is not normally repeated. If it is necessary to refer to a procedure already given this is done by quoting the original chapter, section and sometimes paragraph number.

The reference is given thus: Chapter No./Section No. Paragraph No. For example chapter 3, section 6 would be given as: Chapter 2/6. Chapter 2, Section 6, Paragraph 5 would be given as Chapter 2/6:5. If more than one section is involved the reference would be written: Chapter 2/6 to 7 or where the section is not consecutive 2/6 and 9. To refer to several paragraphs within a section the reference is given thus: Chapter 2/6. 2 and 4.

To refer to a section within the same chapter the chapter number is usually dropped. Thus a reference in a chapter merely reads 'see Section 8', this refers to Section 8 in that same chapter.

All references to components on the right or left-hand side are made as if looking forward to the bonnet from the rear of the car.

CORTINA SUPER ESTATE CAR

CORTINA DE LUXE ESTATE CAR

CORTINA 1300 DE LUXE

CORTINA GT

4

CONTENTS

INTRODUCTION

This is a manual for do-it-yourself minded Cortina owners. It shows how to maintain these cars in first class condition and how to carry out repairs when components become worn or break. Regular and careful maintenance is essential if maximum reliability and minimum wear are to be achieved.

The step-by-step photographs show how to deal with the major components and in conjunction with the text and exploded illustrations should make all the work quite clear - even to the novice who has never previously attempted the more complex job.

Although Cortinas are hardwearing and robust it is inevitable that their reliability and performance will decrease as they become older. Repairs and general reconditioning will become necessary if the car is to remain roadworthy. Early models requiring attention are frequently bought by the more impecunious motorist who can least afford the repair prices charged in garages, even though these prices are usually quite fair bearing in mind overheads and the high cost of capital equipment and skilled labour.

It is in these circumstances that this manual will prove to be of maximum assistance, as it is the ONLY workshop manual written from practical experience specially to help Cortina owners.

Manufacturer's official manuals are usually splendid publications which contain a wealth of technical information. Because they are issued primarily to help the manufacturers authorised dealers and distributors they tend to be written in very technical language, and tend to skip details of certain jobs which are common knowledge to garage mechanics. Owner's workshop manuals are different as they are intended primarily to help the owner. They therefore go into many of the jobs in great detail with extensive photographic support to ensure everything is properly understood so that the repair is done correctly.

Owners who intend to do their own maintenance and repairs should have a reasonably comprehensive tool kit. Some jobs require special service tools, but in many instances it is possible to get round their use with a little care and ingenuity. For example a 3½ inch diameter jubilee clip makes a most efficient and cheap piston ring compressor.

Throughout this manual ingenious ways of avoiding the use of special equipment and tools are shown. In some cases the proper tool must be used. Where this is the case a description of the tool and its correct use is included.

When a component malfunctions repairs are becoming more and more a case of replacing the defective item with an exchange rebuilt unit. This is excellent practice when a component is thoroughly worn out, but it is a waste of good money when overall the component is only half worn, and requires the replacement of but a single small item to effect a complete repair. As an example, a non-functioning dynamo can frequently be repaired quite satisfactorily just by fitting new brushes.

A further function of this manual is to show the owner how to examine malfunctioning parts; determine what is wrong, and then how to make the repair.

Given the time, mechanical do-it-yourself aptitude, and a reasonable collection of tools, this manual will show the ordinary private owner how to maintain and repair his car really economically.

ROUTINE MAINTENANCE

The maintenance instructions listed below are basically those recommended by the manufacturer. They are supplemented by additional maintenance tasks which, through practical experience, the author recommends should be carried out at the intervals suggested.

The additional tasks are indicated by an asterisk and are primarily of a preventive nature in that they will assist in eliminating the unexpected failure of a component due to fair wear and tear.

The levels of the engine oil, radiator cooling water, windscreen washer water and battery electrolyte, also the tyre pressures, should be checked weekly or more frequently if experience dictates this to be necessary. Similarly it is wise to check the level of the fluids in the clutch and brake master cylinder reservoirs at monthly intervals. If not checked at home it is advantageous to use regularly the same garage for this work as they will get to know your preferences for particular oils and the pressures at which you like to run your tyres.

6,000 miles

EVERY 6,000 MILES (or every six months if 6,000 miles are not exceeded).

1. Run the engine until it is hot and place a container of at least 8 pints capacity under the sump drain plug, undo and remove the drain plug, and allow the oil to drain for at least 10 minutes. Clean the plug and the area around the plug hole in the sump and replace the plug tightening it firmly. Remove the oil filter element, as described on page 32, and replace the element. Clean the oil filler with petrol, and its surrounding area. Refill the sump with 6 pints of the recommended grade of oil (see page 10) and clean off any oil which may have been spilt over the engine or its components. Check the oil level. The interval between oil changes should be reduced in very hot or dusty conditions or during cold weather with much slow stop/start driving.

2. The fan belt must be tight enough to drive the generator without overloading the generator and water pump bearings. The method of adjusting the fan belt is described on page 54 and is correct when the fan belt can be depressed ½ inch (13 mm) at the mid-point position between the dynamo and water pump pulley wheels.

3. Examine and adjust the distributor contact breaker points gap. Ensure that the moving contact breaker arm locking screws on the fixed contact and move it so that there is a clearance of .025 inches (.64 mm), tighten the locking screws and check the clearance again. At the same time clean any dirt from the inside of the distributor cap and clean the rotor arm. Apply two drops only of engine oil to the pad at the centre of the cam and smear very lightly with grease the cam surface. Wipe off immediately any excess oil or grease.

4. Remove the rubber filler plug from the top of the steering box and top up with a recommended oil (see page 10) and refit the plug.

5. Check the clearances of the valves and adjust if necessary. The correct procedure is described on page 42. Following adjustment, tighten the locknuts and recheck the clearances. Refit the rocker cover and check for oil leaks.

6. Inject a few drops of engine oil through the aperture at the centre of the rear plate of the generator.

7. Unscrew the clamp on top of the fuel pump, detach the glass bowl and clean the sediment from the pump body and the filter screen, using petrol. Check the condition of the gasket and renew if it is hardened or badly ridged. Replace the screen and glass bowl and tighten the clamp nut.

8. Disconnect the hose on the crankcase emission control valve, located to the rear of the carburetter, and pull the valve from the grommet. Remove the valve circlip,

The oil filter

Fan belt free movement

Adjusting the contact breaker gap

seal, valve and valve spring and wash them all in petrol. Reassemble.

9. Remove the top of the air cleaner. If it is of the gauze type wash the element in petrol, allow it to dry, and dip it in engine oil. Shake out the surplus oil and refit the element. Should the element be of paper, withdraw it, shake it out thoroughly and replace it. Refit the top cover and screw.

10 Check the condition of the battery and the tightness of the connections on the terminals. Clean off any dirt with a dry cloth.

11 Remove the plug from the top left-hand side of the gearbox and top up with a recommended oil (see page 10) until the oil just starts to pour out over the threads. Clean the plug and the area around the plug hole and replace the plug tightening it firmly. On cars fitted with automatic transmission check the level of the dipstick, with the engine idling, and top up, if necessary, with the correct fluid (page 10).

12 Remove the plug at the rear of the rear axle casing and top up with a recommended oil (see page 10) until the oil just starts to pour out over the threads. Clean the plug and the area around the plug hole and replace the plug tightening it firmly.

13 Check the rear spring 'U' bolts for tightness. If you have a torque wrench they should be tightened to 20 to 25 lb.ft.

14 Check the condition of the rear spring inserts.

15 Check the tightness of the front suspension crossmember bolts (they should be tightened to a torque of 25 to 30 lb.ft.)

16 Check the condition of the boot type gaiters on the front suspension and steering joints.

17 Jack up the front of the car, remove the road wheels, and measure the thickness of the brake pad material. If it is between 1/8th in. to 1/16th in. the pads must be renewed (further details on page 126). Jack up the rear of the car, remove the road wheels and brake drums, and examine the brake linings, brake drums and the self-adjusting mechanism for wear. Blow out the dust before reassembling.

18 Inspect the brake hoses, during the previous operation, for signs of leaks or chafing.

19 Check the front wheel hub bearings for wear, and adjust if necessary. Further details are given on page 169

20 If a cycle of rotating the road wheels has been decided upon it is wisdom to carry this out at the same time as the three previous operations.

21 Lubricate the handbrake cable at the dash panel grommet on early models, and adjust the cable if necessary.

22 Lubricate all door locks, lock cylinders, bonnet hinges and safety catch, all door and boot hinges etc, with a recommended oil. Smear a very little grease over the door striker wedges.

23 Remove the sparking plugs, clean them and set the gaps to .023 in. (.584 mm). Clean the ceramic insulators and inspect the plug leads for deterioration. Sparking plugs should be renewed at least every 12,000 miles.

24 With the engine at normal running temperature adjust the carburetter slow running screw to obtain the correct idling speed. Unscrew the mixture control screw until the engine 'hunts' and screw it in carefully until the engine runs evenly. Adjust the idling speed again if necessary. It may be necessary to repeat these operations until the engine runs satisfactorily.

25 Check the levels of the hydraulic fluid in the clutch and brake master cylinder reservoirs. Top up if necessary to within ¼ inch of the neck with the recommended fluid and replace the caps.

The filler plug on the gearbox

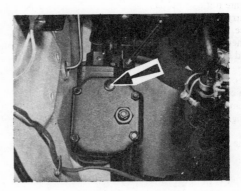

The filler plug on the steering box

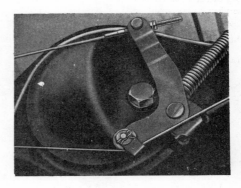

The fillerplug on the rear axle

Rear spring 'U' bolts

26 Check the operation of all lights, instruments and controls.

27 Check the seat belts for security and wear.

28 Give the bodywork and trim a thoroughly good wash and then a wax polish. If chromium cleaner is used to remove rust on any of the car's plated parts remember that the cleaner also removes parts of the chromium and therefore must be used sparingly.

29 Remove the carpets or mats and thoroughly vacuum clean the interior of the car. Beat out or vacuum clean the carpets. If the upholstery is soiled apply an upholstery cleaner with a damp sponge and wipe off with a clean cloth.

18,000 miles

EVERY 18,000 MILES (or every 18 months if 18,000 miles are not exceeded).

1. Carry out all operations listed for the 6,000 miles service.

2. Where a paper element is fitted in the air cleaner this should be discarded and a new one fitted.

3. Inspect the tyres for wear and, if misalignment of the front wheels is suspected, take the car to have the toe-in checked and adjusted at your local Ford agent.

4. Remove the front wheels and repack the front wheel bearings with grease (see page 10) as described on page 169.

*5. The exhaust system should be examined for holes or leaks and defective components replaced.

36,000 miles

EVERY 36,000 MILES (or every 3 years if 36,000 miles are not exceeded).

1. Carry out all operations listed for the 6,000 and 18,000 mile services.

2. All seals, flexible hoses throughout the braking system should be renewed, brake cylinders and pistons examined if wear is found, and brake pipes replaced if damaged. (Further details on page 123).

*3. It is a sound scheme to visit your local main agent and have the underside of the body steam cleaned. This will take about 1½ hours and cost about £4. All traces of dirt and oil will be removed and the underside can then be inspected for rust, *damaged hydraulic pipes, frayed electrical wiring and similar maladies. The car should be greased on completion of this job.

*4. At the same time the engine compartment should be cleaned in a similar manner. If steam cleaning facilities are not available then brush 'Gunk' or a similar cleaner over the whole engine and engine compartment with a stiff brush working it well in where there is an accumulation of oil and dirt. Do not paint the ignition system but protect it with oily rags. As the Gunk is washed away it will take with it all traces of oil and dirt, leaving the engine looking clean and bright.

*5. Drain and refill the gearbox and rear axle with the appropriate grade of oil (page 10). This is recommended so that any minute particles of metal are carried away in the old oil so helping to minimise wear.

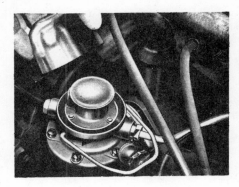

The fuel filter

Generator rear bearing

Adjusting valve clearances

RECOMMENDED LUBRICANTS

COMPONENT		SOME MANUFACTURERS
FRONT WHEEL BEARINGS	Lithium base grease	Ford Part No.EMIC-3
BRAKES AND CLUTCH	Brake fluid	Ford Part No.ME-3833-F
STEERING GEAR	S.A.E.90 E.P.gear oil	Mobil,Shell,Esso,BP,Castrol,Duckhams,Texaco
REAR AXLE	S.A.E.90 Hypoid oil	Mobil,Shell,Esso,BP,Castrol,Duckhams,Texaco
ENGINE)	Ford Specification ESE-M2C101-B	
GENERATOR) SAE Grade	Use between	
DISTRIBUTOR) 5W-20W, 5W-30.	-40⁰ to + 32⁰F	
10W-30	-10⁰ to + 70⁰F... ...	Amoco,Esso,Fina,Texaco,Shell
10W-40	-10⁰ to + 90⁰F...	B.P.
10W-50	-10⁰ to + 120⁰F	Mobil
20W-40	+25⁰ to + 90⁰F	
20W-50	+32⁰ to + 120⁰F	Amoco,BP,Duckhams,Esso,Mobil,Fina,Shell
20W-50 'All season'	+25⁰ to + 120⁰F	Castrol GTX, Texaco
10W	-10⁰ to + 32⁰F	
20W-20	+25⁰ to + 70⁰F.. ...	Amoco, Esso, Texaco
30...	+32⁰ to + 90⁰F	
40...	+50⁰ to + 120⁰F	
GEARBOX	S.A.E.80 gear oil	Mobil,Shell,Esso,BP,Castrol,Duckhams,Texaco
AUTOMATIC TRANSMISSION	Fluid...	Ford Part No.M-2C33-F

Additionally a supply of grease, similar to Ford Part No.68 AB-19D533-AA, is required for the distributor cam, door striker wedges etc. A light oil, such as Mobil Handy Oil or Castrol Everyman oil, is required for door and bonnet hinges and locks, pivots etc.

10

LUBRICATION CHART
EXPLANATION OF SYMBOLS

 CASTROL GTX. An ultra high performance motor oil incorporating for the first time every necessary high performance quality in one oil. Approved for the engine in summer and winter.

 CASTROL HYPOY 90 EP GEAR OIL. A powerful extreme pressure lubricant approved for the rear axle and steering box. CASTROL HYPOY LIGHT 80 EP GEAR OIL is approved for the gearbox.

 CASTROL LM GREASE. A high melting point lithium based grease for use wherever indicated on the chart.

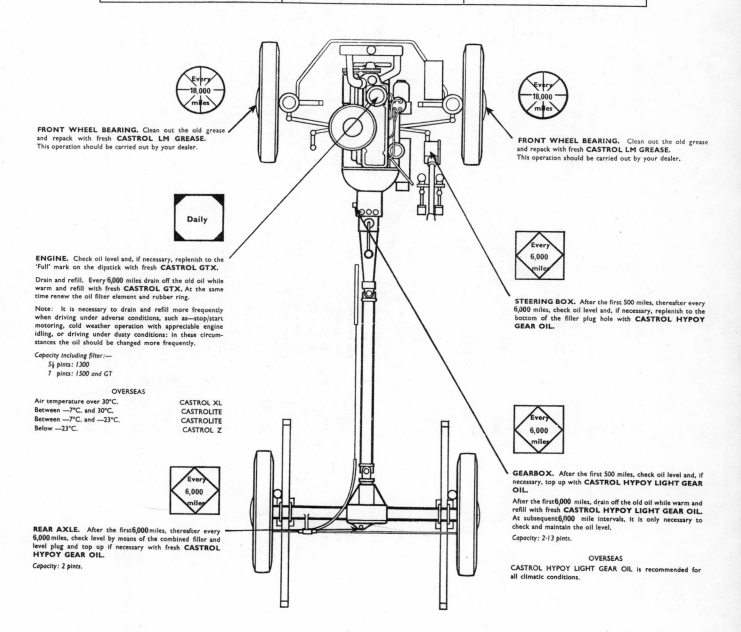

FRONT WHEEL BEARING. Clean out the old grease and repack with fresh **CASTROL LM GREASE.** This operation should be carried out by your dealer.

FRONT WHEEL BEARING. Clean out the old grease and repack with fresh **CASTROL LM GREASE.** This operation should be carried out by your dealer.

ENGINE. Check oil level and, if necessary, replenish to the 'Full' mark on the dipstick with fresh **CASTROL GTX.**

Drain and refill. Every 6,000 miles drain off the old oil while warm and refill with fresh **CASTROL GTX.** At the same time renew the oil filter element and rubber ring.

Note: It is necessary to drain and refill more frequently when driving under adverse conditions, such as—stop/start motoring, cold weather operation with appreciable engine idling, or driving under dusty conditions: in these circumstances the oil should be changed more frequently.

Capacity including filter:—
5½ pints: 1300
7 pints: 1500 and GT

OVERSEAS

Air temperature over 30°C.	CASTROL XL
Between —7°C. and 30°C.	CASTROLITE
Between —7°C. and —23°C.	CASTROLITE
Below —23°C.	CASTROL Z

STEERING BOX. After the first 500 miles, thereafter every 6,000 miles, check oil level and, if necessary, replenish to the bottom of the filler plug hole with **CASTROL HYPOY GEAR OIL.**

GEARBOX. After the first 500 miles, check oil level and, if necessary, top up with **CASTROL HYPOY LIGHT GEAR OIL.**

After the first 6,000 miles, drain off the old oil while warm and refill with fresh **CASTROL HYPOY LIGHT GEAR OIL.** At subsequent 6,000 mile intervals, it is only necessary to check and maintain the oil level.

Capacity: 2·13 pints.

OVERSEAS
CASTROL HYPOY LIGHT GEAR OIL is recommended for all climatic conditions.

REAR AXLE. After the first 6,000 miles, thereafter every 6,000 miles, check level by means of the combined filler and level plug and top up if necessary with fresh **CASTROL HYPOY GEAR OIL.**

Capacity: 2 pints.

ORDERING SPARE PARTS

Always order genuine FoMoCo spare parts from your nearest Ford dealer or local garage. Authorised dealers carry a comprehensive stock of GENUINE PARTS and can supply most items 'over the counter'.

When ordering new parts it is essential to give full details of your car to the storeman. He will want to know the model, type, e.g., 1600 GT and the vehicle number and these are given together with other useful details on a plate which is riveted to the top of the engine side apron panel. If possible take along the part to be replaced.

If you want to retouch the paintwork you can obtain an exact match (providing the original paint has not faded) by quoting the paint code number in conjunction with the vehicle number.

VEHICLE IDENTIFICATION PLATE

A TYPE OF DRIVE. R or 1 Right-hand drive. L or 2 Left-hand drive.

B ENGINE TYPE. Code A 1300 c.c. HC with LC distributor. B 1300 LC. C 1300 c.c. with normal distributor D 1500 c.c. HC with LC distributor. E 1500 c.c. LC. F 1500 c.c. HC with normal distributor. G 1500 c.c. GT. J 1300 c.c. HC. K 1300 c.c. LC. L 1600 c.c. HC. M 1600 c.c. LC. N 1600 c.c. GT.

C TYPE OF TRANSMISSION. A Floor and remote change. B Column change. C Automatic.

D TYPE OF AXLE. A 3.900:1 ratio. B 4.125:1 ratio. C 4.444:1 ratio.

E TRIM. The code, consisting of a letter and three figures, indicates the colour and type of trim.

F SVC indicates when a vehicle is shipped unassembled from factory of origin for assembly at another.

G VEHICLE NUMBER consists of a combination of letters and numbers, referring to factories, body type and sequence number etc., and can be interpreted by a Ford dealer.

H PAINT CODE consisting of letters, indicating colours and type or original paint, and this can be interpreted by a Ford dealer.

CHAPTER ONE

ENGINE

CONTENTS

SPECIFICATIONS
ENGINE SPECIFICATIONS & DATA - 1297 c.c. (Oct '66-Sept '67)

Engine - General

Type	4 cylinder in line pushrod operated O.H.V.
Bore	3.1878 in. (80.970 mm.)
Stoke	2.480 in. (62.99 mm.)
Cubic capacity	1,297 c.c. (79.17 cu.in.)

Compression ratio: High C	9.0 to 1
Low C	7.5 to 1
Compression pressure: High C	175 lb/sq.in. (12.30 kg/sq.cm) at 375 r.p.m.
Low C	155 lb/sq.in. (10.90 kg/sq.cm) at 450 r.p.m.
Maximum B.H.P. : High C	54.0 (nett) at 5,000 r.p.m.
Low C	52.0 (nett) at 5,000 r.p.m.
Maximum Torque: High C	70.5 lb.ft. (9.74 kg.m) at 2,750 r.p.m.
Low C	67.0 lb.ft. (9.26 kg.m) at 2,500 r.p.m.
Engine idle speed - Optimum..	580 to 620 r.p.m.
Location of No.1 cylinder	Next to radiator
Firing order...	1,2,4,3
Engine mountings	3 - one each side of engine, one on op of gearbox extension

Camshaft & Camshaft Bearings

Camshaft drive	Single roller chain from crankshaft
Camshaft bearings	Three steel back white metal replaceable bushes
Bearing oversize available...	.020 in. (.513 mm) oversize on o/d. Standard i/d
Camshaft journal diameter	1.5597 to 1.5605 in. (39.617 to 39.637 mm)
Camshaft bearing internal diameter..	1.5615 to 1.5620 in. (39.662 to 39.675 mm)
Diametrical bearing clearance	.001 to .0023 in. (.025 to .058 mm)
End float	.0025 to .0075 in. (.064 to .191 mm)
Thrust plate thickness	.176 to .178 in. (4.47 to 4.52 mm)
Maximum cam lift - Inlet...	.2108 in. (5.350 mm)
- Exhaust	.2176 in. (5.523 mm)
Cam heel to toe dimension - Inlet	1.3308 in. (33.802 mm)
- Exhaust	1.3176 in. (33.467 mm)

Connecting Rods & Big & Little End Bearings

Connecting rod : Type..	'H' Section steel forging
Length between centres	4.324 to 4.326 in. (109.83 to 109.88 mm)
Big end bearings : Type	Shell
Big end bearings : Material	Steel backed copper/lead, lead/bronze or aluminium/tin
Big end bore..	2.0825 to 2.0830 in. (52.896 to 52.908 mm)
Bearing liner wall thickness	.0719 to .07225 in. (1.8269 to 1.8347 mm)
Undersize bearings available	-.002, -.010, -.020, -.030, -.040 in.
	(-.05, -.25, -.51, -.76, -1.02 mm)
Small end bush : Type..	Steel backed bronze
Small end bush internal diameter	.8121 to .8125 in. (20.630 to 20.638 mm)

Crankshaft & Main Bearings

Number of bearings	5
Main bearing journal diameter - BLUE...	2.1253 to 2.1257 in. (53.983 to 53.993 mm)
- RED	2.1257 to 2.1261 in. (53.993 to 54.003 mm)
- GREEN	2.1153 to 2.1157 in. (53.729 to 53.739 mm)
- YELLOW..	2.1157 to 2.1161 in. (53.739 to 53.749 mm)
Regrind diameters - .010 in. (.25 mm)...	2.1152 to 2.1157 in. (53.726 to 53.739 mm)
- .020 in. (.51 mm)...	2.1055 to 2.1060 in. (53.480 to 53.492 mm)
- .030 in. (.76 mm)...	2.0955 to 2.0960 in. (53.226 to 53.238 mm)
Main journal length - Front	1.219 to 1.239 in. (30.95 to 31.47 mm)
- Centre...	1.247 to 1.249 in. (31.67 to 31.73 mm)
- Rear	1.308 to 1.318 in. (33.22 to 33.48 mm)
- Intermediates..	1.273 to 1.283 in. (32.33 to 32.59 mm)
Crankshaft end thrust	Taken by thrust washers at centre main bearing
Crankshaft end float	.003 to .011 in. (.08 to .28 mm)
Main bearing material...	Steel backed white metal liners
Undersize bearings available	-.010, -.020, -.030 in.
	(-.25, -.51, -.76 mm)

Cylinder Block

Type	Cylinder cast integral with top half of crankcase
Water jackets	Full length
Height, sump face to head face	7.224 to 7.229 in. (183.5 to 183.6 mm)
Cylinder liners available	Standard .020 in. (.51 mm) o/s on O.D.
Bore for cylinder liners	3.3115 to 3.125 in. (84.112 to 84.138 mm) Standard

Cylinder Head

Type	Cast iron with vertical valves
Port arrangement	Separate inlet and exhaust ports on same side
Number of ports - Inlet	4
- Exhaust	4

Gudgeon Pin
Type ... ...   Fully floating retained by end circlips
Material ... ...   Machined seamless steel tubing
Length ... ...   2.80 to 2.81 in. (71.1 to 71.4 mm)
Fit in piston... ... ...   .0001 to .0003 (.0025 to .0076 mm)
Fit in small end bush ... ...   .0001 to .0003 (.0025 to .0076 mm)

Lubrication System
Type ... ...   Pressure and splash. Wet sump
Oil filter ... ...   Full flow with replaceable element
Oil filter capacity ... ...   2/3rds pint (.8 US pint, .38 litres)
Sump capacity ... ...   5½ pints (6.6 US pints, 3.12 litres)
Oil pump type ... ...   Eccentric rotor or sliding vane

Eccentric Rotor Type
Capacity... ... ...   2 gallons per min.(2.4 US galls, 9.085 litres) at 2,000 r.p.m.
Pump body bore diameter ... ...   .500 to .501 in. (12.70 to 12.73 mm)
Drive shaft diameter ... ...   .498 to .4985 in. (12.65 to 12.66 mm)
Drive shaft to body clearance ... ...   .0015 to .003 in. (.038 to .076 mm)
Inner and outer rotor clearance ... ...   .006 in. (.15 mm) maximum
Outer rotor and housing clearance ... ...   .010 in. (.25 mm) maximum
Inner and outer rotor end float ... ...   .005 in. (.13 mm) maximum

Sliding Vane Type
Capacity... ... ...   2.8 galls per min.(3.36 US galls,12.719 litres)at 2,000 r.p.m
Pump body bore diameter ... ...   .500 to .501 in. (12.70 to 12.73 mm)
Drive shaft diameter ... ...   .498 to .4955 in. (12.65 to 12.66 mm)
Drive shaft to body clearance ... ...   .0015 to .003 in. (.003 in. (.038 to .076 mm)
Vane clearance in rotor ... ...   .005 in. (.13 mm) maximum
Rotor and vane end float... ... ...   .005 in. (.13 mm) maximum

Normal oil pressure ... ...   35 to 40 lb/sq.in. (2.46 to 2.81 kg/sq.cm.)

Pistons
Type ... ...   Solid skirt with thermal slots
Material ... ...   Aluminium alloy, tin plated
Clearance in cylinder ... ...   .0005 to .0011 in. (.013 to .028 mm)
Number of rings ... ...   3. Two compression, one oil control
Width of Ring Grooves
- Compression rings ... ...   .0796 to .0806 in. (2.022 to 2.047 mm)
- Oil control ring ... ...   .1578 to .1588 in. (4.008 to 4.034 mm)
Gudgeon pin bore ... ...   Graded
- Grade - white ... ...   .8117 to .8118 in. (20.617 to 20.620 mm)
     - red... ... ...   .8118 to .8119 in. (20.620 to 20.622 mm)
     - yellow.. ... ...   .8119 to .8120 in. (20.622 to 20.625 mm)
     - blue ... ...   .8120 to .8121 in. (20.625 to 20.627 mm)
Piston oversizes available ... ...   +.0025 in., +.005 in., +.015 in., +.030 in., +.045 in.
                                                              (+.064, +.13, +.38, +.76, +1.14 mm)

Piston Rings
Top compression ring... ... ...   Tapered cast iron, chromium plated
Lower compression ring ... ...   Cast iron, stepped on lower face
Top ring width ... ...   .077 to .078 in. (1.96 to 1.98 mm)
Lower ring width ... ...   .077 to .078 in. (1.96 to 1.98 mm)
Top ring fitted gap... ... ...   .009 to .014 in. (.23 to .36 mm)
Lower ring fitted gap ... ...   .009 to .014 in. (.23 to .36 mm)
Groove clearance ... ...   .0016 to .0036 in. (.041 to .091 mm)
Oil control ring... ... ...   'Micro-land' cast iron slotted scraper
Oil control ring - width ... ...   .155 to .156 in. (3.94 to 3.96 mm)
Oil control ring - fitted gap ... ...   .009 to .014 in. (.23 to .36 mm)
Groove clearance ... ...   .0018 to .0038 in. (.046 to .097 mm)

Tappets
Type ... ...   Barrel with flat base
Stem diameter ... ...   .4360 to .4365 in. (11.072 to 11.085 mm)
Length ... ...   1.85 in. (47.0 mm)

Rocker Gear
Rocker shaft diameter.. ... ...   .623 to .624 in. (15.83 to 15.85 mm)
Rocker bore... ... ...   .625 to .626 in. (15.88 to 15.90 mm)

Shaft clearance in rocker...	.001 to .0035 in. (.03 to .09 mm)
Rocker arm ratio	1.54 to 1

Valves

Head diameter - Inlet	1.432 to 1.442 in. (36.37 to 36.63 mm)
- Exhaust	1.183 to 1.193 in. (30.05 to 30.30 mm)
Valve seat angle..	45° to 45° 15'
Stem diameter - Inlet	.3095 to .3105 in. (7.861 to 7.887 mm)
- Exhaust	.3086 to .3096 in. (7.838 to 7.864 mm)
Stem to guide clearance - Inlet	.0008 to .0030 in. (.020 to .08 mm)
- Exhaust	.0017 to .0039 in. (.043 to .099 mm)
Valve lift - Inlet	.315 in. (8.00 mm)
- Exhaust	.319 in. (8.10 mm)

Valve stem to rocker arm clearance (cold)	
- Inlet..	.008 in. to .010 in. (.20 to .25 mm)
- Exhaust..	.018 in. to .020 in. (.46 to .51 mm)

Valve Guides

Type	Machined in cylinder head, guide bushes available
Bore for guide bushes...	.4383 to .4391 in. (11.133 to 11.153 mm)
Valve guide inside diameter	.3113 to .3125 in. (7.907 to 7.938 mm)

Valve Timing

- Inlet valve : Opens	17° B.T.D.C.
: Closes	51° A.B.D.C.
- Exhaust valve : Opens	51° B.B.D.C.
: Closes	17° A.T.D.C.
Timing marks	Lines on camshaft & crankshaft sprockets

Valve Springs

Type	Single valve springs
Free length	1.48 in. (37.6 mm)
Fitted length (valve closed)	1.263 in. (32.08 mm)
Load at fitted length	44 to 49 lb. (19.96 to 22.23 kg.)
Total number of coils...	6

TORQUE WRENCH SETTINGS

Big end bolts	25 to 30 lb/ft. (3.46 to 4.15 kg.m)
Camshaft sprocket...	12 to 15 lb/ft. (1.66 to 2.07 kg.m)
Camshaft thrust plate...	5 to 7 lb/ft. (.69 to .97 kg.m)
Crankshaft pulley	24 to 28 lb/ft. (3.32 to 3.87 kg.m)
Cylinder head bolts	65 to 70 lb/ft. (8.98 to 9.67 kg.m)
Engine front cover	5 to 7 lb/ft. (.69 to .97 kg.m)
Flywheel securing bolts	45 to 50 lb/ft. (6.22 to 6.91 kg.m)
Main bearing bolts...	55 to 60 lb/ft. (7.60 to 8.29 kg.m)
Manifold bolts & nuts...	15 to 18 lb.ft. (2.07 to 2.49 kg.m)
Oil filter centre bolt	12 to 15 lb.ft. (1.66 to 2.07 kg.m)
Oil pump..	12 to 15 lb.ft. (1.66 to 2.07 kg.m)
Rear oil seal retainer	12 to 15 lb.ft. (1.66 to 2.07 kg.m)
Rocker cover	5 to 7 lb.ft. (.69 to .97 kg.m)
Rocker shaft	17 to 22 lb.ft. (2.35 to 3.04 kg.m)
Sump...	6 to 9 lb.ft. (.83 to 1.11 kg.m)
Sump drain plug	20 to 25 lb.ft. (2.76 to 3.46 kg.m)
Tappet adjusting screw locknut...	8 to 12 lb.ft. (1.11 to 1.66 kg.m)

ENGINE SPECIFICATIONS & DATA - 1500 c.c. (Oct.'66-Sept '67)

The engine specification is identical to the 1297 c.c. type except for the differences listed below.

Engine - General

Stroke..	2.867 in. (72.82 mm)
Cubic capacity	1500 c.c. (91.54 cu.in.)
Compression ratio - G.T	9 to 1
Compression pressure - High C	185 lb/sq.in. (13.01 kg/sq.cm) at 400 r.p.m.
- Low C	155 lb/sq.in. (10.90 kg/sq.cm) at 425 r.p.m.
- G.T	185 lb/sq.in. (13.01 kg/sq.cm) at 400 r.p.m.
Maximum BHP - High C	61.5 (nett) at 4,700 r.p.m.
- Low C	57.5 (nett) at 4,700 r.p.m.
- G.T	78.0 (nett) at 5,200 r.p.m.
Maximum torque - High C	83.5 lb/ft. (11.54 kg.m) at 2,500 r.p.m.

- Low C	80.0 lb/ft. (11.06 kg.m) at 2,700 r.p.m.
- G.T	91.0 lb/ft. (12.58 kg.m) at 3,600 r.p.m.
Engine speed - Optimum - G.T	680 to 720 r.p.m.

Maximum Torque

- High C	91.5 lb/ft. (12.64 kg.m) at 2,500 r.p.m.
- E.C. 8.5 to 1	86 lb/ft. (12.0 kg.m) at 2,500 r.p.m.
- Low C	87 lb/ft. (12.1 kg.m) at 2,500 r.p.m.
- G.T	96 lb/ft. (13.26 kg.m) at 3,600 r.p.m.
Engine idle speed - Optimum	
- G.T	680 to 720 r.p.m.
- E.C. 8.5 to 1	700 to 740 r.p.m.

Camshaft & Camshaft Bearings
  Maximum cam lift

G.T only - Inlet	.2309 in. (5.865 mm)
- Exhaust	.2321 in. (5.905 mm)

  Cam heel to toe dimension

G.T only - Inlet	1.3109 in. (33.277 mm)
- Exhaust	1.3121 in. (33.327 mm)

Connecting Rods & Big & Little End Bearings

Length between centres	4.799 to 4.801 in. (121.90 to 121.95 mm)

Crankshaft & Main Bearings

Main bearing material - G.T only	Steel backed copper/lead or lead bronze liners

Cylinder Block

Height sump face to head face	7.891 to 7.896 in. (200.4 to 200.6 mm)

Lubrication System

Sump capacity	7 pints (8.4 US pints, 3.97 litres)

Pistons

Clearance in cylinder - G.T only	.0008 to .0014 in. (.020 to .036 mm)

Valves

Head diameter - G.T only - Inlet	1.405 to 1.415 in. (35.69 to 35.94 mm)
- Exhaust	1.240 to 1.250 in. (31.50 to 31.75 mm)
Valve stem to rocker arm clearance (cold)	
G.T only - Inlet...	.011 to .013 in. (.28 to .33 mm)
- Exhaust	.021 to .023 in. (.53 to .58 mm)

Valve Timing

G.T only - Inlet valve opens	27° B.T.D.C.
closes	65° A.B.D.C.
- Exhaust valve opens	65° B.B.D.C.
closes	27° A.T.D.C.

ENGINE SPECIFICATIONS & DATA - 1297 c.c. (Sept '67 on)

The engine specification is identical to the earlier Oct '66 to Sept '67 1297 c.c. engine except for the differences listed below.

Engine - General

Bore	3.1881 in. (80.978 mm)
Compression ratio - High C	9 to 1
- Low C	8 to 1
Compression pressure - High C	168 lb/sq.in. (11.81 kg/sq.cm) at 360 r.p.m.
- Low C	157 lb/sq.in. (11.04 kg/sq.cm) at 360 r.p.m.
Maximum B.H.P - High C	58 (nett) at 5,000 r.p.m.
- Low C	53.5 (nett) at 5,000 r.p.m.
Maximum torque - High C	71.5 lb/ft. (9.88 kg.m) at 2,500 r.p.m.
- Low C	68.0 lb/ft. (9.45 kg.m) at 2,500 r.p.m.

Connecting Rods & Big & Little End Bearings

Length between centres	4.133 to 4.135 in. (104.98 to 105.03 mm)

Cylinder Head

Port arrangement	Separate inlet & exhaust ports on opposite side

Lubrication System
    Sump capacity ... ...   6.4 pints (7.7 US pints, 3.63 litres)

Pistons
    Combustion bowl depth - High C ... ...   .540 to .548 in. (13.72 to 13.92 mm)
                       - Low C ... ...   .640 to .648 in. (16.26 to 16.46 mm)

Gudgeon Pin Bore
    Grade - W.. ... ...   .8120 to .8121 in. (20.625 to 20.627 mm)
         - One spot ... ...   .8117 to .8118 in. (20.617 to 20.620 mm)
         - Two spot ... ...   .8118 to .8119 in. (20.620 to 20.622 mm)
         - Three spot... ... ...   .8119 to .8120 in. (20.622 to 20.625 mm)
    Piston oversizes available ... ...   +.0025, +.015. +.030 in.
                                                (+.064, +.38, +.76 mm)
    Clearance in cylinder ... ...   .0019 to .0025 in. (.0483 to .0635 mm)

Valves
    Head diameter - Inlet ... ...   1.405 to 1.415 in. (35..69 to 35.94 mm)
                   - Exhaust ... ...   1.240 to 1.250 in. (31.50 to 31.75 mm)

ENGINE SPECIFICATIONS & DATA - 1598 c.c. (Sept '67 on)

The engine specification is identical to the 1297 c.c. engine (Sept '67 on) except for the differences listed below.

Engine - General
    Stroke.. ... ...   3.056 in. (77.62 mm)
    Cubic capacity ... ...   1598 c.c. (97.51 cu.in.)
    Compression ratio:
    High C ... ...   9 to 1
    Emission controlled (E.C.) ... ...   8.5 to 1
    Low C ... ...   8 to 1
    G.T. ... ...   9 to 1
    Compression pressure:
    High C & G.T ... ...   188 lb/sq.in. (13.22 kg/sq.cm) at 300 r.p.m.
    E.C. 8.5 to 1.. ... ...: ... ... :.. ... ...   180 lb/sq.in. (12.65 kg/sq.cm) at 300 r.p.m.
    Low C ... ...   170 Ib/sq.in. (11.95 kg/sq.cm) at 300 r.p.m.

Maximum B.H.P.
    High C ... ...   71 (nett) at 5,000 r.p.m.
    E.C. 8.5 to 1.. ... ...   62.5 (nett) at 5,000 r.p.m.
    Low C ... ...   69.5 (nett) at 5,000 r.p.m.
    G.T ... ...   88 (nett) at 5,400 r.p.m.

Camshaft & Camshaft Bearings
    Maximum cam lift
                 - G.T only - Inlet ... ...   .2309 in. (5.865 mm)
                          - Exhaust ... ...   .2321 in. (5.905 mm)
    Cam heel to toe dimension
                 - G.T only - Inlet ... ...   1.3109 in. (33.277 mm)
                          Exhaust ... ...   1.3121 in. (33.327 mm)

Connecting Rods & Big & Little End Bearings
    Length between centres ... ...   4.927 to 4.929 in. (125.15 to 125.20 mm)

Crankshaft & Main Bearings
    Main bearing material - G.T only ... ...   Steel backed copper/lead or lead/bronze or aluminium/tin liners

Cylinder Block
    Height sump face to head face ... ...   8.326 to 8.331 in. (211.48 to 211.61 mm)

Lubrication System
    Sump capacity ... ...   7.2 pints (8.6 US pints, 4.09 litres)

Pistons
    Combustion bowl depth
     - High C & G.T ... ...   .496 to .504 in. (12.60 to 12.80 mm)
     - E.C. 8.5 to 1 ... ...   .554 to .546 in. (14.07 to 13.87 mm)
     - Low C ... ...   .599 to .607 in. (15.22 to 15.42 mm)
    Clearance in cylinder ... ...   .0013 to .0019 in. (.0330 to .0483 mm)

Valves

Head diameter - Inlet	1.497 to 1.507 in. (38.02 to 38.28 mm)
- Exhaust	1.240 to 1.250 in. (31.50 to 31.75 mm)
Valve lift - G.T only - Inlet	.3420 in. (8.69 mm)
- Exhaust	.3367 in. (8.55 mm)

Valve stem to rocker arm clearance (cold)

G.T only - Inlet...	.011 to .013 in. (.28 to .33 mm)
- Exhaust	.021 to .023 in. (.53 to .58 mm)

TORQUE WRENCH SETTINGS
(1297 c.c. & 1598 c.c. engines where different from pre Sept '67 settings)

Big end bolts	30 to 35 lb/ft. (4.15 to 4.84 kg.m)
Camshaft thrust plate...	2.5 to 3.5 lb/ft. (.35 to .48 kg.m)
Main bearing nuts	65 to 70 lb/ft. (8.98 to 9.67 kg.m)
Rocker cover	2.5 to 3.5 lb/ft. (.35 to .48 kg.m)

1. GENERAL DESCRIPTION

The engine fitted may be any one of six different units depending on year and model, but in each case they are of the in line four cylinder overhead valve type. The engine is supported by rubber mountings in the interests of silence and lack of vibration.

Fitted from October 1966 to September 1967 were engines known as the 1300, 1500 and 1500 G.T. of 1297 c.c. and 1498 c.c. respectively. On these units the inlet and exhaust ports are both on the same side of the cylinder head. From September 1967 engines known as the 1300, 1600 and 1600 G.T. were fitted of 1297 c.c. and 1598 c.c. capacity. The cylinder head on these models is of the crossflow type with inlet ports on one side and exhaust ports on the other.

The bore on all models is identical the variations in capacity being achieved by different crankshaft strokes. Excluding the cylinder head and pistons all six engines are identical in design and differ only in the size of some of the components used, e.g. the crankshaft and block.

Two valves per cylinder are mounted vertically in the cast iron cylinder head and run in integral valve guides. They are operated by rocker arms, pushrods and tappets from the camshaft which is located at the base of the cylinder bores in the right-hand side of the engine. The correct valve stem to rocker arm pad clearance can be obtained by the adjusting screws in the ends of the rocker arms.

On pre-September 1967 models the cylinder head has four inlet and four exhaust ports on the left-hand side. Post-1967 models which make use of the crossflow cylinder head have four inlet ports on the right-hand side and four exhaust on the left. High or low compression ratios may be used.

The cylinder block and the upper half of the crankcase are cast together. The height of the block varies depending on the stroke of the crankshaft fitted. The open half of the crankcase is closed by a pressed steel sump.

The pistons are made from anodised aluminium alloy with solid skirts. Two compression rings and a slotted oil control ring are fitted. The gudgeon pin is retained in the little end of the connecting rod by circlips. On crossflow engines the combustion chamber is machined in the piston crown and a different piston is used for each engine capacity and compression ratio. The bearings are all steel backed and may be of copper/lead, lead/bronze, or aluminium tin.

At the front of the engine a single chain drives the camshaft via the camshaft and crankshaft chain wheels which are enclosed in a pressed steel cover.

The chain is tensioned automatically by a snail cam which bears against a pivoted tensioner arm. This presses against the non driving side of the chain so avoiding any lash or rattle.

The camshaft is supported by three renewable bearings located directly in the cylinder block. Endfloat is controlled by a plate bolted to the front of the cylinder block and positioned between the front bearing journal and the chain wheel flange.

The statically and dynamically balanced forged steel crankshaft is supported by five renewable thinwall shell main bearings which are in turn supported by substantial webs which form part of the crankcase. Crankshaft endfloat is controlled by semi-circular thrust washers located on each side of the centre main bearing. The main bearings fitted are of the white metal type except on the G.T. when they are of the copper/lead or lead/bronze sort.

The centrifugal water pump and radiator cooling fan are driven, together with the dynamo, from the crankshaft pulley wheel by a rubber/fabric belt. The distributor is mounted towards the front of the right-hand side of the cylinder block and advances and retards the ignition timing by mechanical and vacuum means. The distributor is driven at half crankshaft speed from a skew gear on the camshaft.

The oil pump is mounted externally on the right-hand side of the engine under the distributor and is driven by a short shaft from the same skew gear on the camshaft as for the distributor and may be of the eccentric bi-rotor or sliding vane type.

Bolted to the flange on the end of the crankshaft is the flywheel to which is bolted in turn the clutch. Attached to the rear of the engine is the gearbox bellhousing.

2. ROUTINE MAINTENANCE

1. Once a week or daily if experience dictates this necessary remove the dipstick, wipe it, replace it and remove it again to check the engine oil level which should be at the 'FULL' mark. Top up if the oil level is at the 'FILL' mark with one of the recommended lubricants on page 10. On no account allow the oil level to drop into the very bottom portion of the dipstick marked 'DANGER'. The amount of oil needed to bring the level up from the 'FILL' to the 'FULL' marks is 1½ pints. Do not overfill as the oil will only be wasted.

2. Every 6,000 miles run the engine till it is hot; place a container with a capacity of at least 8 pints under the sump drain plug; undo and remove the drain plug; and allow at least 10 minutes for all the oil to drain. While the oil is draining renew the filter element as described in Section 24.

3. Clean the drain plug, ensure the washer is in place, and return the plug to the sump, tightening the plug

firmly. Refill the sump with 5½ pints of the recommended grade of oil (see page 10 for details).

4. In very hot or dusty conditions, or in cold weather with much slow stop/start driving, with much use of the choke, it is beneficial to change the engine oil every 3,000 miles.

5. Every 6,000 miles the following operations should also be made:-

a) Adjust the fan belt tension as described in Chapter 2, Section 10.

b) Check and adjust the valve to rocker arm clearances as described in Section 70.

c) Clean the oil filler cap on early engines, and the crankcase emission valve on later models See Section 23.

3. MAJOR OPERATIONS WITH ENGINE IN PLACE

The following major operations can be carried out to the engine with it in place in the body frame:-

1. Removal and replacement of the cylinder head assembly.

2. Removal and replacement of the sump.

3. Removal and replacement of the big end bearings.

4. Removal and replacement of the pistons and connecting rods.

5. Removal and replacement of the timing chain and gears.

6. Removal and replacement of the oil pump.

7. Removal and replacement of the engine front mountings.

8. Removal and replacement of the engine/gearbox rear mounting.

4. MAJOR OPERATIONS WITH ENGINE REMOVED

The following major operations can be carried out with engine out of the body frame and on the bench or floor:-

1. Removal and replacement of the main bearings.

2. Removal and replacement of the crankshaft.

3. Removal and replacement of the flywheel.

4. Removal and replacement of the crankshaft rear bearing oil seal.

5. Removal and replacement of the camshaft.

5. METHOD OF ENGINE REMOVAL

The engine complete with gearbox can be lifted as a unit from the engine compartment. Alternatively the engine and gearbox can be split at the front of the bellhousing, a stand or jack placed under the gearbox to provide additional support, and the engine lifted out. The easiest method of engine removal is to remove the engine leaving the gearbox in place in the car. If the engine and gearbox are removed as a unit they have to be lifted out at a very steep angle which can be difficult.

6. ENGINE REMOVAL WITHOUT GEARBOX

1. The average do-it-yourself owner should be able to remove the engine fairly easily in about 3½ hours. It is essential to have a good hoist, and two strong axle stands if an inspection pit is not available. Engine removal will be much easier if you have a friend to help you.

2. Open the bonnet and undo and remove the two bolts and washers from the bonnet side of each of the two hinges (photo). Lift the bonnet off and place it somewhere it will not fall over or be bumped into.

3. Open the water drain plug on the left-hand side of the underside of the radiator and with a spanner turn on the water drain plug in the left-hand rear side of the block (photo). Do not drain the water in your garage or the place where the engine is going to be removed if receptacles are not at hand to catch the water. Re-use the water if it is full of anti-freeze. Drain the engine oil by removing the drain plug on the bottom of the sump and drain the oil from the gearbox if the latter is being removed with the engine.

4. It is best to remove the battery from the engine compartment. Undo the winged nut which secures the clamp (photo) to the ledge on the base of the battery.

5. Disconnect the main lead and then the earth lead from the top of the battery and lift the battery out of the car, (photo) and store it in the boot for safe keeping.

6. To remove the air cleaner undo the screw in the centre of the air cleaner cover and take off the bolt from the cleaner support strap on the rear of the inlet manifold (photo). Lift away the air cleaner. (On certain G.T. models the retaining bolts are inside the cleaner and access is gained to them after removing the air cleaner cover).

7. Unscrew the H.T. lead from the centre of the coil (photo). NOTE on some models the lead is a simple push fit.

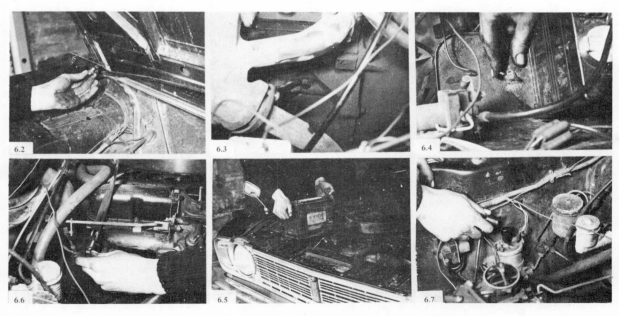

6.2   6.3   6.4

6.6   6.5   6.7

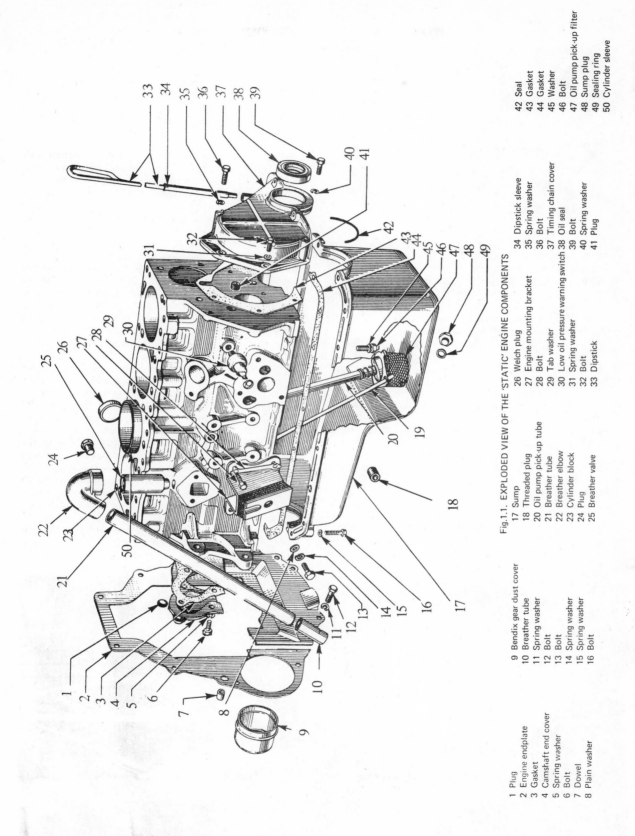

Fig.1.1. EXPLODED VIEW OF THE 'STATIC' ENGINE COMPONENTS

1 Plug	9 Bendix gear dust cover	17 Sump	26 Welch plug	34 Dipstick sleeve	42 Seal
2 Engine endplate	10 Breather tube	18 Threaded plug	27 Engine mounting bracket	35 Spring washer	43 Gasket
3 Gasket	11 Spring washer	20 Oil pump pick-up tube	28 Bolt	36 Bolt	44 Gasket
4 Camshaft end cover	12 Bolt	21 Breather tube	29 Tab washer	37 Timing chain cover	45 Washer
5 Spring washer	13 Bolt	22 Breather elbow	30 Low oil pressure warning switch	38 Oil seal	46 Bolt
6 Bolt	14 Spring washer	23 Cylinder block	31 Spring washer	39 Bolt	47 Oil pump pick-up filter
7 Dowel	15 Spring washer	24 Plug	32 Bolt	40 Spring washer	48 Sump plug
8 Plain washer	16 Bolt	25 Breather valve	33 Dipstick	41 Plug	49 Sealing ring
					50 Cylinder sleeve

8. Pull the small wire and connector off the CB tag on the coil (photo).

6.8

9. Pull the two wires by their tags off the Lucar connectors on the back of the dynamo (photo).

10 Disconnect the wire from the oil pressure sender unit on the side of the block (photo).

11 Loosen the clamp screw which secures the choke cable outer cover (photo). NOTE On cars with automatic transmission disconnect the automatic choke.

12 Then undo the screw (arrowed) which secures the choke wire to the lever (photo) and pull the wire free.

13 Carefully prise apart the accelerator linkage at the bulkhead (photo).

14 Then with the aid of a stubby screwdriver spring out the accelerator rod from its attachment to the carburetter (photo).

15 Undo the clip from the thermostat end of the top hose (photo) and pull the hose off the thermostat outlet pipe leaving the other end connected to the radiator.

16 Loosen the clip on the hose leading to the water pump and pull the hose off (photo).

17 Then pull the rubber overflow pipe off the outlet on the neck of the radiator filler pipe (photo). Disconnect the distributor advance and retard pipe.

18 Undo the two bolts on each side of the radiator which hold it in place. The photo shows the removal of the top right-hand bolt.

19 Carefully lift the radiator out of the car (photo) complete with top and bottom hoses.

20 Disconnect the water temperature wire from the sender unit (photo).

21 Turning to the heater hoses, undo the clips which hold

hold them to the inlet manifold (photo) and pull them away.

22 Pull the heater hose off the water pump (photo) after loosening the clip which holds the hose in place.

23 Disconnect the hoses from the clips on the side of the engine (photo).

24 Undo the union nut which secures the fuel inlet pipe to the fuel pump (photo) and pull the pipe clear.

25 Undo the exhaust pipe clamp bolts (photo) and free the exhaust pipe from the manifold. On G.T. models jack up the car and place stands underneath before attempting this operation.

26 Undo the nut holding the starter cable to the starter motor. (photo). Take off the engine earth lead next. It will be attached to one of the top bellhousing bolts.

27 Jack up the front of the car and place stands under the crossmember (photo). Undo the two bolts holding the starter motor in place and remove the motor.

28 Undo the lower clutch bellhousing bolts and take off the cover. Note that on cars fitted with automatic transmission this operation also disconnects the reinforcing bracket. On cars using automatic transmission turn the engine as required to gain access to the drive plate to torque converter bolts which must be undone.

29 Undo the bolts which hold the engine endplate to the bellhousing.

30 Jack up the front of the car, remove the stands and lower the car to the ground. On cars fitted with automatic transmission support the gearbox.

31 Attach a lifting chain or strong rope round the engine, and take the weight on suitable lifting tackle. Undo the bolt on each side which holds the front engine mountings in place (photo). These bolts are not very accessible and may take some time to remove.

32 Slightly raise the engine, and pull the engine forwards and up until the clutch is free from the first motion shaft in the gearbox. It is important that no excess load is placed on the clutch so take great care at this stage. Once clear of the bellhousing pull the engine forwards tilting the front further upwards to clear the front of the car and wind the engine out of the car. (Photo).

7. **ENGINE REMOVAL WITH GEARBOX**

1. Follow the instructions in Section 6 showing how to remove the engine without the gearbox omitting paragraphs 28,29 and 30. Ensure that the gearbox has been drained of oil. Do not start the work listed in paragraphs 31 and 32 until the following operations have been completed.

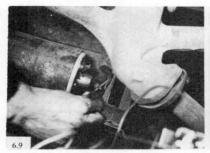
6.9

6.10

6.11

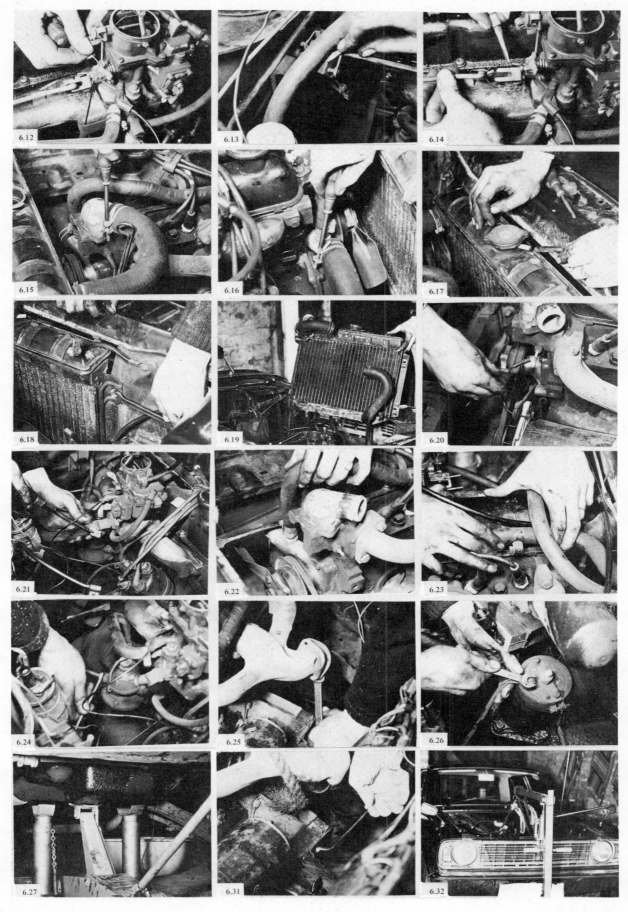

2. To avoid having to bleed the clutch slave cylinder on reassembly, an excellent tip worth following is to place a piece of scrap polythene under the clutch master cylinder filler cap and screw the cap down tight. (Photo). This will prevent any fluid running out of the master cylinder when the clutch pipe is disconnected.

3. Undo the union nut on the master cylinder to free the pipe which runs to the slave cylinder (photo). Blank off the end of the pipe.

4. Undo the screws which hold the rubber cover on the base of the gear lever to the transmission tunnel (photo). On G.T. and Super models it may be necessary to first remove the crossheaded screws which hold the centre console in place. Undo the gear lever knob locknut and unscrew the knob and nut.

5. Lift back the carpeting and with the aid of a hammer and metal drift (an old screwdriver is ideal) tap the gear-change lever retaining cover anti-clockwise until it starts to move (photo) and then unscrew it completely. On later G.T., Super and Deluxe models take off the circlip which holds the gearlever spring in compression. Turn up the lock tab and undo the plastic dome nut.

6. Lift off the retaining cover, inner plate, spring (photo) and then the gearlever. This clears the interior of the car from obstructions.

7. On models fitted with a column change free the lower end of the gear selector rod from the gear selector cross-shaft by removing the spring clip. Then free the cross-shaft from the pivot on the gearbox casing by taking off the spring clip, two flat washers and the wavy washer. Finally disconnect the gate selector lever on top of the gearbox from the gate selector rod.

8. Place a jack under the gearbox. Then from under the car undo the four bolts, two at each end of the gearbox crossmember which hold the crossmember to the body-shell (photo).

9. With the aid of a socket spanner undo and remove the sunken bolt in the centre of the crossmember (photo).

10 With a pair of pliers remove the retaining clip which holds the speedometer drive gear to the side of the gearbox.

11 With the jack still taking the weight of the gearbox now follow the instructions in paragraphs 31 and 32 of Section 6. Note that the rope or chain should be positioned fairly far forward so that it is possible to lift the engine/gearbox unit out at an angle of about 75° (photo).

12 With the engine out (photo) to finally complete the job clear out any loose nuts and bolts from the engine compartment and lightly screw them back from where they were removed or place them where they will not become lost.

8. DISMANTLING THE ENGINE - GENERAL

1. It is best to mount the engine on a dismantling stand but if one is not available, then stand the engine on a strong bench so as to be at a comfortable working height. Failing this, the engine can be stripped down on the floor.

2. During the dismantling process the greatest care should be taken to keep the exposed parts free from dirt. As an aid to achieving this, it is a sound scheme to

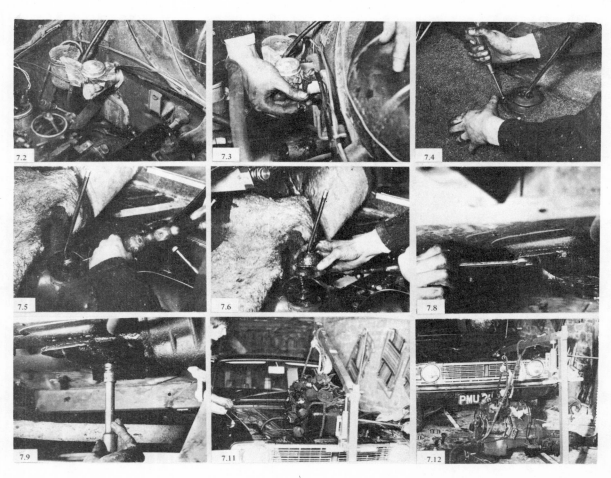

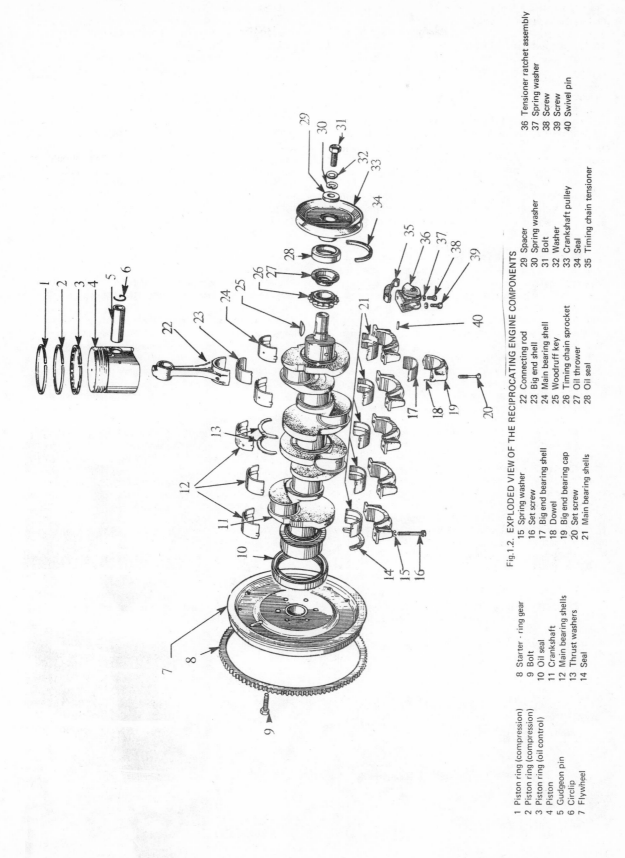

Fig.1.2. EXPLODED VIEW OF THE RECIPROCATING ENGINE COMPONENTS

1 Piston ring (compression)
2 Piston ring (compression)
3 Piston ring (oil control)
4 Piston
5 Gudgeon pin
6 Circlip
7 Flywheel

8 Starter - ring gear
9 Bolt
10 Oil seal
11 Crankshaft
12 Main bearing shells
13 Thrust washers
14 Seal

15 Spring washer
16 Set screw
17 Big end bearing shell
18 Dowel
19 Big end bearing cap
20 Set screw
21 Main bearing shells

22 Connecting rod
23 Big end shell
24 Main bearing shell
25 Woodruff key
26 Timing chain sprocket
27 Oil thrower
28 Oil seal

29 Spacer
30 Spring washer
31 Bolt
32 Washer
33 Crankshaft pulley
34 Seal
35 Timing chain tensioner

36 Tensioner ratchet assembly
37 Spring washer
38 Screw
39 Screw
40 Swivel pin

25

thoroughly clean down the outside of the engine, removing all traces of oil and congealed dirt.

3. Use paraffin or a good grease solvent such as 'Gunk'. The latter compound will make the job much easier, as, after the solvent has been applied and allowed to stand for a time, a vigorous jet of water will wash off the solvent and all the grease and filth. If the dirt is thick and deeply embedded, work the solvent into it with a wire brush.

4. Finally wipe down the exterior of the engine with a rag and only then, when it is quite clean should the dismantling process begin. As the engine is stripped, clean each part in a bath of paraffin or petrol.

5. Never immerse parts with oilways in paraffin, i.e. the crankshaft, but to clean wipe down carefully with a petrol dampened rag. Oilways can be cleaned out with pipe cleaners. If an air line is present all parts can be blown dry and the oilways blown through as an added precaution.

6. Re-use of old engine gaskets is a false economy and can give rise to oil and water leaks, if nothing worse. To avoid the possibility of trouble after the engine has been reassembled ALWAYS use new gaskets throughout.

7. Do not throw the old gaskets away as it sometimes happens that an immediate replacement cannot be found and the old gasket is then very useful as a template. Hang up the old gaskets as they are removed on a suitable hook or nail.

8. To strip the engine it is best to work from the top down. The sump provides a firm base on which the engine can be supported in an upright position. When the stage where the sump must be removed is reached, the engine can be turned on its side and all other work carried out with it in this position.

9. Wherever possible, replace nuts, bolts and washers finger-tight from wherever they were removed. This helps avoid later loss and muddle. If they cannot be replaced then lay them out in such a fashion that it is clear from where they came.

10 If the engine was removed in unit with the gearbox separate them by undoing the nuts and bolts which hold the bellhousing to the engine endplate (photo).

11 Also undo the three bolts holding the starter motor in place and lift off the motor (photo).

12 Carefully pull the gearbox and bellhousing off the engine to separate them (photo).

9. REMOVING ANCILLARY ENGINE COMPONENTS

1. Before basic engine dismantling begins the engine should be stripped of all its ancillary components. These items should also be removed if a factory exchange reconditioned unit is being purchased. The items comprise:-

Dynamo and dynamo brackets.
Water pump and thermostat housing.
Starter motor.
Distributor and sparking plugs.
Inlet and exhaust manifold and carburetters.
Fuel pump and fuel pipes.
Oil filter and dipstick.
Oil filler cap.
Clutch assembly.
Engine mountings.
Oil pressure sender unit/pressure gauge adaptor (G.T. Models).
Oil separator unit (positive ventilation systems only).

2. Without exception all these items can be removed with the engine in the car if it is merely an individual item which requires attention. (It is necessary to remove the gearbox if the clutch is to be renewed with the engine 'in situ').

3. Remove the dynamo after undoing the nuts and bolts which secure it in place. Remove the dynamo securing straps.

4. Remove the distributor by disconnecting the vacuum pipe, unscrew the single bolt at the clamp plate and lift out the distributor.

5. Remove the oil pump and filter assembly by unscrewing the three securing bolts with their lockwashers.

6. Unscrew the two bolts securing the fuel pump.

7. Unscrew the oil pressure gauge unit or the oil pressure sender unit depending on model.

8. Remove the inlet and exhaust manifolds together with the carburetter by undoing the bolts and nuts which hold the units in place.

9. Unbolt the securing bolts of the water elbow and lift out the thermostat.

10 Bend back the tab lockwashers where fitted and undo the bolts which hold the water pump and engine mountings in place.

11 Undo the bolts which hold the clutch cover flange to the flywheel a third of a turn each in a diagonal sequence repeating until the clutch and driven plate can be lifted off.

12 Loosen the clamp which secures the rubber tube from the oil separator unit to the inlet manifold and pull off the tube (where a positive ventilation system is fitted). Remove the oil separator located on the fuel pump mounting pad by carefully prising it off.

13 On 1300 and 1500 models an open ventilation system consisting of an oil filler cap breather and a road draught tube is usually fitted. The tube is secured by one or two clutch housing bolts.

14 The engine is now stripped of ancillary components and ready for major dismantling to begin.

8.10

8.11

8.12

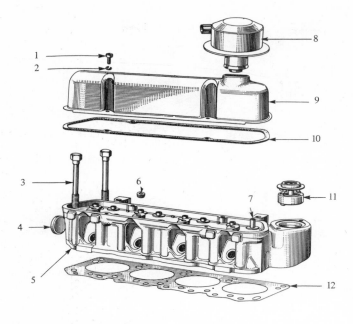

Fig.1.3. EXPLODED VIEW OF THE NON-CROSSFLOW CYLINDER HEAD

1 Screw	4 Welch plug	7 Valve guide	10 Rocker cover gasket
2 Spring washer	5 Cylinder head	8 Oil filler cap & breather	11 Thermostat
3 Cylinder head bolt	6 Threaded plug	9 Rocker cover	12 Head gasket

10. CYLINDER HEAD REMOVAL - ENGINE ON BENCH

1. Undo the four screw headed bolts and flat washers which hold the flange of the rocker cover to the cylinder head and lift off the rocker cover and gasket.

2. Unscrew the four rocker shaft pedestal bolts evenly and remove together with their washers.

3. Lift off the rocker assembly as one unit (photo) NOTE Photographs in this section depict the earlier non-crossflow cylinder head. Instructions for removal of the crossflow head are identical.

4. Remove the pushrods, (photo), keeping them in the relative order in which they were removed. The easiest way to do this is to push them through a sheet of thick paper or thin card in the correct sequence.

5. Undo the cylinder head bolts half a turn at a time (photo) in the reverse order shown in Fig.1.4. When all the bolts are no longer under tension they may be screwed off the cylinder head one at a time.

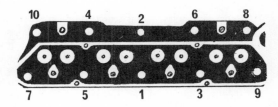

Fig.1.4. Cylinder head bolts tightening and loosening sequence

6. The cylinder head can now be removed by lifting upwards. If the head is jammed, try to rock it to break the seal. Under no circumstances try to prise it apart from the block with a screwdriver or cold chisel as damage may be done to the faces of the head or block. If the head

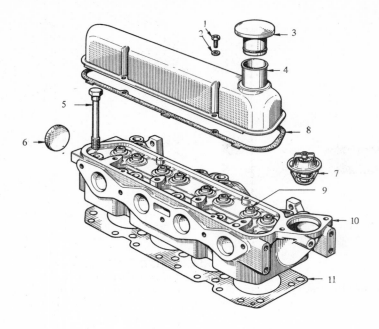

Fig.1.5. EXPLODED VIEW OF THE CROSSFLOW CYLINDER HEAD

1 Screw	4 Rocker cover	7 Thermostat	10 Cylinder head
2 Spring washer	5 Cylinder head bolt	8 Rocker cover gasket	11 Head gasket
3 Oil filler cap	6 Welch plug	9 Valve guide	

will not readily free, turn the engine over by the flywheel as the compression in the cylinders will often break the cylinder head joint. If this fails to work, strike the head sharply with a plastic headed hammer, or with a wooden hammer, or with a metal hammer with an interposed piece of wood to cushion the blows. Under no circumstances hit the head directly with a metal hammer as this may cause the iron casting to fracture. Several sharp taps with the hammer at the same time pulling upwards should free the head. Lift the head off and place on one side (photo).

10.6

7. On crossflow engines on no account lay the cylinder head face downwards unless the plugs have been removed. (The plugs protrude and can be easily damaged.)

11. CYLINDER HEAD REMOVAL - ENGINE IN CAR

To remove the cylinder head with the engine still in

the car the following additional procedure to that above must be followed. This procedure should be carried out before that listed in Section 10.

1. Disconnect the battery by removing the lead from the negative terminal.

2. Drain half the water (approx. 5 pints) by undoing the drain plug at the base of the radiator.

3. Take off the carburetter air cleaner and undo the two bolts which hold the thermostat housing in place. Remove the thermostat.

4. Undo the clips which hold the heater hoses and the vacuum hose to the inlet manifold. The automatic choke hoses should now be disconnected (where fitted).

5. Undo the bolts which hold the exhaust manifold to the exhaust pipe and on the G.T. engine undo the nuts bolts and washers which hold the exhaust manifold to the cylinder head.

6. Pull the cable away from the temperature gauge sender unit.

7. On cars fitted with automatic transmission disconnect the change-down cable from the carburetter.

8. Also free from the carburetter the throttle cable and linkage, the petrol pipe, the distributor vacuum pipe and the choke cable (where fitted). On certain early G.T. models undo and remove the bolt from the inlet manifold support stay (photo).

9. On models other than G.T. unclip from the rocker cover the carburetter ventilation pipe.

10 Pull the leads off the sparking plugs and flip back the clips which hold the distributor cover in place. Place the cover and leads to one side.

11 The procedure is now the same as for removing the cylinder head when on the bench. One tip worth noting is that should the cylinder head refuse to free easily, the battery can be reconnected up, and the engine turned

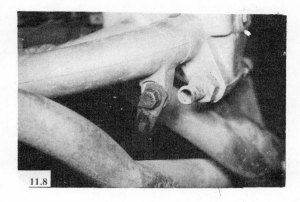

11.8

over on the solenoid switch. Under no circumstances turn the ignition on and ensure the fuel inlet pipe is disconnected from the mechanical fuel pump.

12. VALVE REMOVAL

1. The valves can be removed from the cylinder head by the following method. Compress each spring in turn with a valve spring compressor until the two halves of the collets can be removed. Release the compressor and remove the spring and spring retainer.

2. If, when the valve spring compressor is screwed down, the valve spring retaining cap refuses to free to expose the split collet, do not continue to screw down on the compressor as there is a likelihood of damaging it.

3. Gently tap the top of the tool directly over the cap with a light hammer. This will free the cap. To avoid the compressor jumping off the valve spring retaining cap

when it is tapped, hold the compressor firmly in position with one hand.

4. Slide the rubber oil control seal off the top of each inlet valve stem and then drop out each valve through the combustion chamber.

5. It is essential that the valves are kept in their correct sequence unless they are so badly worn that they are to be renewed. If they are going to be kept and used again, place them in a sheet of card having eight holes numbered 1 to 8 corresponding with the relative positions the valves were in when fitted. Also keep the valve springs, washers etc., in the correct order. Make No.1 hole the one at the front of the cylinder head.

13. DISMANTLING THE ROCKER ASSEMBLY

1. Pull out the split pin from either end of the rocker shaft and remove the flat washer, crimped spring washer and the remaining flat washer.

2. The rocker arms, rocker pedestals, and distance springs can now be slid off the end of the shaft.

14. TIMING COVER, GEARWHEEL & CHAIN REMOVAL

1. The timing cover, gear wheels, and chain can be removed with the engine in the car providing the radiator, fan, and water pump are first removed. See Chapter 2, Sections 6 and 8 for details.

2. Undo the bolt from the centre of the crankshaft fan belt pulley wheel noting the spring and large flat washer under the bolts head.

3. The crankshaft pulley wheel may pull off quite easily. If not place two large screwdrivers behind the wheel at 180° to each other, and carefully lever off the wheel. It is preferable to use a proper pulley extractor if this is available, but large screwdrivers or tyre levers are quite suitable, providing care is taken not to damage the pulley

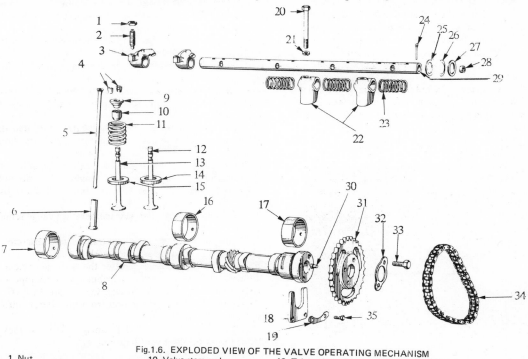

Fig.1.6. EXPLODED VIEW OF THE VALVE OPERATING MECHANISM

1 Nut	10 Valve stem seal	19 Tab washer	28 Plug
2 Rocker arm adjusting screw	11 Valve spring	20 Bolt	29 Rocker shaft
3 Rocker arm	12 Valve	21 Spring washer	30 Dowel pin
4 Valve collets	13 Valve	22 Rocker pedestals	31 Timing chain sprocket
5 Pushrod	14 Inserts	23 Rocker arm spacer springs	32 Tab washer
6 Cam follower	15	24 Split pin	33 Bolt
7 Camshaft bearings	16 Centre camshaft bearing	25 Spacer	34 Timing chain
8 Camshaft	17 Front camshaft bearing	26 Shim	35 Bolt
9 Spring retainer	18 Camshaft thrust plate	27 Spacer	

flange.

4. Undo the bolts which hold the timing cover in place noting that four sump bolts must also be removed before the cover can be taken off.

5. Check the chain for wear by measuring how much it can be depressed. More than ½ in. means a new chain must be fitted on reassembly.

6. With the timing cover off, take off the oil thrower. NOTE that the concave side faces outwards.

7. With a drift or screwdriver tap back the tabs on the lockwasher under the two camshaft gearwheel retaining bolts and undo the bolts.

8. To remove the camshaft and crankshaft timing wheels complete with chain, ease each wheel forward a little at a time levering behind each gear wheel in turn with two large screwdrivers at 180° to each other. If the gearwheels are locked solid then it will be necessary to use a proper gearwheel and pulley extractor, and if one is available this should be used anyway in preference to screwdrivers. With both gearwheels safely off, remove the woodruff key from the crankshaft with a pair of pliers and place it in a jam jar for safe keeping.

15. CAMSHAFT REMOVAL

1. The camshaft cannot be removed with the engine in place in the car primarily because of the restriction imposed by the inverted umbrella shaped tappets which can only be removed downwards i.e. towards the camshaft.

2. With the engine inverted and sump, rocker gear, pushrods, timing cover, oil pump, gearwheels and timing chain removed take off the chain tensioner and arm.

3. Knock back the lockwasher tabs from the two bolts which hold the horseshoe shaped camshaft retainer in place behind the camshaft flange and slide out the retainer.

4. Rotate the camshaft so that the tappets are fully home and then withdraw the camshaft from the block. Take great care that the cam lobe peaks do not damage the camshaft bearings as the shaft is pulled forward.

16. SUMP REMOVAL

1. The sump can be removed with the engine in or out of the car. If out of the car it is only necessary to follow the instructions in paragraph 7. If the engine is in the car the following additional instructions apply.

2. Disconnect the battery and drain the cooling water and engine oil.

3. Undo the clips retaining the top and bottom radiator hoses at the engine end and pull the hoses away from the engine. Disconnect the throttle linkage at the carburetter.

4. Apply the handbrake firmly, jack up the front of the car and fit stands under frame rails at each side. Remove the jack and place it under the front of the gearbox bellhousing.

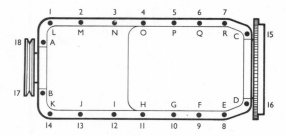

Fig.1.7. Sump retaining bolts tightening and loosening sequence

5. Undo the front engine mounting bolts and the sump shield if fitted. On cars fitted with automatic transmission it is necessary to also remove the dynamo and support bracket.

6. Undo the three bolts holding the starter motor in place (two bolts only if the pre-engaged type is fitted), undo the cable to the starter motor and lift the motor off. Jack up the engine two to three inches.

7. Undo the 18 sump bolts in reverse sequence to that shown in Fig.1.7 and remove the sump from under the car. If necessary jack up the engine further during this process.

17. PISTON, CONNECTING ROD & BIG END BEARING REMOVAL

1. The pistons and connecting rods can be removed with the engine still in the car or with the engine on the bench.

2. With the cylinder head and sump removed undo the big end retaining bolts.

3. The connecting rods and pistons are lifted out from the top of the cylinder block.

4. Remove the big end caps one at a time, taking care to keep them in the right order and the correct way round. Also ensure that the shell bearings are kept with their correct connecting rods and caps unless they are to be renewed. Normally, the numbers 1 to 4 are stamped on adjacent sides of the big end caps and connecting rods, indicating which cap fits on which rod and which way round the cap fits. If no numbers or lines can be found then with a sharp screwdriver or file scratch mating marks across the joint from the rod to the cap. One line for connecting rod No.1, two for connecting rod No.2 and so on. This will ensure there is no confusion later as it is most important that the caps go back in the correct position on the connecting rods from which they were removed.

5. If the big end caps are difficult to remove they may be gently tapped with a soft hammer.

6. To remove the shell bearings, press the bearing opposite the groove in both the connecting rod, and the connecting rod caps and the bearings will slide out easily.

7. Withdraw the pistons and connecting rods upwards and ensure they are kept in the correct order for replacement in the same bore. Refit the connecting rod caps and bearings to the rods if the bearings do not require renewal to minimise the risk of getting the caps and rods muddled.

18. GUDGEON PIN - REMOVAL

1. To remove the gudgeon pin to free the piston from the connecting rod remove one of the circlips at either end of the pin with a pair of circlips pliers.

2. Press out the pin from the rod and piston with your finger.

3. If the pin shows reluctance to move, then on no account force it out, as this could damage the piston. Immerse the piston in a pan of boiling water for three minutes. On removal the expansion of the aluminium should allow the gudgeon pin to slide out easily.

4. Make sure the pins are kept with the same piston for ease of refitting.

19. PISTON RING REMOVAL

1. To remove the piston rings, slide them carefully over the top of the piston, taking care not to scratch the aluminium alloy. Never slide them off the bottom of the piston skirt. It is very easy to break the iron piston rings if they are pulled off roughly so this operation should be done with extreme caution. It is helpful to make use of an old hacksaw blade, or better still, an old

.020 in. feeler gauge.

2. Lift one end of the piston ring to be removed out of its groove and insert the end of the feeler gauge under it.

3. Turn the feeler gauge slowly round the piston and as the ring comes out of its groove apply slight upward pressure so that it rests on the land above. It can then be eased off the piston with the feeler gauge stopping it from slipping into any empty groove if it is any but the top piston ring that is being removed.

20. FLYWHEEL REMOVAL

1. Remove the clutch as described in Chapter 5.5.

2. No lock tabs are fitted under the six bolts which hold the flywheel to the flywheel flange on the rear of the crankshaft.

3. Unscrew the bolts and remove them.

4. Lift the flywheel away from the crankshaft flange. NOTE Some difficulty may be experienced in removing the bolts by the rotation of the crankshaft every time pressure is put on the spanner. To lock the crankshaft in position while the bolts are removed, wedge a block of wood between the crankshaft and the side of the block inside the crankcase.

21. MAIN BEARING & CRANKSHAFT REMOVAL

1. With the engine out of the car and the timing gears, sump, flywheel, connecting rods and pistons removed, undo evenly the ten bolts retaining the five main bearing caps in place.

2. Lift out the bolts and lock washers and remove the main bearing caps together with the bottom halves of each shell bearing. Take great care to keep the caps the correct way round and in their right order, and the shells in the right caps, Mark No.1 cap as such.

3. Remove the semi-circular thrust washers fitted to the centre main bearing.

4. Remove the crankshaft by lifting it out from the crankcase.

22. TIMING CHAIN TENSIONER - REMOVAL

1. Undo the two bolts and washers which hold the timing chain tensioner in place. Lift off the tensioner.

2. Pull the timing chain tensioner arm off its hinge pin on the front of the block.

23. LUBRICATION & CRANKCASE VENTILATION SYSTEMS - DESCRIPTION

1. A forced feed system of lubrication is fitted with oil circulated round the engine by a pump draining from the sump below the block.

2. The full flow filter and oil pump assembly is mounted externally on the right-hand side of the cylinder block. The pump is driven by means of a short shaft and skew gear off the camshaft.

3. Oil reaches the pump via a tube pressed into the cylinder block sump face. Initial filtration is provided by a spring loaded gauge on the end of the tube. Drillings in the block carry the oil under pressure to the main and big end bearings. Oil at a reduced pressure is fed to the valve and rocker gear and the timing chain and gearwheels.

4. One of two types of oil pump may be fitted. The eccentric bi-rotor type can be identified by four recesses cast in the cover whereas the vane type cover is flat. The pumps are directly interchangeable.

5. On non crossflow engines an open crankcase ventilation system consisting of a breather in the oil filler cap and a road draught tube were fitted as standard. On non crossflow 1300 engines the road draught tube emerges from an oil separator mounted on the top of the fuel pump attachment lug.

6. Non crossflow G.T. models use a closed crankcase ventilation system (See Fig.1.8). This comprises the oil separator as fitted to 1300 engines but the outlet is connected to the inlet manifold via an emission control valve.

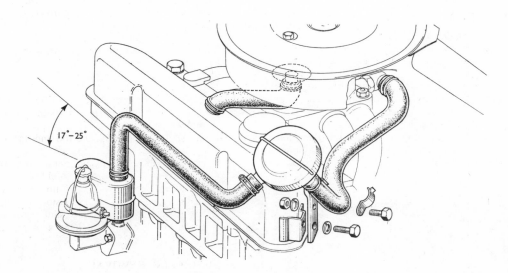

Fig.1.8. The closed positive ventilation system fitted to non-crossflow G.T. models

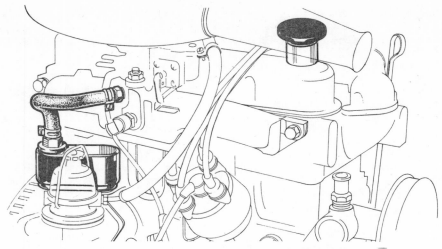

Fig.1.9. The semi-closed positive ventilation system fitted to crossflow engines

7. On crossflow engines a semi-closed positive ventilation system is fitted as standard (See Fig.1.9). This consists of a breather in the oil filler cap, an oil separator mounted on top of the fuel pump attachment lug, an emission control valve fitted into a grommet on the top of the oil separator, and a pipe leading from the valve to the inlet manifold.

24. OIL FILTER - REMOVAL & REPLACEMENT

1. The full flow oil filter is attached to the oil pump on the right-hand side of the engine towards the front. The element is removed by unscrewing the long centre bolt which holds the filter bowl to the filter head. With the bolt released carefully lift away the filter bowl which contains the filter and will also be full of oil. It is helpful to have a large basin under the filter body to catch the amount which is bound to spill.

2. Throw the old filter element away and thoroughly clean down the filter bowl, the bolt and associated parts with petrol and when perfectly clean wipe dry with a non-fluffy rag.

3. A rubber sealing ring is located in a groove round the head of the oil filter and forms an effective leak-proof joint between the filter head and the filter bowl. A new rubber sealing ring is supplied with each new filter element.

4. Carefully prise out the old sealing ring from the locating groove. If the ring has become hard and is difficult to move take great care not to damage the sides of the sealing ring groove.

5. With the old ring removed, fit the new ring (photo) in the groove at four equidistant points and press it home a segment at a time. Do not insert the ring at just one point and work round the groove pressing it home as, using this method, it is easy to stretch the ring and be left with a small loop of rubber which will not fit into the locating groove.

6. Offer up the bowl to the rubber sealing ring (photo) and before finally tightening down the centre bolt, check that the lip of the filter bowl is resting squarely on the rubber sealing ring and is not offset and off the ring. If the bowl is not seating properly, rotate it until it is.

7. Tighten down the centre bolt (photo) and run the engine to check the bowl for leaks.

25. OIL PUMP OVERHAUL

1. If the oil pump is worn it is best to purchase an exchange reconditioned unit as a good oil pump is at the very heart of long engine life. Generally speaking an exchange or overhauled pump should be fitted at a major engine reconditioning. If it is wished to overhaul the oil pump, detach the pump and filter unit from the cylinder block, and remove the filter body and element.

2. Remove the four bolts and lockwashers securing the end plate and remove the plate. Lift away the 'O' ring from the sealing groove in the body.

3. Check the clearance between the lobes of the inner and outer rotors in the positions shown in Fig.1.11. parts 2 and 3, and the clearance must not exceed 0.006 inches.

4. Replacement rotors are only supplied as a matched pair so that, if the clearance is excessive, a new rotor assembly must be fitted.

5. Lay a straight edge across the face of the pump in order to check the clearance between the faces of the rotors and the bottom of the straight edge. This

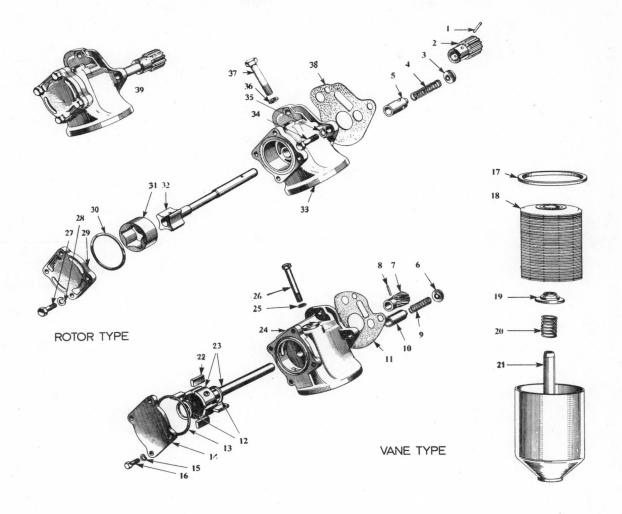

ROTOR TYPE

VANE TYPE

Fig.1.10. EXPLODED VIEW OF THE ROTOR AND VANE OIL PUMPS AND THE OIL FILTER

1 Locking pin	11 Gasket	21 Oil filter bowl	31 Rotor
2 Oil pump drive gear	12 Spacer	22 Rotor blade	32 Rotor shaft
3 Oil pressure relief valve retainer	13 Oil pump cover sealing ring	23 Rotor and shaft assembly	33 Pump body
4 Relief valve spring	14 Cover	24 Pump assembly	34 Bolt
5 Relief valve plunger	15 Spring washer	25 Spring washer	35 Spring washer
6 Oil pressure relief valve plunger	16 Bolt	26 Bolt	36 Spring washer
7 Oil pump drive gear	17 Filter sealing ring	27 Bolt	37 Securing bolt
8 Locking pin	18 Oil filter element	28 Spring washer	38 Gasket
9 Relief valve spring	19 Seat	29 Cover	39 Complete pump assembly
10 Relief valve plunger	20 Spring	30 Sealing ring	

Fig.1.11. MEASURING THE OIL PUMP CLEARANCES
(A) Measuring rotor endfloat. (B) Measuring clearance between inner & outer rotors. (C) Measuring clearance between outer rotor and pump body

clearance should not exceed 0.005 in. If the clearance is excessive the face of the pump body can be carefully lapped on a flat surface.

6. When it is necessary to renew the rotors, drive out the pin securing the skew gear and pull the gear from the shaft. Remove the inner rotor and drive shaft and withdraw the outer rotor. Install the outer rotor with the chamfered end towards the pump body.

7. Fit the inner rotor and drive shaft assembly, position the skew gear and install the pin. Tap over each end of the pin to prevent it loosening in service. Position a new 'O' ring in the groove in the pump body, fit the end plate in position and secure with the four bolts and lockwashers.

8. Refit the oil pump assembly together with a new gasket and secure in place with three bolts and lockwashers.

26. ENGINE FRONT MOUNTINGS - REMOVAL & REPLACEMENT

1. With time the bonded rubber insulators, one on each of the front mountings, will perish causing undue vibration and noise from the engine. Severe juddering when reversing or when moving off from rest is also likely and is a further sign of worn mounting rubbers.

2. The front mounting rubber insulators can be changed with the engine in the car.

3. Apply the handbrake firmly, jack up the front of the car, and place stands under the front of the car.

4. Lower the jack, take off the engine sump shield where fitted, and place the jack under the sump to take the weight of the engine.

5. Undo the large bolt which holds each of the engine mountings to the body crossmember. Then knock back the locking tabs and undo the four bolts holding each of the engine mountings in place (photo).

26.5

6. Fit new mountings using new tab washers, tighten the four bolts down firmly and turn up the tabs on the washers. Refit the large crossmember to mounting bolt on each side, remove the stands and lower the car to the ground.

27. EXAMINATION & RENOVATION - GENERAL

With the engine stripped down and all parts thoroughly cleaned, it is now time to examine everything for wear. The following items should be checked and where necessary renewed or renovated as described in the following sections.

28. CRANKSHAFT EXAMINATION & RENOVATION

1. Examine the crankpin and main journal surfaces for signs of scoring or scratches. Check the ovality of the crankpins at different positions with a micrometer. If more than 0.001 in. out of round, the crankpins will have to be reground. It will also have to be reground if there are any scores or scratches present. Also check the journals in the same fashion.

2. If it is necessary to regrind the crankshaft and fit new bearings your local Ford garage or engineering works will be able to decide how much metal to grind off and the size of new bearing shells.

29. BIG END & MAIN BEARINGS - EXAMINATION & RENOVATION

Big end bearing failure is accompanied by a noisy knocking from the crankcase, and a slight drop in oil pressure. Main bearing failure is accompanied by vibration which can be quite severe as the engine speed rises and falls and a drop in oil pressure.

Bearings which have not broken up, but are badly worn and give rise to low oil pressure and some vibration. Inspect the big ends, main bearings, and thrust washers for signs of general wear, scoring, pitting and scratches. The bearings should be matt grey in colour. With lead-indium bearings should a trace of copper colour be noticed the bearings are badly worn as the lead bearing material has worn away to expose the indium underlay. Renew the bearings if they are in this condition or if there is any sign of scoring or pitting.

The undersizes available are designed to correspond with the regrind sizes, i.e. - .010 in. bearings are correct for a crankshaft reground - .010 in. undersize. The bearings are in fact, slightly more than the stated undersize as running clearances have been allowed for during their manufacture.

Very long engine life can be achieved by changing big end bearings at intervals of 30,000 miles and main bearings at intervals of 50,000 miles, irrespective of bearing wear. Normally, crankshaft wear is infinitesimal and a change of bearings will ensure mileages of between 80,000 to 100,000 miles before crankshaft regrinding becomes necessary. Crankshafts normally have to be reground because of scoring due to bearing failure.

30. CYLINDER BORES - EXAMINATION & RENOVATION

1. The cylinder bores must be examined for taper, ovality, scoring and scratches. Start by carefully examining the top of the cylinder bores. If they are at all worn a very slight ridge will be found on the thrust side. This marks the top of the piston ring travel. The owner will have a good indication of the bore wear prior to dismantling the engine, or removing the cylinder head. Excessive oil consumption accompanied by blue smoke from the exhaust is a sure sign of worn cylinder bores and piston rings.

2. Measure the bore diameter just under the ridge with a micrometer and compare it with the diameter at the bottom of the bore, which is not subject to wear. If the difference between the two measurements is more than .006 in. then it will be necessary to fit special pistons and rings or to have the cylinders rebored and fit oversize pistons. If no micrometer is available remove the rings from a piston and place the piston in each bore in turn about ¾ in. below the top of the bore. If an 0.010 feeler gauge can be slid between the piston and the cylinder wall on the thrust side of the bore then remedial action must be taken. Oversize pistons are available in the following sizes:-

+ .010 in. (254 mm), + .020 in. (.508 mm),
+ .030 in. (.762 mm).

3. These are accurately machined to just below these measurements so as to provide correct running clearances in bores bored out to the exact oversize dimensions.

4. If the bores are slightly worn but not so badly worn as to justify reboring them, then special oil control rings and pistons can be fitted which will restore compression and stop the engine burning oil. Several different types are available and the manufacturers instructions concerning their fitting must be followed closely.

5. If new pistons are being fitted and the bores have not been reground, it is essential to slightly roughen the hard glaze on the sides of the bores with fine glass paper so the new piston rings will have a chance to bed in properly.

31. PISTONS & PISTON RINGS - EXAMINATION & RENOVATION

1. If the old pistons are to be refitted, carefully remove the piston rings and then thoroughly clean them. Take particular care to clean out the piston ring grooves. At the same time do not scratch the aluminium in any way. If new rings are to be fitted to the old pistons then the top ring should be stepped so as to clear the ridge left above the previous top ring. If a normal but oversize new ring is fitted, it will hit the ridge and break, because the new ring will not have worn in the same way as the old, which will have worn in unison with the ridge.

2. Before fitting the rings on the pistons each should be inserted approximately 2 in. down the cylinder bore and the gap measured with a feeler gauge. This should be between .009 in. and .014 in. It is essential that the gap should be measured at the bottom of the ring travel, as if it is measured at the top of a worn bore and gives a perfect fit, it could easily seize at the bottom. If the ring gap is too small rub down the ends of the ring with a very fine file until the gap, when fitted, is correct. To keep the rings square in the bore for measurement line each up in turn by inserting an old piston in the bore upside down, and use the piston to push the ring down

about 2 inches. Remove the piston and measure the piston ring gap.

3. When fitting new pistons and rings to a rebored engine the piston ring gap can be measured at the top of the bore as the bore will not now taper (photo). It is not necessary to measure the side clearance in the piston ring grooves with the rings fitted as the groove dimensions are accurately machined during manufacture. When fitting new oil control rings to old pistons it may be necessary to have the grooves widened by machining to accept the new wider rings. In this instance the manufacturers representative will make this quite clear and will supply the address to which the pistons must be sent for machining.

32. CAMSHAFT & CAMSHAFT BEARINGS - EXAMINATION & RENOVATION

1. Carefully examine the camshaft bearings for wear. If the bearings are obviously worn or pitted then they must be renewed. This is an operation for your local Ford dealer or the local engineering works as it demands the use of specialised equipment. The bearings are removed with a special drift after which new bearings are pressed in, care being taken to ensure the oil holes in the bearings line up with those in the block.

2. The camshaft itself should show no signs of wear, but, if very slight scoring on the cams is noticed, the score marks can be removed by very gentle rubbing down with a very fine emery cloth. The greatest care should be taken to keep the cam profiles smooth.

3. Examine the skew gear for wear, chipped teeth or other damage.

4. Carefully examine the camshaft thrust plate. Excessive wear will be visually self evident and will require the fitting of a new plate.

33. VALVES & VALVE SEATS - EXAMINATION & RENOVATION

1. Examine the heads of the valves for pitting and burning, especially the heads of the exhaust valves. The valve seatings should be examined at the same time. If the pitting on valve and seat is very slight the marks can be removed by grinding the seats and valves together with coarse, and then fine, valve grinding paste.

2. Where bad pitting has occured to the valve seats it will be necessary to recut them and fit new valves. If the valve seats are so worn that they cannot be recut, then it will be necessary to fit new valve seat inserts. These latter two jobs should be entrusted to the local Ford agent or engineering works. In practice it is very seldom that the seats are so badly worn that they require renewal. Normally, it is the valve that is too badly worn for replacement, and the owner can easily

purchase a new set of valves and match them to the seats by valve grinding.

3. Valve grinding is carried out as follows:-

Smear a trace of coarse carborundum paste on the seat face and apply a suction grinder tool to the valve head. With a semi-rotary motion, grind the valve head to its seat, lifting the valve occasionally (photo) to re-distribute the grinding paste. When a dull matt even surface finish is produced on both the valve seat and the valve, then wipe off the paste and repeat the process with fine carborundum paste, lifting and turning the valve to redistribute the paste as before. A light spring placed under the valve head will greatly ease this operation. When a smooth unbroken ring of light grey matt finish is produced, on both valve and valve seat faces, the grinding operation is completed.

33.3

4. Scrape away all carbon from the valve head and the valve stem. Carefully clean away every trace of grinding compound, taking great care to leave none in the ports or in the valve guides. Clean the valves and valve seats with a paraffin soaked rag then with a clean rag, and finally, if an air line is available, blow the valves, valve guides and valve ports clean.

34. TIMING GEARS & CHAIN - EXAMINATION & RENOVATION

1. Examine the teeth on both the crankshaft gear wheel and the camshaft gear wheel for wear. Each tooth forms an inverted 'V' with the gearwheel periphery, and if worn the side of each tooth under tension will be slightly concave in shape when compared with the other side of the tooth, i.e. one side of the inverted 'V' will be concave when compared with the other. If any sign of wear is present the gearwheels must be renewed.

2. Examine the links of the chain for side slackness and renew the chain if any slackness is noticeable when compared with a new chain. It is a sensible precaution to renew the chain at about 30,000 miles and at a less mileage if the engine is stripped down for a major overhaul. The actual rollers on a very badly worn chain may be slightly grooved.

35. ROCKERS & ROCKER SHAFT - EXAMINATION & RENOVATION

1. Thoroughly clean the rocker shaft and then check the shaft for straightness by rolling it on the bench. It is most unlikely that it will deviate from normal, but, if it does, then a judicious attempt must be made to straighten it. If this is not successful purchase a new shaft. The surface of the shaft should be free from any worn ridges caused by the rocker arms. If any wear is present, renew the shaft.

Check the rocker arms for wear of the rocker bushes, for wear at the rocker arm face which bears on the valve stem, and for wear of the adjusting ball ended screws. Wear in the rocker arm bush can be checked by gripping the rocker arm tip and holding the rocker arm in place on the shaft, noting if there is any lateral rocker arm shake. If shake is present, and the arm is very loose on the shaft, a new bush or rocker arm must be fitted.

Check the tip of the rocker arm where it bears on the valve head for cracking or serious wear on the case hardening. If none is present reuse the rocker arm. Check the lower half of the ball on the end of the rocker arm adjusting screw. Check the pushrods for straightness by rolling them on the bench. Renew any that are bent.

36. TAPPETS - EXAMINATION & RENOVATION

Examine the bearing surface of the mushroom tappets which lie on the camshaft. Any indentation in this surface or any cracks indicate serious wear and the tappets should be renewed. Thoroughly clean them out, removing all traces of sludge. It is most unlikely that the sides of the tappets will prove worn, but, if they are a very loose fit in their bores and can readily be rocked, they should be exchanged for new units. It is very unusual to find any wear in the tappets, and any wear is likely to occur only at very high mileages.

37. CONNECTING RODS - EXAMINATION & RENOVATION

1. Examine the mating faces of the big end caps to see if they have ever been filed in a mistaken attempt to take up wear. If so the offending rods must be renewed.

2. Insert the gudgeon pin into the little end of the connecting rod. It should go in fairly easily, but if any slackness is present then take the rod to your local FORD dealer or engineering works and exchange it for a rod of identical weight.

38. FLYWHEEL STARTER RING - EXAMINATION & RENOVATION

1. If the teeth on the flywheel starter ring are badly worn, or if some are missing then it will be necessary to remove the ring and fit a new one.

2. The number of teeth on the ring varies depending on the type of starter motor fitted. With the more usual inertia type starter (3 bolt fixing) the ring gear has 110 teeth. With the pre-engaged starter (2 bolt fixing) the ring gear has 132 teeth.

3. The flywheel on G.T. models weighs 18.5 lbs. as opposed to 26 lbs. for all other models.

4. Either split the ring with a cold chisel after making a cut with a hacksaw blade between two teeth, or use a soft headed hammer (not steel) to knock the ring off, striking it evenly and alternately, at equally spaced points. Take great care not to damage the flywheel during this process.

5. Clean and polish with emery cloth four evenly spaced areas on the outside face of the new starter ring.

6. Heat the ring evenly with an oxyacetylene flame until the polished portions turn dark blue. Hold the ring at this temperature for five minutes and then quickly fit it to the flywheel so the chamfered portion of the teeth faces the gearbox side of the flywheel.

7. The ring should be tapped gently down onto its register and left to cool naturally when the contraction of the metal on cooling will ensure that it is a secure and permanent fit. Great care must be taken not to overheat the ring, indicated by it turning light metallic blue, as

if this happens the temper of the ring will be lost.

8. It does not matter which way round the 132 toothed ring is fitted as it has no chamfers on its teeth. This also makes for quick identification between the two rings.

39. CYLINDER HEAD - DECARBONISATION

1. This can be carried out with the engine either in or out of the car. With the cylinder head off carefully remove with a wire brush mounted in an electric drill (photo) and blunt scraper, all traces of carbon deposits from the combustion spaces and the ports. The valve head stems and valve guides should also be freed from any carbon deposits. Wash the combustion spaces and ports down with petrol and scrape the cylinder head surface free of any foreign matter with the side of a steel rule, or a similar article.

39.1

2. Clean the pistons and top of the cylinder bores. If the pistons are still in the block then it is essential that great care is taken to ensure that no carbon gets into the cylinder bores as this could scratch the cylinder walls or cause damage to the piston and rings. To ensure this does not happen, first turn the crankshaft so that two of the pistons are at the top of their bores. Stuff rag into the other two bores or seal them off with paper and masking tape. The waterways should also be covered with small pieces of masking tape to prevent particles of carbon entering the cooling system and damaging the water pump.

3. There are two schools of thought as to how much carbon should be removed from the piston crown. One school recommends that a ring of carbon should be left round the edge of the piston and on the cylinder bore wall as an aid to low oil consumption. Although this is probably true for early engines with worn bores, on later engines the thought of the second school can be applied; which is that for effective decarbonisation all traces of carbon should be removed.

4. If all traces of carbon are to be removed, press a little grease into the gap between the cylinder walls and the two pistons which are to be worked on. With a blunt scraper carefully scrape away the carbon from the piston crown, taking great care not to scratch the aluminium. Also scrape away the carbon from the surrounding lip of the cylinder wall. When all carbon has been removed, scrape away the grease which will now be contaminated with carbon particles, taking care not to press any into the bores. To assist prevention of carbon build-up the piston crown can be polished with a metal polish such as Brasso. Remove the rags or masking tape from the other two cylinders and turn the crankshaft so that the two pistons which were at the bottom are now at the top. Place rag or masking tape in the cylinders which have been decarbonised and proceed as just described.

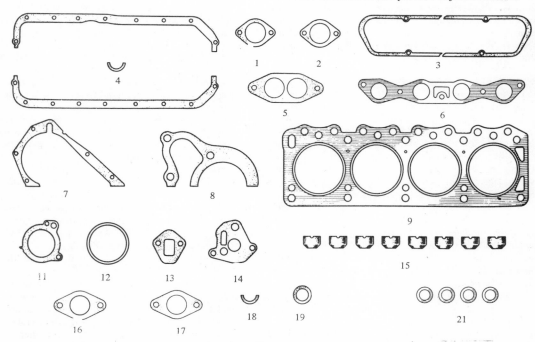

Fig.1.12. VIEW OF THE ITEMS COMPRISED IN A COMPLETE ENGINE GASKET SET

1 Carb/manifold gasket	6 Inlet manifold gasket	12 Sealing ring	17 Exhaust manifold gaskets-outer
2 Water outlet elbow gasket	7 Front cover gasket	13 Fuel pump gasket	18 Sump seal
3 Rocker cover gasket	8 Rear bearing oil seal gasket	14 Oil pump to cylinder block gasket	19 Sump drain plug gasket
4 Sump seal	9 Head gasket	15 Valve stem oil seals	21 Spark plug gaskets
5 Exhaust manifold gasket-centre	11 Water pump gasket	16 Exhaust manifold	

5. If a ring of carbon is going to be left round the piston then this can be helped by inserting an old piston ring into the top of the bore to rest on the piston and ensure that the carbon is not accidentally removed. Check that there are no particles of carbon in the cylinder bores. Decarbonising is now complete.

40. VALVE GUIDES - EXAMINATION & RENOVATION

1. Examine the valve guides internally for scoring and other signs of wear. If a new valve is a very loose fit in a guide and there is a trace of lateral rocking then new guides will have to be fitted.

2. The fitting of new guides is a job which should be done by your local FORD dealer or local engineering works.

41. ENGINE REASSEMBLY - GENERAL

1. To ensure maximum life with minimum trouble from a rebuilt engine, not only must everything be correctly assembled, but everything must be spotlessly clean, all the oilways must be clear, locking washers and spring washers must always be fitted where indicated and all bearing and other working surfaces must be thoroughly lubricated during assembly.

2. Before assembly begins renew any bolts or studs the threads of which are in any way damaged, and whenever possible use new spring washers.

3. Apart from your normal tools, a supply of clean rag, an oil can filled with engine oil (an empty plastic detergent bottle thoroughly cleaned and washed out, will invariably do just as well), a new supply of assorted spring washers, a set of new gaskets, and a torque spanner, should be collected together.

42. ASSEMBLING THE ENGINE

1. Thoroughly clean the block and ensure all traces of old gaskets etc., are removed.

2. Fit a new rear main oil seal bearing retainer gasket to the rear end of the cylinder block (photo). NOTE Later engines make use of a non split circular seal retainer housing. The seal is a press fit in the retainer on these models.

3. Then fit the rear main oil seal bearing retainer housing (photo of early model shown).

4. Do up the four retaining bolts with spring washers under their heads noting that the two bolts (arrowed), nearest the edge of the crankcase are dowelled to ensure correct alignment, and should be tightened first.

5, On early models with non circular seals turn the block upside down and fit the crankshaft rear bearing oil seal to its housing and make sure that the ends of the seal do not project more than 1/32 in. above the face of the housing (photo). Oil the seal generously.

6. Position the upper halves of the shell bearings in their correct positions so that the tabs of the shells engage in the machined keyways in the sides of the bearing locations (photo).

7. Oil the main bearing shells after they have been fitted in position (photo).

8. Thoroughly clean out the oilways in the crankshaft with the aid of a thin wire brush or pipe cleaners (photo).

9. To check for the possibility of an error in the grinding of the crankshaft journal (presuming the crankshaft has been reground) smear engineers blue evenly over each big end journal in turn (photo) with the crankshaft end flange held firmly in position in a vice.

10 With new shell bearings fitted to the connecting rods fit the correct rod to each journal in turn (photo) fully tightening down the securing bolts.

11 Spin the rod on the crankshaft a few times and then remove the big end cap. A fine unbroken layer of engineers blue should cover the whole of the journal. If the blue is much darker on one side than the other or if the blue has disappeared from a certain area (ignore the very edges of the journal) then something is wrong and the journal will have to be checked with a micrometer.

12 The main journals should also be checked in similar fashion with the crankshaft in the crankcase. On completion of these tests remove all traces of the engineers blue.

13 The crankshaft can now be lowered carefully into place (photo).

14 Fit new end float thrust washers. These locate in recesses on either side of the centre main bearing in the cylinder block and must be fitted with the oil grooves facing the crankshaft flange. With the crankshaft in position check for float which should be between 0.003 and 0.011 in. (0.076 to 0.279 mm). If the end float is incorrect remove the thrust washers and select suitable washers to give the correct end float (photo).

15 Place the lower halves of the main bearing shells in their caps making sure that the locking tabs fit into the machined grooves. Refit the main bearing caps ensuring that they are the correct way round and that the correct cap is on the correct journal. The two front caps are marked 'F' (photo), the centre cap 'CENTRE' and the two rear caps 'R'. Tighten the cap bolts to a torque of 55 to 60 lbs.ft. (7.604 to 8.295 kg.m.) Spin the crankshaft to make certain it is turning freely.

16 Check that the piston ring grooves and oilways are thoroughly clean and unblocked. Piston rings must always be fitted over the head of the piston and never from the bottom. The easiest method to use when fitting rings is to wrap a .020 feeler gauge round the top of the piston and place the rings one at a time, starting with the bottom oil control ring, over the feeler gauge.

17 The feeler gauge, complete with ring, can then be slid down the piston over the other piston ring grooves until the correct groove is reached. The piston ring is then slid gently off the feeler gauge into the groove.

18 An alternative method is to fit the rings by holding them slightly open with the thumbs and both of your index fingers (photo). This method requires a steady hand and great care as it is easy to open the ring too much and break it.

19 When assembling the rings note that the compression rings are marked 'top', (photo) and that the upper ring is chromium plated. The ring gaps should be spaced equally round the piston.

20 If the same pistons are being used, then they must be mated to the same connecting rod with the same gudgeon pin. If new pistons are being fitted it does not matter which connecting rod they are used with. Note that the word FRONT is stamped on one side of each of the rods. (Photo). On reassembly the side marked 'FRONT' must be towards the front of the engine.

21 Fit a gudgeon pin circlip in position at one end of the gudgeon pin hole in the piston and fit the piston to the connecting rod by sliding in the gudgeon pin (photo). The arrow on the crown of each piston must be on the same side as the word 'FRONT' on the connecting rod.

22 Fit the second circlip in position (photo). Repeat this procedure for the remaining three pistons and connecting rods.

23 Fit the connecting rod in position and check that the oil hole (arrowed), (photo) in the upper half of each bearing aligns with the oil squirt hole in the connecting rod.

24 With a wad of clean rag wipe the cylinder bores

clean, and then oil them generously. The pistons complete with connecting rods, are fitted to their bores from above (photo). As each piston is inserted into its bore ensure that it is the correct piston/connecting rod assembly for that particular bore and that the connecting rod is the right way round, and that the front of the piston is towards the front of the bore, i.e. towards the front of the engine.

25 The piston will only slide into the bore as far as the oil control ring. It is then necessary to compress the piston rings in a clamp (photo).

26 Gently tap the piston into the cylinder bore with a wooden or plastic hammer (photo). If a proper piston ring clamp is not available then a suitable jubilee clip does the job very well.

27 Note that on crossflow engines the directional arrow may be on the side of the piston (photo).

28 Fit the shell bearings to the big end caps so the tongue on the back of each bearing lies in the machined recess (photo).

29 Generously oil the crankshaft connecting rod journals and then replace each big end cap on the same connecting rod from which it was removed. Fit the locking plates under the head of the big end bolts, tap the caps right home on the dowels and then tighten the bolts to a torque of 20 to 25 lbs.ft. Lock the bolts in position by knocking up the tabs on the locking washers (photo).

30 The semi rebuilt engine will now look like this (photo) and is ready for the cam followers and cam to be fitted.

31 Fit the eight cam followers into the same holes in the block from which each was removed (photo). The cam followers can only be fitted with the block upside down.

32 Fit the woodruff key in its slot on the front of the crankshaft and then press the timing sprocket into place so the timing mark faces forward. Oil the camshaft shell bearings and insert the camshaft into the block (which should still be upside down). (Photo).

33 Make sure the camshaft turns freely and then fit the thrust plate behind the camshaft flange as shown (photo) Measure the endfloat with a feeler gauge - it should be between 0.0025 and 0.0075 in. If this is not so then renew the plate.

34 Fit the two camshaft flange bolts into their joint

washer and screw down the bolts securely (photo).

35 Turn up the tab (arrowed in photo) under the head of each bolt to lock it in place.

36 When refitting the timing chain round the gearwheels and to the engine, the two timing lines (arrowed) must be adjacent to each other on an imaginary line passing through each gearwheel centre.

37 With the timing marks correctly aligned turn the camshaft until the protruding dowel locates in the hole (arrowed) in the camshaft sprocket wheel.

38 Tighten the two retaining bolts and bend up the tabs on the lockwasher (photo).

39 Fit the oil slinger to the nose of the crankshaft, concave side facing outwards. The cut out (arrowed in photo) locates over the woodruff key.

40 Then slide the timing chain tensioner arm over its hinge pin on the front of the block (photo).

41 Turn the tensioner back from its free position so it will apply pressure to the tensioner arm and replace the tensioner on the block sump flange (photo).

42 Bolt the tensioner to the block using spring washers under the heads of the two bolts (arrowed in photo).

43 Remove the front oil seal from the timing chain cover and with the aid of a vice carefully press a new seal into position. (Photo). Lightly lubricate the face of the seal which will bear against the crankshaft.

44 Using jointing compound fit a new gasket in place. (Photo).

45 Fit the timing chain cover replacing and tightening the two dowel bolts first. These fit in the holes nearest the sump flange and serve to align the timing cover correctly. Ensure spring washers are used and then tighten the bolts evenly.

46 Refit the tube or oil breather device to its recess in the top of the petrol pump housing on the block tapping it gently into place. (Photo). Replace the oil pump suction pipe using a new tab washer and position the gauze head so it clears the crankshaft throw and the oil return pipe (where fitted). Tighten the nut and bend back the tab of the lockwasher.

47 Clean the flanges of the sump and fit new gaskets in place. Fit a new oil seal to the flange at the rear of the crankcase and at the front (photo).

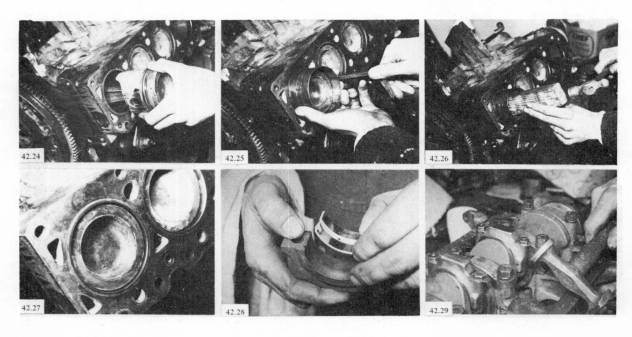

42.24   42.25   42.26

42.27   42.28   42.29

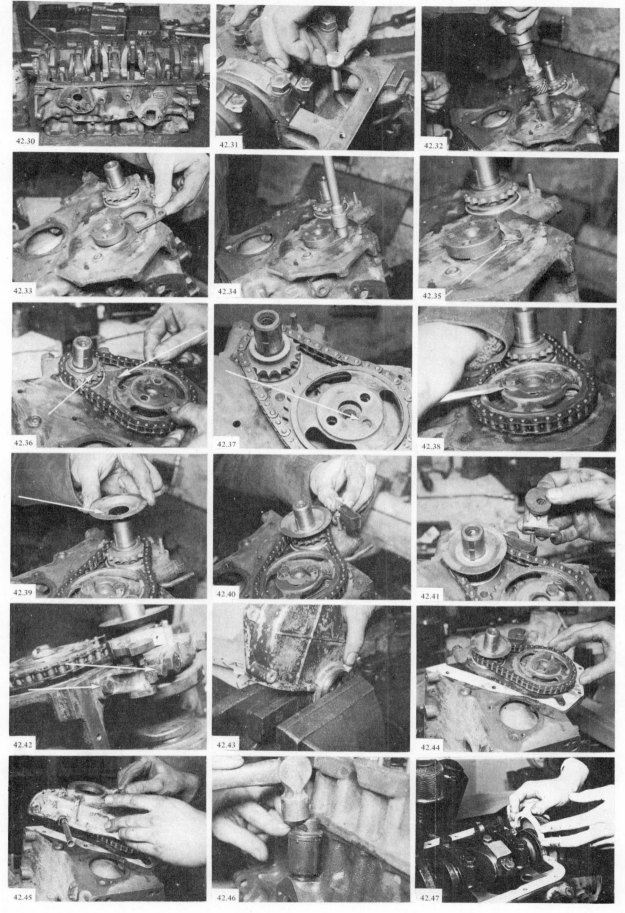

42.30

42.31

42.32

42.33

42.34

42.35

42.36

42.37

42.38

42.39

42.40

42.41

42.42

42.43

42.44

42.45

42.46

42.47

48 Replace the flywheel and tighten down the six securing bolts to a torque of 45 to 50 lb.ft. Carefully replace the sump (photo) taking care not to dislodge the gaskets.
49 Replace the bolts holding the sump in place (photo) in the order shown in Fig.1.7. The two longer sump bolts are fitted at the rear.
50 The engine can now be turned over so it is the right way up. Coat the oil pump flanges with jointing compound (photo).
51 Fit a new gasket in place on the oil pump (photo).
52 Position the oil pump against the block ensuring the skew gear teeth on the drive shaft mate with those on the camshaft (photo).
53 Replace the three securing bolts and spring washers and tighten them down evenly (photo).
54 Moving to the front of the engine align the slot in the crankshaft pulley wheel with the key on the crankshaft and gently tap the pulley wheel home (photo).
55 Secure the pulley wheel by fitting the large flat washer, the spring washer and then the bolt which should be tightened securely (photo).
56 The next step is to thoroughly clean the faces of the block and cylinder head. Then fit a new cylinder head gasket (photo).
57 With the cylinder head on its side lubricate the valve stems and refit the valves to their correct guides (photo). The valves should previously have been ground in. (See Section 33).
58 Then fit the valve stem umbrella oil seals open ends down (photo).
59 Next slide the valve spring into place (photo).
60 Slide the valve spring retainer over the valve stem (photo).
61 Compress the valve spring with a compressor as shown in the photograph.
62 Then refit the split collets (photo). A trace of grease will help to hold them to the valve stem recess until the spring compressor is slackened off and the collets are wedged in place by the spring.
63 Carefully lower the cylinder head onto the block (photo).
64 Replace the cylinder head bolts and screw them down finger tight. Note that two of the bolts are of a different length and should be fitted to the holes indicated in the photograph.

65 With a torque wrench tighten the bolts to 65 to 70 lbs/ft. (photo) in the order shown in Fig.1.4.

66 Fit the pushrods into the same holes in the block from which they were removed. Make sure the pushrods seat properly in the cam followers (photo).

67 Reassemble the rocker gear into the rocker shaft and fit the shaft to the cylinder head. (Photo). Ensure that the oil holes are clear and that the cut-outs for the securing bolts lie facing the holes in the brackets.
68 Tighten down the four rocker bracket washers and bolts to a torque of 17-22 lbs/ft. (photo).
69 The valve adjustments should be made with the engine cold. The importance of correct rocker arm/valve stem clearances cannot be overstressed as they vitally affect the performance of the engine. If the clearances are set too open, the efficiency of the engine is reduced as the valves open late and close earlier than was intended. If, on the other hand the clearances are set too close there is a danger that the stems will expand upon heating and not allow the valves to close properly which will cause burning of the valve head and seat and possible warping. If the engine is in the car access to the rockers is by removing the two holding down studs from the rocker cover, and then lifting the rocker cover and gasket away.
70 It is important that the clearance is set when the tappet of the valve being adjusted is on the heel of the cam, (i.e. opposite the peak). This can be ensured by carrying out the adjustments in the following order (which also avoids turning the crankshaft more than necessary):-

Valve fully open	Valve to adjust
No. 8	No. 1
No. 6	No. 3
No. 4	No. 5
No. 7	No. 2
No. 1	No. 8
No. 3	No. 6
No. 5	No. 4
No. 2	No. 7

The valve clearances are given in the specification Section at the beginning of the Chapter.

71 Working from the front of the engine (No. 1 valve) the correct clearance is obtained by slackening the hexagon locknut with a spanner while holding the ball pin against rotation with a screwdriver. Then, still pressing down with the screwdriver, insert a feeler gauge in the gap between the valve stem head and the rocker arm and adjust the ball pin until the feeler gauge will just move in and out without nipping (photo). Then, still holding the ball pin in the correct position, tighten the locknut. An alternative method is to set the gaps with the engine running and although this may be faster it is no more reliable.
NOTE: Some later engines are fitted with self locking valve clearance adjuster screws in place of the usual screw and locknut. To adjust the valve clearance, simply rotate the adjustment screw with a ring spanner until the correct clearance is obtained.

42.48

42.49

42.50

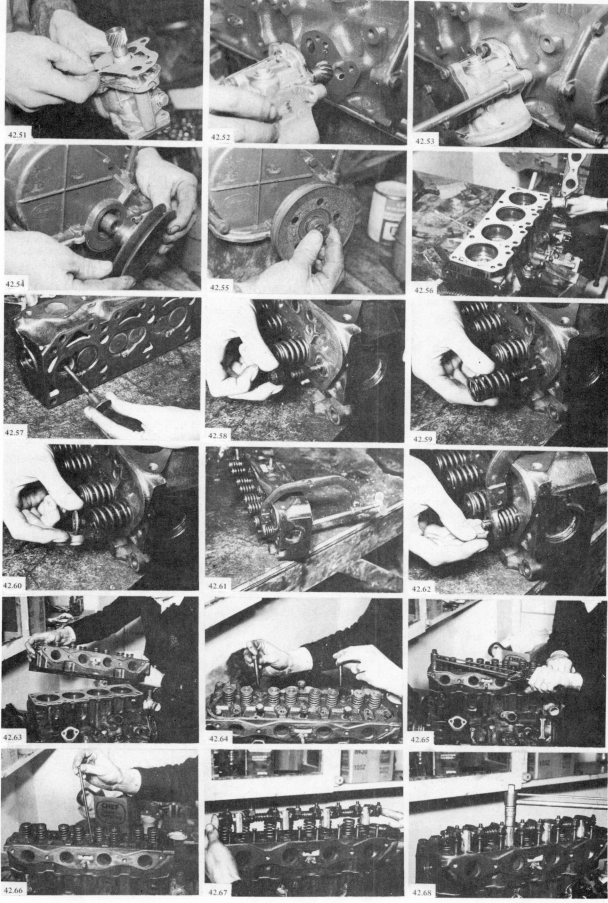

42.51

42.52

42.53

42.54

42.55

42.56

42.57

42.58

42.59

42.60

42.61

42.62

42.63

42.64

42.65

42.66

42.67

42.68

72 Do not refit the rocker cover before replacing the distributor and setting the ignition timing. It is important to set the distributor drive correctly as otherwise the ignition timing will be totally incorrect. It is possible to set the distributor drive in apparently the right position, but, in fact, 180° out, by omitting to select the correct cylinder which must not only be at T.D.C. but must also be on its firing stroke with both valves closed. The distributor drive should therefore not be fitted until the cylinder head is in position and the valves can be observed. Alternatively, if the timing cover has not been replaced, the distributor drive can be replaced when the lines on the timing wheels are adjacent to each other.

Fig.1.13. VIEW OF THE IGNITION TIMING MARKS
Arrows indicate 10° and 6° B.T.D.C., timing cover markings

73 Rotate the crankshaft so that No.1 piston is at T.D.C. and on its firing stroke (the lines in the timing gears will be adjacent to each other). When No.1 piston is at T.D.C. both valves will be closed and both rocker arms will 'rock' slightly because of the stem to arm pad clearance.

74 Note the two timing marks on the timing case (arrowed in photo) and the notch on the crankshaft wheel periphery. When the cut-out is in line with the timing mark on the left this indicates 10° B.T.D.C. and when in line with the one on the right 6° B.T.D.C. Set the crankshaft so the cut-out is in the right position of initial advance which varies depending on the model and is detailed below:-

1297 c.c. & 1500 c.c. H/C up to Sept '67.. 6°   B.T.D.C.
1297 c.c. & 1500 c.c. L/C up to Sept '67..10°   B.T.D.C.
1500 G.T. up to Sept '67 .. ..10°   B.T.D.C.
1297 c.c. & 1598 c.c. H/C from Sept '67..10°   B.T.D.C.
1598 c.c. L/C from Sept '67.. .. .. .. 6°   B.T.D.C.
1598 c.c. G.T. from Sept '67. .. .. .. 8°   B.T.D.C.
1598 c.c. with emission control .. .. .. 4°   B.T.D.C.

75 Hold the distributor in place so the vacuum unit is towards the rear of the engine and at an angle of about 30° to the block. Do not yet engage the distributor drive gear with the skew gear on the camshaft.

76 Turn the rotor arm so that it points towards No.2 plug hole on non crossflow engines and No.2 inlet port on crossflow engines (photo).

77 Push the distributor shaft into its bore and note, as the distributor drive gear and skew gear on the camshaft mate, that the rotor arm turns so that it assumes a position of approximately 90° to the engine (photo). Fit the bolt and washer which holds the distributor clamp plate to the block.

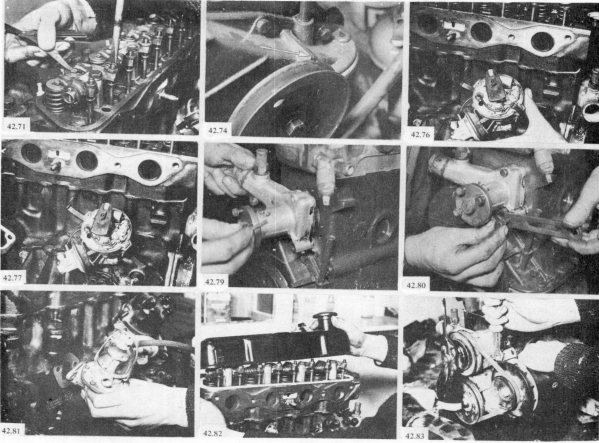

78 Loosen the clamp on the base of the distributor and slightly turn the distributor body until the points just start to open while holding the rotor arm against the direction of rotation so no lost motion is present. Tighten the clamp. For a full description of how to do this accurately see Chapter 4/10.

79 Fit a new gasket to the water pump and attach it to the front of the cylinder block (photo).

80 Note that the dynamo support strap fits under the head of the lower bolt on the water pump as shown. (Photo).

81 Replace the fuel pump using a new gasket and tighten up the two securing bolts (photo).

82 Fit the thermostat and thermostat gasket to the cylinder head and then replace the thermostat outlet pipe. Replace the sparking plugs and refit the rocker cover using a new gasket (photo).

83 Refit the dynamo and adjust it so there is ½ in. play in the fan belt between the water pump and dynamo pulleys (photo). Refit the vacuum advance pipe to the distributor and refit the sender units.

43. FINAL ASSEMBLY

1. Reconnect the ancillary components to the engine in the reverse order to which they were removed.

2. It should be noted that in all cases it is best to reassemble the engine as far as possible before refitting it to the car. This means that the inlet and exhaust manifolds (photo), carburetter, dynamo, water thermostat, oil filter, distributor and engine mounting brackets, should all be in position. Ensure that the oil filter is filled with engine oil, as otherwise there will be a delay in the oil reaching the bearings while the oil filter refills.

43.2

44. ENGINE REPLACEMENT- GENERAL

1. Although the engine can be replaced with one man and a suitable winch, it is easier if two are present. One to lower the engine into the engine compartment and the other to guide the engine into position and to ensure it does not foul anything.

2. At this stage one or two tips may come in useful. Ensure all the loose leads, cables, etc. are tucked out of the way. If not it is easy to trap one and so cause much additional work after the engine is replaced. Smear grease on the tip of the gearbox input shaft before fitting the gearbox.

3. Always fit a new fan belt and new cooling hoses and jubilee clips as this will help eliminate the possibility of failure while on the road. An exchange rebuilt carburetter also helps!

4. Two pairs of hands are better than one when refitting the bonnet. Do not tighten the bonnet securing bolts fully until it is ascertained that the bonnet is on straight.

45. ENGINE REPLACEMENT WITHOUT GEARBOX

1. Position a sling around the engine and support its weight on suitable lifting tackle. If using a fixed hoist raise the engine and then roll the car under it. Place a jack under the gearbox.

2. Lower the engine into the engine compartment ensuring that nothing is fouling. Line up the engine and gearbox raising the height of the gearbox if necessary with the jack until the splines on the gearbox input shaft mate with the splined grooves in the clutch disc centre.

3. To line up the mounting bracket holes it may be necessary to move the engine about slightly and this will be found to be much easier if the lifting slings are still in position and taking most of the weight.

4. Replace the bolts and washers - one on each side - which hold the engine mountings to the bodyframe (photo).

45.4

5. Do up those engine to clutch housing bolts which are accessible from above. The earth strap for the engine is secured by the top left hand bolt. If automatic transmission is fitted turn the engine as required so that the drive plate to torque converter bolts can be fitted. Remove the slings from the engine, and jack up the front of the car securely so it can be worked on from underneath.

6. Working underneath the car replace the lower clutch housing cover and all the lower clutch housing bolts. Do up the bolts holding the clutch housing to the rear of the engine. Replace the clutch slave cylinder and secure it with its circlip (if removed).

7. Refit the starter motor, replace the three retaining bolts, and the starter cable which is held in place with a nut and washer.

8. Replace the engine breather pipe on the clutch housing, (where fitted) and reconnect the fuel lines.

9. Reconnect the high tension lead to the coil centre terminal and the low tension lead to the terminal on the side of the distributor. Refit the ignition distributor cap and connect the H.T. leads to the plugs (if not already done).

10 Reconnect the exhaust downpipe to the exhaust manifold; and secure the throttle linkage and choke control to the carburetter.

11 Replace the temperature gauge sender unit lead.

12 Replace the radiator and reconnect the top and bottom hoses and the heater hoses (on models fitted with a heater unit).

13 Replace the engine splash shield (where fitted); the air

cleaner; the bonnet; and reconnect the two leads to the rear of the dynamo.

14 Reconnect the battery.

15 Check that the drain taps are closed and refill the cooling system with water and the engine with the correct grade of oil. Start the engine and carefully check for oil or water leaks. There should be no oil or water leaks if the engine has been reassembled carefully, all nuts and bolts tightened down correctly, and new gaskets and joints used throughout.

46. ENGINE REPLACEMENT WITH GEARBOX

1. Position a sling round the engine/gearbox unit and support its weight on suitable lifting tackle. If using a fixed hoist raise the power unit and roll the car under it so the power unit will easily drop into the engine compartment.

2. Lower the power unit into position (photo) moving the car forward at the same time. When the engine is ¾ in it will be found helpful to place a trolley jack under the gearbox.

3. Follow the instructions in Chapter 1/45 paragraphs 3 to 5.

4. Reposition the jack under the rear of the engine and

46.2

replace the rear support crossmember tightening down the bolts and locking washers. Refit the gearlever and gaiter. Refit the propeller shaft.

5. Replace the clutch slave cylinder and speedometer drive, and then follow the instructions given in Chapter 1/45, paragraphs 7 to 15.

FAULT FINDING CHART

Cause	Trouble	Remedy
SYMPTOM:	ENGINE FAILS TO TURN OVER WHEN STARTER BUTTON PULLED	
No current at starter motor	Flat or defective battery Loose battery leads Defective starter solenoid or switch or broken wiring Engine earth strap disconnected	Charge or replace battery. Push-start car. Tighten both terminals and earth ends of earth lead. Run a wire direct from the battery to the starter motor or by-pass the solenoid. Check and retighten strap.
Current at starter motor	Jammed starter motor drive pinion Defective starter motor	Place car in gear and rock from side to side. Alternatively, free exposed square end of shaft with spanner. Remove and recondition.
SYMPTOM:	ENGINE TURNS OVER BUT WILL NOT START	
No spark at sparking plug	Ignition damp or wet Ignition leads to spark plugs loose Shorted or disconnected low tension leads Dirty, incorrectly set, or pitted contact breaker points Faulty condenser Defective ignition switch Ignition leads connected wrong way round Faulty coil Contact breaker point spring earthed or broken	Wipe dry the distributor cap and ignition leads. Check and tighten at both spark plug and distributor cap ends. Check the wiring on the CB and SW terminals of the coil and to the distributor. Clean, file smooth, and adjust. Check contact breaker points for arcing, remove and fit new. By-pass switch with wire. Remove and replace leads to spark plugs in correct order. Remove and fit new coil. Check spring is not touching metal part of distributor. Check insulator washers are correctly placed. Renew points if the spring is broken.
No fuel at carburettor float chamber or at jets	No petrol in petrol tank Vapour lock in fuel line (In hot conditions or at high altitude) Blocked float chamber needle valve Fuel pump filter blocked Choked or blocked carburettor jets Faulty fuel pump	Refill tank! Blow into petrol tank, allow engine to cool, or apply a cold wet rag to the fuel line. Remove, clean, and replace. Remove, clean, and replace. Dismantle and clean. Remove, overhaul, and replace. Check CB points on S.U. pumps.
Excess of petrol in cylinder or carburettor flooding	Too much choke allowing too rich a mixture to wet plugs Float damaged or leaking or needle not seating Float lever incorrectly adjusted	Remove and dry sparking plugs or with wide open throttle, push-start the car. Remove, examine, clean and replace float and needle valve as necessary. Remove and adjust correctly.
SYMPTOM:	ENGINE STALLS & WILL NOT START	
No spark at sparking plug	Ignition failure - Sudden Ignition failure - Misfiring precludes total stoppage Ignition failure - In severe rain or after traversing water splash	Check over low and high tension circuits for breaks in wiring Check contact breaker points, clean and adjust. Renew condenser if faulty. Dry out ignition leads and distributor cap.
No fuel at jets	No petrol in petrol tank Petrol tank breather choked Sudden obstruction in carburettor(s) Water in fuel system	Refill tank. Remove petrol cap and clean out breather hole or pipe. Check jets, filter, and needle valve in float chamber for blockage Drain tank and blow out fuel lines

ENGINE FAULT FINDING CHART

Cause	Trouble	Remedy
SYMPTOM:	ENGINE MISFIRES OR IDLES UNEVENLY	
Intermittent sparking at sparking plug	Ignition leads loose	Check and tighten as necessary at spark plug and distributor cap ends.
	Battery leads loose on terminals	Check and tighten terminal leads.
	Battery earth strap loose on body attachment point	Check and tighten earth lead to body attachment point.
	Engine earth lead loose	Tighten lead.
	Low tension leads to SW and CB terminals on coil loose	Check and tighten leads if found loose.
	Low tension lead from CB terminal side to distributor loose	Check and tighten if found loose.
	Dirty, or incorrectly gapped plugs	Remove, clean, and regap.
	Dirty, incorrectly set, or pitted contact breaker points	Clean, file smooth, and adjust.
	Tracking across inside of distributor cover	Remove and fit new cover.
	Ignition too retarded	Check and adjust ignition timing.
	Faulty coil	Remove and fit new coil.
Fuel shortage at engine	Mixture too weak	Check jets, float chamber needle valve, and filters for obstruction. Clean as necessary. Carburettor(s) incorrectly adjusted.
	Air leak in carburettor(s)	Remove and overhaul carburettor.
	Air leak at inlet manifold to cylinder head, or inlet manifold to carburettor	Test by pouring oil along joints. Bubbles indicate leak. Renew manifold gasket as appropriate.
Mechanical wear	Incorrect valve clearances	Adjust rocker arms to take up wear.
	Burnt out exhaust valves	Remove cylinder head and renew defective valves.
	Sticking or leaking valves	Remove cylinder head, clean, check and renew valves as necessary.
	Weak or broken valve springs	Check and renew as necessary.
	Worn valve guides or stems	Renew valve guides and valves.
	Worn pistons and piston rings	Dismantle engine, renew pistons and rings.
SYMPTOM:	LACK OF POWER & POOR COMPRESSION	
Fuel/air mixture leaking from cylinder	Burnt out exhaust valves	Remove cylinder head, renew defective valves.
	Sticking or leaking valves	Remove cylinder head, clean, check, and renew valves as necessary.
	Worn valve guides and stems	Remove cylinder head and renew valves and valve guides.
	Weak or broken valve springs	Remove cylinder head, renew defective springs.
	Blown cylinder head gasket (Accompanied by increase in noise)	Remove cylinder head and fit new gasket.
	Worn pistons and piston rings	Dismantle engine, renew pistons and rings.
	Worn or scored cylinder bores	Dismantle engine, rebore, renew pistons & rings.
Incorrect Adjustments	Ignition timing wrongly set. Too advanced or retarded	Check and reset ignition timing.
	Contact breaker points incorrectly gapped	Check and reset contact breaker points.
	Incorrect valve clearances	Check and reset rocker arm to valve stem gap.
	Incorrectly set sparking plugs	Remove, clean and regap.
	Carburation too rich or too weak	Tune carburettor(s) for optimum performance.
Carburation and ignition faults	Dirty contact breaker points	Remove, clean, and replace.
	Fuel filters blocked causing top end fuel starvation	Dismantle, inspect, clean, and replace all fuel filters.
	Distributor automatic balance weights or vacuum advance and retard mechanisms not functioning correctly	Overhaul distributor.
	Faulty fuel pump giving top end fuel starvation	Remove, overhaul, or fit exchange reconditioned fuel pump.

ENGINE

Cause	Trouble	Remedy
SYMPTOM:	**EXCESSIVE OIL CONSUMPTION**	
Oil being burnt by engine	Badly worn, perished or missing valve stem oil seals	Remove, fit new oil seals to valve stems.
	Excessively worn valve stems and valve guides	Remove cylinder head and fit new valves and valve guides.
	Worn piston rings	Fit oil control rings to existing pistons or purchase new pistons.
	Worn pistons and cylinder bores	Fit new pistons and rings, rebore cylinders.
	Excessive piston ring gap allowing blow-by	Fit new piston rings and set gap correctly.
	Piston oil return holes choked	Decarbonise engine and pistons.
Oil being lost due to leaks	Leaking oil filter gasket	Inspect and fit new gasket as necessary.
	Leaking rocker cover gasket	" " " " " " "
	Leaking tappet chest gasket	" " " " " " "
	Leaking timing case gasket	" " " " " " "
	Leaking sump gasket	" " " " " " "
	Loose sump plug	Tighten, fit new gasket if necessary.
SYMPTOM:	**UNUSUAL NOISES FROM ENGINE**	
Excessive clearances due to mechanical wear	Worn valve gear (Noisy tapping from rocker box)	Inspect and renew rocker shaft, rocker arms, and ball pins as necessary.
	Worn big end bearing (Regular heavy knocking)	Drop sump, if bearings broken up clean out oil pump and oilways, fit new bearings. If bearings not broken but worn fit bearing shells.
	Worn timing chain and gears (Rattling from front of engine)	Remove timing cover, fit new timing wheels and timing chain.
	Worn main bearings (Rumbling and vibration)	Drop sump, remove crankshaft, if bearings worn but not broken up, renew. If broken up strip oil pump and clean out oilways.
	Worn crankshaft (Knocking, rumbling and vibration)	Regrind crankshaft, fit new main and big end bearings.

CHAPTER TWO

COOLING SYSTEM

CONTENTS

SPECIFICATIONS

Type of system	Pressurised, pump impellor and fan assisted
Thermostat - Type	Wax
Thermostat - Location	In cylinder head
Starts to open	85° to 89°C (185° to 190°F)
Fully open	99° to 102°C (210° to 216°F)

Radiator Pressure Cap Opens

Pre Sept '67 models	10 lb/sq.in. (.7031 kg/cm^2)
After Sept '67 models	13 lb/sq.in. (.91 kg/cm^2)

Fan - Type

Standard all models	2 blades. 11 in. (27.9 cm)
Heavy duty (available Sept '67 on)	8 blades. 12 in. (30.48 cm)
Width of fan belt	.38 in. (9.7 mm)
Outside length of fan belt	29 in. (74 cm)
Tension of fan belt	½ in. (12.8 mm) free play between dynamo & water pump pulley wheel
Water pump drive	Belt from crankshaft pulley

Coolant capacity

1297 c.c. models (with heater)	10.20 pints (12.24 US pints, 5.81 litres)
1500 & 1598 c.c. models (with heater)	11.45 pints (13.74 US pints, 6.53 litres)
Radiator type	Corrugated high efficiency fin

Core Height

1297 c.c. model up to Sept '67	11.75 in. (29.85 cm)
1500 c.c. model	14.12 in. (35.87 cm)
1297 c.c. & 1598 c.c. from Sept '67	12.00 in. (30.50 cm)

TORQUE WRENCH SETTINGS

Water pump nuts	5 to 7 lb/ft. (.69 to .97 kg.m)
Fan blade to pulley	5 to 7 lb/ft. (.69 to .97 kg.m)
Thermostat housing	12 to 15 lb/ft. (1.66 to 2.07 kg.m)

GENERAL DESCRIPTION

The engine cooling water is circulated by a thermo-syphon, water pump assisted system, and the whole system is pressurised. This is both to prevent the loss of water down the overflow pipe with the radiator cap in position and to prevent premature boiling in adverse conditions. The radiator cap on models produced before September 1967 was pressurised to 10 lb/sq.in. On later models it is pressurised to 13 lb/sq.in, this has the effect of considerably increasing the boiling point of the coolant. If the water temperature goes above this increased boiling point the extra pressure in the system forces the internal part of the cap off its seat, thus exposing the overflow pipe down which the steam from the boiling water escapes thereby relieving the pressure. It is therefore important to check that the radiator cap is in good condition and that the spring behind the sealing washer has not weakened. Most garages have a special machine in which radiator caps can be tested. The cooling system comprises the radiator, top and bottom water hoses, heater hoses, the impellor water pump, (mounted on the front of the engine, it carries the fan blades, and is driven by the fan belt) the thermostat and the two drain taps. On cars fitted with the 1300 c.c. and 1600 c.c. crossflow engines from September 1967 on the inlet manifold is water heated.

The system functions in the following fashion. Cold water in the bottom of the radiator circulates up the lower radiator hose to the water pump where it is pushed round the water passages in the cylinder block, helping to keep the cylinder bores and pistons cool.

The water then travels up into the cylinder head and circulates round the combustion spaces and valve seats absorbing more heat, and then, when the engine is at its proper operating temperature, travels out of the cylinder head, past the open thermostat into the upper radiator hose and so into the radiator header tank.

The water travels down the radiator where it is rapidly cooled by the in-rush of cold air through the radiator core, which is created by both the fan and the motion of the car. The water, now cold, reaches the bottom of the radiator, when the cycle is repeated.

When the engine is cold the thermostat (which is a valve which opens and closes according to the temperature of the water) maintains the circulation of the same water in the engine.

Only when the correct minimum operating temperature has been reached, as shown in the specification, does the thermostat begin to open, allowing water to return to the radiator.

2. ROUTINE MAINTENANCE

1. Check the level of the coolant in the radiator at least once a week or more frequently if high mileages are being done, and top up with soft water (rain water is excellent) as required.
2. Once every 6,000 miles check the fan belt for wear and correct tension and renew or adjust the belt as necessary. (See Sections 10 & 11 for details).

3. COOLING SYSTEM - DRAINING

1. With the car on level ground drain the system as follows:-
2. If the engine is cold remove the filler cap from the radiator by turning the cap anti-clockwise. If the engine is hot having just been run, then turn the filler cap very slightly until the pressure in the system has had time to disperse. Use a rag over the cap to protect your hand from escaping steam. If, with the engine very hot, the cap is released suddenly, the drop in pressure can result in the water boiling. With the pressure released the cap can be removed.
3. If anti-freeze is in the radiator drain it into a clean bucket or bowl for re-use.
4. Remove the two drain plugs and ensure that the heater control is in the hot position. The radiator plug is

removed by hand, by unscrewing the wing nut, but the cylinder block plug must be removed with the aid of a spanner. The drain plugs are located at the bottom of the radiator and at the rear on the left hand side of the block.
5. When the water has finished running, probe the drain tap orifices with a short piece of wire to dislodge any particles or rust or sediment which may be blocking the taps and preventing all the water draining out.

4. COOLING SYSTEM - FLUSHING

1. With time the cooling system will gradually lose its efficiency as the radiator becomes choked with rust scales, deposits from the water and other sediment. To clean the system out, remove the radiator cap and the drain plugs and leave a hose running in the radiator cap orifice for ten to fifteen minutes.
2. Then close the drain taps and refill with water and a proprietary cleansing compound. Run the engine for 10 to 15 minutes and then drain it and flush out thoroughly for a further ten minutes. All sediment and sludge should now have been removed.
3. In very bad cases the radiator should be reverse flushed. This can be done with the radiator in position. The cylinder block plug is closed and a hose placed over the open radiator drain plug. Water, under pressure, is then forced up through the radiator and out of the header tank filler orifice.
4. The hose is then removed and placed in the filler orifice and the radiator washed out in the usual fashion.

5. COOLING SYSTEM - FILLING

1. Close the two drain taps.
2. Fill the system slowly to ensure that no air locks develop. If a heater is fitted, check that the valve to the heater unit is open, otherwise an air lock may form in the heater. The best type of water to use in the cooling system is rain water, so use this whenever possible.
3. Do not fill the system higher than within ½ in. of the filler orifice. Overfilling will merely result in wastage, which is especially to be avoided when anti-freeze is in use.
4. Only use anti-freeze mixture with a glycerine or ethylene base.
5. Replace the filler cap and turn it firmly clockwise to lock it in position.

6. RADIATOR - REMOVAL, INSPECTION, CLEANING & REPLACEMENT

1. To remove the radiator first drain the cooling system as described in Section 3.
2. Undo the wire clips which hold the top and bottom radiator hoses on the radiator and then pull off the two hoses.
3. Undo and remove the two bolts and washers on either side of the radiator which hold it in place. It may be helpful to remove the battery to give better access to the top right hand bolt.
4. Having removed the bolts lift the radiator out of the engine compartment.
5. With the radiator out of the car any leaks can be soldered up or repaired with a substance such as 'cataloy'. Clean out the inside of the radiator by flushing as detailed in the section before last. When the radiator is out of the car it is advantageous to turn it upside down for reverse flushing. Clean the exterior of the radiator by hosing down the radiator matrix with a strong jet of water to clear away road dirt, dead flies etc.
6. Inspect the radiator hoses for cracks, internal or external perishing, and damage caused by over-tightening

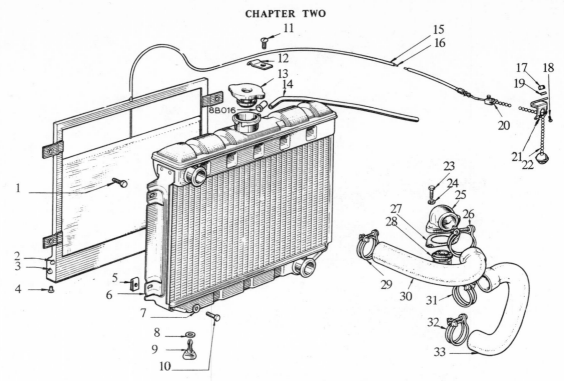

Fig.2.1. EXPLODED VIEW OF THE RADIATOR, HOSES & OPTIONAL BLIND

1 Bolt	10 Bolt	19 Washer	28 Thermostat
2 Pins	11 Screw	20 Chain clamp	29 Hose clip
3	12 Cable clamp	21 Bracket	30 Top hose
4 Rivet	13 Pressure cap	22 Blind control chain	31 Hose clip
5 Screw	14 Overflow pipe	23 Bolt	32 Hose clip
6 Radiator	15 Outer cable	24 Spring washer	33 Bottom hose
7 Washer	16 Inner cable	25 Outlet elbows	
8 Sealing washer	17 Nut	26 Hose clip	
9 Drain plug	18 Screw	27 Gasket	

of the securing clips. Replace the hoses as necessary. Examine the radiator hose securing clips and renew them if they are rusted or distorted. The drain taps should be renewed if leaking, but ensure the leak is not because of a faulty washer behind the tap. If the tap is suspected try a new washer to see if this clears the trouble first.

7. Replacement is a straightforward reversal of the removal procedure.

7. THERMOSTAT - REMOVAL, TESTING & REPLACEMENT

1. To remove the thermostat partially drain the cooling system (4 pints is enough) then loosen the wire clip retaining the top radiator hose to the outlet elbow and pull the hose off the elbow.

2. Undo the two bolts holding the elbow to the cylinder head and remove the elbow and gasket (photo).

3. The thermostat can now be lifted out (photo). Occasionally it will be found that the thermostat has to be gently levered out with a screwdriver due to corrosion. If this operation damages the thermostat in any way always replace it with a new unit.

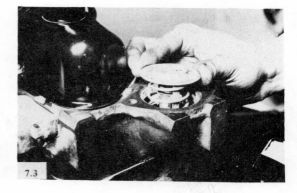

7.3

4. Test the thermostat for correct functioning by dangling it by a length of string in a saucepan of cold water together with a thermometer.

5. Heat the water and note when the thermostat begins to open. This temperature is stamped on the flange of the thermostat, and is also given in the specifications.

6. Discard the thermostat if it opens too early. Continue heating the water until the thermostat is fully open.

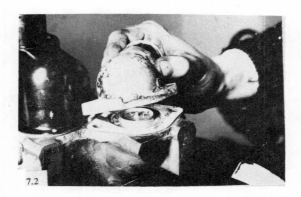

7.2

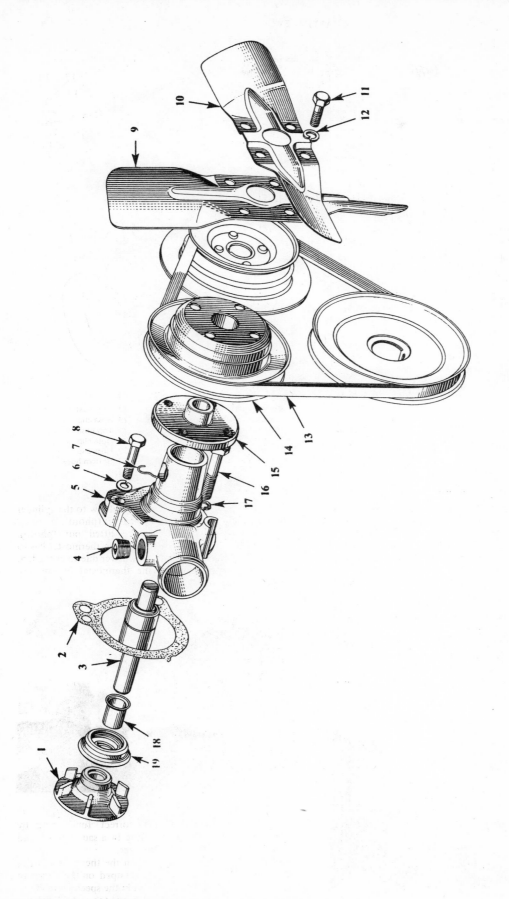

Fig.2.2. EXPLODED VIEW OF THE WATER PUMP

1 Impellor
2 Gasket
3 Spindle & bearing
4 Plug

5 Water pump body
6 Spring washer
7 Bearing securing wire

8 Bolt
9 Fan blade
10 Additional fan blade—(Expt)

11 Bolt
12 Spring washer
13 Fan belt

14 Fan & water pump pulley
15 Hub pulley
16 Bolt

17 Spring washer
18 Slinger
19 Seal

Then let it cool down naturally. If the thermostat will not open fully in boiling water, or does not close down as the water cools, then it must be exchanged for a new one.

7. If the thermostat is stuck open when cold this will be apparent when removing it from the housing.

8. Replacing the thermostat is a reversal of the removal procedure. Remember to use a new gasket between the elbow and the cylinder head. If any pitting or corrosion is apparent it is advisable to apply a layer of sealing compound such as Hermatite to the metal surfaces before reassembly. If the elbow is badly eaten away it must be replaced with a new unit.

8. WATER PUMP - REMOVAL & REPLACEMENT

1. Drain the cooling system as described in Section 3, then loosen the spring clip on the bottom radiator hose at the pump inlet and pull off the hose. Also undo the clip on the small heater hose if fitted and pull off the hose.

2. All numbers used in this section and Section 9 refer to Fig.2.2. Loosen the dynamo securing bolts and swing the dynamo in towards the cylinder block. This frees the fan belt (13) which can now be removed.

3. Undo the four bolts and washers (11,12) which hold the fan blades (9,10) and the pulley wheel (14) in place. Some models may have an eight bladed plastic fan.

4. Remove the fan blades (9,10) and the pulley wheel (14) and then undo the three bolts holding the water pump in place and withdraw the pump together with its gasket.

5. Replacement is a reversal of the above procedure but always remember to use a new gasket.

9. WATER PUMP - DISMANTLING & REASSEMBLY

1. Remove the hub (15) from the water pump shaft (3) either by judicious levering or by using a suitable hub puller such as Ford Tools CPT8000 and P8000 - 4.

2. Carefully pull out the bearing retainer wire (7) and then with the aid of two blocks (a small mandrel and a large vice, if the proper tools are not available) press out the shaft and bearing assembly (3) together with the impellor (1) and seal from the water pump body (5).

3. The impellor vane is removed from the spindle by careful tapping or levering or preferably to ensure no damage and for ease of operation, with an extractor.

4. Remove the seal (19) and the slinger (18) by splitting the later with the aid of a sharp cold chisel.

5. The repair kit available comprises a new shaft and bearing assembly, a slinger, seal, bush, clip and gasket.

6. To reassemble the water pump, press the shaft and bearing assembly (3) into the housing with the short end of the shaft to the front, until the groove in the shaft is in line with the groove in the housing. The bearing retainer wire (7) can then be inserted.

7. Press the pulley hub (15) on to the front end of the shaft (3) until the end of the shaft is half an inch from the outer face of the hub.

8. Fit the new slinger bush (18) with the flanged end first on to the rear of the shaft (3) and refit the pump seal (19) with the thrust face towards the impellor (1). Press the impellor (1) onto the shaft (3) until a clearance of 0.030 in. (0.76 mm) is obtained between the impellor blades and the housing face as shown in Fig.2.3.

10 It is important to check at this stage that the pump turns freely and smoothly before replacement onto the block as detailed in Section 8. After replacement check carefully for leaks.

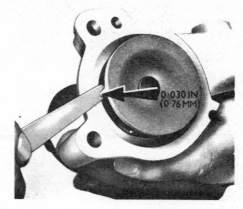

Fig.2.3.   Checking the clearance between the impeller blades and the pump body

10. FAN BELT - ADJUSTMENT

1. The fan belt tension is correct when there is ½ in. of lateral movement at the mid point position of the belt between the dynamo pulley wheel and the water pump pulley wheel.

2. To adjust the fan belt, slacken the dynamo securing bolts as indicated in Fig.2.4. and move the dynamo either in or out until the correct tension is obtained. It is easier if the dynamo securing bolts are only slackened slightly so it requires some force to move the dynamo. In this way the tension of the belt can be arrived at more quickly than by making frequent adjustments.

Fig.2.4.   View of the three dynamo securing bolts and correct fan belt tension

3. If difficulty is experienced in moving the dynamo away from the engine, a long spanner or screwdriver placed behind the dynamo and resting against the cylinder block serves as a very good lever and can be held in this position while the dynamo securing bolts are tightened down.

11. FAN BELT - REMOVAL & REPLACEMENT

1. If the fan belt is worn or has stretched unduly it should be replaced. The most usual reason for replacement is that the belt has broken in service. It is therefore recommended that a spare belt is always carried. Replacement is a reversal of the removal sequence, but as replacement due to breakage is the most usual operation, it is described below.

2. To remove the belt loosen the dynamo securing bolts and push the dynamo in towards the engine.

3. Slip the old belt over the crankshaft, dynamo and water pump pulley wheels and lift it off over the fan blades.

4. Put on a new belt in the same way and adjust it as described in the previous section. NOTE after fitting a new belt it will require adjustment due to its initial stretch after about 250 miles.

12. TEMPERATURE GAUGE - FAULT FINDING

1. If the temperature gauge fails to work either the gauge, the sender unit, the wiring or the connections are at fault.

2. It is not possible to repair the gauge or the sender unit and they must be replaced by new units if at fault.

3. First check the wiring connections and if sound check the wiring for breaks using an ohmmeter. The sender unit and gauge should be tested by substitution.

13. TEMPERATURE GAUGE & SENDER UNIT - RE-MOVAL & REPLACEMENT

1. For details of how to remove and replace the temperature gauge see Chapter 10, Sections 42 and 45.

2. To remove the sender unit disconnect the wire leading into the unit as its connector and undo the unit with a spanner. The unit is located in the cylinder head just below the water outlet elbow on the left side. Replacement is a reversal of the above procedure.

14. ANTI-FREEZE MIXTURE

1. In circumstances where it is likely that the temperature will drop to below freezing it is essential that some of the water is drained and an adequate amount of ethylene glycol anti-freeze such as Fords Long Life Anti-freeze Ford Part No.M97B18-C or Bluecol is added to the cooling system.

2. If either of the above anti-freezes are not available at the time any anti-freeze which conforms with specification BS3151 or BS3152 can be used. Never use an anti-freeze with an alcohol base as evaporation is too high.

3. Either of the above mentioned anti-freezes can be left in the cooling system for up to two years, but after six months it is advisable to have the specific gravity of the coolant checked at your local garage, and thereafter once every three months.

4. Below are the amounts of anti-freeze by percentage volume which should be added to ensure adequate protection down to the temperature given.

Amount of A.F.	Protection to
50%	-37°C (-34°F)
40%	-25°C (-13°F)
30%	-16°C (+3°F)
25%	-13°C (+9°F)
20%	-9°C (+15°F)
15%	-7°C (+20°F)
10%	-4°C (+25°F)

FAULT FINDING CHART

Cause	Trouble	Remedy
SYMPTOM: OVERHEATING		
Heat generated in cylinder not being successfully disposed of by radiator	Insufficient water in cooling system	Top up radiator
	Fan belt slipping (Accompanied by a shrieking noise on rapid engine acceleration	Tighten fan belt to recommended tension or replace if worn.
	Radiator core blocked or radiator grill restricted	Reverse flush radiator, remove obstructions.
	Bottom water hose collapsed, impeding flow	Remove and fit new hose.
	Thermostat not opening properly	Remove and fit new thermostat.
	Ignition advance and retard incorrectly set (Accompanied by loss of power, and perhaps, misfiring)	Check and reset ignition timing.
	Carburettor(s) incorrectly adjusted (mixture too weak)	Tune carburettor(s).
	Exhaust system partially blocked	Check exhaust pipe for constrictive dents and blockages.
	Oil level in sump too low	Top up sump to full mark on dipstick.
	Blown cylinder head gasket (Water/steam being forced down the radiator overflow pipe under pressure)	Remove cylinder head, fit new gasket.
	Engine not yet run-in	Run-in slowly and carefully.
	Brakes binding	Check and adjust brakes if necessary.
SYMPTOM: UNDERHEATING		
Too much heat being dispersed by radiator	Thermostat jammed open	Remove and renew thermostat.
	Incorrect grade of thermostat fitted allowing premature opening of valve	Remove and replace with new thermostat which opens at a higher temperature.
	Thermostat missing	Check and fit correct thermostat.
SYMPTOM LOSS OF COOLING WATER		
Leaks in system	Loose clips on water hoses	Check and tighten clips if necessary.
	Top, bottom, or by-pass water hoses perished and leaking	Check and replace any faulty hoses.
	Radiator core leaking	Remove radiator and repair.
	Thermostat gasket leaking	Inspect and renew gasket.
	Radiator pressure cap spring worn or seal ineffective	Renew radiator pressure cap.
	Blown cylinder head gasket (Pressure in system forcing water/steam down overflow pipe	Remove cylinder head and fit new gasket.
	Cylinder wall or head cracked	Dismantle engine, dispatch to engineering works for repair.

CHAPTER THREE

FUEL SYSTEM AND CARBURATION

CONTENTS

SPECIFICATIONS

Fuel pump	Mechanical, driven from eccentric on camshaft
Delivery pressure	1 to 2 lb/sq.in. (.07 to .14 kg/cm^2)
Later models..	3½ to 5 lb/sq.in. (.25 to .35 kg/cm^2)
Inlet vacuum	8.5 in. (21.6 cm) Hg
Diaphragm Spring	
Test length, except later G.T..	.468 in. (11.88 mm)
Test length, later G.T	.641 in. (16.27 mm)
Test pressure, except later G.T	3¼ to 3½ lb. (1.47 to 1.59 kg)
Test pressure, later G.T	9¼ to 10 lb. (4.31 to 4.54 kg)
Rocker Arm Spring	
Test length all models...	.44 in. (11.18 mm)
Test pressure all models	5 to 5½ lb. (2.27 to 2.5 kg)
Tank Capacity	
Saloons	10 gallons (12 US gallons, 45.4 litres)
Estate cars	8 gallons (9.6 US gallons, 36.3 litres)

Carburetters

1297 c.c. & 1500 c.c. up to Sept '67 except G.T

Type ... ... Ford single choke downdraught

	Manual Choke		Automatic Choke
	1297 c.c.	1500 c.c.	1500 c.c.
Number - Standard..	C6BH-9510-A	C6BH-9510-B	C6BH-9510-C
- Emission controlled	C6BH-9510-D	C6BH-9510-E	C6BH-9510-F
Throttle barrel diameter		34 mm.	34 mm.
Choke diameter..	24 mm.	27.5 mm.	27.5 mm.
Main jet - Standard..	1.25 mm.	1.45 mm.	1.42 mm.
- Emission controlled	1.30 mm.	1.50 mm.	1.47 mm.
Idling speed...	All models 580 to 620 r.p.m.		
Fast idle speed	950 to 1,050 r.p.m.		2,000 to 2,200 r.p.m
Float setting - Inverted	1.12 to 1.14 in.(28.5 to 29 mm)		All models
- Upright	1.38 to 1.40 in.(35.0 to 35.5 mm)		All models
Choke plate pull down..	.14 to .16 in. (3.5 to 4.0 mm)		.15 to .17 in (3.8 to 4.3mm)
Accelerator pump stroke	.126 to .136 in.(3.2 to 3.5 mm)		.146 to .156 in(3.7 to 4.0)
Accelerator pump spring	Red	Red	
De-choke..	-		.18 to .20 in. (4.60 to 5.10 mm)
Vacuum piston link hole	-		Inner
Thermostatic spring slot	-		Centre

1500 G.T. model

Type ... ... Weber twin choke downdraught
Number - Standard.. ... ... 28/36 DCD 23
    - Emission controlled ... ... 28/36 DCD 38

	Primary	Secondary
Choke diameter..	26	27
Auxilary choke diameter...	4.5	4.5
Main jet	140	155
Air correction jet	230	180
Emulsion tube type	F30	F30
Idling jet...	50	70
Needle valve...	1.75 mm	
Float level ...	5.5 mm	
Float stroke...	8.5 mm	
Starter jet ...	190	
Starter air correction jet ...	100	
Accelerator pump jet	60	
Throttle plate chamfer	78°	

1297 c.c. & 1598 c.c. models from Sept '67 except G.T.

Type ... ... Ford single choke downdraught

	1300 c.c.	1600 c.c.	1600 cc emiss.cont.
Number			
Manual transmission	C7BH-9510-A	C7BH-9510-B	C7BH-9510-A
Auto transmission	C7BH-9510-C	C7BH-9510-D	C7BH-9510-B
Throttle barrel diameter	34 mm.	36 mm.	34 mm.
Choke diameter..	25 mm.	28 mm.	26 mm.

Main Jet

Manual	1.32 mm.	1.50 mm.	1.42 mm.
Automatic	1.27 mm.	1.47 mm.	1.37 mm.
Idling speed...	580 to 620 r.p.m.	700 to 740 r.p.m.	
Fast idle speed - Manual	1300 to 1500 "	900 to 1100 r.p.m	1600 to 1800 r.p.m
- Auto...	Home trade 1850 to 2050 r.p.m.		1700 to 1900 "
	Export 2300 to 2350 r.p.m.		
Float setting (up)	1.12 to 1.14 in. (28.5 to 29.0 mm)		1.07 to 1.09 (27.18 to 27.69 mm)
(down)	1.30 to 1.40 in. (35.0 to 35.5 mm)		1.33 to 1.35 in. 33.78 to 34.29 mm)

Choke plate pull down

Manual	.14 to .16 in. (3.5 to 4.0 mm)	.16 to .18 in. 4.0 to 4.6 mm)	.15 to .17 in. 3.18 to 4.32 mm)
Automatic	.13 to .15 in. 3.3 to 3.8 mm)		.15 to .17 in. 3.18 to 4.32 mm)
De-choke (automatic only)	.170 to .210 in. (4.32 to 5.08 mm.)		.20 to .24 in. (5.08 to 6.096 mm)

Accelerator pump stroke

Manual	.145 to .155 in. (3.68 to 3.93 mm)	.135 to .145 in. (3.43 to 3.68 mm)	.120 to .130 in. (3.05 to 3.30 mm)

Automatic	.145 to .155 in.	.170 to .180 in.	.120 to .130 in.
	(3.68 to 3.93 mm)	(4.32 to 4.57 mm)	(3.05 to 3.30 mm)
Accelerator pump lever	.40 in.(10.16 mm)	.30 in. (&.62 mm)	.30 in. (7.62 mm)
Accelerator pump spring	Red		
Vacuum piston link hole	Inner		
Thermostatic spring slot	Centre		

1598 G.T. Model

Type	Weber twin choke downdraught			
Number - Standard..	32 - DFM			
- Emission controlled	32 - DFD			

	32 - DFM		32 - DFD	
	Primary	Secondary	Primary	Secondary
Choke diameter..	26	27	26	27
Main jet	150	155	140	162
Air correction jet	160	140	160	140
Emulsion tube type	F6	F6	F6	F6
Idling jet...	50	45	55	50
Accelerator pump jet				65
Needle valve...	1.75 mm.		1.75 mm.	
Idling speed...	700 to 740 r.p.m.		700 to 740 r.p.m.	
Fast idle speed	2500 r.p.m.		2500 to 2900 r.p.m.	
Fast idle setting..	.95 to 1.05 mm.		.95 to 1.05 mm.	
Float level	7 to 7.5 mm.		6.25 to 6.75 mm.	
Float stroke...	15.00 to 15.50 mm.		15.00 to 15.50 mm.	
Choke plate pull down..	5 mm.		5 mm.	
Choke plate opening	7.5 to 8.5 mm. with lever backed off 10 mm.			
Accelerator pump lever fulcrum..	No.2 hole for cold and temperate climates			

Air Cleaners

Up to Sept '67	Wire gauze or replaceable paper element
From Sept '67	Replaceable paper element

TORQUE WRENCH SETTINGS

Fuel pump	12 to 15 lb/ft. (1.66 to 2.07 kg.m)
Manifolds - Nuts & Bolts	15 to 18 lb/ft. (2.07 to 2.49 kg.m)

1. GENERAL DESCRIPTION

1. The fuel system of all saloon models consists of a ten gallon fuel tank, a mechanically operated fuel pump, a single venturi downdraught Ford carburetter (G.T. models use a Weber twin choke downdraught carburetter) and the necessary fuel lines between the tank and the pump and the pump and the carburetter.

2. Estate car models are fitted with an eight gallon fuel tank which is mounted under the rear floor pan. The remainder of the fuel system is identical in layout to saloon models

2. AIR CLEANERS - REMOVAL, REPLACEMENT & SERVICING

1. Several different types of air cleaner were fitted depending on year of manufacture and the type of carburetter used. The four different air cleaners used are illustrated in Figs.3.3. and 3.4.

2. Two main types of cleaner were employed. Those fitted to G.T. models make use of a paper element, while those fitted to all other models make use of either an oil wetted gauge or paper element.

3. The air cleaners should be serviced at intervals of 6,000 miles and the paper element type renewed at intervals of 18,000 miles.

4. Undo the bolts (or nuts depending on model) which hold the air cleaner cover to the air cleaner body and lift the cover away.

5. Lift out the element from the air cleaner body making a careful note of the sealing ring positions.

6. In the case of the gauze type of cleaner to service it thoroughly wash the element in petrol, re-oil it with engine oil, let it drain, and then refit it to the air cleaner body.

7. To service the upper element type first clean the interior of the air cleaner cover, and blow, shake, and gently brush out the dust from the folds of the air cleaner element. Every 18,000 miles or earlier if the element becomes torn renew the paper filter.

3. FUEL PUMP - ROUTINE SERVICING

1. At intervals of 6,000 miles unscrew the clamp nut on top of the fuel pump, pull aside the clamp and remove the glass bowl.

2. Thoroughly clean the glass bowl inside and out, and use a paintbrush and petrol to clean any sediment from the pump body and filter screen.

3. Ensure that the gasket which seats under the glass bowl is not pitted or split, refit the glass bowl, pull over the retaining clamp and tighten down the clamp nut.

4. CARBURETTER - ROUTINE SERVICING

1. At intervals of 6,000 miles check the carburetter idling mixture setting and adjust as necessary as described in Section 21.

5. A.C. FUEL PUMP - DESCRIPTION

1. The mechanically operated A.C. fuel pump is actuated through a spring loaded rocker arm. One arm of the rocker (20) bears against an eccentric on the camshaft and the other arm (21) operates a diaphragm pull rod. NOTE all references in brackets should be co-related with Fig.3.1.

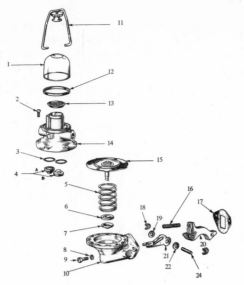

Fig.3.1. EXPLODED VIEW OF THE A.C. TYPE FUEL PUMP

1 Glass dome	13 Filter element
2 Screw	14 Upper pump body
3 Valve gasket	15 Diaphragm
4 Inlet & outlet valves	16 Actuating arm return spring
5 Diaphragm return spring	17 Gasket
6 Spring seats	18 Actuating arm swivel pin re-
7	taining plates
8 Spring washer	19 Shim
9 Bolt	20 Primary actuating arm
10 Lower pump body	21 Secondary actuating arm
11 Dome retaining clamp	22 Shim
12 Dome to body sealing ring	24 Actuating arm swivel pin

2. As the engine camshaft rotates, the eccentric moves the pivoted rocker arm outwards which in turn pulls the diaphragm pull rod and the diaphragm (15) down against the pressure of the diaphragm spring (5).

3. This creates sufficient vacuum in the pump chamber to draw in fuel from the tank through the fuel filter gauze (13), and non-return valve (4A).

4. The rocker arm is held in constant contact with the eccentric by an anti-rattle spring (16), and as the engine camshaft continues to rotate the eccentric allows the rocker arm to move inwards. The diaphragm spring (5) is thus free to push the diaphragm (15) upwards forcing the fuel in the pump chamber out to the carburetter through the non-return outlet valve (4B). On some models a different make of fuel pump may be fitted (see Fig.3.2.). Its system of operation and constructional features are virtually identical to the A.C. unit.

5. When the float chamber in the carburetter is full the float chamber needle valve will close so preventing further flow from the fuel pump.

6. The pressure in the delivery line will hold the diaphragm downwards against the pressure of the diaphragm spring, and it will remain in this position until the needle valve in the float chamber opens to admit more petrol.

6. A.C. FUEL PUMP - REMOVAL & REPLACEMENT

1. Remove the fuel inlet and outlet pipes by unscrewing the union nuts. On some models it is easier to undo the securing clips which hold the flexible pipes to the metal pipes which emerge from the pump.

2. Undo the two bolts which hold the pump in place and then lift the pump together with the gasket away from the crankcase (photo).

3. Replacement of the pump is a reversal of the above process. Remember to use a new crankcase to fuel pump gasket to ensure no oil leaks, ensure that both faces of

the flange are perfectly clean, and check that the rocker arm lies on top of the camshaft eccentric and not underneath it.

7. A.C. FUEL PUMP TESTING

Presuming that the fuel lines and unions are in good condition and that there are no leaks anywhere, check the performance of the fuel pump in the following manner. Disconnect the fuel pipe at the carburetter inlet union, and the high tension lead to the coil, and with a suitable container or a large rag in position to catch the ejected fuel, turn the engine over on the starter motor solenoid. A good spurt of petrol should emerge from the end of the pipe every second revolution.

8. A.C. FUEL PUMP DISMANTLING

1. Unscrew the finger nut on top of the bowl and push the clamp aside. Lift off the glass cover.

2. Remove the cork sealing washer and the fine mesh filter gauze.

3. If the condition of the diaphragm is suspect or for any other reason it is wished to dismantle the pump fully, proceed as follows:- Mark the upper and lower flanges of the pump that are adjacent to the flange on the diaphragm and to each other. Unscrew the five screws and spring washers which hold the two halves of the pump body together. Separate the two halves with great care, ensuring that the diaphragm does not stick to either of the two flanges.

4. Unscrew the screws which retain the valve plate and remove the plate and gasket together with the inlet and outlet valves (Some later pumps have a simplified valve plate arrangement which is released by one screw. Still later models use staking to hold the valves in place).

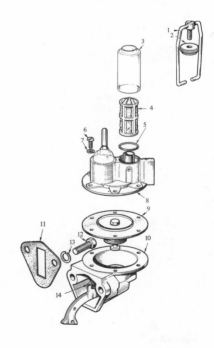

Fig.3.2. EXPLODED VIEW OF THE LATER TYPE OF FUEL PUMP

1 Dome retaining clamp	8 Upper pump body
2 Finger nut	9 Diaphragm
3 Glass dome	10 Lower pump body
4 Filter element	11 Gasket
5 Dome to body retaining ring	12 Bolt
6 Screw	13 Spring washer
7 Spring washer	14 Actuating arm return spring

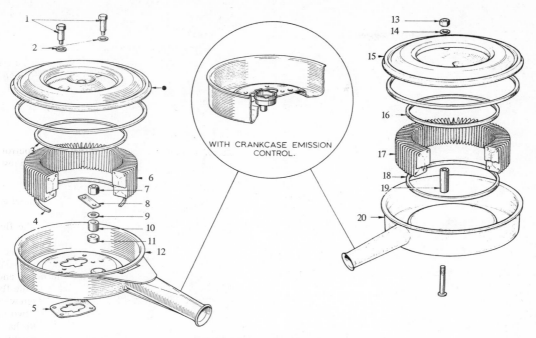

Fig.3.3. EXPLODED VIEW OF THE AIR CLEANER – G.T.

1 Air cleaner top retaining bolts	6 Paper element	11 Rubber washer	16 Paper element top sealing ring
2 Plain washers	7 Nut	12 Aircleaner body	17 Paper element
3 Paper element top sealing ring	8 Tab washer	13 Nut	18 Paper element bottom sealing
4 Paper element bottom sealing ring	9 Plain washer	14 Plain washer	19 Spacer ring
5 Aircleaner/manifold gasket	10 Spacer	15 Aircleaner top	20 Aircleaner body

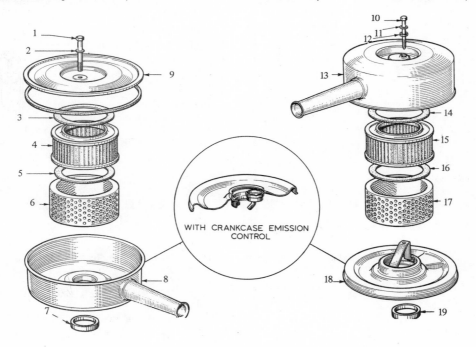

Fig.3.4. EXPLODED VIEW OF AIR CLEANERS – EXCEPT G.T.

1 Air cleaner through bolt	6 Alternative oil wetted gauze	10 Aircleaner through bolt	15 Paper element
2 Plain washer	type element	11 Plain washer	16 Element sealing ring-bottom
3 Paper element top sealing ring	7 Gasket	12 Fibre washer	17 Alternative oil wetted gauze type
4 Paper element	8 Aircleaner body	13 Aircleaner body	18 Aircleaner base plate
5 Paper element bottom sealing ring	9 Aircleaner top	14 Element sealing ring-top	19 Gasket

5. Press down and rotate the diaphragm a quarter of a turn (in either direction) to release the pull rod from the operating lever, and lift away the diaphragm and pull rod (which is securely fixed to the diaphragm and cannot be removed from it). Remove the diaphragm spring and the metal and fibre washer underneath it.

6. If it is necessary to dismantle the rocker arm assembly, remove the retaining circlips and washer from the rocker arm pivot rod and slide out the rod which will then free the rocker arm, operating rod, and anti-rattle spring.

9. A.C. FUEL PUMP EXAMINATION & REASSEMBLY

1. Check the condition of the glass bowl cover sealing washer, and if it is hardened or broken it must be replaced. The diaphragm should be checked similarly and replaced if faulty. Clean the pump thoroughly and agitate the valves in paraffin to clean them out. This will also improve the contact between the valve seat and the valve. It is unlikely that the pump body will be damaged, but check for fractures and cracks.

2. To reassemble the pump proceed as follows:- Replace the rocker arm assembly comprising the operating link, rocker arm, anti-rattle spring and washer in their relative positions in the pump body. Align the holes in the operating link, rocker arm, and washers with the holes in the body and insert the pivot pin.

3. Refit the circlips to the grooves in each end of the pivot pin.

4. Earlier pumps used valves which had to be built up, while later versions used ready assembled valves which are merely dropped into place in the inlet and outlet ports. Ensure that the correct valve is dropped into each port. Stake the valves into place where this method of attachment is used.

5. Reassemble the earlier type of valve as follows:- Position the delivery valve in place on its spring. Place the inlet valve in position in the pump body and then fit the spring. Place the small four legged inlet valve spring retainer over the spring with the legs positioned towards the spring.

6. Place the valve retaining gasket in position, replace the plate, and tighten down the three securing screws. (Or single screw in the case of some models). Check that the valves are working properly with a suitable piece of wire.

7. Position the fibre and steel washer in that order in the base of the pump and place the diaphragm spring over them.

8. Replace the diaphragm and pull rod assembly with the pull rod downwards and the small tab on the diaphragm adjacent to the centre of the flange and rocker arm.

9. With the body of the pump held so that the rocker arm is facing away from one, press down the diaphragm, turning it a quarter of a turn to the left at the same time. This engages the slot on the pull rod with the operating lever. The small tab on the diaphragm should now be at an angle of 90° to the rocker arm and the diaphragm should be firmly located.

10 Move the rocker arm until the diaphragm is level with the body flanges and hold the arm in this position. Reassemble the two halves of the pump ensuring that the previously made marks on the flanges are adjacent to each other.

11 Insert the five screws and lockwashers and tighten them down finger tight.

12 Move the rocker arm up and down several times to centralise the diaphragm, and then with the arm released, tighten the screws securely in a diagonal sequence.

13 Replace the gauze filter in position and fit a new

glass dome seal. Refit the glass dome to the pump body, pull over the clamp and tighten down the finger nut.

10. SALOON FUEL TANK - REMOVAL & REPLACEMENT

1. The fuel tank is positioned in the middle of the boot and the top surface of the tank acts as part of the boot floor. Remove the filler cap and with a 4 ft. length of rubber tubing syphon the petrol tank contents into a suitable container. (No drain plug is fitted).

2. Disconnect the battery. Then jack up the rear of the car and support on stands. Referring to Fig.3.5. undo the clip which secures the fuel pipe (3) to the sender unit (16). Disconnect the fuel gauge wire from the sender unit terminal.

3. Open the boot, take out the rubber floor covering (if fitted), and undo the two clips (34) which hold the rubber hose to the filler pipe (33) and tank neck. Slide the rubber hose and filler pipe out of the way.

4. If a fuel tank shield (5) is fitted, this must first be removed. Then undo from inside the boot the self tapping bolts and washers which hold the fuel tank to the floor pan. The tank is then lifted out from inside the boot.

5. Replacement is quite straightforward and is a reversal of the removal sequence. To ensure no water enters the boot clean the floor pan and tank mating flanges and apply a continuous bead of Bostik No.6 to the floor pan flange before refitting the tank.

11. ESTATE CAR FUEL TANK - REMOVAL & REPLACEMENT

1. The fuel tank is located under the rear floor pan, and unlike on the car has to be removed from beneath the vehicle. Remove the filler cap and with a 4 ft. length of rubber tubing syphon the petrol tank contents into a suitable container. (No drain plug is fitted). Disconnect the battery.

2. Jack up the rear of the car and support securely on stands. Remove the spare wheel.

3. Referring to Fig.3.6. undo the clips (6,10) which secure the rubber connector hose (9) to the filler pipe (4) and tank neck. Pull off the rubber hose (9).

4. Release one of the clips (16,17) which holds the adaptor hose (20) between the fuel tank outlet pipe (on top of the sender unit) and the tank to pump feed pipe, and disconnect the latter.

5. Undo the nuts and bolts which hold the tank and where fitted the body tray in place, partially lower the tank so as to gain access to its top surface so the sender unit wire and the vent pipe can be disconnected.

6. The fuel tank can now be removed from underneath the car.

7. Replacement is quite straightforward and is a reversal of the removal sequence.

12. FUEL GAUGE SENDER UNIT - REMOVAL & REPLACEMENT

1. On Saloon car models the sender unit can be removed with the fuel tank in place but on Estate cars the fuel tank has to be removed as described in Section 11.

2. On the saloon disconnect the battery, syphon the fuel into a suitable container, jack up the rear of the car and support on stands to provide good access. Disconnect the fuel gauge unit wire and the fuel pipe from the sender unit.

3. On both saloon and estate car models with a cold chisel carefully unscrew the sender unit retainer ring and then remove the sender unit and sealing ring from the tank.

4. Replacement is a straightforward reversal of the

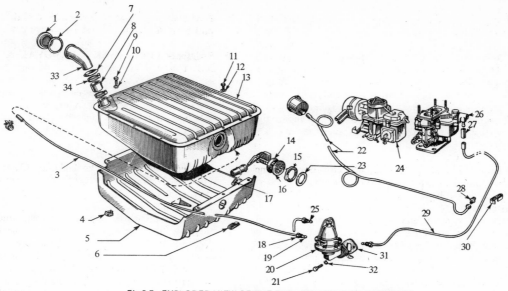

Fig.3.5. EXPLODED VIEW OF THE FUEL SYSTEM & OIL PRESSURE
INDICATOR SYSTEM — SALOON MODELS

1 Cap	10 Washer	19 Olive	28 Adaptor
2 Cap sealing ring	11 Bolt	20 Fuel pump	29 Pump to carburetter
3 Tank to pump feed	12 Washer	21 Bolt	feed pipe
pipe	13 Petrol tank	22 Engine to gauge feed	30 Clip
4 Clip	14 Gasket	pipe	31 Gasket
5 Body tray	15 Sender unit retaining	23 Ring	32 Spring washer
6 Clip	plate	24 Carburetter	33 Filler tube
7 Grommet	16 Tank sender unit	25 Union	34 Hose clip
8 Hose	17 Float	26 Carburetter	
9 Bolt	18 Union	27 Adaptor	

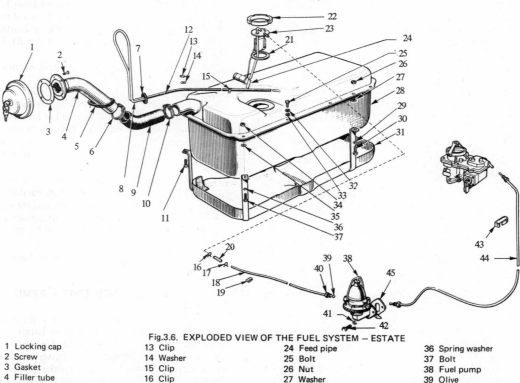

Fig.3.6. EXPLODED VIEW OF THE FUEL SYSTEM — ESTATE

1 Locking cap	13 Clip	24 Feed pipe	36 Spring washer
2 Screw	14 Washer	25 Bolt	37 Bolt
3 Gasket	15 Clip	26 Nut	38 Fuel pump
4 Filler tube	16 Clip	27 Washer	39 Olive
5 Grommet	17 Clip	28 Fuel tank	40 Union
6 Hose clip	18 Tank to pump feed	29 Spring washer	41 Spring washer
7 Grommet	pipe	30 Bolt	42 Bolt
8 Air vent	19 Clip	31 Body tray	43 Clip
9 Flexible hose	20 Adaptor	32 Washers	44 Pump to carburetter
10 Hose clip	21 Gasket	33	feed pipe
11 Screw	22 Sender unit retainer	34 Nut	45 Gasket
12 Tubing	23 Sender unit	35 Washer	

removal sequence. Always fit a new seal to the recess in the tank to ensure no leaks develop.

13. FUEL TANK CLEANING

1. With time it is likely that sediment will collect in the bottom of the fuel tank. Condensation, resulting in rust and other impurities, will usually be found in the fuel tank of any car more than three or four years old.

2. When the tank is removed it should be vigorously flushed out and turned upside down, and if facilities are available, steam cleaned.

14. CARBURETTERS - GENERAL DESCRIPTION

1. A Ford single choke downdraught carburetter is fitted to all except G.T. models. The same basic Ford carburetter is used irrespective of whether it is fitted to a 1300, 1500, or 1600 c.c. engine. Internally different sized jets and chokes cater for the variations in engine capacity. If ever purchasing an exchange carburetter, as they all look identical it is essential to check the part number (See specifications) to ensure a carburetter with the correct jets and choke is obtained.

2. Certain models are fitted with the same carburetter, but with an automatic choke. The addition of this device makes no difference to the internal layout of the unit.

3. The carburetter fitted to G.T. models may be either the Weber 28/36 DCD23 or 38, or the Weber 32-DFM or DFD (See specifications on page 58 for model applicability).

4. Both types of Weber carburetter are of the vertical downdraught twin choke type.

5. Small auxiliary venturi tubes are located at the top of each barrel and these discharge fuel into the narrowest parts of the larger venturis which are located further down the barrels.

6. The throttle plate in one barrel opens before that in the other barrel to ensure good performance at high revolutions as well as smooth progression when the throttle is operated at low engine speeds.

7. At about every 6,000 miles this carburetter should be checked for slow running, and at the same time the float level needs to be checked to ensure that the correct amount of fuel is being retained. At the same time the float bowl is cleaned of any sediment which may have collected.

15. FORD SINGLE CHOKE CARBURETTER - REMOVAL & REPLACEMENT

1. Open the bonnet, take off the air cleaner as described in Section 2, and disconnect the vacuum and fuel pipes at the carburetter.

2. Referring to Fig.3.7 free the throttle control rod (26). from the throttle lever and place the two spring clips used on the nylon linkage in a safe place where they will not become lost.

3. On cars fitted with a manual choke undo the screw of the trunnion on the choke lever to free the inner choke cable. Then slacken the screw which clamps the outer cable to the upper carburetter body cable bracket to free the outer cable.

4. On cars fitted with an automatic choke carburetter partially drain the cooling system and simply free the two hoses from the automatic choke unit.

5. On all models undo the two nuts and spring washers which hold the carburetter to the inlet manifold and remove the carburetter.

6. Replacement is a straightforward reversal of the removal sequence but note the following points:-

a) Remove the old inlet manifold to carburetter gasket, clean the mating flanges and fit a new gasket in place.

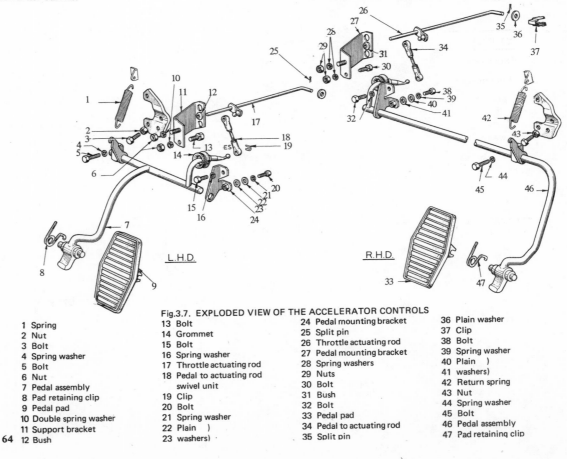

L.H.D.   R.H.D.

Fig.3.7. EXPLODED VIEW OF THE ACCELERATOR CONTROLS

1 Spring	13 Bolt	24 Pedal mounting bracket	36 Plain washer
2 Nut	14 Grommet	25 Split pin	37 Clip
3 Bolt	15 Bolt	26 Throttle actuating rod	38 Bolt
4 Spring washer	16 Spring washer	27 Pedal mounting bracket	39 Spring washer
5 Bolt	17 Throttle actuating rod	28 Spring washers	40 Plain)
6 Nut	18 Pedal to actuating rod	29 Nuts	41 washers)
7 Pedal assembly	swivel unit	30 Bolt	42 Return spring
8 Pad retaining clip	19 Clip	31 Bush	43 Nut
9 Pedal pad	20 Bolt	32 Bolt	44 Spring washer
10 Double spring washer	21 Spring washer	33 Pedal pad	45 Bolt
11 Support bracket	22 Plain)	34 Pedal to actuating rod	46 Pedal assembly
12 Bush	23 washers)	35 Split pin	47 Pad retaining clip

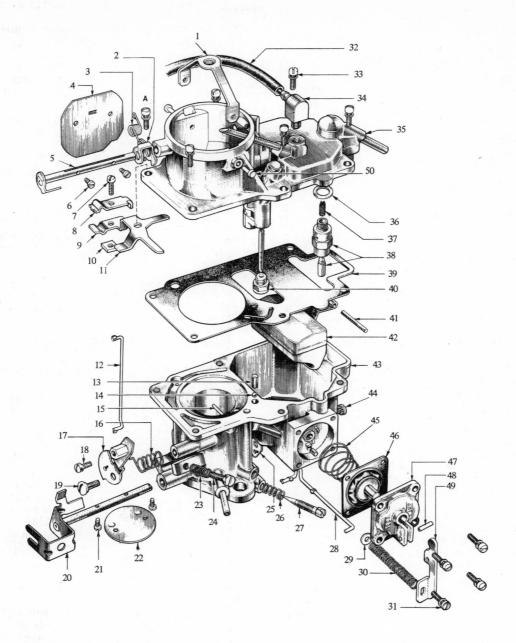

Fig.3.8. EXPLODED VIEW OF CARBURETTER WITH MANUAL CHOKE — EXCEPT G.T.

1 Air cleaner retaining bracket
2 Choke control lever
3 Spring
4 Choke plate
5 Choke spindle
6 Plate to spindle retaining screws
7 Screw
8 Cable clamp—top
9 Cable clamp—bottom
10 Nut
11 Bracket
12 Choke control rod
13 Pump discharge ball weight

14 Discharge ball valve
16 Spring
17 Fast idle cam
18 Screw
19 Screw
20 Throttle lever & spindle assembly
21 Plate retaining screws
22 Throttle plate
23 Spring
24 Throttle stop screw
25 Pump control lever
26 Spring
27 Idling mixture adjustment needle

28 Accelerator pump link to
   lever rod
29 Washer
30 Spring
31 Screw
32 Overflow pipe
33 Screw
34 Adaptor
35 Carburetter top cover
36 Washer
37 Filter
38 Needle valve
39 Gasket

40 Main metering jet
41 Float pivot pin
42 Float
43 Carburetter body
44 Screw
45 Diaphragm return spring
46 Accelerator pump diaphragm
47 Accelerator pump cover
48 Actuating lever pivot pin
49 Actuating lever
50 Aircleaner bracket retaining
   pin

b) After reconnecting the manual choke ensure that the choke opens and closes fully with slack in the cable when the choke control is pushed right in.

16. WEBER TWIN CHOKE CARBURETTER - REMOVAL & REPLACEMENT

1. The Weber carburetter is removed and replaced in exactly the same way as the single choke carburetter (See Section 15) but note the following points:-

2. The carburetter is retained to the inlet manifold by four nuts.

3. When refitting the air cleaner first fit a rubber gasket to the top of the carburetter. Then fit the air cleaner body placing a rubber insulator round each mounting stud and a sleeve through each insulator. Place a flat washer and then double type tab washers over the studs and tighten down the securing nuts. Turn up the tab washers to lock the nuts in position.

17. CARBURETTERS - DISMANTLING & REASSEMBLY - GENERAL

1. With time the component parts of the Ford or Weber carburetter will wear and petrol consumption will increase. The diameter of drillings and jets may alter, and air and fuel leaks may develop round spindles and other moving parts. Because of the high degree of precision involved, in the authors opinion it is best to purchase an exchange rebuilt carburetter. This is one of the few instances where it is better to take the latter course rather than to rebuild the component oneself.

2. It may be necessary to partially dismantle the carburetter to clear a blocked jet or to renew the accelerator pump diaphragm. The accelerator pump itself may need attention and gaskets may need renewal. Providing care is taken there is no reason why the carburetter may not be completely reconditioned at home, but ensure a full repair kit can be obtained before you strip the carburetter down. NEVER poke out jets with wire or similar to clean them but blow them out with compressed air or air from a car tyre pump.

18. FORD SINGLE CHOKE CARBURETTER - DISMANTLING & REASSEMBLY

1. The instructions in this section apply to all non G.T. models including cars with automatic transmissions which make use of the same basic carburetter fitted with an external automatic choke. All numerical references are to Fig.3.8. unless otherwise stated.

2. Undo the six screws and washers (33) which hold the carburetter top (35) to the main body (43).

3. Lift off the top (35) from the main body (43) at the same time unlatching the choke control rod (12). Ensure that the gasket (39) comes off with the top cover (35). On cars fitted with an automatic choke undo the screw which holds the fast idle cam and rod assembly to the lower body.

4. From the top cover pull out the float pivot pin (41) and remove the float (42). The needle valve and body (38) can then be unscrewed and the gasket (36) removed.

5. Only on cars fitted with an automatic choke undo the screw which holds the choke piston lever. Then take off the lever, the link, the choke control lever and finally the piston from the inner housing. Undo the two screws holding the inner housing to the carburetter, remove the housing and gasket, the choke housing lever, shaft assembly, choke control rod, and the Teflon bush.

6. On all models remove the accelerator pump discharge ball valve (14) and weight (13).

7. If it is wished to remove the choke plate (4) first cut the heads off the retaining pins (50) which hold the air cleaner retainer bracket in place (1). Next undo the grub screws (6) which hold the plate to the spindle (5) and pull out the spindle.

8. Carefully smooth away the burrs from around the choke plate screw holes on the spindle and pull out the choke spindle at the same time sliding the choke control lever (2) and spring (3) off.

9. The main jet (40) can now be unscrewed from the top cover (35).

10 Undo the screw which holds the pushrod arm of the accelerator pump to the throttle spindle, and then detach the arm, pushrod (28) and spring (30).

11 The four screws and split washers (31) which hold the accelerator pump cover (47) in place can now be undone and the cover, operating arm (49), diaphragm (46), and return spring (45) removed.

12 Undo the cheese head pivot screw (19) and remove the choke lever (17) and the return spring (16).

13 Undo the two grub screws (21) which hold the choke plate (22) in position on the spindle (20), and remove the plate.

14 Carefully file down any burrs round the grub screw holes on the spindle and slide the spindle out of the main body. Undo the idling mixture adjustment needle (27) and spring (26), and the throttle stop screw (24) and spring (23).

15 Reassembly commences by refitting the throttle stop screw (24) and spring (23), and the idling mixture adjustment needle (27) and spring (26). Screw in the latter so it just seats and then back off one turn.

16 Slide the choke spindle (5) into place on the top cover (35) after ensuring the spring (3) and choke control lever (2) are in position.

17 Refit the choke plate (4) so the small rectangular stamping on the plate faces upwards and is adjacent to the spindle (5) when the plate is in the closed position. Tighten down the two grub screws (6) which hold the plate in place.

18 Refit the air cleaner retaining bracket (1) and tap in two new retaining pins.

19 Screw the main jet (40) into position and then replace the needle valve housing (38). Fit a new gasket on the top cover (35) and then refit the needle, sharp end upwards, to the valve housing.

20 Replace the float (42) securing it in position with the pin (41). Check the float and fuel level setting as described in Section 19.

21 Position the return spring (16) on the bearing abutment on the lower body (43), and refit the choke lever (17) retaining it in place by its pivot screw (19). On automatic choke carburetters only fit the piston, piston lever and link in the inner position to the inner housing. Refit the choke thermostat lever and then screw it into the inner housing. Next position the choke control rod in the choke lever and with the vacuum gasket in place refit the inner housing with the two screws. Finally ensure when the outer housing assembly is fitted to the inner housing that the index marks align, the gasket is in place, and the three securing screws are tightened down evenly.

22 Carefully replace the accelerator pump discharge ball valve (14) and weight (13), Slide one end of the choke control lever into the pull down stop and the other end into the fast idle cam, and with a new gasket (39) positioned between the upper cover (35) and lower body (43) and with the choke plate closed fit the two halves together and retain with five of the six screws. Note that the sixth screw (A) holds the choke cable bracket in place.

23 Slide the throttle spindle (20) into the main body and

refit the throttle plate (22) so the two recessed indentations as the plate are adjacent to the recesses of the screw heads when the throttle plate is closed. Ensure the throttle plate is fully centralised.

24 Fit the accelerator pump diaphragm (46) to the pump cover (47), replace the return spring (45) larger diameter against the carburetter body and secure the assembly in place by means of the four screws and lockwashers (31).

25 The spring (30) and pushrod (28) are then connected to the accelerator pump lever (49) and the gooseneck end of the pushrod attached to the throttle arm. The arm is secured to the throttle spindle end with a screw and lockwasher.

26 This now completes the reassembly operations, but the fast idle setting, accelerator pump stroke, and choke plate pull down must be checked and adjusted as required. (See Sections 20 to 22).

19. FORD CARBURETTER - FUEL LEVEL SETTING

1. Since the height of the float is important in the maintenance of a correct flow of fuel, the correct height is determined by measurement and by bending the tab which rests on the end of the needle valve. If the height of the float is incorrect there will either be fuel starvation symptoms or fuel will leak from the joint of the float chamber. All numbers in brackets refer to Fig.3.8.

2. To check the float first remove the air cleaner as described in Section 2.

3. Undo the choke cable clamp screw (7) and the six screws and washers (33) which hold the carburetter top cover (35) in place.

4. Remove the cover (35) taking care that the gasket (39) does not stick to the main carburetter body (43) and at the same time unlatch the choke link rod (12).

5. The float (42) can now be examined. Shake it to ensure there is no fuel in it and if it has been punctured discard immediately. Check too that the float arm is not bent or damaged.

6. To check the fuel level setting turn the cover (35) upside down so that the float closes the needle valve by its own weight. This corresponds to its true position in the float chamber when the needle valve is closed and no more fuel can enter the chamber.

7. Measure the distance from the normal base of the float to the mating surface of the gasket which should be between 1.12 and 1.14 in. (28.5 to 29.0 mm.) as shown in Fig.3.9. If this measurement is not correct then bend

the tab which rests on the fuel inlet needle valve as required until the correct measurement is obtained. Turn the cover the right way up and take the same measurement with the float in the fully open position. The measurement should now be between 1.38 and 1.40 in. (35.0 to 35.5 mm.) as shown in Fig.3.10. Bend the other tab (the hinge tab) as required.

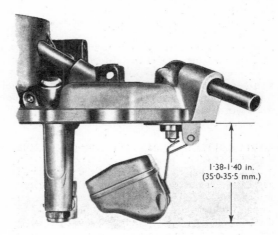

Fig.3.10. Float setting fully open - Autolite carburetter

20. FORD CARBURETTER - ACCELERATOR PUMP ADJUSTMENT

1. Under normal conditions the accelerator pump requires no adjustment. If it is wished to check the accelerator pump action first slacken the throttle stop screw (24 in Fig.3.8.) so the throttle plate is completely closed.

2. Press in the diaphragm plunger fully and check that there is then a .126 to .136 in. clearance between the operating lever and the plunger. The clearance is most easily checked by using a suitably sized drill.

3. To shorten the stroke open the gooseneck of the pump pushrod, and to lengthen the stroke close the gooseneck.

4. If poor acceleration can be tolerated for maximum economy disconnect the operating lever to the accelerator pump entirely.

Fig.3.9. Float setting open - Autolite carburetter

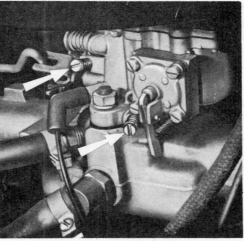

Fig.3.11. Slow running adjustment screws - Autolite carburetter

21.   FORD CARBURETTER - IDLING ADJUSTMENT

1. If available the idling adjustment is best made with the aid of a vacuum gauge. Disconnect the blanking plug on the inlet manifold and connect a suitable adaptor and gauge.

2. Ensure the engine is at its normal operating temperature and then turn in the throttle stop screw (24) to obtain a fast idle.

3. Turn the volume control screw (27) in either direction until a maximum reading is obtained on the gauge.

4. Re-adjust the idling speed as required and continue these adjustments until the maximum vacuum reading is obtained with the engine running smoothly at about 600 r.p.m.

5. To adjust the slow running without a vacuum gauge turn the throttle stop screw (24) clockwise so the engine is running at a fast idle, then turn the volume control screw (27) in either direction until the engine just fires evenly. Continue the adjustments until the engine will run as slowly as possible, but smoothly, with regular firing and no hint of stalling.

22.   FORD CARBURETTER - CHOKE & FAST IDLING ADJUSTMENT

1. To check the choke control first take off the air cleaner as described in Section 2, and then rotate the choke lever until it is against its stop.

2. Depress the choke plate and check the gap between the edge of the plate and the side of the carburetter air intake as shown in Fig.3.12. The gap is correct when it measures 5/32nd inch. (3.5 mm.) using the shank of a drill of this size as the measuring instrument.

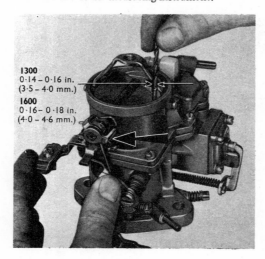

1300
0·14 - 0·16 in.
(3·5 - 4·0 mm.)

1600
0·16 - 0·18 in.
(4·0 - 4·6 mm.)

Fig.3.12.   Choke plate pull-down adjustment - Autolite carburetter

3. If the gap is incorrect bend the tab on the choke spindle until the drill will just fit.

4. The fast idle check and any necessary adjustment should only be made after the choke has been checked and adjusted.

5. If the engine is cold run it until it reaches its normal operating temperature and then allow it to idle naturally.

6. Hold the choke plate in the fully open vertical position and turn the choke lever until it is stopped by the choke linkage. With the choke lever in this position the engine speed should rise to about 1,000 r.p.m. as the fast idle cam will have opened the throttle flap very slightly.

Fig.3.13.   Fast idle adjustment - Autolite carburetter

7. Check how much radial movement is needed on the throttle lever to obtain this result and then stop the engine.

8. With a pair of mole grips clamp the throttle lever fully open on the stop portion of the casting boss and bend down the tab to decrease, or up to increase, the fast idle speed.

9. Remove the grips and check again if necessary repeating the operation until the fast idling is correct. It may also be necessary to adjust the slow idling speed and recheck the choke.

23.   FORD CARBURETTER - AUTOMATIC CHOKE ADJUSTMENT

1. The automatic choke (see Fig.3.14.) fitted to certain models is mounted on the side of the Ford single choke carburetter. The choke works by means of a water actuated bi-metallic spring (15) which turns the choke spindle (2) which in turn opens and closes the choke plate (3).

2. The slow running fuel level, and accelerator pump adjustments are identical to those made for the non-automatic carburetter (see sections 19,20 and 21) with one exception. The gap between the operating lever and plunger when checking accelerator pump operation should be 0.146 to 0.156 in. (3.7 to 4.0 mm.) and not 0.136 in. (3.2 to 3.5 mm).

3. To adjust the choke take off the outer choke housing (14) and open the throttle plate (26).

4. The piston should now be held in the fully depressed position and the choke plate (3) closed manually until further movement is prevented by the linkage. The bottom edge of the choke plate (3) mounted with a 5/32nd inch (4.0 mm.) drill should now be 0.150 to 0.170 in. (3.80 to 4.30 mm.) from the side of the carburetter (0.13 to 0.15 in. 3.3 to 3.8 mm. on emission reduction versions).

5. If the clearance needs to be adjusted bend the extension part of the choke thermostat lever which rests against the choke piston lever until the correct measurement is obtained.

6. The fast idle should only be checked after the choke adjustment has been made.

7. Hold the choke in the full down position and note that the fast idle tab of the throttle lever should be in the first high speed step in the fast idle cam. The engine speed should be about 2,100 r.p.m. Should the tab be incorrectly positioned in relation to the high speed step

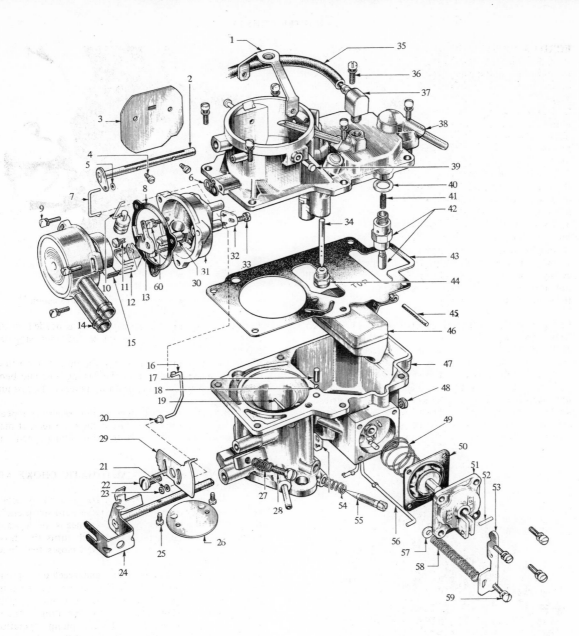

Fig.3.14. EXPLODED VIEW OF CARBURETTER WITH AUTOMATIC CHOKE — EXCEPT G.T.

1 Air filter
2 Choke spindle
3 Choke plate
4 Plate retaining screw
5 Clip
6 Gasket
7 Choke control rod
8 Gasket
9 Screw
10 Automatic)
11 choke   )
12 assembly)
13   )
14 Auto-choke housing cover
15 Bi-metallic spring
16 Fast idler cam rod

17 Pump discharge ball weight
18 Pump discharge ball
20 Bush
21 Washer
22 Screw
23 Shakeproof washer
24 Throttle lever and
      spindle assembly
25 Plate retaining screw
26 Throttle plate
27 Spring
28 Throttle stop screw
30 Spindle
31 Auto-choke housing
32 Bracket
33 Screw

34 Main metering jet tube
35 Overflow pipe
36 Screw
37 Adaptor
38 Carburetter horn assembly
39 Air filter bracket retaining
      pin
40 Washer
41 Filter
42 Needle valve assembly
43 Gasket
44 Main metering jet
45 Float pivot spindle
46 Float
47 Carburetter body
48 Screw

49 Diaphragm return spring
50 Diaphragm
51 Accelerator pump cover
52 Lever pivot pin
53 Accelerator pump actuating
      lever
54 Spring
55 Idling mixture adjustment
      screw
56 Pump to lever rod
57 Spring retaining washer
58 Spring
59 Screw
60 Screw

in the cam, with a pair of pliers increase or decrease the existing bend on the fast idle cam rod. To obtain the correct engine speed, bend the throttle lever fast idle tab.

8. Finally hold the throttle fully open against its stop and check with a 3/16 in. (4.76 mm.) drill that the gap between the bottom edge of the choke plate and the side of the carburetter is between 0.180 and 0.200 in. (4.60 to 5.08 mm.) To adjust the gap bend the projection of the fast idle cam actuated by the throttle lever arm.

24. WEBER CARBURETTER - REMOVAL & REPLACEMENT

1. Take off the air cleaner cover and remove the element as described in Section 2. Remove the air cleaner body after releasing the tab washers and undoing the four nuts which hold the air cleaner to the carburetter. Note the rubber insulators and sleeves and the rubber gasket.

2. Free the throttle control linkage from the throttle lever and disconnect both the fuel line from the float chamber and the vacuum pipe from the carburetter.

3. Loosen the clamp screw which holds the choke cable outer cover in place and the screw which secures the inner cable to the choke lever (where fitted).

4. The carburetter is held to the inlet manifold by four nuts. Undo and remove these and lift the carburetter and gasket away.

5. Replacement is a straightforward reversal of the removal sequence. Ensure a new carburetter to inlet manifold gasket is always used and that the air cleaner cover is replaced with the arrow adjacent to the air intake tube.

25. WEBER 28/36 DCD CARBURETTER - DISMANTLING OVERHAUL & REASSEMBLY

1. All numerical references in brackets refer to Fig.3.15. Undo the fuel inlet strainer plug (54) and washer (55) and remove the cap (56) and gauze element (57).

2. Undo the six screws (3) which holds the carburetter cover (5) to the main carburetter body, and peel away the gasket (58).

3. The pin (69) which retains the floats (70) to the cover (5) can now be pushed out and the floats and needle valve (68) removed. Unscrew the needle valve housing (67) and remove with the washer (66).

4. In the centre of the main body of the carburetter will be seen the inverted 'U' portion of the accelerator pump operating rod (59). Pull out this rod together with the spring retainer (60), spring (61), and piston (64).

5. The accelerator pump delivery valve (10) can now be removed from between the top of the choke tubes, followed by the inlet valve (65) from the bottom of the float chamber. The accelerator pump jet (13) is now free to be extracted from the carburetter body.

6. Unscrew the starter air adjuster jet (62) from the top of the carburetter between the float chamber and the choke tubes and remove together with the starter jet (63). Separation of the starter jet and air adjuster jet is made simply by pulling.

7. From between the float chamber and the choke tubes undo and remove the primary air correction jet (48), and the emulsion tube assembly (49), and follow this with the secondary air correction jet (50) and emulsion tube assembly (51).

8. Undo the idling jet holders (16,84) from each side of the carburetter, and the idling jets (18,82) and sealing rings (17,83).

9. The hexagonal main jet holders (20,87) can now be unscrewed from each side of the body, and the main jets (21,86) undone in turn. Carefully note the numbers on the main jets, 140 indicating the primary, and 155

the secondary main jet. Remove the throttle plates (36,42) by undoing the retaining grub screws (32,41). It should not be necessary to strip the carburetter any further.

10 Thoroughly clean out the drillings and passageways in the carburetter body by swilling in clean petrol and blowing clear with an air line. This process should also be used to clean the jets, accelerator pump, float chamber and floats.

11 Check the condition of all the parts and if any require renewal ensure new parts are to hand before reassembly commences. Always renew the washer and gaskets and the float chamber needle and housing. If a carburetter has been stripped after a relatively high mileage it is best to also renew all the jets.

12 Reassembly commences by screwing the primary main jet (86) and the secondary main jet (21) into their respective holder (87,20). Check the condition of the two copper washers (19,85), renew if necessary, and then screw the main jet holders (87,20) into the carburetter.

13 Note that the number 50 is stamped on the primary idling jet (82) and the number 70 on the secondary idling jet (18). Check the condition of the sealing rings (17,83), and then push the correct jet into each of the two circular headed jet holders and screw the holders into place.

14 Note that the primary air correction jet (48) is numbered 230, and the secondary air correction jet (50) 180. Screw the correct jet into each emulsion tube (48 into 49 and 50 into 51) and screw the assemblies into place between the float chamber and the choke tubes.

15 Push the starter air jet (62) into the starter petrol jet (63) open end first, and then screw the unit into the counterbored hole between the float chamber and the choke tubes.

16 To replace the accelerator pump jet (13), and delivery valve (10), start by placing a washer (14) in the recess between the two choke tubes. Then fit the pump jet (13) so the lug on the jet fit into the notch on the float chamber side of the recess. Place the other fibre washer (12) on top of the jet (13); give the delivery valve (10) a shake to check the valve ball is loose; insert it through the centre of the delivery jet (13) and screw into the carburetter body.

17 Shake the inlet valve (65) to check that the valve ball moves freely and screw the valve into the bottom of the float chamber.

18 Now fit the accelerator pump piston (64), spring (61) and pump operating rod (59) in place securing the latter with the split retainer (60).

19 Moving to the carburetter cover fit a new needle valve housing washer (66) in place, and screw in the housing (67). Fit the needle valve (68) and then the floats (70) retaining the latter with the hinge pins (69). Check the float level settings as described in Section 26.

20 Fit a new gasket (58) between the carburetter top cover (5) and the carburetter body, join the cover and body and secure with the six holding down screws.

21 Thoroughly wash the gauze (57), and replace in the top cover followed by the filter cap (56), and washer (55), and then screw in the retaining plug (54). Check that the air valve assembly (1,2,52,53) is correctly in place. Assembly is now complete and if new parts have been used throughout the carburetter should give thousands of miles of useful service.

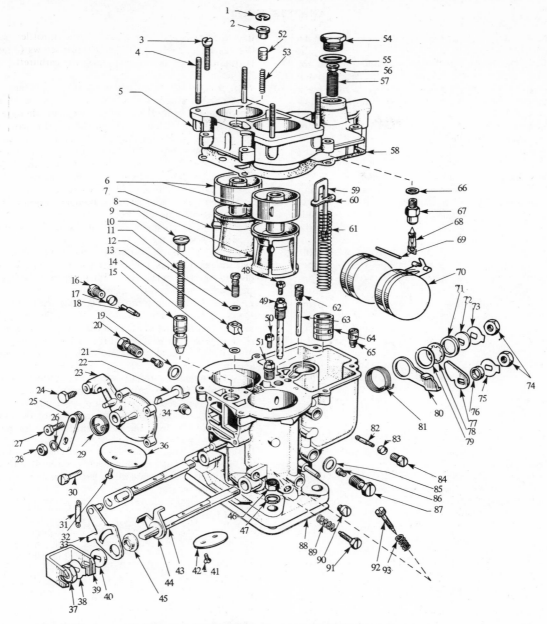

Fig.3.15. EXPLODED VIEW OF THE WEBER 28/36 DCD CARBURETTER
FITTED TO G.T. MODELS FROM 1966 TO 1968

1 Spring washer	24 Cable retaining screw	48 Air correction jet	70 Float
2 Starter plunger seat	25 Choke actuating lever	49 Main emulsion tube	71 Washer
3 Screw	26 Washer	50 Secondary air correction jet	72 Spacer
4 Stud	27 Cable retaining bolt	51 Secondary emulsion tube	73 Tab washer
5 Carburetter cover	28 Nut	52 Carburetter starter plunger	74 Nuts
6 Venturis	29 Spring	53 Starter valve spring retainer	75 Tab washer
7 Venturi insert	30 Screw	54 Fuel inlet strainer plug	76 Spacer
8 Venturi insert	31 Spring	55 Gasket	77 Accelerator pump link
9 Starter valve spring retainer	32 Plate retaining screw	56 Filter cap	78 Shakeproof washer
10 Pump discharge valve	33 Throttle actuating lever	57 Filter element	79 Washer
11 Spring	34 Plug	58 Gasket	80 Accelerator pump lever
12 Gasket	36 Throttle plate - secondary	59 Pump operating rod	81 Spring
13 Pump discharge jet	37 Nut	60 Spring retainer	82 Idling jet
14 Gasket	38 Tab washer	61 Spring	83 Cover
15 Starter valve	39 Throttle lever	62 Starter air adjuster jet	84 Idling jet holder
16 Idling jet holder	40 Spacer	63 Starting jet	85 Washer
17 Sealing ring	41 Plate retaining screw	64 Accelerator pump piston assembly	86 Main metering jet
18 Idling jet	42 Throttle plate primary	65 Accelerator pump inlet valve	87 Main jet holder
19 Washer	43 Throttle spindle	66 Washer	88 Gasket
20 Main jet holder	44 Fast idling adjustment lever	67 Needle valve housing	89 Spring
21 Main metering jet	45 Bush	68 Needle valve	90 Idling adjustment screw
22 Choke spindle	46 Nut	69 Float pivot pin	91 Throttle adjustment screw
23 Choke housing cover	47 Spring washer		92 Idling mixture adjustment screw
			93 Spring

26. WEBER 28/36 DCD CARBURETTER - FUEL LEVEL SETTING

1. Since the height of the float is important in the maintenance of a correct flow of fuel, the correct height is obtained by measurement and adjustment. This is particularly the case if fuel is leaking from the joint of the float chamber.

2. First carefully remove the cover which contains the float and the flow control valve. Hold the cover vertically so that the float hangs down, and it will be seen that a tab, hooked to the needle control valve is in light contact with the ball, and this should be perpendicular.

3. The distance between the float and the cover at this stage should be 5.5 mm. as shown in Fig.3.16.

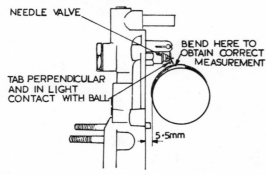

Fig.3.16. Carburetter float level dimension

4. If this measurement is not correct, then the tabs should be carefully bent at the float end until the distance is obtained.

5. Since the stroke of the float is 8.5 mm. it follows that when the needle valve is at its extreme as seen in Fig.3.17. then the distance should be 14 mm.

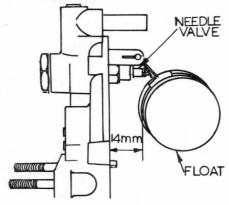

Fig.3.17. Carburetter float-stroke dimension

6. From time to time it may be necessary to replace the sealing washers, and when any part is renewed, then this float adjustment is essential.

27. WEBER 28/36 DCD CARBURETTER - SLOW RUNNING

1. Slow running adjustment is best performed with the aid of a vacuum gauge as described in Section 21. Should a vacuum gauge not be available then turn the throttle stop screw so the engine when warm runs at a fast idle.

2. Turn the volume control screw in or out until the engine runs really smoothly and fires evenly. While this is being done adjust the throttle stop screw until the correct idling speed is obtained which on G.T. engines

is about 800 r.p.m.

3. Do not try and set the idling speed too slow and if necessary check the ignition timing.

28. WEBER 32-DFM CARBURETTER - DISMANTLING & REASSEMBLY

1. All numbers in brackets in this section refer to Fig.3.18 Undo the plug (4) and take out the gauze petrol filter (3). Free the choke actuating arm (22) at its lower end by removing the split pin (27) and nylon washer.

2. Undo the screws and spring washers (2) which hold the top cover (24) in place and lift off the cover and the gasket (25).

3. Pull out the pin (29) which retains the float (5) in place, lift out the needle valve (28) and unscrew the needle valve housing (28) from the top cover. Remove the small washer (26).

4. On the side of the carburetter undo the four screws and washers (13) which hold the accelerator pump cover (14) in place. Remove the cover (14), diaphragm (15) and the diaphragm return spring (16).

5. If the accelerator pump lever is badly worn drive out the pivot pin from the plain end.

6. Pull out the split pin (21) which holds the upper end of the choke actuating arm (22) to the choke spindle (20); undo the choke plate retaining grub screws (19); and pull out the choke plates (18). The choke spindle (20) can now be removed from the side of the carburetter.

7. Unscrew from the bottom of the float chamber the primary (8) and secondary (6) main jets.

8. With a screwdriver undo the accelerator pump discharge valve (31) from the middle of the carburetter and take off the pump discharge nozzle (33) and the gasket (34).

9. Directly behind the discharge nozzle orifice lie the two air correction jets (30) and their emulsion tubes (32). Unscrew the air correction jet (30), turn the carburetter upside down and shake out the emulsion tubes (32).

10 From either side of the carburetter (only one side is shown) unscrew the two idling jet holders (36) and the idling jets (39). From the bottom of the carburetter undo and remove the volume control screw (39) and the spring (40).

11 Take off from between the carburetter body and the secondary throttle lever the return spring.

12 Turn back the lock tab (65) on the primary throttle shaft (10) unscrew the nut (67) and pull off the throttle control lever (64), bush (63), secondary throttle control lever, and the other components.

13 Then disconnect the fast idle connecting rod (47), and remove the bush, washers and fast idle lever.

14 With all the levers, springs and bushes removed from the throttle spindles (9,10) undo the grub screws (12) which hold the butterfly valves (11) to the spindles, remove the valves (11) and slide the spindles out of the carburetter.

15 Finally undo the retaining screw and take off the choke operating lever, spring, and washer.

16 Reassembly commences with refitting the cleaned gauze filter (3) to the top cover (24), and securing the filter in place with the large brass plug(4).

17 Slide the choke spindle (20) into its bore in the top cover (24) so the lever on the spindle lies adjacent to the secondary choke. Replace the choke plates (18) ensuring that the smaller portion faces the rear and that when closed the plate chamfers are parallel to the sides of the air intake. Centralise and secure with grub screws (19). Peen over the ends of the screws to ensure no possibility of their working loose.

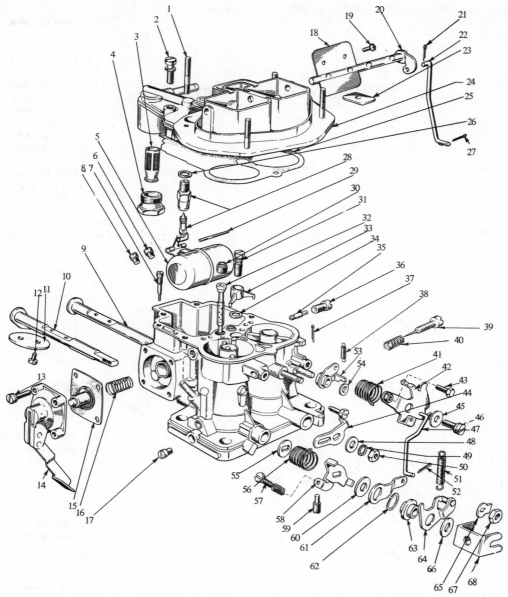

Fig.3.18. EXPLODED VIEW OF THE WEBER 32—DFM CARBURETTER — FITTED
TO LATER G.T. MODELS

1 Stud	18 Choke spindle plate	35 Secondary idling jet
2 Screw	19 Plate retaining screw	36 Idling jet holder
3 Gauze filter element	20 Choke spindle	37 Split pin
4 Plug	21 Split pin	38 Spring
5 Float	22 Choke actuating arm	39 Volume control screw
6 Main metering jet	23 Dust seal	40 Spring
7 Accelerator pump blanking	24 Carburetter top cover	41 Spring
needle	25 Gasket	42 Choke control lever
8 Main metering jet	26 Washer	43 Bolt
9 Spindle	27 Split pin	44 Throttle stop lever
10 Spindle	28 Needle valve	45 Washer
11 Throttle plate or butterfly	29 Float pivot spindle	46 Screw
valve	30 Starting air adjusting	47 Fast idle rod
12 Screw	jet	48 Washer
13 Screw	31 Accelerator pump dis-	49 Spring washer
14 Accelerator pump cover	charge valve	50 Nut
15 Diaphragm	32 Starting jet	51 Spring
16 Diaphragm return spring	33 Pump discharge nozzle	52 Split pin
17 Plug	34 Gasket	53 Choke relay lever

54 Nylon washer
55 Slotted washer
56 Spring
57 Idling adjustment lever
screw
58 Idling adjustment lever
59 Adjuster
60 Spacer
61 Choke/throttle inter-
connecting fast idle lever
62 Washer
63 Bush
64 Throttle control lever
65 Tab washer
66 Washer
67 Nut
68 Throttle lever assembly

18 The dust seal (23) can now be fitted to the top cover flange and the choke rod (22) passed through the seal and the flange and connected by means of the split pin (21) to the choke spindle (20).

19 Fit the choke relay lever (53) and washer (54) to the spindle on the carburetter body and retain in place with the split pin (37).

20 Now assemble the fast idle rod (47) and the toggle spring to the choke control lever (42) and fit the return spring (41) around the carburetter body pivot boss, so the straight end rests in the location hole.

21 Place the choke control lever (42) on the pivot boss, and fix the toggle spring to the relay lever (53). Make sure that the relay lever toggle spring arm lies against the cam portion of the choke control lever (42) and that the fast idle rod lies between the two throttle spindle bosses. The screw (46) flat and spring washers which secure the lever (42) in place now now be refitted.

22 The end of the return spring should be hooked under the fast idle rod bracket.

23 Slide the primary (10) and secondary (9) throttle spindles into the carburetter, turning the spindles until the slots are parallel with the choke bore and the threaded holes face inwards. Slide the butterfly valves into the slots so the faces marked '78°' are facing outwards with the numbers below the spindles. Ensure that the valves are centralised and then retain them in place with the grub screws (12). Peen over the threaded ends of the screws to ensure they will not loosen.

24 To the secondary throttle spindle (9) fit the throttle lever (44) so the abutment rests against the stop. Replace the plain and spring washer (48,49) and do up the retaining nut (50).

25 Close the secondary throttle and then check with a feeler gauge the clearance between the carburetter barrel at its widest point and the butterfly valve. Adjust the stop to give a clearance of 0.0015 in. (0.038 mm).

26 Fit the slotted washer (55), return spring (56), and idling adjustment lever (58) to the primary throttle spindle (10) wrapping the hooked end of the spring around the lower arm of the idling adjustment lever, the other straight end resting on top of the flange between the two chokes.

27 Slide the plain washer (60), fast idle lever (61), wave washer (62), and bush (63) onto the primary throttle spindle (10). Fit the fast idle rod (47) to the fast idle lever (61), securing the split pin (52).

28 The throttle relay lever (64) can now be fitted to the bush (63) so the peg on the relay lever fits into the slot in the secondary throttle lever (44).

29 Now fit the plain washer (66) throttle lever (88) and the tab washer (65) and tighten down the retaining nut (67). Turn up the tab on the lockwasher.

30 Fit the secondary idling jet (35) '45' to the secondary idling holder (36), and the primary idling jet '50' to its idling holder, and screw the holders one into each side of the float chamber.

31 The main primary (8) '150', and main secondary (6) '155' jets can now be screwed into their recesses in the float chamber.

32 Slide the emulsion tubes into their wells and screw down the primary (32) '160' and secondary '140' air correction jets.

33 Fit a new accelerator pump discharge jet washer (34) to the carburetter, position the jet (33) and secure with the discharge valve (31).

34 Slide the accelerator pump spring (16) into the recess in the carburetter and place the diaphragm (15) against the pump cover (14) so the plunger lies in the operating lever recess.

35 Fit the accelerator pump cover assembly (14) in place so the operating lever engages the cam. Now insert and tighten down the four securing screws and washers (13) at the same time pulling the lever away from the cam to the limit of the diaphragm travel.

36 Fully screw in the volume control screw (39) and then undo it 1½ turns. Screw in a further half turn the throttle stop screw when it just contacts the throttle top lever.

37 Fit a new gasket (26) to the threaded end of the needle valve housing (28) and screw the housing into the float chamber cover (24).

38 Place a new gasket (25) on the underside of the carburetter top cover, fit the needle valve to the housing, and then replace the float (5) and pivot pin (29). Check the fuel level setting as described in Section 29.

38 Bring together the top cover and the main carburetter body at the same time connecting the relay lever (53) to the choke plate operating rod (22). Evenly tighten down the securing screws and spring washers. Reassembly is now complete.

29. WEBER 32 DFM CARBURETTER - FUEL LEVEL SETTING

1. The fuel level setting is made in exactly the same way as described in Section 26 for the Weber 28/36 DCD carburetter.

2. Before the float chamber cover can be removed the fuel pipe must be disconnected and the split pin holding the choke operating rod removed at its lower end, so the rod can be disengaged from the relay lever.

3. The measurements between the float and cover gasket are different to those in Section 26. With the float in the closed position i.e. the cover held vertical, the dimension between the float and gasket should be 7 mm. (See Fig.3.19.).

Fig.3.19. Float and fuel level setting

4. The travel of the float should be 8 mm. i.e. 15 mm. from the cover gasket (see Fig.3.20).

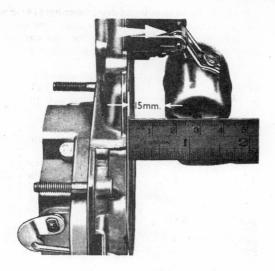

Fig.3.20. Carburetter float stroke dimension

30. WEBER 32 DFM CARBURETTER - SLOW RUNNING ADJUSTMENT

1. The slow running adjustment is made in exactly the same way as for the Weber 28/36 DCD carburetter.
2. See Section 27 and Fig.3.21 for details.

Fig.3.21. Slow running adjustment screws

31. WEBER 32 DFM CARBURETTER - CHOKE ADJUSTMENT

1. If the choke is not working correctly the choke plate pull down and the choke plate opening must be checked.
2. Close the choke and hold the choke lever against its stop. The choke plates should now be opened against the resistance of the toggle spring. The distance between the bottom edge of the plates and the side of the inside choke wall should be 5 mm. checked with a correctly sized drill. If necessary bend the choke lever stop until the gap is correct.
3. To verify the choke plate opening from the fully closed position move the lever back 10 mm. which can be most easily measured along the line of the choke cable. The distance between the bottom edge of the plates and the inside choke wall should be 7.5 to 8.5 mm. checked with a drill of this size.
4. If the gap is incorrect bend the tag marked 'A' in Fig.3.22. in towards the cam to increase the opening, and

away from it to decrease it. NOTE Bend the tag a very small amount at a time as a very small difference to the tag position will make a considerable difference to the position of the chokes.

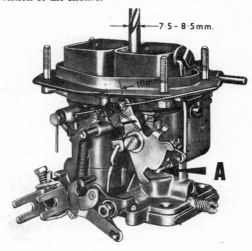

Fig.3.22. Choke plate opening adjustment

32. FUEL SYSTEM - FAULT FINDING

There are three main types of fault the fuel system is prone to, and they may be summarised as follows:-

a) Lack of fuel at engine
b) Weak mixture
c) Rich mixture

33. LACK OF FUEL AT ENGINE

1. If it is not possible to start the engine, first positively check that there is fuel in the fuel tank, and then check the ignition system as detailed in Chapter 4. If the fault is not in the ignition system then disconnect the fuel inlet pipe from the carburetter and turn the engine over by the starter relay switch.
2. If petrol squirts from the end of the inlet pipe, reconnect the pipe and check that the fuel is getting to the float chamber. This is done by unscrewing the bolts from the top of the float chamber, and lifting the cover just enough to see inside.
3. If fuel is there then it is likely that there is a blockage in the starting jet, which should be removed and cleaned.
4. No fuel in the float chamber, is caused either by a blockage in the pipe between the pump and float chamber or a sticking float chamber valve. Alternatively on the twin choke G.T. carburetter the gauze filter at the top of the float chamber may be blocked. Remove the securing nut and check that the filter is clean. Washing in petrol will clean it.
5. If it is decided that it is the float chamber valve that is sticking, remove the fuel inlet pipe, and lift the cover, complete with valve and floats, away.
6. Remove the valve spindle and valve and thoroughly wash them in petrol. Petrol gum may be present on the valve or valve spindle and this is usually the cause of a sticking valve. Replace the valve in the needle valve assembly, ensure that it is moving freely, and then re-assemble the float chamber. It is important that the same washer be placed under the needle valve assembly as this determines the height of the floats and therefore the level of petrol in the chamber.
7. Reconnect the fuel pipe and refit the air cleaner.

8. If no petrol squirts from the end of the pipe leading to the carburetter then disconnect the pipe leading to the inlet side of the fuel pump. If fuel runs out of the pipe then there is a fault in the fuel pump, and the pump should be checked as has already been detailed.

9. No fuel flowing from the tank when it is known that there is fuel in the tank indicates a blocked pipe line. The line to the tank should be blown out. It is unlikely that the fuel tank vent would become blocked, but this could be a reason for the reluctance of the fuel to flow. To test for this, blow into the tank down the fill orifice. There should be no build up of pressure in the fuel tank, as the excess pressure should be carried away down the vent pipe.

34. WEAK MIXTURE

1. If the fuel/air mixture is weak there are six main clues to this condition:-

a) The engine will be difficult to start and will need much use of the choke, stalling easily if the choke is pushed in.
b) The engine will overheat easily.
c) If the sparking plugs are examined (as detailed in the section on engine tuning), they will have a light grey/white deposit on the insulator nose.
d) The fuel consumption may be light.
e) There will be a noticeable lack of power.
f) During acceleration and on the overrun there will be a certain amount of spitting back through the carburetter.

2. As the carburetters are of the fixed jet type, these faults are invariably due to circumstances outside the carburetter. The only usual fault likely in the carburetter is that one or more of the jets may be partially blocked. If the car will not start easily but runs well at speed, then it is likely that the starting jet is blocked, whereas if the engine starts easily but will not rev. then it is likely that the main jets are blocked.

3. If the level of petrol in the float chamber is low this

is usually due to a sticking valve or incorrectly set floats.
4. Air leaks either in the fuel lines, or in the induction system should also be checked for. Also check the distributor vacuum pipe connection as a leak in this is directly felt in the inlet manifold.
5. The fuel pump may be at fault as has already been detailed.

35. RICH MIXTURE

1. If the fuel/air mixture is rich there are also six main clues to this condition:-

a) If the sparking plugs are examined they will be found to have a black sooty deposit on the insulator nose.
b) The fuel consumption will be heavy.
c) The exhaust will give off a heavy black smoke, especially when accelerating.
d) The interior deposits on the exhaust pipe will be dry, black and sooty (if they are wet, black and sooty this indicates worn bores, and much oil being burnt).
e) There will be a noticeable lack of power.
f) There will be a certain amount of back-firing through the exhaust system.

2. The faults in this case are usually in the carburetter and the most usual is that the level of petrol in the float chamber is too high. This is due either to dirt behind the needle valve, or a leaking float which will not close the valve properly, or a sticking needle.
3. With a very high mileage (or because someone has tried to clean the jets out with wire), it may be that the jets have become enlarged.
4. If the air correction jets are restricted in any way the mixture will tend to become very rich.
5. Occasionally it is found that the choke control is sticking or has been maladjusted.
6. Again, occasionally the fuel pump pressure may be excessive so forcing the needle valve open slightly until a higher level of petrol is reached in the float chamber.

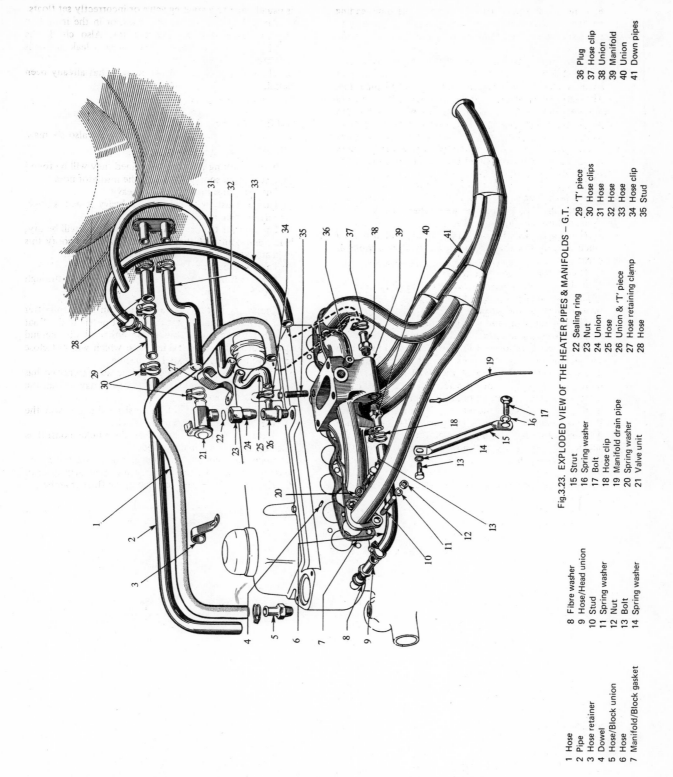

Fig.3.23. EXPLODED VIEW OF THE HEATER PIPES & MANIFOLDS – G.T.

1 Hose	15 Strut	29 'T' piece
2 Pipe	16 Spring washer	30 Hose clips
3 Hose retainer	17 Bolt	31 Hose
4 Dowel	18 Hose clip	32 Hose
5 Hose/Block union	19 Manifold drain pipe	33 Hose
6 Hose	20 Spring washer	34 Hose clip
7 Manifold/Block gasket	21 Valve unit	35 Stud
8 Fibre washer	22 Sealing ring	36 Plug
9 Hose/Head union	23 Nut	37 Hose clip
10 Stud	24 Union	38 Union
11 Spring washer	25 Hose	39 Manifold
12 Nut	26 Union & 'T' piece	40 Union
13 Bolt	27 Hose retaining clamp	41 Down pipes
14 Spring washer	28 Hose	

FUEL SYSTEM AND CARBURATION

FAULT FINDING CHART

Cause	Trouble	Remedy
SYMPTOM:	FUEL CONSUMPTION EXCESSIVE	
Carburation and ignition faults	Air cleaner choked and dirty giving rich mixture	Remove, clean and replace air cleaner.
	Fuel leaking from carburettor(s), fuel pumps, or fuel lines	Check for and eliminate all fuel leaks. Tighten fuel line union nuts.
	Float chamber flooding	Check and adjust float level.
	Generally worn carburettor(s)	Remove, overhaul and replace.
	Distributor condenser faulty	Remove, and fit new unit.
	Balance weights or vacuum advance mechanism in distributor faulty	Remove, and overhaul distributor.
Incorrect adjustment	Carburettor(s) incorrectly adjusted mixture too rich	Tune and adjust carburettor(s).
	Idling speed too high	Adjust idling speed.
	Contact breaker gap incorrect	Check and reset gap.
	Valve clearances incorrect	Check rocker arm to valve stem clearances and adjust as necessary.
	Incorrectly set sparking plugs	Remove, clean, and regap.
	Tyres under-inflated	Check tyre pressures and inflate if necessary.
	Wrong sparking plugs fitted	Remove and replace with correct units.
	Brakes dragging	Check and adjust brakes.
SYMPTOM:	INSUFFICIENT FUEL DELIVERY OR WEAK MIXTURE DUE TO AIR LEAKS	
Dirt in system	Petrol tank air vent restricted	Remove petrol cap and clean out air vent.
	Partially clogged filters in pump and carburettor(s)	Remove and clean filters.
	Dirt lodged in float chamber needle housing	Remove and clean out float chamber and needle valve assembly.
	Incorrectly seating valves in fuel pump	Remove, dismantle, and clean out fuel pump.
Fuel pump faults	Fuel pump diaphragm leaking or damaged	Remove, and overhaul fuel pump.
	Gasket in fuel pump damaged	Remove, and overhaul fuel pump.
	Fuel pump valves sticking due to petrol gumming	Remove, and thoroughly clean fuel pump.
Air leaks	Too little fuel in fuel tank (Prevalent when climbing steep hills)	Refill fuel tank.
	Union joints on pipe connections loose	Tighten joints and check for air leaks.
	Split in fuel pipe on suction side of fuel pump	Examine, locate, and repair.
	Inlet manifold to block or inlet manifold to carburettor(s) gasket leaking	Test by pouring oil along joints - bubbles indicate leak. Renew gasket as appropriate.

CHAPTER FOUR

IGNITION SYTEM

CONTENTS

SPECIFICATIONS

Sparking Plugs
Size … … … .. … … … … … … … … … … … … … … … … .14 mm.

Type
1297 & 1500 up to Sept '67… … … … … … … … … … … … Autolite AG32
Gap … .020 to .024 in. (.508 to .610 mm.)
G.T up to Sept '67… … … … … … … … … … … … … … … Autolite AG22
Gap … .023 to .027 in. (.584 to .686 mm.)
All models after Sept '67… … … … … … … … … … … … … Autolite AG22
Gap … .023 in. (.584 mm.)
Firing order… … … … … … … … … … … … … … … … … … 1,2,4,3

Coil
Type … 12 volt oil filled
Resistance at 20°C (68°F)
Primary … … … … … … … … … … … … … … … … … … … 3.1 to 3.5 ohms
Secondary … … … … … … … … … … … … … … … … … … 4.750 to 5.750 ohms
Output … … … … … … … … … … … … … … … … … … … 30 k.v.
Distributor … … … … … … … … … … … … … … … … … … Ford
Contact points gap setting … … … … … … … … … … … … .025 in. (.64 mm.)
Rotation of rotor … … … … … … … … … … … … … … … … Anti-clockwise
Automatic advance.. … … … … … … … … … … … … … … Mechanical & vacuum
Condenser capacity.. … … … … … … … … … … … … … … .21 to .25 microfarad
Contact breaker spring tension … … … … … … … … … … 17 to 21 ozs. (481,9 to 567.0 gms.)

Identification Numbers
1297 c.c. & 1500 High C up to Sept '67 … … … … … … … … C6AH-A
1297 c.c. & 1500 Low C up to Sept '67 … … … … … … … … C6AH-B
1500 G.T.. … … … … … … … … … … … … … … … … … … C6BH-C
1297 c.c. High C from Sept '67… … … … … … … … … … … C7AH-A
1297 c.c. Low C from Sept '67 … … … … … … … … … … … C7AH-B
1598 c.c. High C … … … … … … … … … … … … … … … C7BH-A
1598 c.c. Low C … … … … … … … … … … … … … … … … C7BH-B
1598 c.c. G.T … … … … … … … … … … … … … … … … … C7BH-C
1598 c.c. 8.5 Emission controlled … … … … … … … … … … C8EH-G
1598 c.c. G.T Emission controlled … … … … … … … … … … C7BH-K

Identification Colour
High C ... ...   Red
Low C ... ...   Green
G.T ... ...   Blue

Initial Advance
1297 c.c. & 1500 c.c. High C up to Sept '67 ... ...   6° B.T.D.C.
1297 c.c. & 1500 c.c. Low C up to Sept '67 ... ...   10° B.T.D.C.
1500 G.T.. ... ...   10° B.T.D.C.
1297 c.c. & 1598 c.c. High C from Sept '67 ... ...   6° B.T.D.C. on 94 octane fuel
                                                              10° B.T.D.C. on 97 octane fuel
1297 c.c. Low C from Sept '67 ... ...   4° B.T.D.C. on 86 octane fuel
                                                              10° B.T.D.C. on 89 octane fuel
1598 c.c. Low C ... ...   6° B.T.D.C. on 86 octane fuel
                                                              10° B.T.D.C. on 89 octane fuel
1598 c.c. G.T ... ...   8° B.T.D.C.
1598 c.c. 8.5 Emission controlled ... ...   4° B.T.D.C.
1598 c.c. G.T Emission controlled ... ...   4° B.T.D.C.
Dwell angle ... ...   30° to 40°
Ignition timing ... ...   Marks on timing cover and mark on crankshaft pulley

	C6AH-A	C6AH-B	C6BH-C	C7AH-A C7BH-A	C7AH-B C7BH-B	C7BH-C
Auto advance commences (distributor r.p.m.)	600	700	550	600	650	600
Maximum advance - crankshaft degrees ... ...:	14°	14°	12½°	14°	13°	8°
at distributor r.p.m..	2500	2500	2750	2750	2250	2500
Vacuum advance crankshaft degrees at - ins of mercury ...	10° @ 15	12° @ 15	7° @ 20	7° @ 9	7° @ 9	7° @ 9

NOTE: C6AH,C6BH,C7AH,C7BH distributors are identical for all practical purposes. The few differences have no effect on the procedures used when dismantling or rebuilding the unit.

1. **GENERAL DESCRIPTION**

In order that the engine can run correctly it is necessary for an electrical spark to ignite the fuel/air mixture in the combustion chamber at exactly the right moment in relation to engine speed and load. The ignition system is based on feeding low tension voltage from the battery to the coil where it is converted to high tension voltage. The high tension voltage is powerful enough to jump the sparking plug gap in the cylinders many times a second under high compression pressures, providing that the system is in good condition and that all adjustments are correct.

The ignition system is divided into two circuits. The low tension circuit and the high tension circuit.

The low tension (sometimes known as the primary) circuit consists of the battery, lead to the control box, lead to the ignition switch, lead from the ignition switch to the low tension or primary coil windings (terminal SW), and the lead from the low tension coil windings (coil terminal CB) to the contact breaker points and condenser in the distributor.

The high tension circuit consists of the high tension or secondary coil windings, the heavy ignition lead from the centre of the coil to the centre of the distributor cap, the rotor arm, and the sparking plug leads and sparking plugs.

The system functions in the following manner. Low tension voltage is changed in the coil into high tension voltage by the opening and closing of the contact breaker points in the low tension circuit. High tension voltage is then fed via the carbon brush in the centre of the distributor cap to the rotor arm of the distributor cap, and each time it comes in line with one of the four metal segments in the cap, which are connected to the sparking plug leads, the opening and closing of the contact breaker points causes the high tension voltage to build up, jump the gap from the rotor arm to the appropriate metal segment and so via the sparking plug lead to the sparking plug, where it finally jumps the spark plug gap

before going to earth.

The ignition is advanced and retarded automatically, to ensure the spark occurs at just the right instant for the particular load at the prevailing engine speed.

The ignition advance is controlled both mechanically and by a vacuum operated system. The mechanical governor mechanism comprises two lead weights, which move out from the distributor shaft as the engine speed rises due to centrifugal force. As they move outwards they rotate the cam relative to the distributor shaft, and so advance the spark. The weights are held in position by two light springs and it is the tension of the springs which is largely responsible for correct spark advancement.

The vacuum control consists of a diaphragm, one side of which is connected via a small bore tube to the carburetter, and the other side to the contact breaker plate. Depression in the inlet manifold and carburetter, which varies with engine speed and throttle opening, causes the diaphragm to move, so moving the contact breaker plate, and advancing or retarding the spark. A fine degree of control is achieved by a spring in the vacuum assembly.

2. **CONTACT BREAKER ADJUSTMENT**

1. To adjust the contact breaker points to the correct gap, first pull off the two clips securing the distributor cap to the distributor body, and lift away the cap. Clean the cap inside and out with a dry cloth. It is unlikely that the four segments will be badly burned or scored, but if they are the cap will have to be renewed.
2. Inspect the carbon brush contact located in the top of the cap - see that it is unbroken and stands proud of the plastic surface.
3. Check the contact spring on the top of the rotor arm. It must be clean and have adequate tension to ensure good contact.
4. Gently prise the contact breaker points open to examine the condition of their faces. If they are rough, pitted, or dirty, it will be necessary to remove them for

Fig.4.1. Adjusting contact breaker points

resurfacing, or for replacement points to be fitted.

5. Presuming the points are satisfactory, or that they have been cleaned and replaced, measure the gap between the points by turning the engine over until the heel of the breaker arm is on the highest point of the cam.

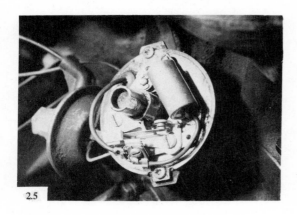

6. A .025 in. (.64 mm) feeler gauge should now just fit between the points. (See Fig.4.1.)

7. If the gap varies from this amount slacken the contact plate securing screw. (See photo).

8 Adjust the contact gap by inserting a screwdriver in the notched hole (see photo) in the breaker plate. Turn clockwise to increase and anti-clockwise to decrease the gap. When the gap is correct tighten the securing screw and check the gap again. Before replacing the distributor cap, check the ignition timing as detailed in Section 12. This is particularly important in later models, where adjustment of the CB points can alter the ignition timing by as much as 8°.

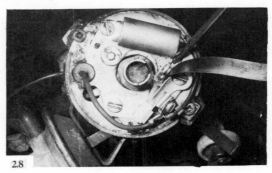

9. Making sure the rotor is in position replace the distributor cap and clip the spring blade retainers into position.

3. REMOVING & REPLACING CONTACT BREAKER POINTS

1. If the contact breaker points are burned, pitted or badly worn, they must be removed and either replaced, or their faces must be filed smooth.

2. Lift off the rotor arm by pulling it straight up from the spindle.

3. Slacken the self-tapping screw holding the condenser and low tension leads to the contact breaker and slide out the forked ends of the leads.

4. Remove the points by taking out the two retaining screws and lifting off the points assembly.

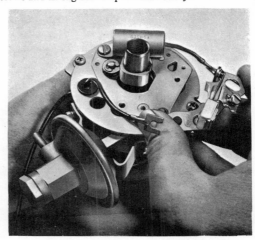

Fig.4.2. Fitting the contact breaker assembly

5. Replacing the points assembly is a reversal of the removal procedure. Take care not to trap the wires between the points and the breaker plate.

6. When the points are replaced the gap should be set as described in the previous section.

7. Finally replace the rotor arm and then the distributor cap.

NOTE Should the contact points be badly worn, a new set should be fitted. As an emergency measure clean the faces with fine emery paper folded over a thin steel ruler. It is necessary to completely remove the built-up deposits, but not necessary to rub the pitted point right down to the stage where all the pitting has disappeared. When the surfaces are flat a feeler gauge can be used and the gap set as above.

4. CONDENSER REMOVAL, TESTING & REPLACEMENT

1. The purpose of the condenser, (sometimes known as a capacitor) is to ensure that when the contact breaker points open there is no sparking across them which would waste voltage and cause wear.

2. The condenser is fitted in parallel with the contact breaker points. If it develops a short circuit, it will cause ignition failure as the points will be prevented from interrupting the low tension circuit.

3. If the engine becomes very difficult to start or begins to miss after several miles running and the breaker points show signs of excessive burning, then the condition of the condenser must be suspect. A further test can be made by separating the points by hand with the ignition switched on. If this is accompanied by a flash it is indicative that the condenser has failed.

4. Without special test equipment the only sure way to diagnose condenser trouble is to replace a suspected unit with a new one and note if there is any improvement.

5. To remove the condenser from the distributor take off the distributor cap and rotor arm. Slacken the self-tapping screw holding the condenser lead and low tension lead to the points, and slide out the fork on the condenser lead. Undo the condenser retaining screw and remove the condenser from the breaker plate.

6. To refit the condenser simply reverse the order of removal. Take care that the condenser lead is clear of the moving part of the points assembly.

5. DISTRIBUTOR LUBRICATION

1. It is important that the distributor cam is lubricated with petroleum jelly at the specified mileages, and that the breaker arm, governor weights, and cam spindle, are lubricated with engine oil once every 6,000 miles.

2. Great care should be taken not to use too much lubricant, as any excess that finds its way onto the contact breaker points could cause burning and misfiring.

3. To gain access to the cam spindle, lift away the rotor arm. Drop no more than two drops of engine oil onto the felt pad. This will run down the spindle when the engine is hot and lubricate the bearings.

4. To lubricate the automatic timing control allow a few drops of oil to pass through the hole in the contact breaker base plate through which the four sided cam emerges. Apply not more than one drop of oil to the pivot post and remove any excess.

6. DISTRIBUTOR REMOVAL

1. To remove the distributor from the engine pull off the four leads from the sparking plugs.

2. Disconnect the high tension and low tension leads from the distributor.

3. Pull off the rubber union holding the vacuum pipe to the distributor vacuum advance housing.

4. Remove the distributor body clamp bolt which holds the distributor clamp plate to the engine and lift out the distributor. BUT SEE NOTE BELOW BEFORE REMOVAL.

NOTE: If it is not wished to disturb the timing under no circumstances should the body clamp pinch bolt be loosened. For the same reason the precise direction in which the rotor arm points should be noted before it is removed. This enables the drive gear to be settled on the same tooth when the distributor is refitted. While the distributor is removed care must be taken not to turn the engine. If these precautions are observed there will be no need to retime the ignition.

7. DISTRIBUTOR DISMANTLING

1. With the distributor on the bench - pull off the two spring clips retaining the cover and lift the cover off.

2. Pull the rotor arm off the distributor cam shaft.

3. Remove the points from the breaker plate as detailed in Section 3.

4. Undo the condenser retaining screw and take off the condenser.

5. Next prise off the small circlip from the vacuum unit pivot post.

7.5

6. Take out the two screws holding the breaker plate to the distributor body and lift away.

7. Take off the circlip flat washer and wave washer from the pivot post. Separate the two plates by bringing the holding down screw through the keyhole slot in the lower plate. Be careful not to lose the spring now left on the pivot post.

8. Pull the low tension wire and grommet from the lower plate.

9. Undo the two screws holding the vacuum unit to the body. Take off the unit.

Fig.4.3. Breaker plate & vacuum unit assembly

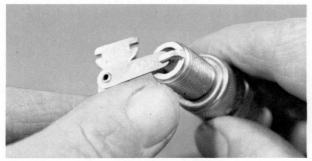

Measuring plug gap. A feeler gauge of the correct size (see ignition system specifications) should have a slight 'drag' when slid between the electrodes. Adjust gap if necessary

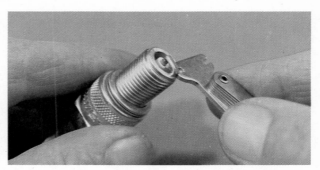

Adjusting plug gap. The plug gap is adjusted by bending the earth electrode inwards, or outwards, as necessary until the correct clearance is obtained. Note the use of the correct tool

Normal. Grey-brown deposits lightly coated core nose. Gap increasing by around 0.001 in (0.025 mm) per 1000 miles (1600 km). Plugs ideally suited to engine and engine in good condition

Carbon fouling. Dry, black, sooty deposits. Will cause weak spark and eventually misfire. Fault: over-rich fuel mixture. Check: carburettor mixture settings, float level and jet sizes; choke operation and cleanliness of air filter. Plugs can be re-used after cleaning

Oil fouling. Wet, oily deposits. Will cause weak spark and eventually misfire. Fault: worn bores/piston rings or valve guides; sometimes occurs (temporarily) during running-in period. Plugs can be re-used after thorough cleaning

Overheating. Electrodes have glazed appearance, core nose very white - few deposits. Fault: plug overheating. Check: plug value, ignition timing, fuel octane rating (too low) and fuel mixture (too weak). Discard plugs and cure fault immediately

Electrode damage. Electrodes burned away; core nose has burned, glazed appearance. Fault: initial pre-ignition. Check: as for 'Overheating' but may be more severe. Discard plugs and remedy fault before piston or valve damage occurs

Split core nose (may appear initially as a crack). Damage is self-evident, but cracks will only show after cleaning. Fault: pre-ignition or wrong gap-setting technique. Check: ignition timing, cooling system, fuel octane rating (too low) and fuel mixture (too weak). Discard plugs, rectify fault immediately

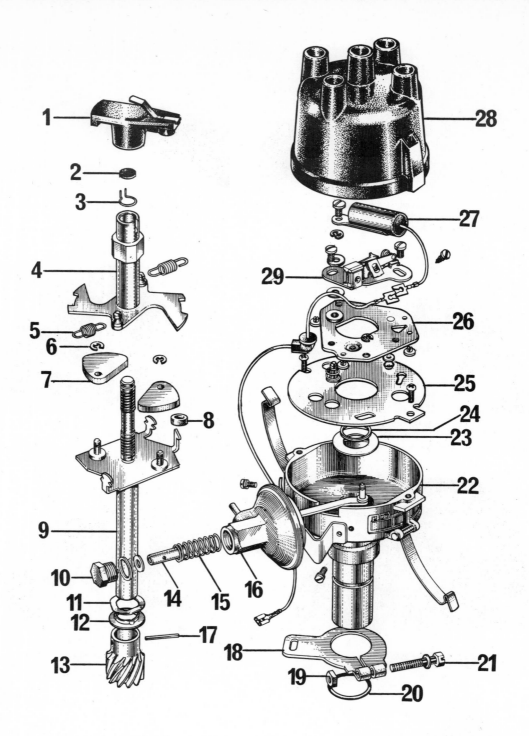

Fig.4.4. EXPLODED VIEW OF THE AUTOLITE DISTRIBUTOR

1 Rotor arm	8 Stop	16 Vacuum advance retard unit	24 Washer
2 Oil pad	9 Action plate & main shaft	17 Skew gear retaining pin	25 Lower C.B.plate
3 Spring clip	10 Shim retaining bolt	18 Clamp plate	26 Upper contact breaker
4 Mechanical advance & cam	11 Wave washer	19 Nut	plate
assembly	12 Thrust washer	20 'O' ring oil seal	27 Capacitor
5 Flyweight tension spring	13 Skew gear	21 Bolt & washer	28 Distributor cap
6 Circlip	14 Stop	22 Distributor body	29 Contact breaker assembly
7 Flyweight	15 Spring	23 Washer	

10 To dismantle the vacuum unit unscrew the bolt on the end of the unit and withdraw the vacuum spring, stop, and shims.

11 The mechanical advance is next removed but first make a careful note of the assembly particularly which spring fits which post and the position of the advance springs. Then remove the advance springs.

12 Prise off the circlips from the governor weight pivot pins and take out the weights.

13 Dismantle the shaft by taking out the felt pad in the top of the spindle. Expand the exposed circlip and take it out.

14 Now mark which slot in the mechanical advance plate is occupied by the advance stop which stands up from the action plate, and lift off the cam spindle.

15 It is only necessary to remove the lower shaft and action plate if it is excessively worn. If this is the case, with a small punch drive out the gear retaining pin and remove the gear with the two washers located above it.

16 Withdraw the shaft from the distributor body and take off the two washers from below the action plate. The distributor is now completely dismantled.

8. DISTRIBUTOR INSPECTION & REPAIR

1. Check the points as described in Section 3. Check the distributor cap for signs of tracking, indicated by a thin black line between the segments. Replace the cap if any signs of tracking are found.

2. If the metal portion of the rotor arm is badly burned or loose, renew the arm. If only slightly burned clean the end with a fine file. Check that the contact spring has adequate pressure and the bearing surface is clean and in good condition.

3. Check that the carbon brush in the distributor cap is unbroken and stands proud of its holder.

4. Examine the fly weights and pivots for wear and the advance springs for slackness. They can best be checked by comparing with new parts. If they are slack they must be renewed.

5. Check the points assembly for fit on the breaker plate, and the cam follower for wear.

6. Examine the fit of the lower shaft in the distributor body. If this is excessively worn it will be necessary to fit a new assembly

9. DISTRIBUTOR REASSEMBLY

1. Reassembly is a straightforward reversal of the dismantling process, but there are several points which must be noted.

2. Lubricate with S.A.E.20 engine oil the balance weights and other parts of the mechanical advance mechanism, the distributor shaft, and the portion of the shaft on which the cam bears, during assembly. Do not oil excessively but ensure these parts are adequately lubricated.

3. When fitting the lower shaft, first replace the thrust washers below the action plate before inserting into the distributor body. Next fit the wave washer and thrust washer at the lower end and replace the drive gear. Secure it with a new pin.

4. Assemble the upper and lower shaft with the advance stop in the correct slot (the one which was marked) in the mechanical advance plate.

5. After assembling the advance weights and springs check that they move freely without binding.

6. Before assembling the breaker plates make sure that the three nylon bearing studs are properly located in their holes in the upper breaker plate, and that the small earth spring is fitted on the pivot post.

7. As you refit the upper breaker plate pass the holding

down spindle through the keyhole slot in the lower plate.

8. Hold the upper plate in position by refitting the wave washer, flat washer and large circlip.

9. When all is assembled, remember to set the contact breaker gap to .025 in. (0.64 mm) as described in Section 2.8.

10 If a new gear or shaft is being fitted it is necessary to drill a new pin hole. Proceed this way.

11 Make a .015 in. (0.38 mm) forked shim to slide over the drive shaft. (Fig.4.5.)

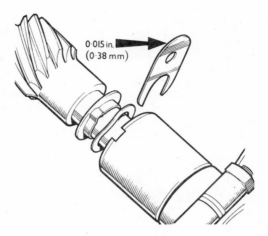

Fig.4.5. Setting distributor shaft endfloat

12 Assemble the shaft, wave washer, thrust washer, shim and gear wheel in position in the distributor body.

13 Hold the assembly in a large clamp such as a vice or carpenters clamp using only sufficient pressure to take up all end play.

14 There is a pilot hole in a new gear wheel for drilling the new hole. Set this pilot hole at 90° to the existing hole in an old shaft if the old one is being reused. Drill a 1/8th inch (3.18 mm) hole through both gear and shaft.

15 Fit a new pin in the hole. Release the clamp and remove the shim. The shaft will now have the correct amount of clearance.

16 When fitting an existing gear wheel still in good condition to a new shaft drill a new pin hole through the gear wheel at 90° to the existing hole. Secure with a new pin.

10. REFITTING DISTRIBUTOR

1. If a new shaft or gear wheel has not been fitted i.e. the original parts are still being used, it will not be necessary to retime the ignition.

2. Insert the distributor with the vacuum advance assembly to the rear and the mounting plate against the engine block.

3. Notice that the rotor arm rotates as the gears mesh. The rotor arm must settle in exactly the same direction that it was in before the distributor was removed. To do this lift out the assembly far enough to rotate the shaft one tooth at a time lowering it home to check the direction of the rotor arm. When it points in the desired direction with the assembly fully home fit the distributor clamp plate bolt.

4. With the distributor assembly fitted reconnect the low tension lead from the side of the distributor to the CB terminal on the coil. Reconnect the H.T. lead between the centre of the distributor cover and the centre of the coil, and refit the rubber union of the vacuum pipe

which runs from the induction manifold to the side of the vacuum advance unit.

11. SPARKING PLUGS & LEADS

1. The correct functioning of the sparking plugs are vital for the correct running and efficiency of the engine.

2. At intervals of 6,000 miles the plugs should be removed, examined, cleaned, and if worn excessively, replaced. The condition of the sparking plugs will also tell much about the overall condition of the engine.

3. If the insulator nose of the sparking plug is clean and white, with no deposits, this is indicative of a weak mixture, or too hot a plug. (A hot plug transfers heat away from the electrode slowly - a cold plug transfers it away quickly).

4. The plugs fitted as standard are AUTOLITE as listed in Specifications at the head of this chapter. If the tip and insulator nose is covered with hard black looking deposits, then this is indicative that the mixture is too rich. Should the plug be black and oily, then it is likely that the engine is fairly worn, as well as the mixture being too rich.

5. If the insulator nose is covered with light tan to greyish brown deposits, then the mixture is correct and it is likely that the engine is in good condition.

6. If there are any traces of long brown tapering stains on the outside of the white portion of the plug, then the plug will have to be renewed, as this shows that there is a faulty joint between the plug body and the insulator, and compression is being allowed to leak away.

7. Plugs should be cleaned by a sand blasting machine, which will free them from carbon more thoroughly than cleaning by hand. The machine will also test the condition of the plugs under compression. Any plug that fails to spark at the recommended pressure should be renewed.

8. The sparking plug gap is of considerable importance, as, if it is too large or too small, the size of the spark and its efficiency will be seriously impaired. The sparking plug gap should be set to the figure given in Specifications at the beginning of this chapter.

9. To set it, measure the gap with a feeler gauge, and then bend open, or close, the outer plug electrode until the correct gap is achieved. The centre electrode should never be bent as this may crack the insulation and cause plug failure if nothing worse.

10 When replacing the plugs, remember to use new plug washers, and replace the leads from the distributor in the correct firing order, which is 1,2,4,3, No.1 cylinder being the one nearest the radiator. No.1 lead from the distributor runs from the 1.0'clock position when looking down on the distributor cap. 2,3 & 4 are anti-clockwise from No.1.

11 The plug leads require no routine attention other than being kept clean and wiped over regularly and kept clean. At intervals of 6,000 miles, however, pull the leads off the plugs and distributor one at a time and make sure no water has found its way onto the connections. Remove any corrosion from the brass ends, wipe the collars on top of the distributor, and refit the leads.

12. IGNITION TIMING

1. When a new gear or shaft has been fitted or the engine has been rotated, or if a new assembly is being fitted it will be necessary to retime the ignition. Carry it out this way:-

2. Look up the initial advance for the particular model in the Specifications at the beginning of this chapter.

3. Turn the engine until No.1 piston is coming up to T.D.C. on the compression stroke. This can be checked by removing No.1 sparking plug and feeling the pressure being developed in the cylinder, or by removing the rocker cover and noting when the valves in No.4 cylinder are rocking, i.e. the inlet valve just opening and exhaust valve just closing. If this check is not made it is all too easy to set the timing 180° out, as both No.1 and 4 cylinders come up to T.D.C. at the same time, but only one is on the firing stroke. The engine can most easily be turned by engaging top gear and edging the car along.

4. Continue turning the engine until the appropriate timing mark on the timing cover is in line with the notch on the crankshaft pulley (arrowed). This setting must be

Fig.4.6. Ignition timing marks

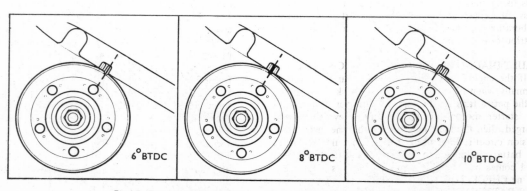

Fig.4.7. Diagrams showing the different degrees of ignition timing possible.

correct for the initial advance for the engine which has already been looked up.

5. Now with the vacuum advance unit pointing to the rear of the car insert the distributor assembly so that the rotor points to No.2 sparking plug on non-crossflow engines, No.2 inlet port on crossflow engines. The rotor will rotate slightly as the gear drops into mesh.

6. Fit the clamp plate retaining bolt to hold the assembly to the engine block and tighten it.

7. Slacken the distributor clamp pinch bolt.

8. Gently turn the distributor body until the contact breaker points are just opening when the rotor is pointing at the contact in the distributor cap which is connected to No.1 sparking plug. A convenient way is to put a mark on the outside of the distributor body in line with the terminal on cover, so that it shows when the cover is removed.

9. If this position cannot easily be reached check that the drive gear has meshed on the correct tooth by lifting out the distributor once more. If necessary rotate the drive shaft one tooth and try again.

10 Tighten the distributor body clamp enough to hold the distributor, but do not overtighten.

11 Set in this way the timing should be correct, but small adjustments may be made by slackening the distributor clamp bolt once more and rotating the distributor body clockwise to advance and anti-clockwise to retard.

12 The setting of a distributor including the amount of vacuum and mechanical advance can only be accurately carried out on an electronic tester. Alterations to the vacuum advance shims or tension on the mechanical advance unit springs will change the characteristics of the unit.

13 Since the ignition timing setting enables the firing point to be correctly related to the grade of fuel used, the fullest advantage of a change of grade from that recommended for the engine will only be attained by re-adjustment of the ignition setting.

13. IGNITION SYSTEM FAULT FINDING

By far the majority of breakdown and running troubles are caused by faults in the ignition system either in the low tension or high tension circuits.

14. IGNITION SYSTEM FAULT SYMPTOMS

There are two main symptoms indicating ignition faults. Either the engine will not start or fire, or the engine is difficult to start and misfires. If it is a regular misfire, i.e. the engine is only running on two or three cylinders the fault is almost sure to be in the secondary, or high tension circuit. If the misfiring is intermittent, the fault could be in either the high or low tension circuits. If the car stops suddenly, or will not start at all, it is likely that the fault is in the low tension circuit. Loss of power and overheating, apart from faulty carburation settings, are normally due to faults in the distributor or incorrect ignition timing.

15. FAULT DIAGNOSIS - ENGINE FAILS TO START

1. If the engine fails to start and the car was running normally when it was last used, first check there is fuel in the petrol tank. If the engine turns over normally on the starter motor and the battery is evidently well charged, then the fault may be in either the high or low tension circuits. First check the H.T. circuit. NOTE: If the battery is known to be fully charged; the ignition light comes on, and the starter motor fails to turn the engine CHECK THE TIGHTNESS OF THE LEADS ON THE BATTERY TERMINALS and also the secureness

of the earth lead to its CONNECTION TO THE BODY. It is quite common for the leads to have worked loose, even if they look and feel secure. If one of the battery terminal posts gets very hot when trying to work the starter motor this is a sure indication of a faulty connection to that terminal.

2. One of the commonest reasons for bad starting is wet or damp sparking plug leads and distributor. Remove the distributor cap. If condensation is visible internally dry the cap with a rag and also wipe over the leads. Replace the cap.

3. If the engine still fails to start, check that current is reaching the plugs, by disconnecting each plug lead in turn at the sparking plug end, and hold the end of the cable about 3/16th inch away from the cylinder block. Spin the engine on the starter motor.

4. Sparking between the end of the cable and the block should be fairly strong with a regular blue spark. (Hold the lead with rubber to avoid electric shocks). If current is reaching the plugs, then remove them and clean and regap them to 0.025 in. The engine should now start.

5. If there is no spark at the plug leads take off the H.T. lead from the centre of the distributor cap and hold it to the block as before. Spin the engine on the starter once more. A rapid succession of blue sparks between the end of the lead and the block indicate that the coil is in order and that the distributor cap is cracked the rotor arm faulty or the carbon brush in the top of the distributor cap is not making good contact with the spring on the rotor arm. Possibly the points are in bad condition. Clean and reset them as described in this chapter section 2:5 to 9.

6. If there are no sparks from the end of the lead from the coil check the connections at the coil end of the lead. If it is in order start checking the low tension circuit.

7. Use a 12v voltmeter on a 12v bulb and two lengths of wire. With the ignition switch on and the points open test between the low tension wire to the coil (it is marked S.W. or +) and earth. No reading indicates a break in the supply from the ignition switch. Check the connections at the switch to see if any are loose. Refit them and the engine should run. A reading shows a faulty coil or condenser or broken lead between the coil and the distributor.

8. Take the condenser wire off the points assembly and with the points open test between the moving point and earth. If there now is a reading then the fault is in the condenser. Fit a new one and the fault is cleared.

9. With no reading from the moving point to earth, take a reading between earth and the CB or - terminal of the coil. A reading here shows a broken wire which will need to be replaced between the coil and distributor. No reading confirms that the coil has failed and must be replaced, after which the engine will run once more. Remember to refit the condenser wire to the points assembly. For these tests it is sufficient to separate the points with a piece of dry paper while testing with the points open.

16. FAULT DIAGNOSIS - ENGINE MISFIRES

1. If the engine misfires regularly run it at a fast idling speed. Pull off each of the plug caps in turn and listen to the note of the engine. Hold the plug cap in a dry cloth or with a rubber glove as additional protection against a shock from the H.T. supply.

2. No difference in engine running will be noticed when the lead from the defective circuit is removed. Removing the lead from one of the good cylinders will accentuate the misfire.

3. Remove the plug lead from the end of the defective plug and hold it about 3/16th inch away from the block. Restart the engine. If the sparking is fairly strong and regular the fault must lie in the sparking plug.

4. The plug may be loose, the insulation may be cracked, or the points may have burnt away giving too wide a gap for the spark to jump. Worse still, one of the points may have broken off. Either renew the plug, or clean it, reset the gap, and then test it.

5. If there is no spark at the end of the plug lead, or if it is weak and intermittent, check the ignition lead from the distributor to the plug. If the insulation is cracked or perished, renew the lead. Check the connections at the distributor cap.

6. If there is still no spark, examine the distributor cap carefully for tracking. This can be recognised by a very thin black line running between two or more electrodes, or between an electrode and some other part of the distributor. These lines are paths which now conduct electricity across the cap thus letting it run to earth. The only answer is a new distributor cap.

7. Apart from the ignition timing being incorrect, other causes of misfiring have already been dealt with under the section dealing with the failure of the engine to start. To recap - these are that:-

a) The coil may be faulty giving an intermittent misfire.
b) There may be a damaged wire or loose connection in the low tension circuit.
c) The condenser may be short circuiting.
d) There may be a mechanical fault in the distributor (Broken driving spindle or contact breaker spring).

8. If the ignition timing is too far retarded, it should be noted that the engine will tend to overheat, and there will be a quite noticeable drop in power. If the engine is overheating and the power is down, and the ignition timing is correct, then the carburetter should be checked, as it is likely that this is where the fault lies.

CHAPTER FIVE

CLUTCH AND ACTUATING MECHANISM

CONTENTS

SPECIFICATIONS

Clutch type... ... ... Single dry plate diaphragm spring
Actuation ... ... Hydraulic
Clutch lining diameter.. ... ... 7.5 in. (19.1 cm)
Total friction area... ... ... 44.17 sq.in. (284.98 cm^2)
Number of damper springs 4
Master cylinder bore ... ... 70 in. (17.78 mm)
Slave cylinder bore.. ... ... 875 in. (22.22 mm)

TORQUE WRENCH SETTINGS

Clutch pressure plate cover to flywheel ... ... 12 to 15 lb/ft. (1.66 to 2.0 kg.m)

1. GENERAL DESCRIPTION

1. All models are fitted with a 7½ in. single dry plate diaphragm clutch. The unit comprises a steel cover which is dowelled and bolted to the rear face of the flywheel, and contains the pressure plate, pressure plate diaphragm spring, and fulcrum rings.

2. The clutch disc is free to slide along the splined first motion shaft and is held in position between the flywheel and the pressure plate by the pressure of the pressure plate spring. Friction lining material is riveted to the clutch disc and it has a spring cushioned hub to absorb transmission shocks and to help ensure a smooth take-off.

3. The circular diaphragm spring is mounted on shouldered pins and held in place in the cover by two fulcrum rings. The spring is also held to the pressure plate by three spring steel clips which are riveted in position.

4. The clutch is actuated hydraulically. The pendant clutch pedal, is connected to the clutch master cylinder and hydraulic fluid reservoir by a short pushrod. The master cylinder and hydraulic reservoir are mounted on the engine side of the bulkhead in front of the driver.

5. Depressing the clutch pedal moves the piston in the master cylinder forwards, so forcing hydraulic fluid through the clutch hydraulic pipe to the slave cylinder.

6. The piston in the slave cylinder moves forward on the entry of the fluid and actuates the clutch release arm by means of a short pushrod.

7. The release arm pushes the release bearing forwards to bear against the release plate, so moving the centre of the diaphragm spring inwards. The spring is sandwiched between two annular rings which act as fulcrum points. As the centre of the spring is pushed in the outside of the spring is pushed out, so moving the pressure plate backwards and disengaging the pressure plate from the clutch disc.

8. When the clutch pedal is released the diaphragm spring forces the pressure plate into contact with the high friction linings on the clutch disc and at the same time pushes the clutch disc a fraction of an inch forwards on its splines so engaging the clutch disc with the flywheel. The clutch disc is now firmly sandwiched between the pressure plate and the flywheel so the drive is taken up.

9. As the friction linings on the clutch disc wear the pressure plate automatically moves closer to the disc to compensate. There is therefore no need to periodically adjust the clutch

2. ROUTINE MAINTENANCE

1. Routine maintenance consists of checking the level of the hydraulic fluid in the master cylinder every 6,000 miles and topping up with hydraulic fluid if the level falls.

2. If it is noted that the level of the liquid has fallen then an immediate check should be made to determine the source of the leak.

3. Before checking the level of the fluid in the master cylinder reservoir, carefully clean the cap and body of the reservoir unit with clean rag so as to ensure that no dirt enters the system when the cap is removed. On no account should paraffin or any other cleaning solvent be used in case the hydraulic fluid becomes contaminated.

4. Check that the level of the hydraulic fluid is up to within ½ in. of the filler neck and that the vent hole in the cap is clear. Do not overfill.

3. CLUTCH SYSTEM - BLEEDING

1. Gather together a clean jam jar, a 9 in. length of rubber tubing which fits tightly over the bleed nipple in the slave cylinder, a tin of hydraulic brake fluid, and a friend to help.

2. Check that the master cylinder is full and if not fill it, and cover the bottom two inches of the jar with hydraulic fluid.

3. Remove the rubber dust cap from the bleed nipple on the slave cylinder and with a suitable spanner open the bleed nipple one turn.

4. Place one end of the tube securely over the nipple and insert the other end in the jam jar so that the tube orifice is below the level of the fluid.

5. The assistant should now pump the clutch pedal up and down slowly until air bubbles cease to emerge from the end of the tubing. He should also check the reservoir frequently to ensure that the hydraulic fluid does not disappear so letting air into the system.

6. When no more air bubbles appear, tighten the bleed nipple on the downstroke.

7. Replace the rubber dust cap over the bleed nipple. Allow the hydraulic fluid in the jar to stand for at least 24 hours before using it, to allow all the minute air bubbles to escape.

4. CLUTCH PEDAL - REMOVAL & REPLACEMENT

1. The clutch pedal is removed and replaced in exactly the same way as the brake pedal.

2. A full description of how to remove and replace the brake pedal can be found in Chapter 9/11.

5. CLUTCH REMOVAL

1. Remove the gearbox as described in Chapter 6, Section 3.

2. Remove the clutch assembly by unscrewing the six bolts holding the cover to the rear face of the flywheel. Unscrew the bolts diagonally half a turn at a time to prevent distortion to the cover flange.

3. With all the bolts and spring washers removed lift the clutch assembly off the locating dowels. The driven plate or clutch disc will fall out at this stage as it is not attached to either the clutch cover assembly or the flywheel (photo).

6. CLUTCH REPLACEMENT

1. It is important that no oil or grease gets on the clutch disc friction linings, or the pressure plate and flywheel faces. It is advisable to replace the clutch with clean hands and to wipe down the pressure plate and flywheel faces with a clean dry rag before assembly begins.

2. Place the clutch disc against the flywheel with the longer end of the hub facing towards the flywheel, (photo). On no account should the clutch disc be replaced with the longer end of the centre hub facing out from the flywheel as on reassembly it will be found quite impossible to operate the clutch with the friction disc in this position.

3. Replace the clutch cover assembly loosely on the dowels, (one dowel is arrowed in the photo). Replace the six bolts and spring washers and tighten them finger tight so that the clutch disc is gripped but can still be moved.

4. The clutch disc must now be centralised so that when the engine and gearbox are mated, the gearbox input shaft splines will pass through the splines in the centre of the driven plate hub.

5. Centralisation can be carried out quite easily by inserting a round bar or long screwdriver through the hole in the centre of the clutch, so that the end of the bar rests in the small hole in the end of the crankshaft containing the input shaft bearing bush. Ideally an old Ford input shaft should be used.

6. Using the input shaft bearing bush as a fulcrum, moving the bar sideways or up and down will move the clutch disc in whichever direction is necessary to achieve centralisation.

7. Centralisation is easily judged by removing the bar and viewing the driven plate hub in relation to the hole in the release bearing. When the hub appears exactly in

5.3

6.2

6.3

6.7

6.8

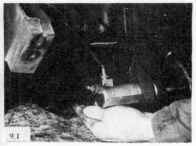

9.1

the centre of the release bearing hole all is correct (photo). Alternatively the input shaft will fit the bush and centre of the clutch hub exactly obviating the need for visual alignment.

8. Tighten the clutch bolts firmly in a diagonal sequence to ensure that the cover plate is pulled down evenly and without distortion of the flange. Finally tighten the bolts down to a torque of 15 lb/ft. (photo).

7. CLUTCH DISMANTLING & REPLACEMENT

1. It is not practical to dismantle the pressure plate assembly and the term clutch dismantling and replacement is the term usually used for simply fitting a new clutch friction plate.

2. If a new clutch disc is being fitted it is a false economy not to renew the release bearing at the same time. This will preclude having to replace it at a later date when wear on the clutch linings is still very small.

3. If the pressure plate assembly requires renewal (See Section 8) an exchange unit must be purchased. This will have been accurately set up and balanced to very fine limits.

8. CLUTCH INSPECTION

1. Examine the clutch disc friction linings for wear and loose rivets and the disc for rim distortion, cracks, broken hub springs, and worn splines. The surface of the friction linings may be highly glazed, but as long as the clutch material pattern can be clearly seen this is satisfactory. Compare the amount of lining wear, with a new clutch disc at the stores in your local garage, and if the linings are more than three quarters worn replace the disc.

2. It is always best to renew the clutch driven plate as an assembly to preclude further trouble, but, if it is wished to merely renew the linings, the rivets should be drilled out and not knocked out with a punch. The manufacturers do not advise that only the linings are renewed and personal experience dictates that it is far more satisfactory to renew the driven plate complete than to try and economise by only fitting new friction linings.

3. Check the machined faces of the flywheel and the pressure plate. If either are grooved they should either be machined until smooth or renewed.

4. If the pressure plate is cracked or split it is essential that an exchange unit is fitted, also if the pressure of the diaphragm spring is suspect.

5. Check the release bearing for smoothness of operation. There should be no harshness and no slackness in it. It should spin reasonably freely bearing in mind it has been prepacked with grease.

9. CLUTCH SLAVE CYLINDER - REMOVAL, DISMANTLING, EXAMINATION & REASSEMBLY

1. The clutch slave cylinder is positioned on the left-hand bottom side of the bellhousing (photo).

2. Before removing the cylinder take off the clutch reservoir cap and place a piece of thin polythene over the top of the reservoir. Screw down the cap tightly.

3. Jack up the front of the car and support on stands to give good access to the slave cylinder.

4. Undo the union nut which holds the hydraulic pipe to the cylinder (the polythene under the cap will prevent the fluid from leaking).

5. Pull the rubber boot back and with a pair of circlip pliers remove the retaining circlip (photo) from round the cylinder body.

6. The slave cylinder can now be removed by pushing forwards out of its location. If very stiff grasp the flats on the cylinder body with a mole wrench and twisting the body backwards and forwards pull it out from the bellhousing.

9.6

7. Referring to Fig.5.2. take out the circlip (38) from the end of the cylinder body.

8. The piston (39), complete with seal (40) and the spring (41) can then be shaken from the slave cylinder bore. Clean all the components thoroughly with hydraulic fluid or methylated spirits and dry them off.

9. Carefully examine the rubber components for signs of swelling, distortion, splitting or other wear, and check the piston and cylinder wall for wear and score marks. Replace any parts that are found faulty.

10 Reassembly is a straightforward reversal of the dismantling procedure, but NOTE the following points:-

a) As the component parts are refitted to the slave cylinder barrel, smear them with hydraulic fluid.

b) When reassembling the operating piston, locate the piston seal on the spigot at the end of the piston so that the recess in the seal is towards the closed end of the slave cylinder bore.

c) On completion of reassembly, top up the reservoir tank with the correct grade of hydraulic fluid and bleed the system, if necessary.

10. CLUTCH MASTER CYLINDER - REMOVAL, DISMANTLING, EXAMINATION & REASSEMBLY

1. Referring to Fig.5.3. disconnect the clutch master cylinder pushrod (1) from the clutch pedal by undoing the nut and removing the spring washer and concentric bolt.

2. Place a rag under the master cylinder to catch any hydraulic fluid which may be spilt. Unscrew the union nut from the end of the hydraulic pipe where it enters the clutch master cylinder and gently pull the pipe clear.

3. Unscrew the two bolts and spring washers holding the clutch cylinder mounting flange to the bulkhead.

4. Remove the master cylinder and reservoir, unscrew the filler cap, and drain the hydraulic fluid into a clean container.

5. Pull off the rubber boot (2) to expose the circlip (3) which must be removed so the pushrod complete with metal retaining washer (1) can be pulled out of the master cylinder (14).

6. The piston and valve assembly can now be shaken from the master cylinder body.

7. With a small electrical screwdriver lift the tag on the spring retainer (6) which engages against the shoulder on the front of the piston shank (4) and separate the piston from the retainer.

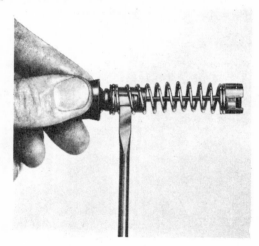

Fig.5.1. Removing the piston valve

8. To dismantle the valve assembly manoeuvre the flange on the valve shank stem (10) through the eccentrically positioned hole in the end face of the spring retainer (6). The spring (7), distance piece (8) and valve spring seal washer (9) can now be pulled off the valve shank stem (10).

9. Carefully ease the rubber seals (12 & 5) from the valve stem (10) and the piston (4) respectively.

10 Clean and carefully examine all the parts, especially the piston cup and rubber washers, for signs of distortion, splitting, or other wear and check the piston and cylinder for wear and scoring. Replace any parts that are faulty.

11 During the inspection of the piston seal it has been found advisable to maintain the shape of this seal as regular as possible and for this reason do not turn it inside out as slight distortion may be caused.

12 Rebuild the piston and valve assembly in the following sequence.

a) Fit the piston seal (5) to the piston (4) so the larger circumference of the rubber lip will enter the cylinder bore first.

b) Fit the valve seal (12) to the valve (10) in the same way.

c) Place the valve spring seal washer (9) so its convex face abuts the valve stem flange, and then fit the seat spacer (8) and spring (7).

d) Fit the spring retainer (6) to the spring (7) which must then be compressed so the valve stem (10) can be reinserted in the retainer (6).

e) Replace the front of the piston (4) in the retainer (6) and then press down the retaining leg so it locates under the shoulder at the front of the piston shank.

f) Generously lubricate the assembly with hydraulic fluid and carefully replace it in the master cylinder taking great care not to damage the rubber seals as they are inserted into the cylinder bore.

g) Fit the pushrod (1) and washer in place and secure with the circlip (3). Replace the rubber boot (2).

12 Replacement of the unit in the car is a straightforward reversal of the removal sequence. Finally, bleed the system as described earlier in Section 3.

11. CLUTCH RELEASE BEARING - REMOVAL & REPLACEMENT

1. With the gearbox and engine separated to provide access to the clutch, attention can be given to the release bearing located in the bellhousing, over the input shaft.

2. The release bearing is a relatively inexpensive but important component and unless it is nearly new it is a mistake not to replace it during an overhaul of the clutch.

3. To remove the release bearing first pull off the release arm rubber gaiter.

4. The release arm and bearing assembly can then be withdrawn from the clutch housing (photo).

11.4

11.5

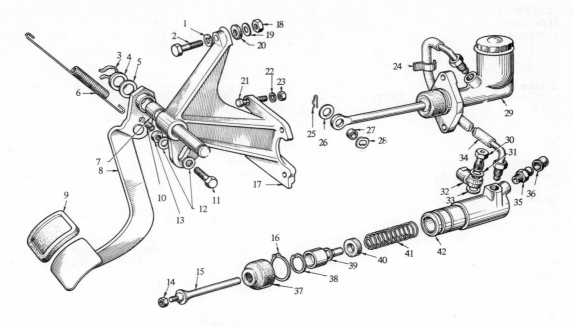

Fig.5.2. EXPLODED VIEW OF THE CLUTCH HYDRAULIC SYSTEM

1 Spring washer
2 Bolt
3 Clip
4 Washer
5 Washer
6 Return spring
7 Bush
8 Clutch pedal
9 Clutch pedal pad
10 Bush
11 Bolt

12 Washers
13 Nut
14 Nut
15 Slave cylinder push rod
16 Circlip
17 Pedal mounting bracket
18 Nut
19 Washer
20 Insulation washer
21 Bracket securing bolt
22 Spring washer

23 Nut
24 Clip
25 Retaining circlip
26 Washer
27 Bush
28 Clip
29 Clutch master cylinder
30 Clutch flexible pipe connector
   bolt (this type not normally
   fitted)
31 Washer

32 Connector
33 Washer
34 Flexible pipe
35 Bleed nipple
36 Bleed nipple cover
37 Rubber boot
38 Circlip
39 Piston
40 Rubber piston seal
41 Return spring
42 Slave cylinder body

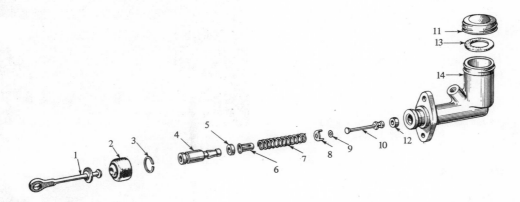

Fig.5.3. EXPLODED VIEW OF THE CLUTCH MASTER CYLINDER

1 Pushrod
2 Rubber boot
3 Pushrod retaining circlip
4 Piston

5 Piston seal
6 Spring retainer
7 Spring
8 Spacer

9 Seal washer
10 Valve shank
11 Cap
12 Valve seal

13 Gasket
14 Master cylinder body

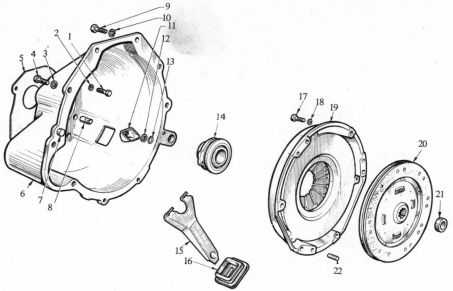

Fig.5.4. EXPLODED VIEW OF THE MAIN CLUTCH COMPONENTS,
BELLHOUSING AND RELEASE MECHANISM

1 Bolt	7 Dowel	13 Spring washer	19 Clutch pressure plate assembly
2 Spring washer	8 Bellhousing pin	14 Clutch release bearing	20 Clutch friction plate
3 Spring washer	9 Bolt	15 Clutch release lever	21 Bush
4 Bolt	10 Spring washer	16 Rubber boot	22 Dowel
5 Gasket	11 Clutch release pivot	17 Bolt	
6 Bellhousing	12 Washer	18 Split washer	

5. To free the bearing from the release arm simply un-hook it, and then with the aid of two blocks of wood and a vice press off the release bearing from its hub.

6. Replacement is a straightforward reversal of these instructions.

12. CLUTCH FAULTS

There are four main faults to which the clutch and release mechanism are prone. They may occur by themselves or in conjunction with any of the other faults. They are clutch squeal, slip, spin, and judder.

13. CLUTCH SQUEAL - DIAGNOSIS & CURE

1. If on taking up the drive or when changing gear, the clutch squeals, this is a sure indication of a badly worn clutch release bearing.

2. As well as regular wear due to normal use, wear of the clutch release bearing is much accentuated if the clutch is ridden, or held down for long periods in gear, with the engine running. To minimise wear of this component the car should always be taken out of gear at traffic lights and for similar hold-ups.

3. The clutch release bearing is not an expensive item, but difficult to get at.

14. CLUTCH SLIP - DIAGNOSIS & CURE

1. Clutch slip is a self-evident condition which occurs when the clutch friction plate is badly worn, the release arm free travel is insufficient, oil or grease have got onto the flywheel or pressure plate faces, or the pressure plate itself is faulty.

2. The reason for clutch slip is that, due to one of the faults listed above, there is either insufficient pressure from the pressure plate, or insufficient friction from the friction plate to ensure solid drive.

3. If small amounts of oil get onto the clutch, they will be burnt off under the heat of clutch engagement, and in the process, gradually darkening the linings. Excessive oil on the clutch will burn off leaving a carbon deposit which can cause quite bad slip, or fierceness, spin and judder.

4. If clutch slip is suspected, and confirmation of this condition is required, there are several tests which can be made.

5. With the engine in second or third gear and pulling lightly up a moderate incline, sudden depression of the accelerator pedal may cause the engine to increase its speed without any increase in road speed. Easing off on the accelerator will then give a definite drop in engine speed without the car slowing.

6. In extreme cases of clutch slip the engine will race under normal acceleration conditions.

7. If slip is due to oil or grease on the linings a temporary cure can sometimes be effected by squirting carbon tetrachloride into the clutch. The permanent cure is, of course, to renew the clutch driven plate and trace and rectify the oil leak.

15. CLUTCH SPIN - DIAGNOSIS & CURE

1. Clutch spin is a condition which occurs when there is a leak in the clutch hydraulic actuating mechanism, the release arm free travel is excessive, there is an obstruction in the clutch either on the primary gear splines, or in the operating lever itself, or the oil may have partially burnt off the clutch linings and have left a resinous deposit which is causing the clutch disc to stick to the pressure plate or flywheel.

2. The reason for clutch spin is that due to any, or a combination of, the faults just listed, the clutch pressure plate is not completely freeing from the centre plate

even with the clutch pedal fully depressed.

3. If clutch spin is suspected, the condition can be confirmed by extreme difficulty in engaging first gear from rest, difficulty in changing gear, and very sudden take-up of the clutch drive at the fully depressed end of the clutch pedal travel as the clutch is released.

4. Check the clutch master and slave cylinders and the connecting hydraulic pipe for leaks. Fluid in one of the rubber boots fitted over the end of either the master or slave cylinders is a sure sign of a leaking piston seal.

5. If these points are checked and found to be in order then the fault lies internally in the clutch, and it will be necessary to remove the clutch for examination.

16. CLUTCH JUDDER - DIAGNOSIS & CURE

1. Clutch judder is a self-evident condition which occurs when the gearbox or engine mountings are loose or too flexible, when there is oil on the faces of the clutch friction plate, or when the clutch pressure plate has been incorrectly adjusted.

2. The reason for clutch judder is that due to one of the faults just listed, the clutch pressure plate is not freeing smoothly from the friction disc, and is snatching.

3. Clutch judder normally occurs when the clutch pedal is released in first or reverse gears, and the whole car shudders as it moves backwards or forwards.

CHAPTER SIX

GEARBOX

CONTENTS

SPECIFICATIONS

Gearbox
Number of gears	4 forward, 1 reverse
Type of gears	Helical constant mesh
Synchromesh	All forward gears

Main Drive Gear
	All models except GT.	GT from Jan 1967
Number of teeth	17	
G.T. from Jan 1967	19	
Layshaft...	All models except GT.	GT from Jan 1967
Number of teeth	32	30
	28	26
	22	22
	17	17
	19	19
End float..	.008 to .020 in. (.203 to .508 mm)	
Thrust washer thickness	.061 to .063 in. (.155 to .160 mm)	
Number of rollers	40	
Layshaft diameter...	.6818 to .6823 in. (1.732 to 1.733 mm)	

First Gear
End float	.005 to .017 in. (.127 to .432 mm)
Number of teeth	32

Second Gear
End float	.005 to .017 in. (.127 to .432 mm)
Number of teeth	28

Third Gear
End float	.005 to .017 in. (.127 to .432 mm)
Number of teeth	21 (later G.T models 23)

Reverse Idler Gear
Number of teeth	22

Gearbox ratios: All 1297 c.c. models:-	Gearbox	Overall
First	3.543 to 1	14.615 to 1
Second	2.396 to 1	9.883 to 1
Third	1.412 to 1	5.824 to 1
Top	1.000 to 1	4.125 to 1
Reverse	3.963 to 1	16.347 to 1

1500 c.c., 1598 c.c., & G.T. models before Jan 1967:-		
First	3.543 to 1	13.818 to 1
Second	2.396 to 1	9.344 to 1

Third	1.412 to 1	5.507 to 1
Top	1.000 to 1	3.900 to 1
Reverse	3.963 to 1	15.456 to 1

G.T. models from Jan 1967

First	2.972 to 1	11.591 to 1
Second	2.010 to 1	7.839 to 1
Third	1.397 to 1	5.448 to 1
Top	1.000 to 1	3.900 to 1
Reverse	3.324 to 1	12.964 to 1

Oil Capacity

Up to Sept '67	2.13 pints (2.56 US pints, 1.21 litres)
From Sept '67 on	1.97 pints (2.40 US pints, 1.11 litres)

TORQUE WRENCH SETTINGS

Gearbox drain and filler plugs	25 to 30 lb/ft. (3.46 to 4.15 kg.m)
Mainshaft assembly retaining nut	20 to 25 lb/ft. (2.76 to 3.46 kg.m)
Gearbox extension to gearbox	20 to 25 lb/ft. (2.76 to 3.46 kg.m)

1. GENERAL DESCRIPTION

1. The gearbox fitted to all models is basically the same although small differences do occur depending on year of manufacture and the capacity and power output of the engine.

2. The main differences lie in the design of the selector mechanism (3 selector rods on early models, 1 selector rod on later models), and the extensive use of circlips on the later models. Figs.6.1. and 6.2. show these differences quite clearly.

3. The gearbox contains four forward and one reverse gear. Synchromesh is fitted between 1st and 2nd, 2nd and 3rd, and 3rd and 4th gears. The cast iron bellhousing is a separate casting to the gearbox case and the mainshaft extension.

4. An oil seal is fitted to the rear of the extension and to the front of the gearbox over the input shaft.

5. All the forward gears are helically cut in the interests of silent operation. Reverse gear is straight cut and meshes via an idler with a straight cut gear with teeth machined on the outside of the 1st and 2nd gear synchroniser sleeve.

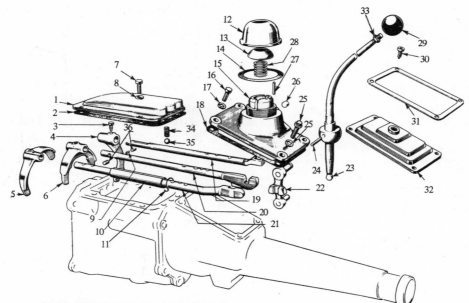

Fig.6.1. EXPLODED VIEW OF THE FLOOR GEARCHANGE MECHANISM FITTED TO ALL EXCEPT G.T. MODELS DURING THE PERIOD SEPTEMBER 1966 TO OCTOBER 1968

1 Gearbox cover	9 Interlock pin	19 Reverse gear selector rod	27 Pin
2 Gasket	10 Interlock plungers	20 First and second gear selector rod	28 Spring
3 Selector fork locking screw	11 Clip	21 Third and fourth gear selector rod	29 Gearlever knob
4 Reverse gear selector fork	12 Gearlever retaining cap		30 Phillips screw
5 Third and fourth gear selector fork	13 Retaining spring seat	22 Gear selector lever	31 Retainer
6 First and second gear selector fork	14 Gasket	23 Gear lever	32 Rubber boot
	15 Gearbox cover	24 Pin	33 Lock nut
7 Bolt	16 Bolt	25 Split washer	34 Detent spring
8 Spring washer	17 Spring washer	26 Gearchange cover cup	35 Detent ball
	18 Gasket		36 Detent plungers

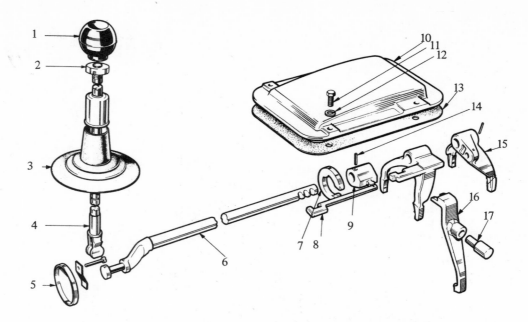

Fig.6.2. EXPLODED VIEW OF THE GEARCHANGE MECHANISM FITTED TO ALL MODELS
FROM OCTOBER 1968 ON

1 Gearlever knob	7 Selector interlock plate	12 Spring washer	17 Fork pivot
2 Knob locknut	8 Third and fourth gearchange	13 Gasket	18 Third and fourth gear
3 Gearlever boot	gate	14 Split locking pin	selector fork
4 Gearlever	9 Selector arm	15 First and second gear selector	
5 Plug	10 Gearbox cover	fork	
6 Gear selector rod	11 Bolt	16 Reverse gear selector fork	

2. ROUTINE MAINTENANCE

1. Once every 6,000 miles check the level of oil in the gearbox by removing the combined oil filler/level plug from the left-hand side of the gearbox. Top up, if necessary, with an SAE 80 Hypoy oil until lubricant just starts to run out of the filler hole. Wipe the filler plug clean and screw it back in to the gearbox securely.

2. In the author's opinion it is good practice to change the oil at least once every 36,000 miles as in this way the majority of abrasive metal particles which are bound to accumulate as the mileage rises, are carried away with the old oil.

3. GEARBOX - REMOVAL & REPLACEMENT

1. The gearbox can be removed in unit with the engine as described in Chapter 1/7 alternatively providing the car can be raised onto stands or ramps, far the easier method is to remove the gearbox from under the car after separating the front of the bellhousing from the rear of the engine.

2. Drain the gearbox oil, open the bonnet and disconnect the leads to the battery.

3. Raise the car on ramps or stands so there is at least a 2½ ft. gap between the bottom of the gearbox and the ground.

4. On ordinary early models with a floor mounted gear-change take off the gearlever knob, remove the screws which hold the metal gaiter securing ring to the floor, pull the ring and gaiter off the gearlever, and unscrew the gearlever turret so the gearlever can be lifted off.

5. From inside the car on G.T. and super models undo the Phillips screws which hold the centre console in place, remove the console and undo the gearlever knob.

6. Lift out the carpet, and release the metal ring which holds the rubber gaiter to the floor pan. Unscrew the gearlever turret and lift out the gearlever.

7. On later models follow the instructions in paragraph 5 where applicable and then with a pair of circlip pliers take off the circlip at the base of the gearlever which holds the lever spring in compression. Bend back the lock tab from the plastic dome nut, unscrew it, and take out the gearlever.

8. On models fitted with a column change first disconnect the lower end of the gear selector rod from the gear selector cross-shaft by pulling off the spring clip. Then free the cross-shaft from the pivot on the gearbox casing by pulling off the spring clip, followed by the two flat washers, and the wave washer. The gate selector lever on top of the gearbox is now disconnected from the gate selector rod.

9. The speedometer cable is held in place on the right-hand side of the gearbox extension by either a circlip or a forked retainer. From under the car remove the circlip or unscrew the forked retainer and pull the speedometer cable clear.

10 Scratch a mating mark across the propeller shaft flange and the rear axle pinion flange and then undo the four nuts and bolts holding the flanges together. Separate the flanges and pull the front yoke of the propeller shaft off the rear of the gearbox.

11 Free the exhaust pipe from the exhaust manifold by undoing the retaining nuts, and remove the slave cylinder after releasing the circlip which holds it to the front of the bellhousing. The slave cylinder may be very difficult to shift. If this is so it is permissible to seal the clutch hydraulic system by placing a thin sheet of polythene under the master cylinder cap which is then screwed down tightly. Undo the clutch hydraulic pipe union nut on the slave cylinder and pull the pipe clear. As the vent hole in the cap is sealed by the polythene no

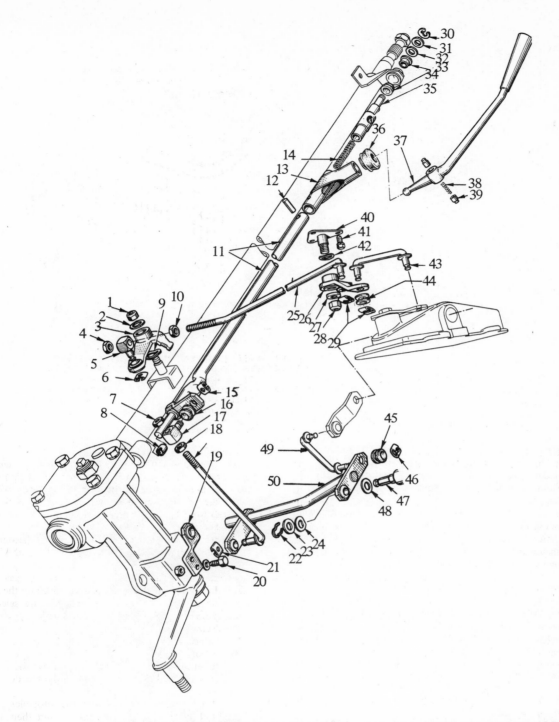

Fig.6.3. EXPLODED VIEW OF THE STEERING COLUMN GEARCHANGE MECHANISM FITTED TO CERTAIN MODELS

1 Nut	14 Spring	27 Washer	41 Bolt
2 Washer	15 Clip	28 Nut	42 Spring washer
3 Lever & bush assembly	16 Bush	29 Clips	43 Gate selector rod (short)
4 Nut	17 Connecting rod adjusting sleeve	30 Clip	44 Washers
5 Connecting rod adjusting sleeve	18 Nut	31 Washer	45 Insulator bush
6 Clip	19 Relay shaft bracket	32 Washer	46 Clip
7 Nut	20 Bolt	33 Bush	47 Relay lever pin
8 Gearchange gate selector	21 Clip	34 Bush	48 Washer
lever bush	22 Circlip	35 Shaft inner	49 Gearchange lever to relay
9 Spring washer	23 Washer	36 Gear lever insulator	shaft rod
10 Nut	24 Spring washer	37 Gearlever	50 Relay shaft lever
11 Gearchange shaft	25 Gearchange gate selector	38 Spring	
12 Pin	rod (long)	39 Trunnion	
13 Socket	26 Gate selector relay lever	40 Bracket	

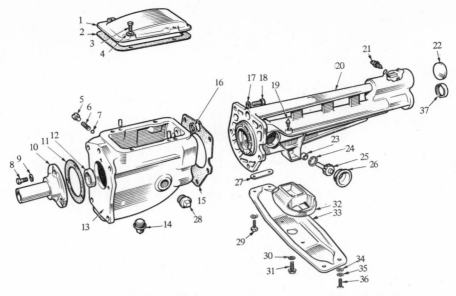

**Fig.6.4. EXPLODED VIEW OF THE GEARBOX EXTERIOR AS FITTED TO ALL MODELS
FROM OCTOBER 1968**

1 Gearbox cover	11 Gasket	21 Reverse light switch	31 Bolt
2 Gasket	12 Oil seal	22 Plug	32 Gearbox rubber mounting
3 Bolt	13 Gearbox casting	23 Seal	33 Crossmember
4 Spring washer	14 Drain plug	24 Circlip	34 Spring washer
5 Plug	15 Gasket	25 Speedometer pinion	35 Flat washer
6 Detent spring	16 Gearbox selector rod seal	26 Speedometer pinion retainer	36 Bolt
7 Detent ball	17 Spring washer	27 Plate	37 Rear oil seal
8 Bolt	18 Bolt	28 Filler plug	
9 Washer	19 Oil vent	29 Bolt	
10 Input shaft bearing retainer	20 Mainshaft extension	30 Washer	

loss of hydraulic fluid should occur.

12 Disconnect the lead to the starter motor and undo the two (or three) bolts which hold the starter motor in place.

13 Undo the bolts round the bellhousing periphery noting that one of the top bolts also secures the engine earth strap. Some of the lower bolts hold the metal dust cover in place. The cover should be slid off and placed on one side when the bolts are undone.

14 Support the rear of the engine by means of a jack placed under the rear of the sump

15 Undo the four bolts, two at each end, from the gearbox crossmember, and then slide the gearbox backwards and remove from under the car. The gearbox is heavy and on no account should it be allowed to hang on the first motion shaft when it is in the half-off position. The safest way to remove it is to have a trolley jack under the gearbox taking the weight.

16 The crossmember can be removed from the gearbox together with the rubber mounting by undoing the nut in the very centre of the crossmember.

17 Replacement is a straightforward reversal of the removal process but note the following points.

a) When refitting the bellhousing to engine securing bolts note that the top two bolts are plain, and not dowelled like the remainder.

b) Do not forget to fit the engine earth strap to one of the plain bellhousing bolts.

c) Ensure the mating lines on the propeller shaft and rear axle flanges are in line - vibration from the propeller shaft may otherwise be noticeable.

d) Refill the gearbox with 2.13 or 1.97 pints of Hypoy SAE 80 oil (see page 97 for model applicability).

Fig.6.5. The gearbox crossmember is held in place by four bolts, (arrowed in the figure), also arrowed is the speedometer drive retaining circlip.

4. GEARBOX DISMANTLING

1. All numbers in brackets refer to Fig.6.6.

2. Undo the four bolts and spring washer (photo) which hold the bellhousing to the front of the gearbox.

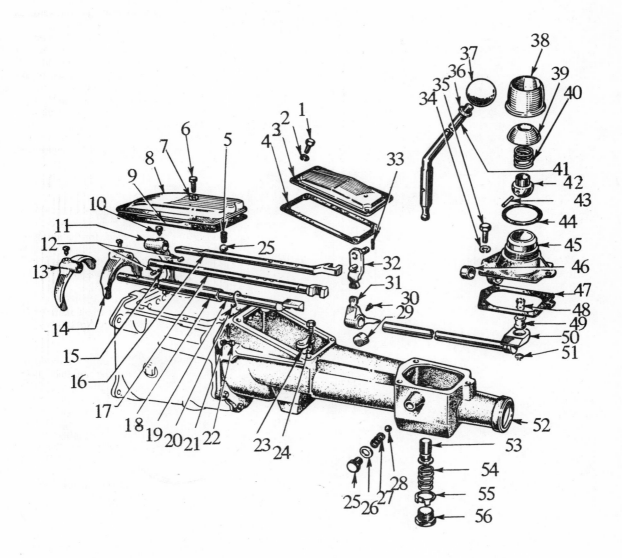

Fig.6.6. EXPLODED VIEW OF THE REMOTE CONTROL GEAR CHANGE MECHANISM FITTED TO G.T. MODELS FROM SEPTEMBER 1966 TO OCTOBER 1968

1 Bolt	16 Reverse gear selector rod	30 Bolt	46 Remote control gearchange housing bush
2 Spring washer	17 First and second gear selector rod	31 Gearchange selector arm	47 Gasket
3 Selector rod cover	18 Sleeve	32 Gear selector lever	48 Gearchange shaft bushing sleeve
4 Gasket	19 Third and fourth gear selector rod	33 Split lock pin	49 Bushing
5 Detent spring	20 Clip	34 Spring washer	50 Gearchange shaft
6 Bolt	21 Spring washer	35 Bolt	51 Sleeve ring
7 Spring washer	22 Bolt	36 Gearlever lock screw	52 Gearbox extension
8 Gearbox cover	23 Gearchange shaft and bridge bearing	37 Gearlever knob	53 Reverse gear stop
9 Gaskt	24 Bolt	38 Turret cover	54 Spring
10 Locknut	25 Plug	39 Retaining spring seat	55 Washer
11 Reverse gear selector fork	26 Washer	40 Spring	56 Plug
12 Interlock plungers	27 Spring	41 Gearlever	
13 Third and fourth gear selector fork	28 Ball	42 Bush	
14 First and second gear selector fork	29 Gearchange cover cup	43 Bush to gearlever locking pin	
15 Interlock pin		44 Sealing ring	
		45 Gearlever turret	

3. With the bolts removed pull the bellhousing away from the front of the gearbox casing (photo).

4. Undo the four bolts and spring washers (6,7) which hold the gearbox cover (8) in place and lift off the cover (photo). Note particularly the detent springs (5) which will pop up as the cover is removed.

5. Lift out the three detent springs (photo).

6. The three balls which lie under the detent springs (25) must now be removed. This is most easily done by tipping the gearbox onto its side and shaking out the balls (photo) one from each drilling.

7. Undo and remove the four bolts and spring washers (1,2) which hold the mainshaft extension inspection cover (3) in place (photo).

8. Undo the two bolts which hold the bridge piece in place (photo) and lift out the bridge piece.

9. Remove the locking wire from the head of the gearchange selector arm (31) bolt (photo).

10 Undo the bolt (photo) and slide the arm off. It is sometimes easier to do this after the selector rods have been removed.

11 Undo the lock wire (photo) from the three square headed selector fork securing bolts (10) which should then be unscrewed and removed.

12 Pull out from the extension inspection hole the left-hand third/fourth gear selector rod (19), and lift the sleeve (18) out of the gearbox.

13 Remove the interlock pin (15) from the end of the central first/second gear selector rod (photo) and withdraw the rod.

14 Undo the three bolts and spring washers (34,35) which hold the gearlever turret (45) in place and take off the turret (photo) together with the gearchange shaft (50).

15 Undo the bolts and spring washers (21,22) which hold the extension (52) to the rear of the gearbox, carefully prise out the speedometer drive gear (photo), and pull the extension complete with the reverse gear selector rod away from the gearbox.

16 The reverse gear selector rod (16) can now be removed from the extension, and the gearchange shaft (50) removed from the turret.

17 Undo the two plugs (25,56) from the rear of the extension and place the washers (55,26), springs (27,54) ball (28), and plunger (53) in a jam jar for safe keeping.

18 Lift out the 1st and 2nd gear selector fork (14), the 3rd and 4th gear selector fork (13), and finally the reverse gear selector fork (11), (photo).

19 All numbers in brackets refer now to Fig.6.7. With a metal rod against the exposed end of the layshaft (31) at the front of the gearbox tap the layshaft out (photo) removing it from the rear of the gearbox.

20 The laygear (17) will now drop out of mesh with the gears on the mainshaft (4), and the mainshaft assembly can be removed from the rear of the gearbox (photo).

21 From the front of the gearbox remove the input shaft cover (photo), where this is fitted.

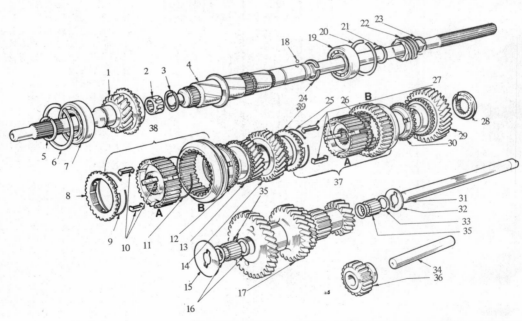

Fig.6.7. EXPLODED VIEW OF THE INTERNAL GEARBOX COMPONENTS FITTED TO ALL MODELS FROM OCTOBER 1968 ON

1 Input shaft	12 Synchroniser ring	22 Speedometer drive gear	32 Laygear thrust washer
2 Caged roller bearing	13 Third gear	23 Circlip	33 Needle roller thrust ring
3 Circlip	14 Second gear	24 Circlip	34 Reverse gear shaft
4 Mainshaft	15 Laygear thrust washer	25 Spring ring	35 Needle roller bearings
5 Small circlip	16 Needle roller bearing thrust	26 Spring ring	36 Reverse gear
6 Bearing retaining circlip	washers	27 Blocker bars	37 First & second gear syn-
7 Input shaft bearing	17 Laygear	28 First gear thrust washer	chroniser assembly
8 Synchroniser ring	18 Ball	29 First gear	38 Third and fourth gear
9 Spring ring	19 Mainshaft ball bearing	30 First & second gear synchroniser	synchroniser assembly
10 Blocker bars	20 Circlip	ring	39 Synchroniser ring
11 Spring ring	21 Circlip	31 Layshaft	

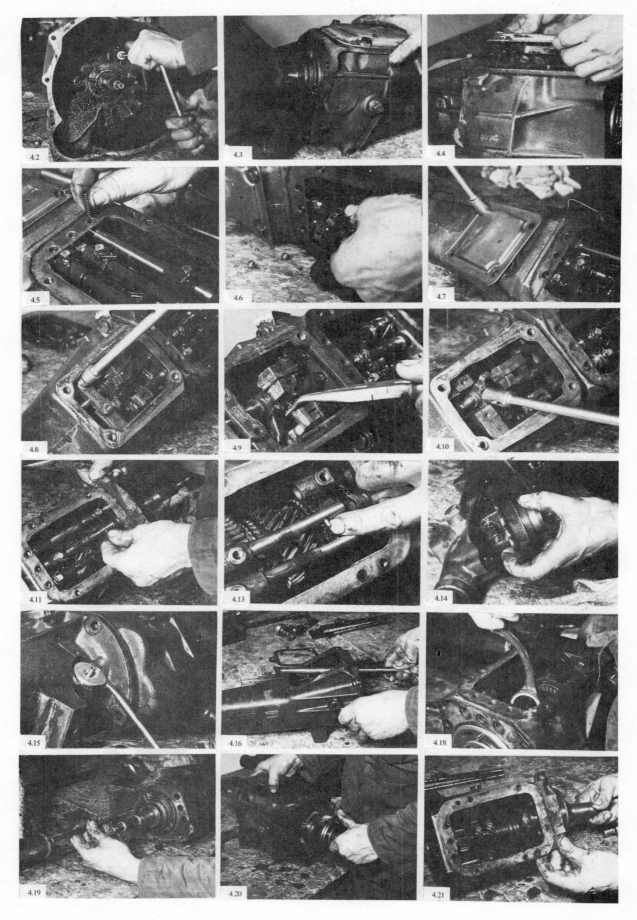

22 Undo the bolts and spring washers holding the input shaft oil seal retainer in place and slide it off the input shaft (photo).

23 With a pair of circlip pliers spring the large circlip (photo) (6) off the periphery of the input shaft bearing (7).

24 Gently tap the outside end of the input shaft with a soft faced hammer and withdraw the input shaft assembly from inside the gearbox (photo).

25 The laygear (17) can now be removed through the hole in the rear of the gearbox (photo). Note the needle rollers in each end of the laygear.

26 Lift out the two laygear thrust washers (15,32) from inside the gearbox (photo).

27 Screw a bolt into the threaded hole in the end of the reverse gear shaft (34) and using an open ended spanner as a lever as shown in the photo start to remove the shaft.

28 Then pull out the shaft and remove the reverse gear idler (36) from inside the gearbox.

29 The gearbox is now stripped right out and must be thoroughly cleaned. If there is any quantity of metal chips and fragments in the bottom of the gearbox casing it is obvious that several items will be found to be badly worn. The component parts of the gearbox should be examined for wear, and the laygear, input shaft and mainshaft assemblies broken down further as described in the following sections.

5. GEARBOX EXAMINATION & RENOVATION

1. Carefully clean and then examine all the component parts for general wear, distortion, slackness of fit, and damage to machined faces and threads.

2. Examine the gearwheels for excessive wear and chipping of the teeth. Renew them as necessary. If the laygear endfloat is above the permitted tolerance of 0.020 in. the thrust washers must be renewed. New thrust washers will almost certainly be required on any car that has completed more than 40,000 miles.

3. Examine the layshaft for signs of wear, where the laygear needle roller bearings bear. If a small ridge can be felt at either end of the shaft it will be necessary to renew it.

4. The four synchroniser rings (8,12,39,30) are bound to be badly worn and it is a false economy not to renew them. New rings will improve the smoothness and speed of the gearchange considerably.

5. The needle roller bearing and cage (2) located between the nose of the mainshaft and the annulus in the rear of the input shaft is also liable to wear, and should be renewed as a matter of course.

6. Examine the condition of the two ball bearing assemblies, one on the input shaft (7) and one on the mainshaft (19). Check them for noisy operation, looseness between the inner and outer races, and for general wear. Normally they should be renewed on a gearbox that is being rebuilt.

7. If either of the synchroniser units (37,38) are worn it will be necessary to buy a complete assembly as the parts are not sold individually.

8. Examine the ends of the selector forks where they rub against the channels in the periphery of the synchroniser units. If possible compare the selector forks with new units to help determine the wear that has occured. Renew them if worn.

9. If the bush bearing in the extension is badly worn it is best to take the extension to your local Ford garage to have the bearing pulled out and a new one fitted.

10 The rear oil seal should be renewed as a matter of course. Drive out the old seal with the aid of a drift or broad screwdriver as shown in the photo.

11 The seal is surrounded by a metal ring and comes out fairly easily (photo).

12 With a piece of wood to spread the load evenly, carefully tap a new seal into place (photo) ensuring it enters its bore in the extension squarely.

13 It is unlikely that any of the mainshaft bearing surfaces will be worn, but if there is any sign of scoring, picking up, or flats on the shaft then it must be renewed.

6. INPUT SHAFT - DISMANTLING & REASSEMBLY

1. The only reasons for dismantling the input shaft is to fit a new ball bearing assembly, or, if the input shaft is being renewed and the old bearing is in excellent condition, then the fitting of a new shaft to an old bearing.

2. With a pair of expanding circlip pliers remove the circlip (5) from the input shaft (photo).

3. With a soft headed hammer gently tap the bearing forward and then remove it from the shaft (photo).

4. When fitting the new bearing ensure that the groove cut in the outer periphery faces away from the gear. If the bearing is fitted the wrong way round it will not be possible to fit the large circlip which retains the bearing in the housing.

5. Using the jaws of a vice as a support behind the bearing tap the bearing squarely into place by hitting the rear of the input shaft with a plastic or hide faced hammer as shown in the photo.

6. Then refit the circlip (5) which holds the bearing to the input shaft.

7. MAINSHAFT - DISMANTLING & REASSEMBLY

1. The mainshaft has to be dismantled before some of the synchroniser rings can be inspected. For dismantling it is best to mount the plain portion of the shaft between two pieces of wood in a vice.

2. From the forward end of the mainshaft pull off the caged roller bearing (2) arrowed in the photo, and the synchro ring (8).

3. With a pair of circlip pliers remove the circlip (3) which holds the third/fourth gear synchroniser hub in place (photo).

4. Ease the hub (38) and third gear (13) forward by gentle leverage with a pair of long nosed pliers (photo).

5. The hub (38) and synchro ring (12) are then removed from the mainshaft (photo).

6. Then slide off third gear (photo). Nothing else can be removed from this end of the mainshaft because of the raised lip on the shaft (arrowed in photo).

7. Turn back the retaining tab from the side of the mainshaft nut and undo the nut with a Stilson wrench or large pair of mole grips (photo). The average owner

7.7

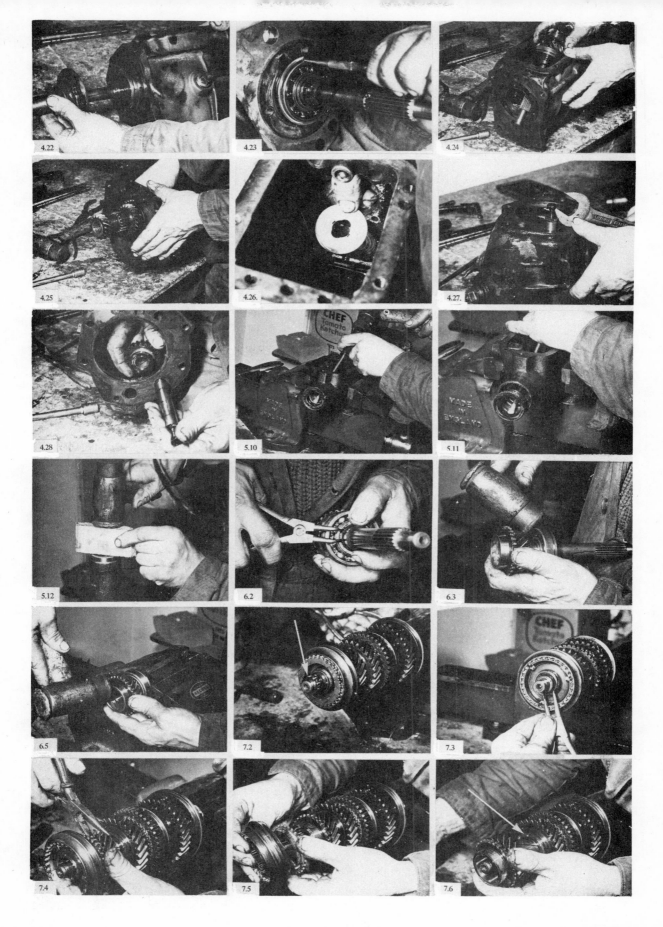

4.22

4.23

4.24

4.25

4.26.

4.27.

4.28

5.10

5.11

5.12

6.2

6.3

6.5

7.2

7.3

7.4

7.5

7.6

is unlikely to have a spanner large enough to move this nut. On some models a circlip (23) is used instead of a nut.

8. Remove the nut or circlip, washer, and speedometer drive, taking care not to drop the ball (arrowed in photo) which locates in a groove in the speedometer drive gear.

9. Where fitted remove the circlip (21), and then with the edges of the bearing housing held by the jaws of a vice tap the shaft backwards out of the bearing (19), (photo).

10 The bearing and housing followed by the large thrust washer (28) can then be pulled off. Follow these items by pulling off first gear (29) and the synchroniser ring (30), (photo).

11 With a pair of circlip pliers remove the circlip (24) which retains the first and second gear synchroniser assembly in place (photo).

12 The first and second gear synchroniser followed by second gear (14) are then simply slid off the mainshaft (photo). The mainshaft is now completely dismantled.

13 If a new synchroniser assembly is being fitted it is necessary to take it to pieces first to clean off all the preservative. These instructions are also pertinent in instances where the outer sleeve has come off the hub accidently during dismantling.

14 To dismantle an assembly for cleaning slide the synchroniser sleeve off the splined hub and clean all the preservative from the blocker bars (27), spring rings (25,26), the hub itself (A), and the sleeve (B).

15 Oil the components lightly and then fit the sleeve (B) to the hub (A) so the lines marked on them (see Fig.6.8) are in line. Note the three slots in the hub and fit a blocker bar in each.

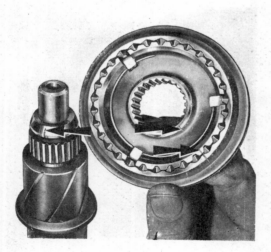

Fig.6.8. The synchroniser assembly alignment marks

16 Fit the two springs (25,26) one on the front and one on the rear face of the inside of the synchroniser sleeve under the blocker bars with the tagged end of each spring locating in the 'U' section of the same bar. One spring must be put on anti-clockwise, and one clockwise when viewed from the side (see Fig.6.9). When either side of the assembly is viewed face on the direction of rotation of the springs should then appear the same.

Fig.6.9. The synchroniser hub springs must be put on as shown in the illustration

17 Reassembly commences by replacing second gear (14), gear teeth facing in, on the rear portion of the mainshaft (4) (photo).

18 Then slide on a new synchroniser ring (39), (photo).

19 Next slide on the first and second gear synchroniser assembly (37) AND MAKE CERTAIN that the cut-outs in the synchroniser ring (arrowed in photo) fit over the blocker bars in the synchroniser hub; that the marks on the mainshaft and hub are in line (where made); and that the reverse gear teeth cut on the synchroniser sleeve periphery face away from second gear.

20 Replace the circlip (24) which holds the synchroniser hub in place (accidentally wrong way round in photo).

21 Then fit another synchroniser ring (30) again ensuring that the cut-outs in the ring fit over the blocker bars in the synchronising hub (photo).

22 Next slide on first gear so the synchronising cone portion lies inside the synchronising ring just fitted (photo).

23 Fit the splined thrust washer (28) to the front of first gear (photo).

24 The mainshaft bearing is then slid on as far as it will go. (photo). On some models ensure the groove for the retaining circlip (20) on the outside periphery of the bearing (19), lies adjacent to first gear.

25 To press the bearing fully home, close the jaws of a vice until they are not quite touching the mainshaft, and with the bearing resting against the side of the vice jaws draw the bearing on by tapping the end of the shaft with a hide or plastic hammer (photo). On some models replace the securing circlip (21).

26 Shown in the photo are the next items to be fitted. These comprise the distance piece, lockwasher, and nut (not fitted to models using circlips for mainshaft bearing retention) and the locating ball and speedometer drive gear.

27 Insert the ball into its hole and where supplied fit the distance piece followed by the speedometer drive gear. Ensure the groove on the inside of the latter slides over the location ball. Fit the retaining circlip (23) where used. Otherwise now slide on the tab washer, followed by the nut (photo).

28 Tighten up the nut securely and then bend down part of the tab washer to lock the nut in place (photo).

29 Moving to the forward end of the mainshaft, slide on third gear (13) so the machined gear teeth lie adjacent to

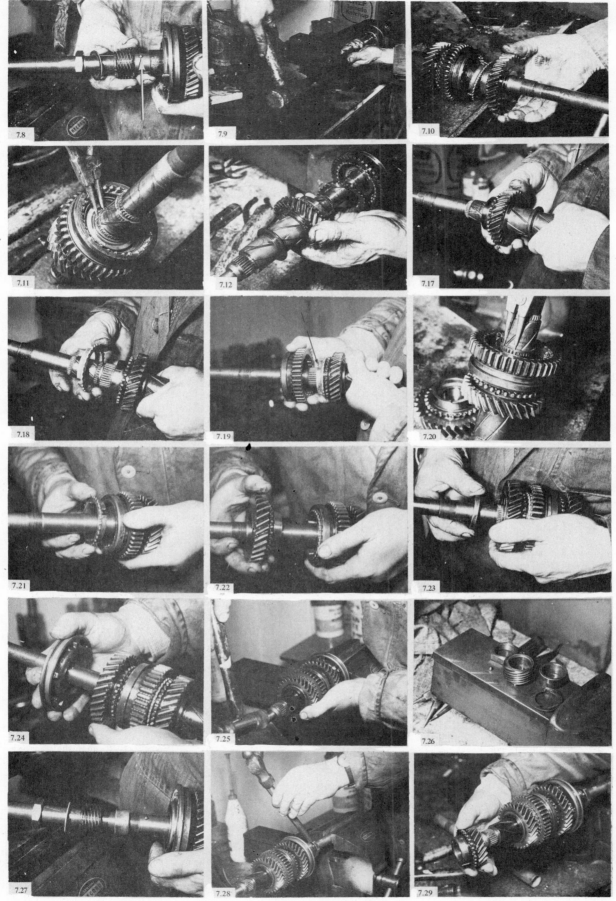

second gear. (photo).

30 Slide on a new synchroniser ring (12) and then fit the third and fourth gear synchroniser assembly (38) (photo) again ensuring that the cut-outs on the ring line up with the blocker bars and that the marks on the hub and mainshaft are adjacent (see Fig.6.8.).

31 With a piece of wood used as a drift tap the synchroniser hub fully home on the mainshaft (photo).

32 Then fit the securing circlip (3) in place (photo). Apart from the needle roller race which rests on the nose of the mainshaft this completes mainshaft re-assembly.

8. GEARBOX - REASSEMBLY

1. Buy a 1 ft. length of mild steel bar as close to the diameter of the layshaft as possible. It must not be any thicker than the layshaft, but can be slightly thinner. Slide the bar into the laygear and cut the bar so it is the exact length of the laygear (photo).

2. Slide a retaining washer (16) into either end of the laygear (photo) so they abut the internal machined shoulders.

3. Smear thick grease in the laygear orifice and fit the needle rollers (35) one at a time until all are in place (photo). The grease will hold the rollers in position. Build up the needle roller bearings in the other end of the laygear in similar fashion.

4. Carefully slide in the dummy layshaft made from the mild steel bar (photo).

5. Then fit the external washers to each end of the laygear.

6. Grease the two thrust washers and position the larger of the two (15) in the front of the gearbox (photo) so the tongues fit into the machined recesses.

7. Fit the smaller of the thrust washers (32) to the rear of the gearbox in similar fashion (photo).

8. Fit the laygear (17) complete with dummy layshaft in the bottom of the gearbox casing taking care not to dislodge the thrust washers (photo).

9. Now fit the reverse idler gear (36) and shaft (34) so the selector fork groove on the gear is towards the rear of the gearbox (photo), and turn the shaft (34) until the flats on the end of the shaft are positioned to fit the recess in the extension housing when the latter is fitted.

10 Now fit the input shaft assembly (1) (photo) and secure it in place with the large circlip (6). Fit a new gasket to the front of the gearbox and fit the input shaft oil seal retainer and cover, and tighten down the bolts and washers.

11 Fit a new extension housing gasket to the rear of the gearbox and then fit the mainshaft to the gearbox ensuring that the needle roller bearings on the nose of the mainshaft enter fully into the orifice in the centre of the input gear shaft.

12 Gently tap the mainshaft (4) into place ensuring that the dowel pin on the rear main bearing carrier lines up with the hole for the centre selector rod.

13 Carefully turn the gearbox upside down so that the laygear (17) drops into mesh with the input and mainshaft gears. From the rear of the gearbox insert the layshaft plain end first and push or tap it carefully home until the front face just protrudes. As the layshaft enters the laygear it will push out the dummy layshaft. Providing care is taken none of the needle roller bearings will be dislodged. Check that the flat on the end of the layshaft is so positioned that it will fit into the recess in the front face of the extension housing.

14 Referring to Fig.6.6. fit the gearchange shaft (50) in the turret housing (45) and fit the turret in place on the extension housing. Secure it in place with the three holding down bolts and spring washers (34,35).

15 Then fit the reverse selector rod (16) in the right-hand hole in the gearbox and slide the rod into the reverse selector fork (11). Then fit the 3rd/4th gear selector fork, and the 1st/2nd gear selector fork (photo). Note that the bosses on all the forks except the reverse fork face towards the rear of the gearbox.

16 Fit a new gasket in place and offer up the extension to the gearbox casing. Ensure the flats on the layshaft and·on the reverse idler shaft mate with the slot cut in the front face of the extension. Otherwise the extension will not fit properly. Tighten up the five securing bolts and washers (21,22).

17 At the rear of the extension fit the reverse gear stop (53) followed by the spring (54). (Photo).

18 Fit the tag washer (55) and screw down the plug (56) tightly (photo). Bend the lock tab over one of the plug flats and the other tab down over the side of the casing (arrowed in photo 8.19).

19 Then fit the ball (28) in place in the drilling in the side of the extension (photo).

20 Secure the ball in place with the spring (27), washer (26) and plug (25).

21 Replace the bearing bridge (23) over the gearchange shaft (50), with the cut-out facing forwards and tighten down the two securing bolts (24).

22 Refit the gearchange selector arm (31) with its arms facing upwards to the gearchange shaft (50) and secure the arm to the shaft with the bolt (30). which must then be locked in place with wire.

23 Note that at the end of the 1st/2nd gear selector rod (17) is a cross drilling. Into this fits a small interlock pin (15) (photo). Do not fit this pin yet.

24 Ensure an interlock plunger (12) is positioned in the horizontal drilling between the 1st/2nd gear selector rod hole and the reverse selector rod hole in the front of the gearbox casing. An interlock plunger should also be fitted to the drilling between the 1st/2nd gear selector rod hole and the 3rd/4th gear selector rod hole.

7.30

7.31

7.32

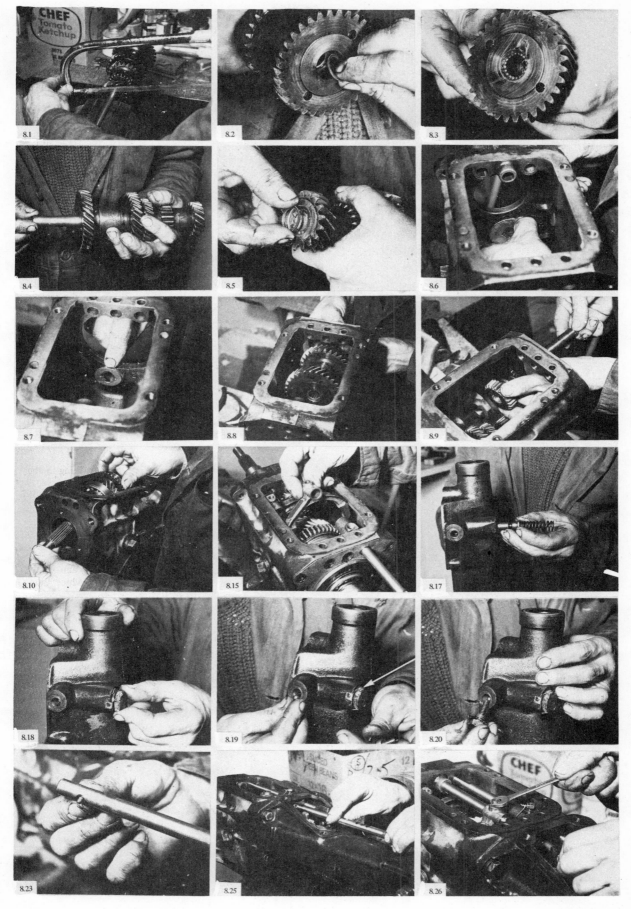

8.1

8.2

8.3

8.4

8.5

8.6

8.7

8.8

8.9

8.10

8.15

8.17

8.18

8.19

8.20

8.23

8.25

8.26

25 Slide the 1st/2nd gear selector rod (17) through the centre hole in the rear of the gearbox casing (photo) and through the 1st/2nd gear selector fork. Make sure that the uppermost arm of the angled gearchange selector arm is to the left of the rail. Then fit the interlock pin and push the rod fully home.

26 Refit the selector fork retaining bolts to the two rods already fitted (photo) and lock the heads of the bolts with wire. Place the two selector rods in neutral.

27 Fit the 3rd/4th gear selector rod (19) through the left-hand hole and slide it through the sleeve (18) (photo) and the 3rd/4th gear selector fork.

8.27

28 Replace the bolt holding the 3rd/4th gear selector fork to the rod and lock the head of the bolt with wire (photo).

29 Drop one detent ball into each of the three holes in the casing above the selector rods (photo).

30 Select third gear, and pressing down on the detent ball measure the gap between the face of the selector fork and the sleeve. Fit a clip (20) of the correct size as specified below:-

Measured Gap	Clip Part No.
Below 0.065 in. (1.651 mm)	2821E - 7K714-G
0.065 - 0.070 in. (1.651 - 1.778 mm)	2821E - 7K714-H
0.070 - 0.075 in. (1.778 - 1.905 mm)	2821E - 7K714-J
0.075 - 0.080 in. (1.905 - 2.032 mm)	2821E - 7K714-K
0.080 - 0.085 in. (2.032 - 2.159 mm)	2821E - 7K714-L
0.085 - 0.090 in. (2.159 - 2.286 mm)	2821E - 7K714-M
0.090 - 0.095 in. (2.286 - 2.413 mm)	2821E - 7K714-N
0.095 - 0.100 in. (2.413 - 2.540 mm)	2821E - 7K714-P
0.100 - 0.105 in. (2.540 - 2.667 mm)	2821E - 7K714-R
0.105 - 0.110 in. (2.667 - 2.794 mm)	2821E - 7K714-S
0.110 - 0.115 in. (2.794 - 2.921 mm)	2821E - 7K714-T
Over 0.115 in. (2.921 mm)	2821E - 7K714-U

31 Place the detent springs in position on top of the balls previously fitted to the casing (photo).

32 Fit a new gasket to the top of the casing and fit the gearbox cover (8) in place so the springs enter the special holes in the cover (photo). Secure the cover in place with the four bolts and spring washers.

33 Fit a new gasket to the front of the gearbox and fit the bellhousing in place (photo).

34 Insert and tighten down the bolts which secure the bellhousing to the gearbox (photo).

35 Fit the clutch release bearing and arm in place as shown in the photo).

36 Replace the nylon speedometer gear in its hole in the front of the extension (photo). Renew the rubber seal in the periphery of the gear body (arrowed) if worn.

37 Refit the selector rod cover (3) using a new gasket and tighten down the four securing bolts and washers (photo). Refit the gearlever and check that all gears are working correctly. **Reassembly is now complete.**

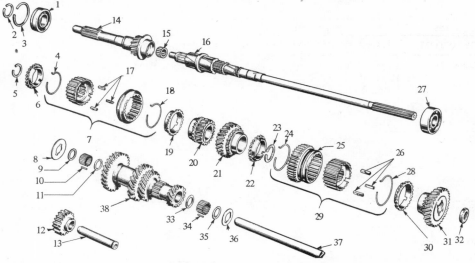

Fig.6.10. EXPLODED VIEW OF THE INTERNAL GEARBOX COMPONENTS FITTED FROM SEPTEMBER 1966 TO OCTOBER 1968

1 Input shaft ball bearing
2 Small circlip
3 Large circlip
4 Wire ring
5 Circlip
6 Third and fourth gear synchroniser cone,
7 Third and fourth gear synchroniser assembly
8 Laygear thrust washer
9 Needle roller thrust washer
10 Needle roller bearings

11 Needle roller thrust washer
12 Reverse gear
13 Reverse gear shaft
14 Input shaft
15 Cage needle roller bearing
16 Mainshaft
17 Blocker bar
18 Wire ring
19 Third and fourth gear synchroniser cone
20 Third gear

21 Second gear
22 First and second gear synchroniser cone
23 Circlip
24 Spring ring
25 Reverse and first and second gear synchroniser sleeve
26 Blocker bars
27 Mainshaft bearing
28 Spring ring
29 First and second gear synchroniser assembly

30 First and second gear synchroniser cone
31 First gear
32 First gear thrust washer
33 Needle roller thrust washer
34 Needle roller bearing
35 Thrust washer
36 Laygear thrust washer
37 Layshaft
38 Laygear

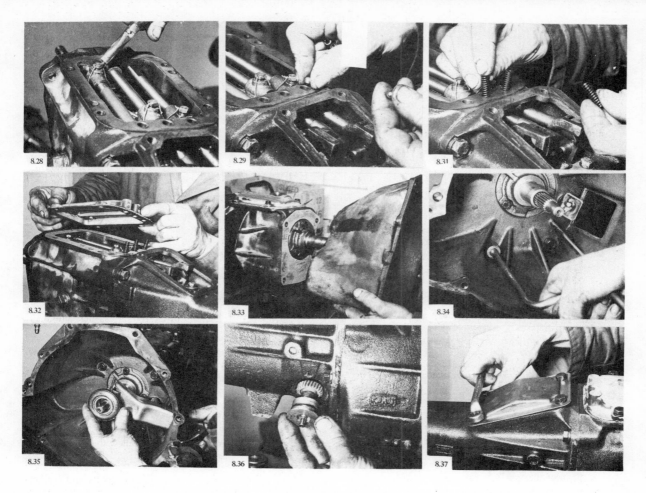

8.28 8.29 8.31
8.32 8.33 8.34
8.35 8.36 8.37

GEARBOX
FAULT FINDING CHART

Cause	Trouble	Remedy
SYMPTOM:	WEAK OR INEFFECTIVE SYNCHROMESH	
General wear	Synchronising cones worn, split or damaged.	Dismantle and overhaul gearbox. Fit new gear wheels and synchronising cones.
	Baulk ring synchromesh dogs worn, or damaged	Dismantle and overhaul gearbox. Fit new baulk ring synchromesh.
SYMPTOM:	JUMPS OUT OF GEAR	
General wear or damage	Broken gearchange fork rod spring	Dismantle and replace spring.
	Gearbox coupling dogs badly worn	Dismantle gearbox. Fit new coupling dogs.
	Selector fork rod groove badly worn	Fit new selector fork rod.
	Selector fork rod securing screw and locknut loose	Remove side cover, tighten securing screw and locknut.
SYMPTOM:	EXCESSIVE NOISE	
Lack of maintenance	Incorrect grade of oil in gearbox or oil level too low	Drain, refill, or top up gearbox with correct grade of oil.
General wear	Bush or needle roller bearings worn or damaged	Dismantle and overhaul gearbox. Renew bearings.
	Gearteeth excessively worn or damaged	Dismantle, overhaul gearbox. Renew gearwheels.
	Laygear thrust washers worn allowing excessive end play	Dismantle and overhaul gearbox. Renew thrust washers.
SYMPTOM:	EXCESSIVE DIFFICULTY IN ENGAGING GEAR	
Clutch not fully disengaging	Clutch pedal adjustment incorrect	Adjust clutch pedal correctly.

CHAPTER SEVEN

PROPELLER SHAFT & UNIVERSAL JOINTS

CONTENTS

1. GENERAL DESCRIPTION

Drive is transmitted from the gearbox to the rear axle by means of a finely balanced tubular propeller shaft. Fitted at each end of the shaft is a universal joint which allows for vertical movement of the rear axle. Each universal joint comprises a four legged centre spider, four needle roller bearings and two yokes.

Fore and aft movement of the rear axle is absorbed by a sliding spline in the front of the propeller shaft which slides over a mating spline on the rear of the gearbox mainshaft. A supply of oil through very small oil holes from the gearbox lubricates the splines.

All models are fitted with the sealed type of universal joint which requires no maintenance.

The propeller shaft is a relatively simple component and to overhaul and repair it is fairly easy.

2. PROPELLER SHAFT - REMOVAL & REPLACEMENT

1. Jack up the rear of the car, or position the rear of the car over a pit or on a ramp.

2. If the rear of the car is jacked up supplement the jack with support blocks so that danger is minimised should the jack collapse.

3. If the rear wheels are off the ground place the car in gear or put the handbrake on to ensure that the propeller shaft does not turn when an attempt is made to loosen the four nuts securing the propeller shaft to the rear axle.

4. Unscrew and remove the four self-locking nuts, bolts, and securing washers which hold the flange on the propeller shaft to the flange on the rear axle.

5. The propeller shaft is carefully balanced to fine limits and it is important that it is replaced in exactly the same position it was in prior to its removal. Scratch a mark on the propeller shaft and rear axle flanges to ensure accurate mating when the times comes for reassembly.

6. Slightly push the shaft forward to separate the two flanges, and then lower the end of the shaft and pull it rearwards to disengage the gearbox mainshaft splines.

7. Place a large can or a tray under the rear of the gearbox extension to catch any oil which is likely to leak through the spline lubricating holes, when the propeller shaft is removed.

8. Replacement of the propeller shaft is a reversal of the above procedure. Ensure that the mating marks scratched on the propeller shaft and rear axle flanges line up.

3. UNIVERSAL JOINTS - INSPECTION & REPAIR

1. Wear in the needle roller bearings is characterised by vibration in the transmission, 'clonks' on taking up the drive, and in extreme cases of lack of lubrication, metallic squeaking, and ultimately grating and shrieking sounds as the bearings break up.

2. It is easy to check if the needle roller bearings are worn with the propeller shaft in position, by trying to turn the shaft with one hand, the other hand holding the rear axle flange when the rear universal is being checked, and the front half coupling when the front universal is being checked. Any movement between the propeller shaft and the front and the rear half couplings is indicative of considerable wear. If worn, the old bearings and spiders will have to be discarded and a repair kit, comprising new universal joint spiders, bearings, oil seals, and retainers purchased. Check also by trying to lift the shaft and noticing any movement in the joints.

3. Examine the propeller shaft splines for wear. If worn it will be necessary to purchase a new front half coupling, or if the yokes are badly worn, an exchange propeller shaft. It is not possible to fit oversize bearings and journals to the trunnion bearing holes.

4. UNIVERSAL JOINTS - DISMANTLING

1. Clean away all traces of dirt and grease from the circlips located on the ends of the bearing cups, and remove the clips by pressing their open ends together with a pair of pliers (photo), and lever them out with a

4.1

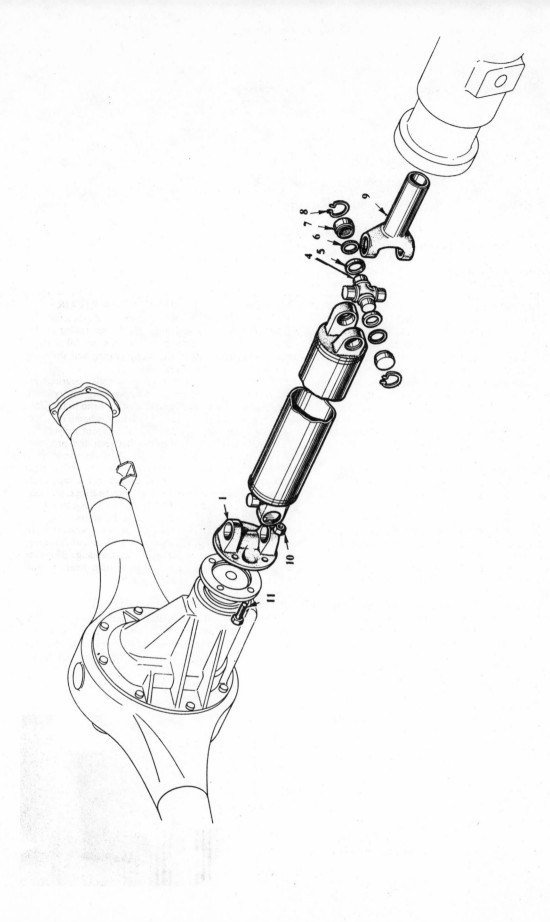

Fig.7.1. EXPLODED VIEW OF THE PROPELLER SHAFT & UNIVERSAL JOINTS

1 Drive shaft flange yoke. 4 Spider. 5 Oil seal retainer. 6 Oil seal. 7 Needle roller bearings and cap. 8 Retaining circlip. 9 Universal joint knuckle. 10 Nut. 11 Bolt.

4.2 4.3 4.4

screwdriver. NOTE If they are difficult to remove tap the bearing cup face resting on top of the spider with a mallet which will ease the pressure on the circlip.

2. Take off the bearing cups on the propeller shaft yoke. To do this select two sockets from a socket spanner set, one large enough to fit completely over the bearing cup and the other smaller than the bearing cup (photo).

3. Open the jaws of the vice and with the sockets opposite each other and the U.J. in between tighten the vice and so force the narrower socket to move the opposite cup partially out of the yoke (photo) into the larger socket.

4. Remove the cup with a pair of pliers (photo). Remove the opposite cup, and then free the yoke from the propeller shaft.

5. To remove the remaining two cups now repeat the instructions in paragraph 3, or use a socket and hammer as illustrated.

5. UNIVERSAL JOINTS - REASSEMBLY

1. Thoroughly clean out the yokes and journals.

2. Fit new oil seals and retainers on the spider journals, place the spider on the propeller shaft yoke, and assemble the needle rollers in the bearing races with the assistance of some thin grease. Fill each bearing about a third full with Castrolease LM or similar, and fill the grease holes in the journal spider making sure all air bubbles are eliminated.

3. Refit the bearing cups on the spider and tap the bearings home so they lie squarely in position. Replace the circlips.

4.5

6. STAKED TYPE UNIVERSAL JOINTS

Some later models have propshafts fitted which incorporate 'staked' universal joints. Unfortunately, it is not possible for the DIY man to dismantle and overhaul this type of universal joint. If heavy universal joint wear is evident it will be necessary to exchange the complete propshaft for a replacement unit.

CHAPTER EIGHT

REAR AXLE

CONTENTS

SPECIFICATIONS

Type	Semi-floating hypoid	
Ratios:	Standard	Optional
1297 c.c. models	4.125 to 1	4.444 to 1
1500 c.c. & 1598 c.c. models..	3.900 to 1	4.125 to 1
G.T. up to Sept '67..	3.900 to 1	-
G.T. from Sept '67..	3.777 to 1	-

Pinion/Crown wheel No. of Teeth	
4.444 to 1 ratio..	9/40
4.125 to 1 ratio..	8/33
3.900 to 1 ratio..	10/39
3.777 to 1 ratio..	9/34

Pinion/Crown wheel backlash	.005 to .007 in. (.127 to .178 mm)
Pinion bearing preload	
All models up to Sept '67..	9 to 11 lb.in. (.104 to .127 kg.m) excluding oil seal
From Sept '67	13 to 19 lb.in. (.150 to .219 kg.m) excluding oil seal
Differential bearing preload (cap spread)	
Up to Sept '67	.005 to .007 in. (.127 to .178 mm)
From Sept '67	.008 to .010 in. (.200 to .250 mm)
(If part used bearings are being used then the preload figures should be set to half those quoted above)	
Differential pinion thrust washer thickness	.030 to .032 in. (.762 to .813 mm)
Oil capacity...	2 pints (2.4 US pints, 1.1 litres)

TORQUE WRENCH SETTINGS

Crown wheel to differential case bolts...	50 to 60 lb/ft. (6.93 to 7.60 kg.m)
Differential carrier to axle housing nuts	15 to 18 lb/ft. (2.07 to 2.50 kg.m)
Differential bearing locking plate bolts	12 to 15 lb/ft. (1.66 to 2.07 kg.m)
Differential bearing cap bolts	45 to 50 lb/ft. (6.22 to 6.93 kg.m)
Axle shaft bearing retainer bolts	15 to 18 lb/ft. (2.07 to 2.50 kg.m)
Universal joint flange to pinion flange	15 to 18 lb/ft. (2.07 to 2.50 kg.m)
Rear axle filler plug	25 to 30 lb/ft. (3.46 to 4.15 kg.m)
Spring 'U' bolt nuts	25 lb/ft. (3.46 kg.m)
G.T. & 1600E radius arms axle mounting...	22 to 27 lb/ft. (3.04 to 3.73 kg.m)
G.T. & 1600E radius arms body mounting	45 to 50 lb/ft. (6.22 to 6.91 kg.m)

1. GENERAL DESCRIPTION

The rear axle is of the semi-floating type and is held in place by two semi-elliptic springs. These provide the necessary lateral and longitudinal support for the axle.

The banjo type casing carries the differential assembly which consists of a hypoid crown wheel and pinion and the two star pinion differential bolted in a carrier to the casing nose piece.

All repairs can be carried out to the component parts of the rear axle without removing the axle casing from the car. It will be found simpler in practice to fit a guaranteed second hand axle from a car breakers yard rather than dismantle the differential unit which calls for special tools which very few garages will have.

As an alternative a replacement differential carrier assembly can be fitted which means that the axle can be left in position and dismantling is reduced to a minimum.

2. REAR AXLE - ROUTINE MAINTENANCE

1. Every 6,000 miles remove the filler plug in the rear axle casing and top up with an S.A.E.90 E.P. gear oil such as Castrol Hypoy. After topping up do not replace the plug for five minutes to allow any excess to run out. If the axle is overfilled there is a possibility that oil will leak out of the ends of the axle casing and ruin the rear brake linings.

2. Every 36,000 miles drain the oil when hot by removing the differential carrier assembly part way as described in Section 6., and refill the axle with 2 pints (2.4 US pints, 1.1 litres) of S.A.E.90 E.P. gear oil. This is not a factory recommended maintenance task, as there will have been no deterioration in the condition of the oil. However, the oil with time will become contaminated with minute particles of metal and for this reason the author prefers to change the rear axle oil once every three years or 36,000 miles rather than leave it in place for the life of the car.

3. REAR AXLE - REMOVAL & REPLACEMENT

1. Remove the rear wheel hub caps and loosen the wheel nuts.

2. Raise and support the rear of the body and the differential casing with chocks or jacks so that the rear wheels are clear of the ground. This is most easily done by placing a jack under the centre of the differential, jacking up the axle and then fitting chocks under the mounting points at the front of the rear springs to support the body.

3. Remove both rear wheels and place the wheel nuts in the hub caps for safe keeping.

4. Mark the propeller shaft and differential drive flanges to ensure replacement in the same relative positions. Undo and remove the nuts and bolts holding the two flanges together.

5. Release the handbrake and by undoing the adjusting nut disconnect the cable at the pivot point at the rear of the axle casing.

6. Unscrew the union on the brake pipe at the junction on the rear axle and have handy either a jar to catch the hydraulic fluid or a plug to block the end of the pipe.

7. Undo the nuts and bolts holding the shock absorber attachments to the spring seats and remove the bolts thus freeing the shock absorbers. It will probably be necessary to adjust the jack under the axle casing to free the bolts.

8. On G.T. and 1600E models only where radius arms are fitted unscrew the nuts and withdraw the bolts holding the radius arms to the rear axle casing.

9. Unscrew the nuts from under the spring retaining plates. These nuts screw onto the ends of the inverted 'U' bolts which retain the axle to the spring.

10 The axle will now be resting free on the jack and can now be removed by lifting it through one of the wheel arches.

11 Reassembly is a direct reversal of the removal procedure, but various points must be carefully noted.

12 The nuts on the 'U' bolts must be tightened to a torque of 25 lb.ft. (3.5 kg.m.).

13 On G.T. and 1600E models the weight of the car must be fully on its wheels before the radius arm securing bolts are fully tightened. The axle mounting bolts should be tightened to a torque of 22 to 27 lb/ft. (3.04 to 3.73 kg.m) and the body mounting bolts to a torque of 45 to 50 lb/ft. (6.22 to 6.91 kg.m.).

14 Bleed the brakes after reassembly as described in Chapter 9, Section 3.

4. HALF SHAFTS - REMOVAL & REPLACEMENT

1. The method described below is normally a very easy way or removing a half shaft together with its combined bearing and oil seal but, should the half shaft fail to move using the method described, it will be necessary to use Ford tool No.P.3072 to ensure success.

2. After jacking up the car and removing the road wheel unscrew the brake drum retaining screw and take off the brake drum.

3. Remove the four self-locking nuts retaining the half shaft bearing housing to the axle casing. These nuts can be reached through the large hole in the half shaft flange.

4. It may be possible at this stage to remove the half shaft by simply pulling on the flange. If this fails replace the road wheel on the studs and tighten the nuts down just enough to prevent movement of the wheel on the studs.

5. Sitting on the ground, with one leg either side of the wheel and braced on the spring, get a firm hold on the outer edges of the tyre and pull straight outwards as hard as possible.

6. Care must be taken not to damage the splines on the end of the half shaft when withdrawing by this method as its release from the axle casing may be a bit sudden.

7. If this method also fails it will be necessary to use Ford tool No.P.3072. Fig.8.2. shows how the tool is attached to two of the wheel studs and how by using the sliding hammer on the tool extension the half shaft can be withdrawn.

8. Replacement is a reversal of the removal procedure but once again care should be taken not to damage the splines on the end of the half shaft.

5. HALF SHAFT COMBINED BEARING & OIL SEAL - REMOVAL & REPLACEMENT

1. To remove and replace the combined bearing and oil seal so as to ensure correct fitting it is necessary to get hold of three Ford tools specially made for the job. They are Tool No.P.4090-2 & 6 which is the half shaft bearing remover; Tool 370 which is a universal taper base to fit a hydraulic press and tool No.P.4084 which is a spring indicator.

2. Locate the adaptors of Tool No.P.4090-6 and a slave ring between the bearing and the half shaft flange then by using the universal taper base No.370 support the whole assembly in a hydraulic press and push the half shaft out of the combined bearing and oil seal.

3. To fit a new bearing locate the bearing retainer plate and the bearing on the half shaft making sure that the oil seal side of the bearing is facing the splined end of the half shaft.

4. Using the adaptors on Tool No.P.4090-2 and a slave ring support the assembly in the bed of a hydraulic press. Fit the spring indicator, Tool No.P.4084 to the ram of the hydraulic press and press the bearing onto the half shaft.

5. The spring indicator should show a minimum pressure of 1,200 lbs. (544 kg.); if the pressure shown is lower this indicates an incorrect fit and another bearing must be tried.

6. DIFFERENTIAL CARRIER - REMOVAL & REPLACEMENT

1. To remove the differential carrier assembly, jack up the rear of the vehicle and remove both rear road wheels, and brake drums and then withdraw both half shafts as described in Section 4.

2. Disconnect the propeller shaft at the rear end as

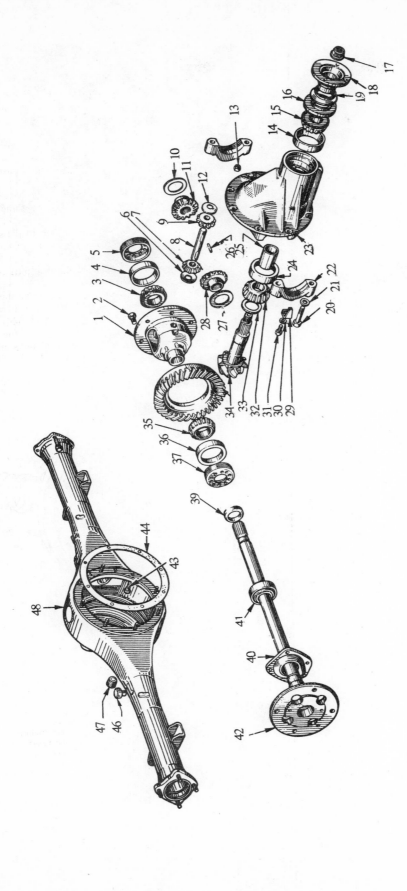

Fig.8.1. 'EXPLODED VIEW OF THE REAR AXLE

1 Differential cage	9 Differential pinion	17 Flange nut
2 Cage to drown wheel bolt	10 Differential gear thrust washer	18 Drive shaft flange
3 Differential roller bearing	11 Differential gear	19 Oil seal dust deflector
4 Differential bearing cup	12 Pinion thrust washer	20 Bearing cap bolt
5 Bearing adjusting nut	13 Nut	21 Washer
6 Pinion thrust washer	14 Driving pinion bearing cup	22 Bearing cap carrier
7 Differential pinion	15 Driving pinion roller bearing	23 Differential carrier
8 Pinion shaft	16 Oil seal	24 Driving pinion bearing cup

25 Driving pinion bearing spacer	33 Bearing adjusting shim	42 Half shaft
26 Pinion shaft lock pin	34 Driving pinion	43 Bolt
27 Differential gear thrust washer	35 Differential roller bearing	44 Gasket
28 Differential gear	36 Cup	46 Vent
29 Lock nut	37 Bearing adjusting cup	47 Filler plug
30 Washer	39 Seal	48 Rear axle housing
31 Bolt	40 Flange	
32 Driving pinion cone roller bearing	41 Bearing	

117

Fig.8.2. Showing the method of attachment and use of Ford Tool No.P.3072 to withdraw the half shafts.

described in Chapter 7, Section 2.

3. Undo the eight self locking nuts holding the differential carrier assembly to the axle casing. Pull the assembly slightly forward and allow the oil to drain away. The carrier complete with the crown wheel can now be lifted clear with the gasket.

4. Before replacement, carefully clean the mating surfaces of the carrier and the axle casing and fit a new gasket. Replacement is then a direct reversal of the above instructions. The eight nuts retaining the differential carrier assembly to axle casing should be tightened to a torque of 50 to 60 lb/ft. (6.93 to 7.60 kg.m.).

CHAPTER NINE

BRAKING SYSTEM

CONTENTS

SPECIFICATIONS

Type ... ...   Disc at front drum at rear
Footbrake ... ...   Hydraulic on all 4 wheels
Handbrake ... ...   Mechanical to rear wheels only

Front Brake Layout
    All G.T models & 1600E... ... ...   Leading callipers
    All other models ... ...   Trailing callipers

Front Brake Dimensions
    Up to Sept '67 except G.T
    Disc diameter ... ...   9.50 in. (24.13 cm.)
    Disc run out (max).. ... ...   .004 in. (.102 mm.)
    Total pad swept area ... ...   171.9 sq.in. (1109 cm^2)
    Pad colour coding ... ...   Red, Yellow, Yellow

    G.T up to Sept '67
    Disc diameter ... ...   9.625 in. (24.45 cm.)
    Disc run out (max).. ... ...   .004 in. (.102 mm.)
    Total pad swept area ... ...   189.5 sq.in. (1220 cm^2)
    Pad colour coding ... ...   Green

    From Sept '67 except G.T & 1600E
    Disc diameter ... ...   9.625 in. (24.45 cm.)
    Disc run out (max).. ... ...   .002 in. (.05 mm.)
    Total pad swept area ... ...   171.9 sq.in. (1109 cm^2)
    Pad colour coding ... ...   Yellow, Red, Red, Yellow

    1598 c.c. G.T & 1600E
    Disc diameter ... ...   9.625 in. (24.45 cm.)
    Disc run out (max).. ... ...   .002 in. (.05 mm.)
    Total pad swept area ... ...   189.5 sq.in. (1220 cm^2)
    Pad colour coding ... ...   Green, Red, Red, Red

Rear Brakes

All cars except G.T & 1600E

Drum diameter & width	8 x 1.5 in. (20.3 x 3.81 cm)
Total shoe swept area...	75.5 sq.in. (487 cm^2)
Wheel cylinder diameter	.70 in. (1.778 cm)

G.T & 1600E

Drum diameter & width	9 x 1.75 in. (22.9 x 4.45 cm)
Total shoe swept area...	99.0 sq.in. (639 cm^2)
Wheel cylinder diameter	.87 in. (2.21 cm)

Master Cylinder Diameter

All models except G.T & 1600E..	.625 in. (1.59 cm)
G.T & 1600E	.70 in. (1.778 cm)
Dual brake lines..	Fitted as optional extra and export models
Servo...	Fitted as standard to G.T, 1600E & Estate cars with dual brake lines
Servo boost ratio	2.2 to 1
Servo diaphragm area	38 sq.in.

TORQUE WRENCH SETTINGS

Brake calliper to front suspension	45 to 50 lb/ft. (6.22 to 6.91 kg.m)
Brake disc to hub	30 to 34 lb/ft. (4.15 to 4.70 kg.m)
Rear brake plate to axle housing	15 to 18 lb/ft. (2.07 to 2.49 kg.m)
Hydraulic unions	5 to 7 lb/ft. (.69 to 1.00 kg.m)
Bleed valves...	5 to 7 lb/ft. (.69 to 1.00 kg.m)

1. DISC/DRUM BRAKES - GENERAL DESCRIPTION

Disc brakes are fitted to the front wheels of all models together with single leading shoe drum brakes at the rear. The mechanically operated handbrake works on the rear wheels only.

The brakes fitted to the front wheels are of the rotating disc and static calliper type, with one calliper per disc, each calliper containing two piston operated friction pads, which on application of the footbrake pinch the disc rotating between them. On G.T & 1600E models the calliper is positioned on the leading edge of the disc but on all other models it is positioned on the trailing edge.

Application of the footbrake creates hydraulic pressure in the master cylinder and fluid from the cylinder travels via steel and flexible pipes to the cylinders in each half of the callipers, thus pushing the pistons, to which are attached the friction pads, into contact with either side of the disc.

Two seals are fitted to the operating cylinders, the outer seal prevents moisture and dirt entering the cylinder. while the inner seal which is retained in a groove inside the cylinder, prevents fluid leakage.

As the friction pads wear so the pistons move further out of the cylinders and the level of the fluid in the hydraulic reservoir drops. Disc pad wear is therefore taken up automatically and eliminates the need for periodic adjustment by the owner.

On earlier G.T. models the handbrake lever is located under the fascia but on all other models and later G.T. models the lever is located between the front seats. A single cable runs from the lever to a compensator mechanism on the back of the rear axle casing. From the compensator a single cable runs to the rear brake drums. As the rear brake shoes wear the handbrake cables operate a self adjusting mechanism in the rear brake drums thus doing away with the necessity for the owner to adjust the brakes on each rear wheel individually. The only adjustment required is on the handbrake compensator mechanism, due to wear in the linkage.

On later G.T., 1600E and Estate models fitted with a dual braking system a mechanical servo of the suspended vacuum type is fitted as standard.

On certain models, in particular those cars for export to the U.S.A. a dual braking system is fitted providing separate hydraulic circuits for the front and rear brakes. Should one circuit fail the other circuit is unaffected and the car can still be stopped. A warning light is fitted on the fascia which illuminates should either circuit fail. The bulb in the light can also be tested by means of the switch provided.

2. BRAKES - MAINTENANCE

1. Every 3,000 miles or more frequently if necessary, carefully clean the top of the brake master cylinder reservoir, remove the cap, and inspect the level of the fluid which should be ¼ in. below the bottom of the filler neck. Check that the breathing holes in the cap are clear.

2. If the fluid is below this level, top up the reservoir with any hydraulic fluid conforming to specification SAE 70 R3. It is vital that no other type of brake fluid is used. Use of a non-standard fluid will result in brake failure caused by the perishing of special seals in the master and brake cylinders. If topping up becomes frequent then check the metal piping and flexible hoses for leaks, and check for worn brake or master cylinders which will also cause loss of fluid.

3. Every 6,000 miles check the front brake disc pads and the rear brake shoes for wear and renew them if necessary. Also check the adjustment on the handbrake cable and adjust if necessary. Due to the self adjusting rear brakes it should not be necessary to adjust the handbrake cable unless wear has taken place in the linkage.

4. Every 36,000 miles or three years whichever comes sooner it is advisable to change the fluid in the braking system and at the same time renew all hydraulic seals and flexible hoses.

3. BLEEDING THE HYDRAULIC SYSTEM

1. Removal of all the air from the hydraulic system is essential to the correct working of the braking system,

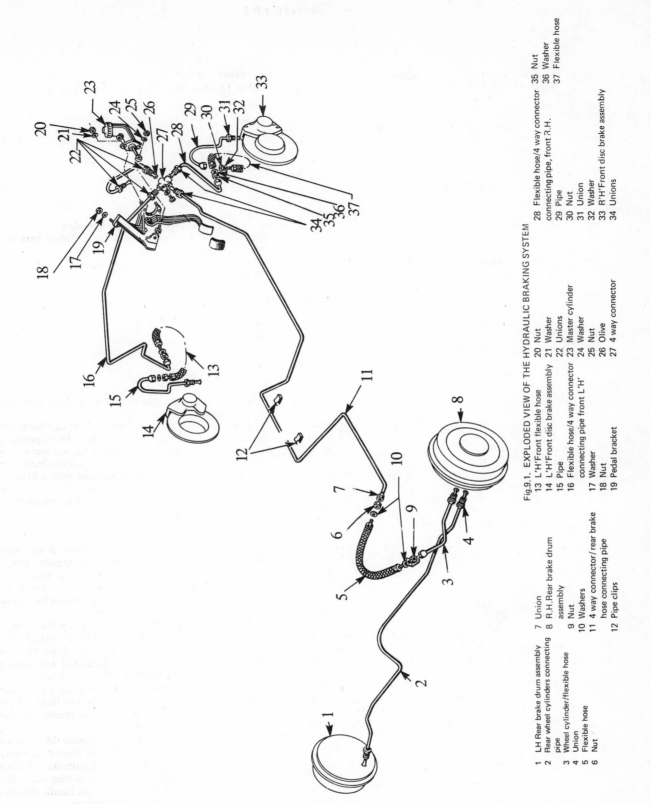

Fig.9.1. EXPLODED VIEW OF THE HYDRAULIC BRAKING SYSTEM

1 LH Rear brake drum assembly
2 Rear wheel cylinders connecting pipe
3 Wheel cylinder/flexible hose
4 Union
5 Flexible hose
6 Nut
7 Union
8 R.H. Rear brake drum assembly
9 Nut
10 Washers
11 4 way connector/rear brake hose connecting pipe
12 Pipe clips
13 L'H'Front flexible hose
14 L'H'Front disc brake assembly
15 Pipe
16 Flexible hose/4 way connector connecting pipe front L'H'
17 Washer
18 Nut
19 Pedal bracket
20 Nut
21 Washer
22 Unions
23 Master cylinder
24 Washer
25 Nut
26 Olive
27 4 way connector
28 Flexible hose/4 way connector connecting pipe, front R.H.
29 Pipe
30 Nut
31 Union
32 Washer
33 R'H'Front disc brake assembly
34 Unions
35 Nut
36 Washer
37 Flexible hose

and before undertaking this examine the fluid reservoir cap to ensure that both vent holes, one on top and the second underneath but not in line, are clear; check the level of fluid and top up if required.

2. Check all brake line unions and connections for possible seepage, and at the same time check the condition of the rubber hoses, which may be perished.

3. If the condition of the wheel cylinders is in doubt, check for possible signs of fluid leakage.

4. If there is any possibility of incorrect fluid having been put into the system, drain all the fluid out and flush through with methylated spirits. Renew all piston seals and cups since these will be affected and could possibly fail under pressure.

5. Gather together a clean jam jar, a 9 in. length of tubing which fits tightly over the bleed nipples, and a tin of the correct brake fluid.

6. To bleed the system clean the areas around the bleed valves, and start on the front brakes first by removing the rubber cup over the bleed valve, if fitted, and fitting a rubber tube in position.

7. Place the end of the tube in a clean glass jar containing sufficient fluid to keep the end of the tube underneath during the operation.

8. Open the bleed valve with a spanner and quickly press down the brake pedal. After slowly releasing the pedal, pause for a moment to allow the fluid to recoup in the master cylinder and then depress again. This will force air from the system. Continue until no more air bubbles can be seen coming from the tube. At intervals make certain that the reservoir is kept topped up, otherwise air will enter at this point again.

9. Repeat this operation on the other front brake and the left-hand rear brake, there being no bleed valve on the right-hand rear brake. When completed, check the

level of the fluid in the reservoir and then check the feel of the brake pedal, which should be firm and free from any 'spongy' action, which is normally associated with air in the system.

4. REAR BRAKE SHOES - INSPECTION, REMOVAL & REPLACEMENT

After high mileages it will be necessary to fit replacement brake shoes with new linings. Refitting new brake linings to old shoes is not always satisfactory, but if the services of a local garage or workshop with brake lining equipment is available, then there is no reason why your own shoes should not be successfully relined.

1. Remove the hub cap, loosen off the wheel nuts, then securely jack up the car, and remove the road wheel. Chock the front wheels and fully release the handbrake.

2. Undo the single domed screw retaining the brake drum and then pull off the drum.

3. Remove the small holding down springs from each shoe by turning two small top washers through 90° degrees.

4. Pull out the ends of each shoe from their locating slots in the fixed pivot on one side of the drum and the wheel cylinder on the other side. When removing the shoes from their slots in the wheel cylinder great care should be taken not to allow the piston to fall out of the wheel cylinder. This can be kept in place by an elastic band.

5. Remove the shoes with the return springs still attached; then take off the return springs noting that they are of different lengths and the positions in which they are fitted.

6. Take the self adjusting ratchet wheel assembly off the wheel cylinder and turn the ratchet wheel until it is right up against the end of the slot headed bolt on

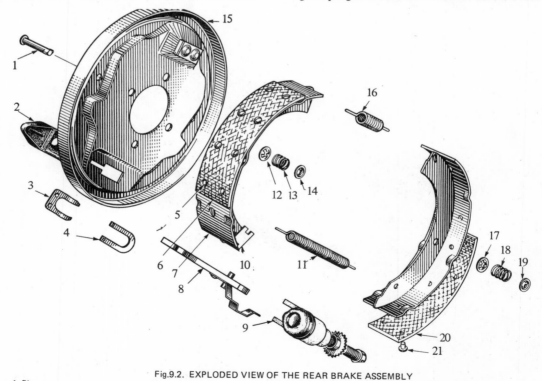

Fig.9.2. EXPLODED VIEW OF THE REAR BRAKE ASSEMBLY

1 Pin	7 Shoe	13 Spring	19 Pin retainer
2 Dust cover	8 Handbrake lever	14 Pin retainer	20 Lining material
3 Cylinder retaining clip	9 Wheel cylinder	15 Backplate	21 Rivet
4 Cylinder retaining clip	10 Shoe support plate	16 Return spring	
5 Rivet	11 Return spring	17 Spring seating washer	
6 Lining mater	12 Spring seating washer	18 Spring	

which it rotates. This has the effect of adjusting the rear brake to the fully off position. If this is not done it may be found difficult to get the brake drum to fit over the new shoes when reassembling.

7. The brake linings should be examined and must be renewed if they are so worn that the rivet heads are flush with the surface of the lining. If bonded linings are fitted these must be renewed when the material has worn down to 1/32nd inch at its thinnest point.

8. Replacement of the shoes is a direct reversal of the removal procedure but great care must be taken to ensure that the return springs are correctly fitted. On G.T. and 1600E models they are fitted from the drum side of the shoe, but on all other models they are fitted on the brake backplate side.

9. When replacement of the shoes is complete, operate the handbrake several times to allow the rear brake self-adjusting mechanism to bring the shoes into the correct position, then road test the car to ensure the brakes are operating correctly.

5. FLEXIBLE HOSES - INSPECTION, REMOVAL & REPLACEMENT

1. Inspect the condition of the flexible hydraulic hoses leading from under the front wings to the brackets on the front suspension units, and also the single hose on the rear axle casing. If they are swollen, damaged or chafed, they must be renewed.

2. Undo the locknuts at both ends of the flexible hoses and then holding the hexagon nut on the flexible hose steady undo the other union nut and remove the flexible hose and washer.

3. Replacement is a reversal of the removal procedure, but carefully check that all the securing brackets are in a sound condition and that the locknuts are tight.

6. REAR BRAKE SEALS - INSPECTION & OVERHAUL

If hydraulic fluid is leaking from one of the rear brake cylinders it will be necessary to dismantle the cylinder and replace the dust cover and piston sealing rubber. If brake fluid is found running down the side of the wheel, or it is noticed that a pool of liquid forms alongside one wheel and the level in the master cylinder has dropped, and the hoses are in good order proceed as follows:-

1. Remove the offending brake drum and shoes as described in Section 4.

2. Remove the small metal clip holding the rubber dust cap in place then prise off the dust cap.

3. Take the piston complete with its seal out of the cylinder bore and then withdraw the spring from the bore as well. Should the piston and seal prove difficult to remove gentle pressure on the brake pedal will push it out of the bore. If this method is used place a quantity of rag under the brake backplate to catch the hydraulic fluid as it pours out of the cylinder.

4. Inspect the cylinder bore for score marks caused by impurities in the hydraulic fluid. If any are found the cylinder and piston will require renewal together as an exchange unit.

5. If the cylinder bore is sound thoroughly clean it out with fresh hydraulic fluid.

6. The old rubber seal will probably be visibly worn or swollen. Detach it from the piston, smear a new rubber seal with hydraulic fluid and assemble it to the piston with the flat face of the seal next to the piston rear shoulder.

7. Reassembly is a direct reversal of the above procedure. If the rubber dust cap appears to be worn or damaged this should also be replaced.

8. Replenish the hydraulic fluid, replace the brake shoes

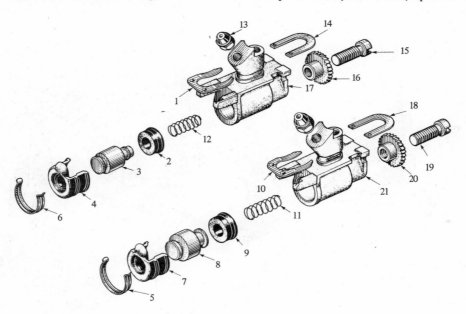

Fig.9.3. EXPLODED VIEW OF THE REAR WHEEL BRAKE CYLINDER

1 Retaining clip	7 Dust cover	13 Bleed nipple	19 Screw
2 Seal	8 Piston	14 Retaining clip	20 Adjusting wheel
3 Piston	9 Seal	15 Screw	21 Body
4 Dust cover	10 Retaining clip	16 Adjusting wheel	
5 Retaining clip	11 Spring	17 Body	
6 Retaining clip	12 Spring	18 Retaining clip	

and drum and bleed the braking system as described in Section 3.

7. REAR WHEEL CYLINDERS - REMOVAL & REPLACEMENT

1. Remove the left or right-hand brake drum and brake shoes as required, as described in Section 4.

2. To avoid having to completely drain the hydraulic system screw down the master cylinder reservoir cap tightly over a piece of polythene.

3. Free the hydraulic pipe from the wheel cylinder at the union, (there are two unions on the right-hand brake-plate).

4. Working on the inside of the brake backplate remove the spring clip and clevis pin from the handbrake link.

5. From the back of the brake backplate prise off and remove the rubber boot on the back of the wheel cylinder.

6. Pull off the two 'U' shaped retainers holding the wheel cylinder to the backplate noting that the spring retainer is fitted from the handbrake link end of the wheel cylinder and the flat retainer from the other end, the flat retainer being located between the spring retainer and the wheel cylinder.

7. Now the wheel cylinder together with the handbrake link can be removed from the brake backplate.

8. Before commencing replacement smear the area where the wheel cylinder slides on the backplate and the brake shoe support pads with Girling white brake grease or other approved brake grease.

9. Replacement is a straight forward reversal of the removal sequence but the following points should be checked with extra care.

10 After fitting the rubber boot, check that the wheel cylinder can slide freely in the carrier plate and that the handbrake link operates the self adjusting mechanism correctly.

11 It is important to note that the self adjusting ratchet mechanism on the right-hand rear brake is right-hand threaded and the mechanism on the left-hand rear brake is left-hand threaded.

12 When replacement is complete, bleed the braking system as described in Section 3.

8. BRAKE MASTER CYLINDER - REMOVAL & REPLACEMENT

1. To remove the master cylinder start by disconnecting the pushrod from the brake pedal inside the car by undoing the single nut and withdrawing the through bolt.

2. Then working under the bonnet disconnect the single hydraulic pipe leading to the master cylinder by undoing the union. Plug the end of the pipe to prevent any dirt entering.

3. Undo the two nuts and spring washers holding the master cylinder to the bulkhead and then remove the master cylinder.

4. Replacement is a reversal of the removal sequence; bleed the brakes after replacement.

9. BRAKE MASTER CYLINDER - DISMANTLING & REASSEMBLY

1. To dismantle the master cylinder pull off the rubber dust cover where the pushrod enters the master cylinder then with a pair of long nosed pliers remove the circlip holding the pushrod in place in the cylinder and remove the pushrod.

2. Now withdraw the piston and valve assembly complete from the master cylinder. The piston is held in the spring retainer by a tab which engages under a shoulder on the front of the piston. Gently lift this tab and

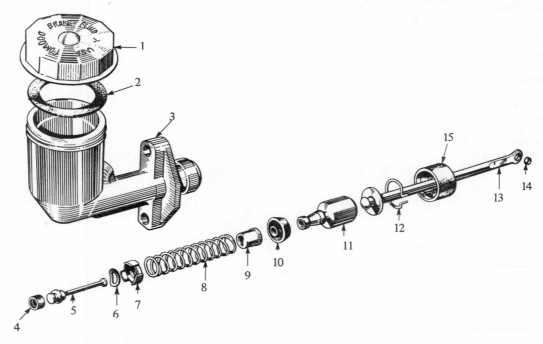

Fig.9.4. EXPLODED VIEW OF THE BRAKE MASTER CYLINDER

1 Cap	5 Valve stem	9 Spring retainer	13 Push rod
2 Sealing ring	6 Spring washer	10 Seal	14 Bush
3 Body	7 Valve spacer	11 Piston	15 Dust cover
4 Valve seal	8 Spring	12 Circlip	

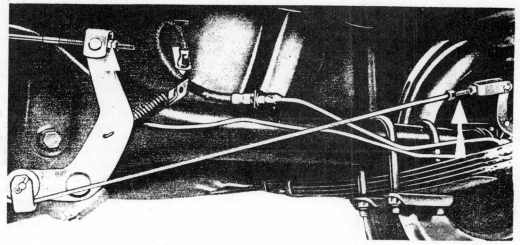

Fig.9.5. Handbrake linkage adjustment points

remove the piston.

3. Carefully compress the spring and move the spring retainer to one side. This will release the end of the valve stem from the retainer.

4. Slide the valve spacer and shim off the valve stem. Remove the rubber seal from the piston and the valve seal off the other end of the valve stem.

5. Examine the bore of the cylinder carefully for any scores or ridges, and if this is found to be smooth all over, new seals can be fitted. If there is any doubt as to the condition of the bore, then a new cylinder must be fitted.

6. If examination of the seals shows them to be apparently oversize, or very loose on their seats, suspect oil contamination in the system. Oil will swell these rubber seals, and if one is found to be swollen, it is reasonable to assume that all seals in the braking system will need attention.

7. Before reassembly wash all parts in methylated spirit, commercial alcohol or approved brake fluid. Do not use any other type of oil or cleaning liquid or the seals will be damaged.

8. To reassemble the master cylinder start by fitting the piston seal to the piston with the sealing lips towards the narrow end and fit the valve seal to the valve stem with the lip towards the front of the valve Fig.9.4.

clearly shows the correct fitting of the seals.

9. Place the shim washer on the valve stem ensuring that the convex face abuts the shoulder flange on the valve stem. Fit the seal spacer onto the valve stem so that the legs of the spacer are facing the valve seal.

10 Refit the spring to the valve stem then insert the spring retainer into the open end of the spring. Compress the spring and engage the small boss on the end of the valve stem into its recess in the spring retainer.

11 Place the narrow end of the piston in its slot in the spring retainer and secure it there by pressing down the tab.

12 Dip the complete assembly in clean approved hydraulic fluid and with the valve leading slide it into the cylinder taking extra care not to damage the piston cylinder as it goes into the cylinder.

13 Replace the piston in the master cylinder and secure it with the circlip. Finally replace the rubber dust cap. The master cylinder can now be refitted to the car as described in Section 8.

10. HANDBRAKE LINKAGE - ADJUSTMENT

1. Fit chocks under front wheels to prevent the car moving then release the handbrake and jack up the rear of the car.

2. Before making any adjustments check that the cable

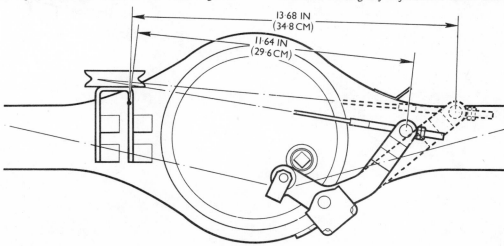

Fig.9.6. Primary cable adjustment dimensions

from the handbrake and that the transverse cable are correctly located in their guides and that the guides are well greased.

3. Slacken the locknut on the main handbrake cable on the relay lever on the rear of the back axle, and turn the adjusting nut until the main cable is reasonably taut.

4. On earlier models the relay lever should be just clear of the stop on the banjo rear axle casing. On later models a measurement can be taken from the inner face of the pulley mounting bracket to the centre of the relay lever trunnion mounting as shown in Fig.9.6. The measurements are as follows:-

Floor mounted handbrakes 11.64 in. (29.6 cm.)
Fascia mounted handbrake 13.68 in. (34.8 cm.)
A tolerance of ¼ in. (0.63 cm) is allowed.

5. To adjust the single transverse cable, slacken the locknut on the end of the cable next to the right-hand rear brake. Check carefully that both handbrake operating levers are back on their stops and in the fully 'off' position then adjust the cable until it is reasonably taut. Check the handbrake operating levers again and finally tighten down the locknut.

6. The effect of adjusting the transverse cable may have upset the adjustment of the main cable so this should be checked again and adjusted as necessary and the locknut tightened down.

7. At frequent intervals during the adjustments it is advisable to check that the handbrake operating levers on both rear brakes have not moved off their stops. If they do move and are left in that position any adjustments made will be of no use and in fact the car will be motoring with the rear brakes partially applied all the time thus causing excessive wear to the brake linings.

11. BRAKE & CLUTCH PEDALS - REMOVAL & REPLACEMENT

1. Both the brake and the clutch pedals pivot about the same pin running through a mounting bracket. The pin being held in position by circlips at either end.

2. To remove the brake pedal take off the nut and knock out the through bolt holding the brake master cylinder pushrod to the pedal, then unhook the pedal return spring.

3. Take the circlip off the main mounting pin together with the washers and slide the pedal off the pin.

4. The clutch pedal is removed in the same manner but the clutch master cylinder pushrod is held in place on the pedal by a clevis pin and split pin instead of a nut and bolt.

5. Replacement of both pedals is a direct reversal of the removal sequence.

12. DISC BRAKE FRICTION PADS - INSPECTION, REMOVAL & REPLACEMENT

1. Remove the front wheels and inspect the amount of friction material left on the friction pads. The pads must be renewed when the thickness of the material has worn down to 1/16th inch. On G.T. and 1600E cars with forward facing callipers it will be necessary to remove the dust cover slotted over the retaining pins in order to examine the friction pads.

2. With a pair of pliers pull out the two small wire clips that hold the main retaining pins in place. (See photo).

3. Remove the main retaining pins which run through the calliper the metal backing of the pads and the shims. (See photo).

4. The friction pads and shims can now be removed from the calliper. If they prove difficult to move by hand a pair of long nosed pliers can be used (see photo).

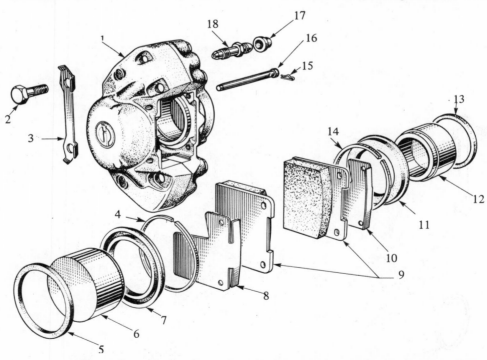

Fig.9.7. EXPLODED VIEW OF THE FRONT BRAKE CALLIPER UNIT — EXCEPT G.T. & 1600E TRAILING TYPE

1 Body	6 Piston	11 Ring seal	16 Pin
2 Bolt	7 Ring seal	12 Piston	17 Dust cap
3 Tab washer	8 Shim	13 Ring seal	18 Bleed nipple
4 Cylinder boot retainer	9 Brake pads	14 Cylinder boot retainer	
5 Ring seal	10 Shim	15 Clip	

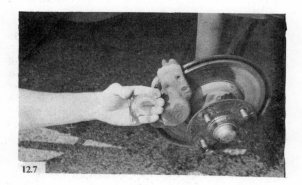

5. Carefully clean the recesses in the calliper in which the friction pads and shims lie, and the exposed faces of each piston from all traces of dirt and rust.

6. Remove the cap from the hydraulic fluid reservoir and place a large rag underneath the unit. Press the pistons in each half of the calliper right in - this will cause the fluid level in the reservoir to rise and possibly spill over the brim onto the protective rag.

7. Fit new friction pads and shims ensuring if working on a rearward facing calliper that the arrow on the shims is pointing in the direction of forward rotation of the wheel. (See photo). On G.T. and 1600E cars with forward facing callipers the shims can be fitted either way up.

8. Insert the main pad retaining pins and secure them with the small wire clips.

13. BRAKE CALLIPER - REMOVAL, DISMANTLING & REASSEMBLY

1. Jack up the car and remove the road wheel, remove the friction pads and shims as described in the previous section and disconnect the hydraulic fluid pipe at either the back of the calliper or at the bracket on the suspension unit.

2. If it is intended to dismantle the calliper after removal; before disconnecting the hydraulic pipe depress

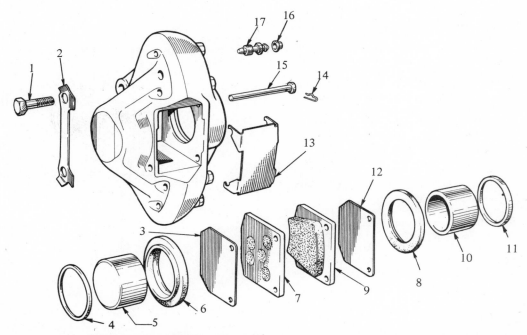

Fig.9.8. EXPLODED VIEW OF THE FRONT BRAKE CALLIPER UNIT – G.T. & 1600E LEADING TYPE

1 Bolt	6 Ring seal	11 Ring seal	16 Dust cap
2 Tab washer	7 Brake pad	12 Shim	17 Bleed nipple
3 Shim	8 Ring seal	13 Dust cover	
4 Ring seal	9 Brake pad	14 Clip	
5 Piston	10 Piston	15 Pin	

the brake pedal to bring the calliper pistons into contact with the disc. This will make it much easier to remove the pistons when the calliper is removed.

3. Knock back the locking tabs on the calliper mounting bolts (see Fig.9.9) undo the bolts and remove the calliper from the disc.

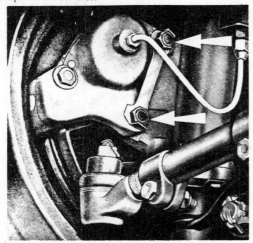

Fig.9.9. Correct staking of the tab washer

4. On all cars except G.T. and 1600E models remove the circlips securing the dust covers to the calliper and pull off the dust covers.

5. The pistons can now be removed from their bores. If they prove difficult to move a small amount of air pressure applied at the hydraulic pipe union will affectively push them out of their bores.

6. Withdraw the piston sealing rings from their locations in the cylinder bores.

7. On G.T. and 1600E models, which do not have a circlip and dust cover as such on each side of the calliper, partially remove one piston from its bore then remove the sealing bellows from its location in the lower part of the piston skirt. The piston can now be removed.

8. Pull the sealing bellows out of their machined location in the cylinder bore and withdraw the piston sealing ring from the cylinder bore. The operation can now be repeated on the other piston and cylinder.

9. On all models the pistons and piston bores should be carefully cleaned with brake fluid and examined for signs of wear, score marks or damage. All rubber seals should be replaced as a matter of course.

10 Reassembly is a direct reversal of the removal sequence on the various models. On the G.T. and 1600E models great care should be taken when passing the piston through the rubber bellows into the cylinder bore as it is very easy at this stage to damage the bellows.

11 Once the calliper has been reassembled, fit it over the disc and tighten down the securing bolts, using a new locking tab, to a torque of 45 to 50 lb/ft. (6.22 to 6.91 kg.m).

12 Reconnect the hydraulic pipe and bleed the brake system as described in Section 3.

14. BRAKE DISC - REMOVAL & REPLACEMENT

1. The brake disc is not normally removed from the hub unless it is to be replaced with a new disc.

2. Remove the hub and disc assembly complete as described in Chapter 11, Section 4.

3. Separate the hub from the disc by knocking back the locking tabs and undoing the four bolts. Discard the disc, bolts and locking tabs.

4. Before fitting a new disc to the hub, thoroughly clean the mating surfaces of both components. If this is not done properly and dirt is allowed to get between the hub and the disc this will seriously affect disc brake run-out when it is checked after reassembly.

5. Align the mating marks on the new disc and the hub and fit the two together using new locking tabs and nuts. Tighten the nuts down to a torque of 30 to 34 lb/ft. (4.15 to 4.70 kg.m) and bend up the locking tabs.

6. Replace the disc and hub assembly and check the disc brake run-out as described in Chapter 11, Section 4.

15. DUAL BRAKING SYSTEM - GENERAL DESCRIPTION

1. Certain models of the Cortina, in particular those built for the U.S.A market, are fitted with separate front and rear braking systems. In this way hydraulic failure when it occurs is never complete, only the front or rear brakes going out of action.

2. A tandem master cylinder is used and both the front and rear systems are connected to the opposite sides of a pressure differential warning actuator. Should either the front or the rear brakes fail the pressure drop on one side of the warning actuator causes a shuttle valve to move from its normal mid position so actuating an electrical switch which brings on a warning light on the fascia.

3. It is possible to check the bulb in the warning light by operating a switch on the fascia.

16. PRESSURE DIFFERENTIAL WARNING ACTUATOR - CENTRALISATION

1. If the shuttle in the pressure differential actuator has moved, either because air has got into one of the braking circuits or because one of the circuits has failed it will be necessary to centralise the shuttle.

2. This can be done by getting hold of an old screwdriver and cutting it down or grinding it into a tool of the dimensions shown in Fig.9.10.

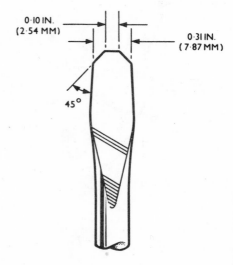

Fig.9.10. Screwdriver special tool dimensions

3. The rubber cover should be removed from the bottom of the pressure differential warning actuator and the tool inserted through the hole where it will engage in a slot in the larger piston thus drawing it into a central position.

4. During bleeding of the brakes the piston must be held in this position throughout the operation or it will prove very difficult to get the warning light to go out and stay out.

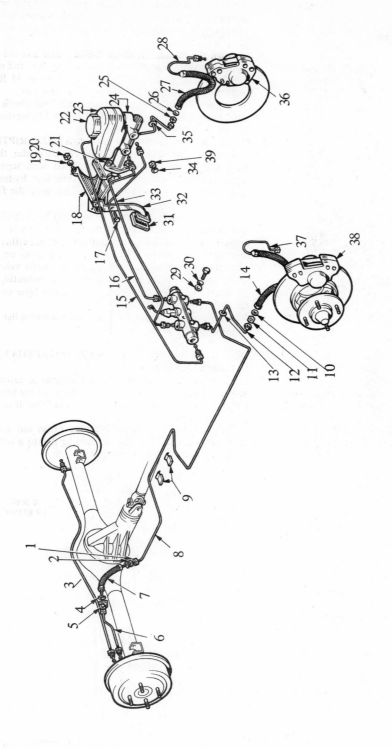

Fig.9.11. EXPLODED VIEW OF THE TANDEM HYDRAULIC BRAKING SYSTEM L.H.D.

1 Union
2 Nut
3 Rear wheel cylinder connecting pipe
4 Washer
5 Nut
6 Wheel cylinder/Flexible hose connecting pipe
7 Flexible hose
8 Front & rear systems connecting pipe
9 Pipe clips
10 Washer
11 Nut
12 Valve & switch unit/flexible hose connecting pipe R.H.
13 Grommet
14 Flexible hose
15 Valve & switch unit/master) cylinder connecting pipes)
16
17 Bolt
18 Pedal bracket
19 Washer
20 Nut
21 Nut
22 Filler cap
23 Reservoir
24 Master cylinder
25 Nut
26 Washer
27 Flexible hose
28 Pipe
29 Washers
30 Washer
31 Pedal rubber
32 Pedal
33 Valve & switch unit/master cylinder connecting pipe
34 Washer
35 Grommet
36 L.H.Front brake disc assembly
37 Pipe
38 R.H.Front brake disc assembly
39 Nut

129

17. PRESSURE DIFFERENTIAL WARNING ACTUATOR-DISMANTLING, EXAMINATION & REASSEMBLY

1. Disconnect the five hydraulic pipes at their unions on the pressure differential warning actuator and to prevent too much loss of hydraulic fluid either place a piece of polythene under the cap of the master cylinder and screw it down tightly or plug the ends of the two pipes leading from the master cylinder.
2. Referring to Fig.9.12. disconnect the wiring from the switch assembly (2).

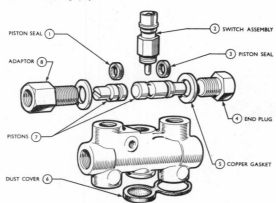

Fig.9.12. Exploded view of the valve and switch unit assembly

3. Undo the single bolt holding the assembly to the rear of the engine compartment and remove it from the car.
4. To dismantle the assembly start by undoing the end plug (4) and discarding the copper gasket (5). Then undo the adaptor (8) and also discard its copper gasket as they must be replaced.
5. Unscrew the switch assembly (2) from the top of the unit then push the small and large pistons (7) out of their bores taking extreme care not to damage the bores during this operation.
6. Take the small seals (1 & 3) from their pistons making a careful note that the seals are slightly tapered and that the large diameter on each seal is fitted to the slotted end of the pistons. Discard the seals as they must be be reused.
7. Pull the dust cover (6) off the bottom of the unit and also discard this component for the same reasons as above.
8. Carefully examine the pistons (7) and the bore of the actuator for score marks scratches or damage; if any are found the complete unit must be exchanged.
9. To test if the switch assembly (2) is working correctly reconnect the wiring and press the plunger against any part of the bare metal of the engine or the bodywork when the warning light should come on. If it does not come on check the switch by substitution and also check the warning lamp bulb.
10 To reassemble the unit start by fitting new seals (1 & 3) to the pistons (7) making sure that they are correctly fitted as detailed in paragraph 6 of this section.
11 With the slotted end outwards, gently push the larger piston into the bore until the groove in the other end of the piston is opposite the hole in which the switch assembly (2) is fitted.
12 Screw the switch assembly (2) into position and tighten it down to a torque of 2 to 2.5 lb/ft. (0.28 to 0.34 kg.m). Then gently push the shorter piston, with the slotted end outwards into the other end of the actuator.
14 Fit new copper washers (5) to the adaptor (8) and the end plug (4) and replace them in the assembly tightening them down to a torque of 16 to 20 lb/ft. (2.22 to 2.80 kg.m). Fit a new dust cover (6) over the bottom aperture.

15 Replacement of the pressure differential warning actuator on the car is a direct reversal of the removal sequence. The brakes must be bled after replacement.

18. TANDEM MASTER CYLINDER - DISMANTLING, EXAMINATION & REASSEMBLY

1. The tandem master cylinder comprises two piston assemblies, one behind the other operating in a common bore. There are two outlets from the master cylinder, one to the front brakes and one to the rear brakes, both going via the pressure differential warning actuator.
2. To remove the tandem master cylinder disconnect the pushrod from the brake pedal, detach the two hydraulic pipes at their unions with the side of the master cylinder and undo the two nuts and spring washers holding the master cylinder to the bulkhead. Plug the loose pipes to prevent entry of dirt.
3. To dismantle the unit, pull off the rubber dust cover and remove the circlip and washer under the dust cover which holds the pushrod in place. Remove the pushrod.
4. Take the hydraulic fluid reservoir off the cylinder assembly by undoing the two screws on either side of the cylinder.
5. From the top of the cylinder remove the circlip and spring from the primary recuperating valve and with a suitable hexagon headed key take out the plug which holds this valve in place then remove the valve assembly.
6. Fit plugs to the two outlet holes and also to the primary recuperating valve aperture, then using a suitable air line blow gently into the other hole on the top of the cylinder. This will remove from the cylinder bore the primary piston and spring, the secondary piston and the secondary recuperating valve assemblies.
7. Remove the piston seal from the primary piston. Lift the tab on the secondary piston spring retainer and remove the piston. Compress the secondary piston spring, move the retainer to one side and remove the secondary recuperating valve stem from the retainer. Then slide the valve spacer and shim from the valve stem, noting the way in which the shim is fitted.
8. Remove the small rubber valve seal and also the secondary piston seal. Examine all the rubber seals for signs of loose fitting or swelling and renew as necessary. Also examining the state of the cylinder bore for signs of scoring or corrosion. If this is damaged in any way a replacement master cylinder must be fitted. It is also advisable to replace all rubber seals as a matter of course whether they are damaged or not.
9. Clean all parts with approved hydraulic fluid prior to reassembly in the cylinder bore.
10 Fit a new seal onto the secondary piston and a new seal to the valve stem. Replace the shim on the valve stem making sure that the convex side faces towards the seal spacer which is fitted next, with its legs towards the valve seal.
11 Refit the secondary piston spring over the valve stem, insert the spring retainer, compress the spring and fit the boss in the valve stem into its location in the spring retainer.
12 Place the narrow end of the secondary piston into the spring retainer and secure it in place by pressing down the tab. Dip the now complete secondary assembly in approved hydraulic fluid and carefully slide it into the cylinder bore with the secondary recuperating valve leading.
13 Place the primary piston spring into the cylinder, fit a new rubber seal to the primary piston, dip it in approved fluid and carefully slide it into the cylinder, drilled end first.

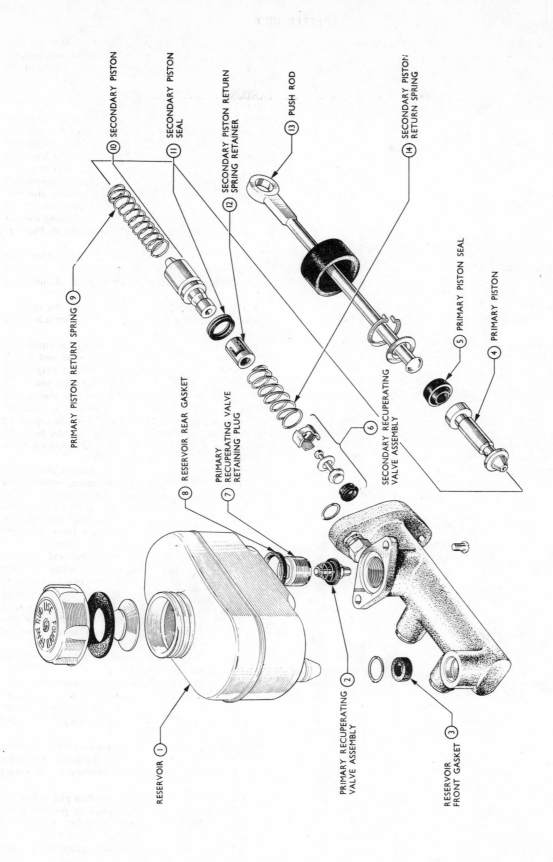

SECONDARY PISTON ⑩

SECONDARY PISTON SEAL ⑪

SECONDARY PISTON RETURN SPRING RETAINER ⑫

PUSH ROD ⑬

SECONDARY PISTON RETURN SPRING ⑭

PRIMARY PISTON SEAL ⑤

PRIMARY PISTON ④

PRIMARY PISTON RETURN SPRING ⑨

RESERVOIR REAR GASKET ⑧

PRIMARY RECUPERATING VALVE RETAINING PLUG ⑦

SECONDARY RECUPERATING VALVE ASSEMBLY ⑥

PRIMARY RECUPERATING VALVE ASSEMBLY ②

RESERVOIR ①

RESERVOIR FRONT GASKET ③

Fig.9.13. EXPLODED VIEW OF THE TANDEM MASTER CYLINDER

14 Fit the pushrod into the end of the primary piston and retain it with the washer and circlip.

15 Place the primary recuperating valve into its location in the top of the cylinder and check that it is properly located by moving the pushrod up and down a small amount. Screw the retaining plug into position and refit the spring and circlip to the valve plunger.

16 Move the pushrod in and out of the cylinder and check that the recuperating valve opens when the rod is fully withdrawn and closes again when it is pushed in.

17 Check the condition of the front and rear reservoir gaskets and if there is any doubt as to their condition they must be replaced. Refit the reservoir to the cylinder with its two retaining screws.

18 Refitting the master cylinder to the car is a reversal of the removal instructions. When replacement is complete bleed the brakes and road test the car.

19. VACUUM SERVO UNIT - REMOVAL & REPLACEMENT

1. Remove the vacuum supply pipe from the servo unit and then undo the brake fluid pipes from the master cylinder. Block the ends of the pipes to prevent the entry of dirt.

2. Take the master cylinder off the front of the servo unit by undoing the two retaining nuts and washers.

3. Detach the servo pushrod from the brake pedal; this may either be held in position by a nut with a bolt running through the pedal, or by a clevis pin and spring clip.

4. On right-hand drive models the servo mounting bracket is much longer than on left-hand drive cars and it is necessary to undo the two nuts and one bolt from under the right-hand wing which hold the bracket to the side panel.

5. On left-hand drive models the bracket is retained to the bulkhead by four nuts which must now be removed; on right-hand drive models there are only two nuts to be removed.

6. Remove the servo unit complete with its mounting bracket from the car. Undo the four nuts and spring washers securing the servo unit to its mounting bracket and separate the two.

7. Replacement of the servo unit is a direct reversal of the above procedure.

20. VACUUM SERVO UNIT - DISMANTLING, EXAMINATION & REASSEMBLY

1. Before starting to dismantle the servo unit it will be necessary to make up two pieces of angle iron or similar metal flat rod about three feet long each with holes drilled in them to fit over the four studs on the pushrod side of the servo unit. You will also require another piece of angle iron about one foot long with holes drilled to coincide with the master cylinder attachment bolts.

2. Scribe marks on both halves of the servo unit so that the shells can be refitted in exactly the same position on reassembly.

3. Fit the three pieces of angle iron to the servo unit as shown in Fig.9.16. and clamp the one foot long piece in a vice so that the servo non-return valve is accessible and pointing downwards. Ensure that the nuts on the angle irons are tight.

4. As it is not possible to separate the two shells with the spring pressure still on the diaphragm it is necessary to create a vacuum behind the diaphragm. This is done by connecting a suitable length of hose to the servo non-return valve and the engine manifold and starting up the engine.

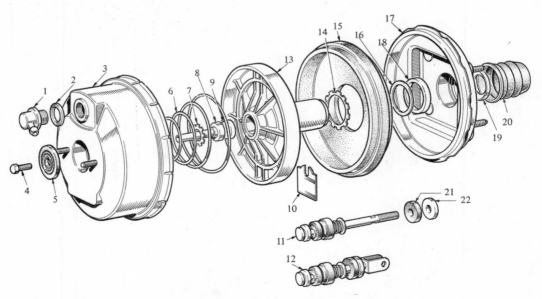

Fig.9.14. EXPLODED VIEW OF THE BRAKE SERVO UNIT

1 Valve union	7 Castellated washer	13 Diaphragm plate	19 Filter retainer
2 Sealing ring	8 Pushrod	14 Castellated washer	20 Dust cover
3 Front housing	9 Seal	15 Diaphragm	21 Filter
4 Bolt	10 Valve plunger stop key	16 Piston guide	22 Pad
5 Seat	11 Plunger assembly R.H.D.	17 Rear body section	
6 Spring	12 Plunger assembly L.H.D.	18 Seal	

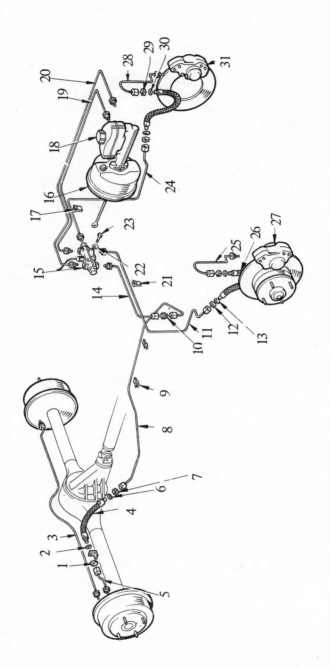

Fig.9.15. EXPLODED VIEW OF THE HYDRAULIC BRAKING SYSTEM — WITH SERVO

1 Nut
2 Washer
3 Rear wheel slave cylinders connection pipe
4 Flexible hose
5 Wheel cylinder/flexible hose. connecting pipe

6 Washer
7 Nut
8 Front & rear systems connecting pipe
9 Pipe clips
10 Union

11 Valve & switch unit/flexible hose connecting pipe R.H.
12 Nut
13 Washer
14 Extension pipe
15 Valve & switch unit

16 Servo unit
17 Clip
18 Filler cap
19 Servo/valve & switch unit)
20 connecting pipes   )
21 Clip

22 Washer
23 Bolt
24 Valve & switch unit/flexible hose connecting pipe L.H.
25 Pipe
26 Flexible hose

27 R.H.Front disc brake assembly
28 Pipe
29 Nut
30 Washer
31 L.H.Front disc brake assembly

Fig.9.16. Method of separating the front and rear shells.

6. Once the two shells have been separated the vacuum can be released and the diaphragm and diaphragm plate assembly, which includes the control rod and valve assembly, can be withdrawn.

7. The control rod and valve assembly should now be removed from the plate and the diaphragm taken from its plate by carefully pulling its centre from its locating groove in the plate.

8. Take off and discard the air filter which is found in the extension flange on the rear edge of the diaphragm plate.

9. Withdraw the seal from the larger front shell and also the internal pushrod and remove the slotted disc from the diaphragm plate.

10 With a screwdriver, prise off the seal retainer from the smaller rear shell and take out the seal.

11 With a suitable spanner, unscrew the non-return valve and its seal from the larger front shell.

12 Carefully examine and clean all parts of the servo before reassembly and as a matter of course replace all rubber parts including the diaphragm. The control and valve assembly are replaced as a unit and should not be broken down.

13 Commence reassembly by fitting a new seal to the non-return valve and replacing the valve in the front shell.

14 Place a new seal into its recess in the rear shell and fit the seal retainer which can be forced into place with a socket just smaller than the retainer.

15 Fit a new air filter to the rear of the diaphragm plate then insert the control rod and valve assembly into the centre of the diaphragm plate and apply a suitable lubricant such as Part No.EM-1C-14 to the bearing surfaces of the control rod and valve assembly. Secure the complete assembly in the plate with the stop key; (See photo).

5. It will probably be necessary to get two assistants to help with the next operation, one to steady the servo unit in the vice and one on the end of one of the longer angle irons. Using the top angle irons as leverage turn the servo top shell in an anti-clockwise direciton until a mark on the top shell aligns with a cut-away on the bottom shell. At this point the shells should separate, but if they fail to do so they can be gently tapped with a soft headed hammer. It is important to keep the vacuum going all the time or the two shells will fly apart under the action of the diaphragm spring causing possible injury and damage.

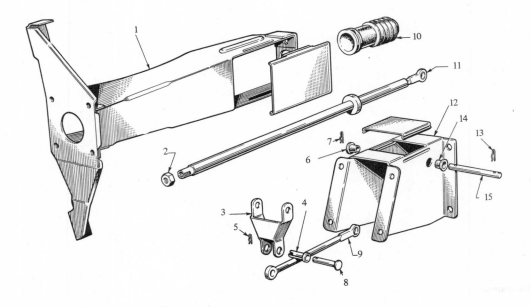

Fig.9.17. EXPLODED VIEW OF THE BRAKE SERVO MOUNTING BRACKET

1 Mounting bracket cover	5 Clip	9 Pushrod	13 Clip
2 Nut	6 Pushrod bush	10 Boot	14 Bush
3 Pusrod relay link	7 Clip	11 Pushrod	15 Pin
4 Bush	8 Clevis pin	12 Mounting bracket cover	

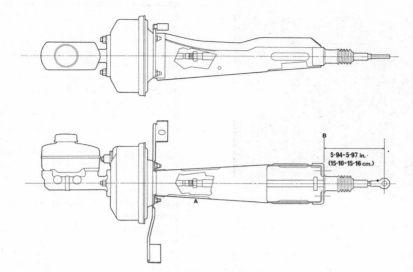

Fig.9.18. SERVO INSTALLATION R.H.D.
The dimension shown at 'B' is achieved by adjusting the pedal pushrod at location 'A'. NOTE: Yellow paint mark on clevis to be towards car centre line.

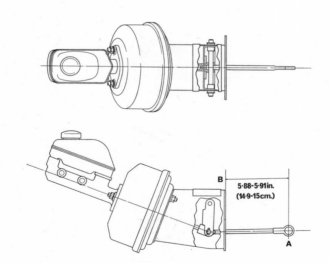

Fig.9.19. SERVO INSTALLATION L.H.D.
The dimension shown at 'B' is achieved by adjusting the pedal pushrod at location 'A'. NOTE: Yellow paint mark on clevis to be towards car centre line.

16 Assemble the new diaphragm to its plate making sure that its centre is correctly located in the groove on the plate. It is advisable to lightly grease the areas of the diaphragm that contact the shells with a grease such as Ford Part No.EM-1C-15. This will help during reassembly and also during later dismantling operations. This grease must not be allowed to come into contact with any of the hydraulic brake system seals or damage will result.

17 Refit the lengths of angle iron as in paragraph 3 and replace the unit in the vice. Reconnect the vacuum pipe, check that the two shells are correctly lined up and start the engine.

18 With the help of the vacuum created and by applying further pressure to the rear shell completely engage the two shells together and with the aid of the angle irons turn the rear shell in a clockwise direction until the scribe marks made prior to dismantling are in line.

19 With the vacuum still being applied check how far the pushrod extends beyond the front shell. This must be from 0.011 to 0.016 in. (0.28 to 0.40 mm.).

20 The unit can now be replaced in the car when the measurements shown in Fig.9.18. for right-hand drive cars and Fig.9.19. for left-hand drive cars must be checked and adjusted as necessary. Also make sure that the yellow paint mark on the retaining clevis pin is towards the centre line of the car.

FAULT FINDING CHART

Cause	Trouble	Remedy
SYMPTOM:	**PEDAL TRAVELS ALMOST TO FLOORBOARDS BEFORE BRAKES OPERATE**	
Leaks and air bubbles in hydraulic system	Brake fluid level too low	Top up master cylinder reservoir. Check for leaks.
	Wheel cylinder leaking	Dismantle wheel cylinder, clean, fit new rubbers and bleed brakes.
	Master cylinder leaking (Bubbles in master cylinder fluid)	Dismantle master cylinder, clean, and fit new rubbers. Bleed brakes.
	Brake flexible hose leaking	Examine and fit new hose if old hose leaking. Bleed brakes.
	Brake line fractured	Replace with new brake pipe. Bleed brakes.
	Brake system unions loose	Check all unions in brake system and tighten as necessary. Bleed brakes.
Normal wear	Linings over 75% worn	Fit replacement shoes and brake linings.
Incorrect adjustment	Brakes badly out of adjustment	Jack up car and adjust brakes.
	Master cylinder push rod out or adjustment causing too much pedal free movement	Reset to manufacturer's specification.
SYMPTOM:	**BRAKE PEDAL FEELS SPRINGY**	
Brake lining renewal	New linings not yet bedded-in	Use brakes gently until springy pedal feeling leaves.
Excessive wear or damage	Brake drums badly worn and weak or cracked	Fit new brake drums.
Lack of maintenance	Master cylinder securing nuts loose	Tighten master cylinder securing nuts. Ensure spring washers are fitted.
SYMPTOM:	**BRAKE PEDAL FEELS SPONGY & SOGGY**	
Leaks or bubbles in hydraulic system	Wheel cylinder leaking	Dismantle wheel cylinder, clean, fit new rubbers, and bleed brakes.
	Master cylinder leaking (Bubbles in master cylinder reservoir)	Dismantle master cylinder, clean, and fit new rubbers and bleed brakes. Replace cylinder if internal walls scored.
	Brake pipe line or flexible hose leaking	Fit new pipeline or hose.
	Unions in brake system loose	Examine for leaks, tighten as necessary.
SYMPTOM:	**EXCESSIVE EFFORT REQUIRED TO BRAKE CAR**	
Lining type or condition	Linings badly worn	Fit replacement brake shoes and linings.
	New linings recently fitted - not yet bedded-in	Use brakes gently until braking effort normal.
	Harder linings fitted than standard causing increase in pedal pressure	Remove linings and replace with normal units.
Oil or grease leaks	Linings and brake drums contaminated with oil, grease, or hydraulic fluid	Rectify source of leak, clean brake drums, fit new linings.
SYMPTOM:	**BRAKES UNEVEN & PULLING TO ONE SIDE**	
Oil or grease leaks	Linings and brake drums contaminated with oil, grease, or hydraulic fluid	Ascertain and rectify source of leak, clean brake drums, fit new linings.
Lack of maintenance	Tyre pressures unequal	Check and inflate as necessary.
	Radial ply tyres fitted at one end of car only	Fit radial ply tyres of the same make to all four wheels.
	Brake backplate loose	Tighten backplate securing nuts and bolts.
	Brake shoes fitted incorrectly	Remove and fit shoes correct way round.
	Different type of linings fitted at each wheel	Fit the linings specified by the manufacturers all round.
	Anchorages for front suspension or rear axle loose	Tighten front and rear suspension pick-up points including spring anchorage.
	Brake drums badly worn, cracked or distorted	Fit new brake drums.

BRAKING SYSTEM

Cause	Trouble	Remedy
SYMPTOM:	BRAKES TEND TO BIND, DRAG, OR LOCK-ON	
Incorrect adjustment	Brake shoes adjusted too tightly Handbrake cable over-tightened Master cylinder push rod out of adjustment giving too little brake pedal free movement	Slacken off brake shoe adjusters two clicks. Slacken off handbrake cable adjustment. Reset to manufacturer's specifications.
Wear or dirt in hydraulic system or incorrect fluid	Reservoir vent hole in cap blocked with dirt Master cylinder by-pass port restricted – brakes seize in 'on' position Wheel cylinder seizes in 'on' position	Clean and blow through hole. Dismantle, clean, and overhaul master cylinder. Bleed brakes. Dismantle, clean, and overhaul wheel cylinder. Bleed brakes.
Mechanical wear	Brake shoe pull off springs broken, stretched or loose	Examine springs and replace if worn or loose.
Incorrect brake assembly	Brake shoe pull off springs fitted wrong way round, omitted, or wrong type used	Examine, and rectify as appropriate.
Neglect	Handbrake system rusted or seized in the 'on' position	Apply 'Plus Gas' to free, clean and lubricate.

CHAPTER TEN

ELECTRICAL SYSTEM

CONTENTS

SPECIFICATIONS

Battery

Type	Lead Acid 12 volt
Earthed Terminal	Negative
Capacity at 20 hr.rate	
Standard...	38 amp/hr.

Cold climate..	57 amp/hr
Plates per cell - standard	9
- cold climate...	13
Specific gravity charged	1.275 to 1.290
Electrolyte capacity - standard	4.5 pints (5.4 US pints, 2.5 litres)
- cold climate	6.4 pints (7.7 US pints, 3.6 litres)
Dynamo	Lucas C40 (C40/L cold start models)
Maximum charge	22 amps
Number of brushes..	2
Brush length new	.718 in. (18.23 mm)
Brush spring tension	18 to 24 ozs.
Field resistance...	6.0 ohms.

Starter motor inertia type

Number of brushes	4
Minimum brush length	.3 in. (7.5 mm)
Brush spring tension	34 ozs. (.96 kg)
Gear ratio	11 to 1
Teeth on pinion	10
Teeth on ring gear	110

NOTE: A pre-engaged type of starter motor is fitted as standard on cars with 'cold start' equipment and can be fitted as an optional extra on other models

Regulator/Control box	Lucas RB 340
Cut-in voltage	12.6 to 13.4 volts
Drop-off voltage	9.25 to 11.25 volts
Armature to cone air gap...	.035 to .045 in. (.89 to 1.14 mm)
Current regulator on load setting	Max. generator output + or - 1½ amps
Armature to cone air gap...	.052 to .056 in. (1.32 to 1.42 mm)
Voltage regulator open circuit setting	13.8 to 14.2 volts at $20^{\circ}C$ ($68^{\circ}F$)
Armature to cone air gap...	.052 to .056 in. (1.32 to 1.42 mm)
Reverse current	3.0 to 5.0 amps
Voltage setting at 2,000 r.p.m.	$10^{\circ}C$ ($50^{\circ}F$) 14.9 to 15.5 volts
	$20^{\circ}C$ ($68^{\circ}F$) 14.7 to 15.3 volts
	$30^{\circ}C$ ($86^{\circ}F$) 14.5 to 15.1 volts
	$40^{\circ}C$ ($104^{\circ}F$) 14.3 to 14.9 volts
Fuses	6 - fitted from 1969 on - 8 amp rating

Bulbs

Headlamps	60/45 watts (sealed beam)
Sidelamps (front)	6 watts
Front flashers	24 watts
Rear flashers	24 watts
Stop/tail lamps...	6/24 watts
Rear number plates	6 watts
Interior light..	3 watts
Instrument warning lights	2.2 watts
Clock (G.T. & 1600E)	1.2 watts

TORQUE WRENCH SETTINGS

Starter motor retaining bolts..	20 to 25 lb/ft. (2.76 to 3.46 kg.m.)
Dynamo pulley...	14 to 17 lb/ft. (1.93 to 2.35 kg.m.)
Dynamo mounting bolts	15 to 18 lb/ft. (2.07 to 2.49 kg.m.)
Dynamo mounting bracket	20 to 25 lb/ft. (2.76 to 3.46 kg.m.)

1. GENERAL DESCRIPTION

The electrical system is of the 12 volt type and the major components comprise: a 12 volt battery with the negative terminal earthed; a voltage regulator and cut-out; a Lucas dynamo which is fitted to the front left-hand side of the engine and is driven by the fan belt from the crankshaft pulley wheel; and a starter motor which is fitted to the clutch bellhousing on the right-hand side of the engine (left-hand side on left-hand drive cars).

The 12 volt battery gives a steady supply of current

for the ignition, lighting, and other electrical circuits, and provides a reserve of electricity when the current consumed by the electrical equipment exceeds that being produced by the dynamo.

The dynamo is of the two brush type and works in conjunction with the voltage regulator and cut-out. The dynamo is cooled by a multi-bladed fan mounted behind the dynamo pulley, and blows air through cooling holes in the dynamo end brackets. The output from the dynamo is controlled by the voltage regulator which ensures a high output if the battery is in a low state of charge or the demands from the electrical equipment high, and a low output if the battery is fully charged and there is little demand from the electrical equipment.

2. BATTERY - REMOVAL & REPLACEMENT

1. The battery is positioned on a tray in the front of the engine compartment forward of the offside suspension.
2. Disconnect the earthed negative lead and then the positive lead by slackening the retaining nuts and bolts or, by unscrewing the retaining screws if these are fitted.
3. Remove the battery clamp and carefully lift the battery off its tray. Hold the battery vertical to ensure that no electrolyte is spilled.
4. Replacement is a direct reversal of this procedure.
   NOTE: Replace the positive lead and the earth (negative) lead, smearing the terminals with petroleum jelly (vaseline) to prevent corrosion. NEVER use an ordinary grease as applied to other parts of the car.

3. BATTERY - MAINTENANCE & INSPECTION

1. Normal weekly battery maintenance consists of checking the electrolyte level of each cell to ensure that the separators are covered by ¼ in. of electrolyte. If the level has fallen top up the battery using distilled water only. Do not overfill. If a battery is overfilled or any electrolyte spilled, immediately wipe away the excess as electrolyte attacks and corrodes any metal it comes into contact with very rapidly.
2. As well as keeping the terminals clean and covered with petroleum jelly, the top of the battery, and especially the top of the cells, should be kept clean and dry. This helps prevent corrosion and ensures that the battery does not become partially discharged by leakage through dampness and dirt.
3. Once every three months remove the battery and inspect the battery securing bolts, the battery clamp plate, tray, and battery leads for corrosion (white fluffy deposits on the metal which are brittle to touch). If any corrosion is found, clean off the deposits with ammonia and paint over the clean metal with an anti-rust/anti-acid paint.
4. At the same time inspect the battery case for cracks. If a crack is found, clean and plug it with one of the proprietary compounds marketed by firms such as Holts for this purpose. If leakage through the crack has been excessive then it will be necessary to refill the appropriate cell with fresh electrolyte as detailed later. Cracks are frequently caused to the top of the battery cases by pouring in distilled water in the middle of winter AFTER instead of BEFORE a run. This gives the water no chance to mix with the electrolyte and so the former freezes and splits the battery case.
5. If topping up the batteries becomes excessive and the cases have been inspected for cracks that could cause leakage, but none are found, the batteries are being overcharged and the voltage regulator will have to be checked and reset.
6. With the batteries on the bench at the three monthly interval check, measure their specific gravity with a hydrometer to determine the state of charge and condition of the electrolyte. There should be very little variation between the different cells and if a variation in excess of 0.025 is present it will be due to either:-

a) Loss of electrolyte from the battery at sometime caused by spillage or a leak resulting in a drop in the specific gravity of the electrolyte, when the deficiency was replaced with distilled water instead of fresh electrolyte.

b) An internal short circuit caused by buckling of the plates or a similar malady pointing to the likelihood of total battery failure in the near future.

7. The specific gravity of the electrolyte for fully charged conditions at the electrolyte temperature indicated, is listed in Table A. The specific gravity of a fully discharged battery at different temperatures of the electrolyte is given at Table B.

TABLE A

Specific Gravity - Battery Fully Charged

1.268 at 100°F or 38°C electrolyte temperature
1.272 at 90°F or 32°C electrolyte temperature
1.276 at 80°F or 27°C electrolyte temperature
1.280 at 70°F or 21°C electrolyte temperature
1.284 at 60°F or 16°C electrolyte temperature
1.288 at 50°F or 10°C electrolyte temperature
1.292 at 40°F or 4°C electrolyte temperature
1.296 at 30°F or -1.5°C electrolyte temperature

TABLE B

Specific Gravity - Battery Fully Discharged

1.098 at 100°F or 38°C electrolyte temperature
1.102 at 90°F or 32°C electrolyte temperature
1.106 at 80°F or 27°C electrolyte temperature
1.110 at 70°F or 21°C electrolyte temperature
1.114 at 60°F or 16°C electrolyte temperature
1.118 at 50°F or 10°C electrolyte temperature
1.122 at 40°F or 4°C electrolyte temperature
1.126 at 30°F or -1.5°C electrolyte temperature

4. ELECTROLYTE REPLENISHMENT

1. If the battery is in a fully charged state and one of the cells maintains a specific gravity reading which is 0.025 or more lower than the others, and a check of each cell has been made with a voltage meter to check for short circuits (a four to seven second test should give a steady reading of between 1.2 to 1.8 volts), then it is likely that electrolyte has been lost from the cell with the low reading at sometime.
2. Top up the cell with a solution of 1 part sulphuric acid to 2.5 parts of water. If the cell is already fully topped up draw some electrolyte out of it with a pipette. The total capacity of each cell is ¾ pint.
3. When mixing the sulphuric acid and water NEVER ADD WATER TO SULPHURIC ACID - always pour the the acid slowly onto the water in a glass container. IF WATER IS ADDED TO SULPHURIC ACID IT WILL EXPLODE.
4. Continue to top up the cell with the freshly made electrolyte and then recharge the battery and check the hydrometer readings.

5. BATTERY CHARGING

1. In winter time when heavy demand is placed upon the battery, such as when starting from cold, and much electrical equipment is continually in use, it is a good idea to occasionally have the battery fully charged from an external source at the rate of 3.5 to 4 amps.
2. Continue to charge the battery at this rate until no further rise in specific gravity is noted over a four hour period.
3. Alternatively, a trickle charger charging at the rate of 1.5 amps can be safely used overnight.
4. Specially rapid 'boost' charges which are claimed to restore the power of the battery in 1 to 2 hours are most dangerous as they can cause serious damage to the

battery plates through over-heating.

5. While charging the battery note that the temperature of the electrolyte should never exceed 100°F.

6. DYNAMO - ROUTINE MAINTENANCE

1. Routine maintenance consists of checking the tension of the fan belt, and lubricating the dynamo rear bearing once every 6,000 miles.

2. The fan belt should be tight enough to ensure no slip between the belt and the dynamo pulley. If a shrieking noise comes from the engine when the unit is accelerated rapidly, it is likely that it is the fan belt slipping. On the other hand, the belt must not be too taut or the bearings will wear rapidly and cause dynamo failure or bearing seizure. Ideally ½ in. of total free movement should be available at the fan belt midway between the fan and the dynamo pulley.

3. To adjust the fan belt tension slightly slacken the three dynamo retaining bolts, and swing the dynamo on the upper two bolts outwards to increase the tension, and inwards to lower it.

4. It is best to leave the bolts fairly tight so that considerable effort has to be used to move the dynamo; otherwise it is difficult to get the correct setting. If the dynamo is being moved outwards to increase the tension and the bolts have only been slackened a little, a long spanner acting as a lever placed behind the dynamo with the lower end resting against the block works very well in moving the dynamo outwards. Retighten the dynamo bolts and check that the dynamo pulley is correctly aligned with the fan belt.

5. Lubrication on the dynamo consists of inserting three drops of S.A.E.30 engine oil in the small oil hole in the centre of the commutator end bracket. This lubricates the rear bearing. The front bearing is pre-packed with grease and requires no attention.

7. DYNAMO - TESTING IN POSITION

1. If, with the engine running, no charge comes from the dynamo, or the charge is very low, first check that the fan belt is in place and is not slipping. Then check that the leads from the control box to the dynamo are firmly attached and that one has not come loose from its terminal.

2. The lead from the 'D' terminal on the dynamo should be connected to the 'D' terminal on the control box, and similarly the 'F' terminals on the dynamo and control box should also be connected together. Check that this is so and that the leads have not been incorrectly fitted.

3. Make sure none of the electrical equipment (such as the lights or radio) is on and then pull the leads off the dynamo terminals marked 'D' and 'F', join the terminals together with a short length of wire.

4. Attach to the centre of this length of wire the positive clip of a 0-20 volts voltmeter and run the other clip to earth on the dynamo yoke. Start the engine and allow it to idle at approximately 750 r.p.m. At this speed the dynamo should give a reading of about 15 volts on the voltmeter. There is no point in raising the engine speed above a fast idle as the reading will then be inaccurate.

5. If no reading is recorded then check the brushes and brush connections. If a very low reading of approximately 1 volt is observed then the field winding may be suspect.

6. If a reading of between 4 to 6 volts is recorded it is likely that the armature winding is at fault.

7. On early dynamos it was possible to remove the dynamo cover band and check the dynamo and brushes in position. With the Lucas C40-1 windowless yoke dynamo it must be removed and dismantled before the brushes and commutator can be attended to.

8. If the voltmeter shows a good reading then, with the temporary link still in position, connect both leads from the control box to 'D' and 'F' on the dynamo ('D' to 'D' and 'F' to 'F'). Release the lead from the 'D' terminal at the control box end and clip one lead from the voltmeter to the end of the cable, and the other lead to a good earth. With the engine running at the same speed as previously, an identical voltage to that recorded at the dynamo should be noted on the voltmeter. If no voltage is recorded then there is a break in the wire. If the voltage is the same as recorded at the dynamo then check the 'F' lead in similar fashion. If both readings are the same as at the dynamo then it will be necessary to test the control box.

8. DYNAMO - REMOVAL & REPLACEMENT

1. Slacken the two dynamo retaining bolts, and the nut on the sliding link, and move the dynamo in towards the engine so that the fan belt can be removed.

2. Disconnect the two leads from the dynamo terminals.

3. Remove the nut from the sliding link bolt, and remove the two upper bolts. The dynamo is then free to be lifted away from the engine.

4. Replacement is a reversal of the above procedure. Do not finally tighten the retaining bolts and the nut on the sliding link until the fan belt has been tensioned correctly. See 10/6.2 for details.

9. DYNAMO - DISMANTLING & INSPECTION

1. Mount the dynamo in a vice and unscrew and remove the two through bolts from the commutator end bracket. (See photo).

9.1

9.2

2. Mark the commutator end bracket and the dynamo casing so the end bracket can be replaced in its

original position. Pull the end bracket off the armature shaft. NOTE some versions of the dynamo may have a raised pip on the end bracket which locates in a recess on the edge of the casing. If so, marking the end bracket and casing is not necessary. A pip may also be found on the drive end bracket at the opposite end of the casing. (See photo).

3. Lift the two brush springs and draw the brushes out of the brush holders (arrowed).

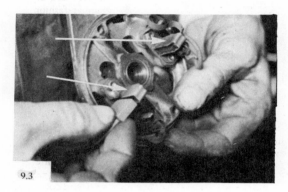

9.3

4. Measure the brushes and, if worn down to 9/32 in. or less, unscrew the screws holding the brush leads to the end bracket. Take off the brushes complete with leads. Old and new brushes are compared in the photograph.

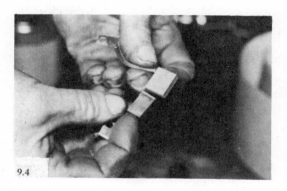

9.4

5. If no locating pip can be found, mark the drive end bracket and the dynamo casing so the drive end bracket can be replaced in its original position. Then pull the drive end bracket, complete with armature, out of the casing. (See photo).

6. Check the condition of the ball bearing in the drive end plate by firmly holding the plate and noting if there is visible side movement of the armature shaft in relation to the end plate. If play is present the armature assembly must be separated from the end plate. If the bearing is sound there is no need to carry out the work described in the following two paragraphs.

7. Hold the armature in one hand (mount it carefully in a vice if preferred) and undo the nut holding the pulley wheel and fan in place. Pull off the pulley wheel and fan.

8. Next remove the woodruff key (arrowed) from its slot in the armature shaft and also the bearing locating ring.

9. Place the drive end bracket across the open jaws of a vice with the armature downwards and gently tap the armature shaft from the bearing (see photo) in the end

plate with the aid of a suitable drift.

10 Carefully inspect the armature and check if for open or short circuited windings. It is a good indication of an open circuited armature when the commutator segments are burnt. If the armature has short circuited the commutator segments will be very badly burnt, and the overheated armature windings badly discoloured. If open or short circuits are suspected then test by substituting the suspect armature for a new one (see photo).

11 Check the resistance of the field coils. To do this, connect an ohmmeter between the field terminal and the yoke and note the reading on the ohmmeter which should be about 6 ohms. If the ohmmeter reading is infinity this indicates an open circuit in the field winding; If the ohmmeter reading is below 5 ohms this indicates that one of the field coils is faulty and must be replaced.

12 Field coil replacement involves the use of a wheel operated screwdriver, a soldering iron, caulking and riveting and this operation is considered to be beyond the scope of most owners. Therefore, if the field coils are at fault either purchase a rebuilt dynamo, or take the casing to a Ford dealer or electrical engineering works for new field coils to be fitted.

13 Next check the condition of the commutator (arrowed). If it is dirty and blackened as shown clean it with a petrol dampened rag. If the commutator is in good condition the surface will be smooth and quite free from pits or burnt areas, and the insulated segments clearly defined.

14 If, after the commutator has been cleaned, pits and burnt spots are still present, wrap a strip of glass paper round the commutator taking great care to move the commutator ¼ of a turn every ten rubs till it is thoroughly clean. (See photo).

15 In extreme cases of wear the commutator can be mounted in a lathe and with the lathe turning at high speed, a very fine cut may be taken off the commutator. Then polish the commutator with glass paper. If the commutator has worn so that the insulators between the segments are level with the top of the segments, then undercut the insulators to a depth of 1/32 in. (.8 mm.). The best tool to use for this purpose is half a hacksaw blade ground to a thickness of the insulator, and with the handle end of the blade covered in insulating tape to make it comfortable to hold. This is the sort of finish the surface of the commutator should have when finished.

16 Check the bush bearing (arrowed) in the commutator end bracket for wear by noting if the armature spindle rocks when placed in it. If worn it must be renewed.

17 The bush bearing can be removed by a suitable extractor or by screwing a 5/8 in. tap four or five times into the bush. The tap complete with bush is then pulled out of the end bracket.

18 NOTE before fitting the new bush bearing that it is of the porous bronze type, and it is essential that it is allowed to stand in S.A.E.30 engine oil for at least 24 hours before fitment. In an emergency the bush can be immersed in hot oil (100ºC) for 2 hours.

19 Carefully fit the new bush into the end plate, pressing it in until the end of the bearing is flush with the inner side of the end plate. If available, press the bush in with a smooth shouldered mandrel the same diameter as the armature shaft.

10. DYNAMO - REPAIR & REASSEMBLY

1. To renew the ball bearing fitted to the drive end bracket drill out the rivets which hold the bearing retainer plate to the end bracket and lift off the plate.

2. Press out the bearing from the end bracket and remove the corrugated and felt washers from the bearing housing.

3. Thoroughly clean the bearing housing, and the new bearing and pack with high melting-point grease.

4. Place the felt washer and corrugated washer in that order in the end bracket bearing housing (see photo).

5. Then fit the new bearing as shown.

6. Gently tap the bearing into place with the aid of a suitable drift. (See photo).

7. Replace the bearing plate and fit three new rivets. (See photo).

8. Open up the rivets with the aid of a suitable cold chisel. (See photo).

9. Finally peen over the open end of the rivets with the aid of a ball hammer as illustrated.

10 Refit the drive end bracket to the armature shaft. Do not try and force the bracket on but with the aid of a suitable socket abutting the bearing tap the bearing on gently, so pulling the end bracket down with it. (See photo).

11 Slide the spacer up the shaft and refit the woodruff key. (See photo).

12 Replace the fan and pulley wheel and then fit the spring washer and nut and tighten the latter. The drive bracket end of the dynamo is now fully assembled as shown.

13 If the brushes are little worn and are to be used again then ensure that they are placed in the same holders from which they were removed. When refitting brushes, either new or old, check that they move freely in their holders. If either brush sticks, clean with a petrol moistened rag and, if still stiff, lightly polish the sides of the brush with a very fine file until the brush moves quite freely in its holders.

14 Tighten the two retaining screws and washers which hold the wire leads to the brushes in place (see photo).

15 It is far easier to slip the end piece with brushes over the commutator if the brushes are raised in their holders

as shown and held in this position by the pressure of the springs resting against their flanks (arrowed).

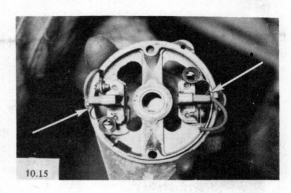
10.15

16 Refit the armature to the casing and then the commutator end plate and screw up the two through bolts.

17 Finally, hook the ends of the two springs off the flanks of the brushes and onto their heads so the brushes are forced down into contact with the armature.

11. INERTIA TYPE STARTER MOTOR - GENERAL DESCRIPTION

The starter motor is held in position by three bolts which also clamp the bellhousing flange.

The motor is of the four field coil, four pole piece type, and utilises four spring-loaded commutator brushes. Two of these brushes are earthed, and the other two are insulated and attached to the field coil ends.

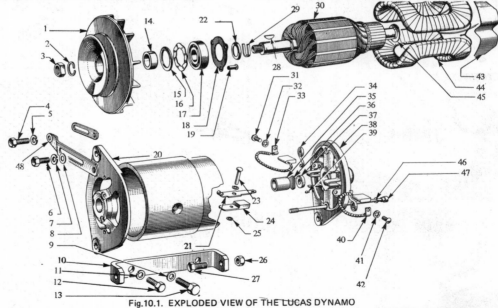

Fig.10.1. EXPLODED VIEW OF THE LUCAS DYNAMO

1 Pulley & fan	13 Bolt	25 Shim	37 Oil retaining felt
2 Lock washer	14 End bearing collar	26 Nut	38 End plate
3 Nut	15 Felt oil retainer	27 Bolt	39 Dowel
4 Bolt	16 Shim	28 Woodruff key	40 Brush assembly
5 Washer	17 Bearing	29 Collar	41 Shakeproof washer
6 Bolt	18 Bearing retaining plate	30 Armature	42 Screw
7 Lock washer	19 Rivet	31 Screw	43 Field coil insulator
8 Plain washer	20 Dynamo end plate	32 Shakeproof washer	44 Field coils
9 Plain washer	21 Connector terminal	33 Brush assembly	45 Washer
10 Dynamo bracket	22 Bearing locating ring retainer	34 Brush retaining spring	46 Lockwasher
11 Lock washer	23 Rivet	35 Plain bearing/bush	47 Dynamo through bolt
12 Bolt	24 Connector insulator	36 Felt retainer	48 Dynamo adjusting bracket

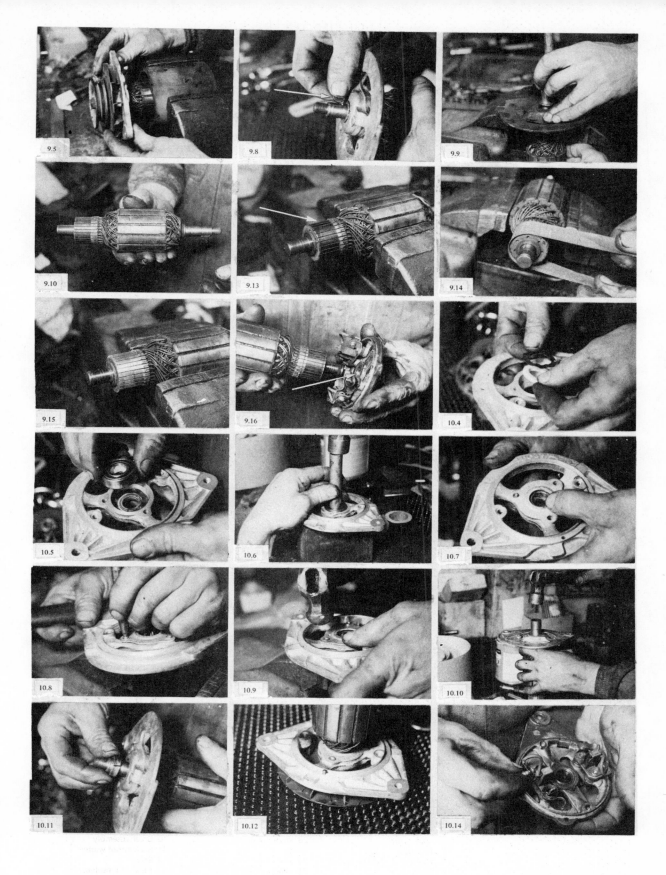

12. STARTER MOTOR - TESTING ON ENGINE

1. If the starter motor fails to operate then check the condition of the battery by turning on the headlamps. If they glow brightly for several seconds and then gradually dim, the battery is in an uncharged condition.

2. If the headlamps glow brightly and it is obvious that that the battery is in good condition, then check the tightness of the battery wiring connections (and in particular the earth lead from the battery terminal to its connection on the bodyframe). If the positive terminal on the battery becomes hot when an attempt is made to work the starter, this is a sure sign of a poor connection on the battery terminal. To rectify remove the terminal, clean the inside of the cap and the terminal post thoroughly and reconnect. Check the tightness of the connections at the relay switch and at the starter motor. Check the wiring with a voltmeter for breaks or shorts.

3. If the wiring is in order then check that the starter motor is operating. To do this, press the rubber covered button in the centre of the solenoid under the bonnet. If it is working the starter motor will be heard to 'click' as it tries to rotate. Alternatively check it with a voltmeter.

If the battery is fully charged, the wiring in order, and the switch working and the starter motor fails to operate, then it will have to be removed from the car for examination. Before this is done, however, ensure that the starter pinion has not jammed in mesh with the flywheel. Check by turning the square end of the armature shaft with a spanner. This will free the pinion if it is stuck in engagement with the flywheel teeth. On some models the square on the end of the shaft will be covered by a metal cap.

13. STARTER MOTOR - REMOVAL & REPLACEMENT

1. Disconnect the battery earth lead from the negative terminal.

2. Disconnect the starter motor cable from the terminal on the starter motor end plate.

3. Remove the upper starter motor securing bolt.

4. Working under the car loosen, and then remove, the two lower starter motor securing bolts taking care to support the motor so as to prevent damage to the drive components.

5. Lift the starter motor out of engagement with the flywheel ring and lower it out of the car.

6. Replacement is a straight forward reversal of the removal procedure.

14. STARTER MOTOR - DISMANTLING & REASSEMBLY

1. With the starter motor on the bench, loosen the screw on the cover band and slip the cover band off. With a piece of wire bent into the shape of a hook, lift back each of the brush springs in turn and check the movement of the brushes in their holders by pulling on the flexible connectors. If the brushes are so worn that their faces do not rest against the commutator, or if the ends of the brush leads are exposed on their working face, they must be renewed.

2. If any of the brushes tend to stick in their holders then wash them with a petrol moistened cloth and, if necessary, lightly polish the sides of the brush with a very fine file, until the brushes move quite freely in their holders.

3. If the surface of the commutator is dirty or blackened, clean it with a petrol dampened rag. Secure the starter motor in a vice and check it by connecting a heavy gauge cable between the starter motor terminal and a 12 volt battery.

4. Connect the cable from the other battery terminal to earth in the starter motor body. If the motor turns at high speed it is in good order.

5. If the starter motor still fails to function, or if it is wished to renew the brushes, it is necessary to further dismantle the motor.

6. Lift the brush springs with the wire hook and lift all four brushes out of their holders one at a time.

7. Remove the terminal nuts and washers from the terminal post on the commutator end bracket.

8. Unscrew the two through bolts which hold the end plates together and pull off the commutator end bracket. Also remove the driving end bracket which will come away complete with the armature.

9. At this stage, if the brushes are to be renewed, their flexible connectors must be unsoldered and the connectors of new brushes soldered in their place. Check that the new brushes move freely in their holders as detailed above. If cleaning the commutator with petrol fails to remove all the burnt areas and spots, then wrap a piece of glass paper round the commutator and rotate the armature. If the commutator is very badly worn, remove the drive gear as detailed in the following section. Then mount the armature in a lathe and with the lathe turning at high speed, take a very fine cut-out of the commutator and finish the surface by polishing with glass paper. DO NOT UNDERCUT THE MICA INSULATORS BETWEEN THE COMMUTATOR SEGMENTS.

10 With the starter motor dismantled, test the four field coils for an open circuit. Connect a 12-volt battery with a 12-volt bulb in one of the leads between the field terminal post and the tapping point of the field coils to which the brushes are connected. An open circuit is proved by the bulb not lighting.

11 If the bulb lights, it does not necessarily mean that the field coils are in order, as there is a possibility that one of the coils will be earthing to the starter yoke or pole shoes. To check this, remove the lead from the brush connector and place it against a clean portion of the starter yoke. If the bulb lights the field coils are earthing. Replacement of the field coils calls for the use of a wheel operated screwdriver, a soldering iron, caulking and riveting operations and is beyond the scope of the majority of owners. The starter yoke should be taken to a reputable electrical engineering works for new field coils to be fitted. Alternatively, purchase an exchange starter motor.

12 If the armature is damaged this will be evident after visual inspection. Look for signs of burning, discolouration, and for conductors that have lifted away from the commutator. Reassembly is a straight reversal of the dismantling procedure.

15. STARTER MOTOR DRIVE - GENERAL DESCRIPTION

1. The starter motor drive is of the outboard type. When the starter motor is operated the pinion moves into contact with the flywheel gear ring by moving in towards the starter motor.

2. If the engine kicks back, or the pinion fails to engage with the flywheel gear ring when the starter motor is actuated no undue strain is placed on the armature shaft, as the pinion sleeve disengages from the pinion and turns independently.

16. STARTER MOTOR DRIVE - REMOVAL & REPLACEMENT

1. When the starter motor is removed the drive should be well washed in petrol or paraffin to remove any grease or oil which may be the cause of a sticking pinion. Under no circumstances should these parts be lubricated.

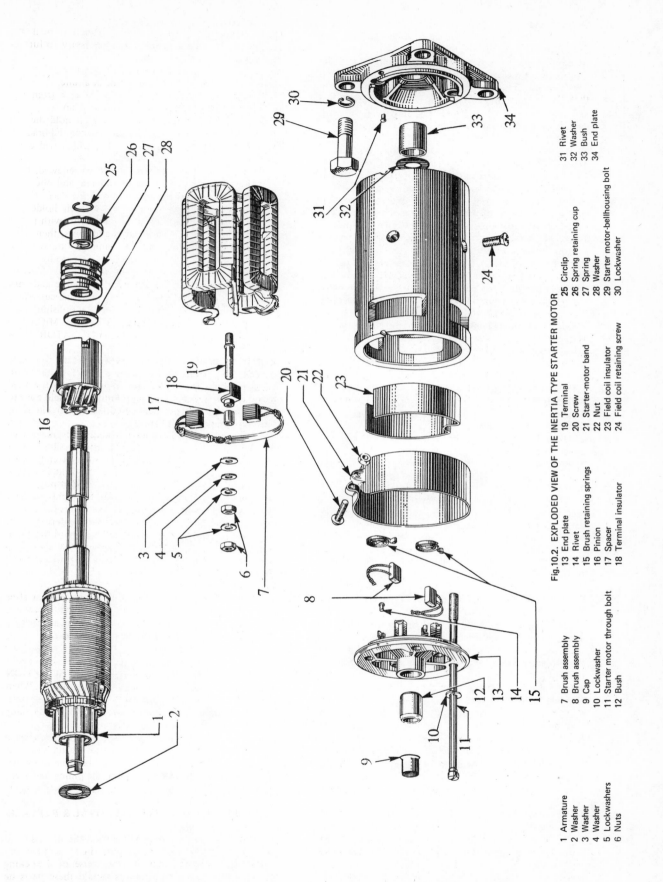

Fig.10.2. EXPLODED VIEW OF THE INERTIA TYPE STARTER MOTOR

1 Armature	13 End plate	25 Circlip
2 Washer	14 Rivet	26 Spring retaining cup
3 Washer	15 Brush retaining springs	27 Spring
4 Washer	16 Pinion	28 Washer
5 Lockwashers	17 Spacer	29 Starter motor-bellhousing bolt
6 Nuts	18 Terminal insulator	30 Lockwasher
7 Brush assembly	19 Terminal	31 Rivet
8 Brush assembly	20 Screw	32 Washer
9 Cap	21 Starter-motor band	33 Bush
10 Lockwasher	22 Nut	34 End plate
11 Starter motor through bolt	23 Field coil insulator	
12 Bush	24 Field coil retaining screw	

147

2. To dismantle the drive, compress the drive spring and cup employing a press for this purpose, and then extract the locking device, pin or circlip.

3. Ease the press and remove the drive spring cup, spring and retaining washer. Pull the drive pinion barrel assembly from the armature shaft. If the pinion is badly worn or broken, this must be replaced as an assembly. When refitting the pinion barrel assembly must be fitted with the pinion teeth toward the armature windings.

17. PRE-ENGAGED STARTER MOTORS - GENERAL DESCRIPTION

This type of starter motor is normally only fitted as original equipment to cars with 'cold start' specifications, but it can be fitted as an optional extra on all other models. Two types of motor may be used, the first type being exactly the same as the inertia type described in the previous sections. The second type is a wave wound motor and uses an end-face commutator instead of the normal drum type. On both types a solenoid is attached to the top of the starter motor which actuates a one way clutch when the starter button is pressed thus engaging the motor to the pinion which is permanently in mesh with the starter ring on the flywheel. The drive to the pinion therefore remains fully engaged until the solenoid is de-activated. The starter motor is attached to the bellhousing by two bolts only and not three as in the inertia type.

18. PRE-ENGAGED STARTER MOTORS - REMOVAL & REPLACEMENT

1. Disconnect the battery by removing the earth lead from the negative terminal.
2. Disconnect the starter motor cable from the terminal on the starter motor end plate.
3. Remove the two solenoid retaining nuts and the connecting strap and lift off the solenoid.
4. Remove the upper starter motor retaining bolt.
5. Working under the car, remove the lower retaining bolt taking care to support the motor so as to prevent damage to the drive components.
6. Withdraw the starter motor from the bellhousing and lower it from the car.
7. Replacement is a straightforward reversal of the removal procedure.

19. ENDFACE COMMUTATOR STARTER MOTOR - DISMANTLING & REASSEMBLY

Due to the fact that this type of starter motor uses a face commutator, on which the brushes make contact end on, a certain amount of thrust is created along the armature shaft. A thrust bearing is therefore incorporated in the motor at the commutator end.

1. Remove the split pin from the end of the shaft and slide off the shim(s), washer and thrust plate.
2. Remove the two screws which retain the end plate and pull off the end plate complete with the brush holders and brushes.
3. Should the brushes have to be renewed follow the instructions given in Section 14, paragraph 9 of this chapter
4. To remove the armature, unscrew the nuts on the holding studs at the drive end bracket.
5. Withdraw the armature complete with the drive and the one way clutch operating lever.
6. Reassembly is a direct reversal of the above procedure, but the armature end float should be measured as indicated in Fig.10.3. The correct end float should be .010 in. (.254 mm.) with an 8 volt current activating the solenoid. If the end float is found to be incorrect it

can be corrected by fitting an appropriate sized shim or shims between the thrust plate and the split pin. NOTE: Never use the same split pin more than once.

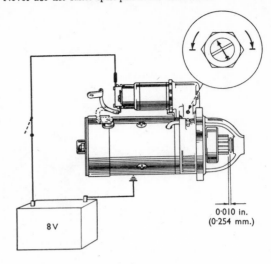

0·010 in.
(0·254 mm.)

8 V

Fig.10.3. Measuring armature endfloat

20. CONTROL BOX - GENERAL DESCRIPTION

1. The control box is positioned on the left-hand wing valance and comprises three units; two separate vibrating armature - type single contact regulators and a cut-out relay. One of the regulators is sensitive to changes in current and the other to changes in voltage.
2. Adjustments can only be made with a special tool which resembles a screwdriver with a multi-toothed blade. This can be obtained through Lucas agents.
3. The regulators control the output from the dynamo depending on the state of the battery and the demands of the electrical equipment, and ensures that the battery is not overcharged. The cut-out is really an automatic switch and connects the dynamo to the battery when the dynamo is turning fast enough to produce a charge. Similarly it disconnects the battery from the dynamo when the engine is idling or stationary so that the battery does not discharge through the dynamo.

21. CUT-OUT & REGULATOR CONTACTS - MAINTENANCE

1. Every 12,000 miles check the cut-out and regulator contacts. If they are dirty or rough or burnt place a piece of fine glass paper. (DO NOT USE EMERY PAPER OR CARBORUNDUM PAPER) between the cut-out contacts, close them manually and draw the glass paper through several times.
2. Clean the regulator contacts in exactly the same way, but use emery or carborundum paper and not glass paper. Carefully clean both sets of contacts from all traces of dust with a rag moistened in methylated spirits.

22. VOLTAGE REGULATOR ADJUSTMENT

1. The regulator requires very little attention during its service life, and should there be any reason to suspect its correct functioning, tests of all circuits should be made to ensure that they are not the reason for the trouble.
2. These checks include the tension of the fan belt, to make sure that it is not slipping and so providing only a very low charge rate. The battery should be carefully checked for possible low charge rate due to a faulty cell, or corroded battery connections.

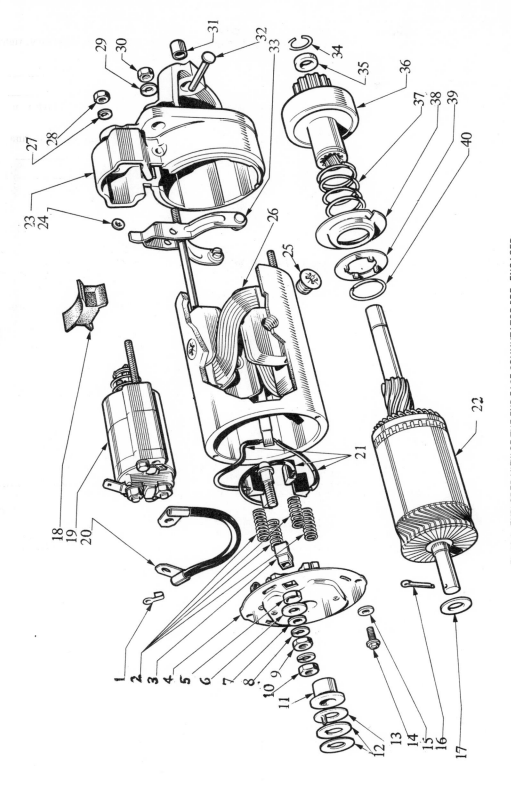

Fig.10.4. EXPLODED VIEW OF THE END FACE COMMUTATOR PRE–ENGAGED TYPE STARTER MOTOR

1 Hook
2 Brush springs
3 Insulator
4 Endplate & brush holder
5 Spacer
6 Washer
7 Washer
8 Lockwasher

9 Nut
10 Nut
11 Bush
12 Washers
13 Tabbed washer
14 Bolt
15 Washer
16 Split pin

17 Washer
18 Grommet
19 Solenoid assembly
20 Cable assembly
21 Brush assembly
22 Armature
23 Starter drive cover and starter motor endplate

24 Pin retaining ring
25 Field coil retaining screw
26 Field coils
27 Washer
28 Nut
29 Lockwasher
30 Nut
3: Bush

32 Lever swivel pin
33 Actuating lever
34 Circlip
35 Spacer
36 Pinion
37 Spring
38 Clutch assembly
39

40 Retaining ring

149

3. The leads from the generator may have been crossed during replacement, and if this is the case then the regulator points will have stuck together as soon as the generator starts to charge. Check for loose or broken leads from the generator to the regulator.

4. If after a thorough check it is considered advisable to test the regulator, this should only be carried out by an electrician who is well acquainted with the correct method, using test bench equipment.

5. Pull off the Lucar connections from the two adjacent control box terminals 'B'. To start the engine it will now be necessary to join together the ignition and battery leads with a suitable wire.

6. Connect a 0-30 volt voltmeter between terminal 'D' on the control box and terminal 'WL'. Start the engine and run it at 2,000 r.p.m. The reading on the voltmeter should be steady and lie between the limits detailed in the specification.

7. If the reading is unsteady this may be due to dirty contacts. If the reading is outside the specified limits stop the engine and adjust the voltage regulator in the following manner.

8. Take off the control box cover and start and run the engine at 2,000 r.p.m. Using the correct tool turn the voltage adjustment cam anti-clockwise to raise the setting and clockwise to lower it. To check that the setting is correct, stop the engine, and then start it and run it at 2,000 r.p.m. noting the reading. Refit the cover and the connections to the 'WL' and 'D' terminals.

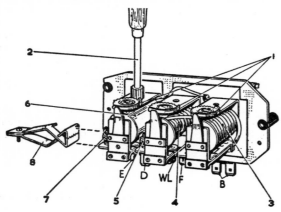

Fig.10.5. THE CONTROL BOX (COVER REMOVED)
1 Adjustment cams. 2 Setting tool. 3 Cut-out relay. 4 Current regulator. 5 Current regulator contacts. 6 Voltage regulator. 7 Voltage regulator contacts. 8 Clip.

23. CURRENT REGULATOR ADJUSTMENT

1. The output from the current regulator should equal the maximum output from the dynamo which is 22 amps. To test this it is necessary to bypass the cut-out by holding the contacts together.

2. Remove the cover from the control box and with a bulldog clip hold the cut-out contacts together. (See Fig.10.5.

3. Pull off the wires from the adjacent terminals 'B' and connect a 0-40 moving coil ammeter to one of the terminals and to the leads.

4. All the other load connections including the ignition must be made to the battery.

5. Turn on all the lights and other electrical accessories and run the engine at 2,000 r.p.m. The ammeter should give a steady reading between 19 and 22 amps. If the needle flickers it is likely that the points are dirty. If the reading is too low turn the special Lucas tool clockwise to raise the setting and anti-clockwise to lower it.

24. CUT-OUT ADJUSTMENT

1. Check the voltage required to operate the cut-out by connecting a voltmeter between the control box terminals 'D' and 'WL'. Remove the control box cover, start the engine and gradually increase its speed until the cut-outs close. This should occur when the reading is between 12.6 to 13.4 volts.

2. If the reading is outside these limits turn the cut-out adjusting cam (1 in the illustration) by means of the adjusting tool, a fraction at a time clockwise to raise the voltage, and anti-clockwise to lower it.

3. To adjust the drop off voltage bend the fixed contact blade carefully. The adjustment to the cut-out should be completed within 30 seconds of starting the engine as otherwise heat build-up from the shunt coil will affect the readings.

4. If the cut-out fails to work, clean the contacts, and, if there is still no response, renew the cut-out and regulator unit.

25. FUSES - GENERAL

Prior to 1969 no fuse box was used in the Cortina electrical circuits. In 1969 a fuse box containing six fuses was fitted and is located on the right-hand wing valance at the rear of the engine compartment. The circuits protected by these fuses are shown in Fig.10.6. If reversing lights are fitted a separate fuse protecting this circuit is located in the boot as a line fuse as shown in Fig.10.6.

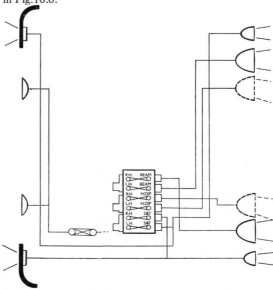

Fig.10.6. Diagram of the circuits protected by fuses

26. FLASHER CIRCUIT - FAULT TRACING & RECTIFICATION

1. The flasher unit is a small cylindrical metal container located under the dashboard on top of the steering column brace and is held in place by one Phillips screw. The unit is actuated by the direction indicator switch.

2. If the flasher unit fails to operate, or works very slowly or rapidly, check out the flasher indicator circuit as detailed below, before assuming that there is a fault in the unit.

a) Examine the direction indicator bulbs both front and rear for broken filaments.

b) If the external flashers are working but either of the internal flasher warning lights have ceased to function, check the filaments in the warning light bulbs and replace with a new bulb if necessary.

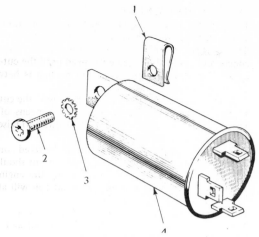

Fig.10.7. VIEW OF THE FLASHER UNIT ASSEMBLY
Clip. 2 Flasher to body retaining screw. 3 Shakeproof washer.
4 Flasher unit.

c) If a flasher bulb is sound but does not work check all the flasher circuit connections with the aid of the wiring diagram found at the end of this chapter.

d) With the ignition switched on check that the current is reaching the flasher unit by connecting a voltmeter between the 'plus' terminal and earth. If it is found that current is reaching the unit connect the two flasher unit terminals together and operate the direction indicator switch. If one of the flasher warning lights comes on this proves that the flasher unit itself is at fault and must be replaced as it is not possible to dismantle and repair it.

27. WINDSCREEN WIPER MECHANISM - MAINTENANCE

1. Renew the windscreen wiper blades at intervals of approximately 12,000 or more frequently if necessary.

2. The washer round the wheelbox spindle can be lubricated with several drops of glycerine every 6,000 miles. The windscreen wiper links can be lightly oiled at the same time.

28. WINDSCREEN WIPER BLADES - REMOVAL & REPLACEMENT

1. Lift the wiper arm away from the windscreen and remove the old blade by turning it in towards the arm and then disengage the arm from the slot in the blade.

2. To fit a new blade, slide the end of the wiper arm into the slotted spring fastening in the centre of the blade. Push the blade firmly onto the arm until the raised portion of the arm is fully home in the hole in the blade.

29. WINDSCREEN WIPER ARMS - REMOVAL & REPLACEMENT

1. Before removing a wiper arm, turn the windscreen wiper switch on and off to ensure the arms are in their normal parked position parallel with the bottom of the windscreen.

2. To remove an arm pivot the arm back and pull the wiper arm head off the splined drive. If the arm proves difficult to remove a screwdriver with a large blade can be used to lever the wiper arm head off the splines. Care must be taken not to damage the splines.

3. When replacing an arm position it, so it is in the correct relative parked position and then press the arm head onto the splined drive until it is fully home on the splines.

30. WINDSCREEN WIPER MECHANISM - FAULT DIAGNOSIS & RECTIFICATION

1. Should the windscreen wipers fail, or work very slowly, then check the terminals on the motor for loose connections, and make sure the insulation of all the wiring is not cracked or broken thus causing a short circuit. If this is in order then check the current the motor is taking by connecting an ammeter in the circuit and turning on the wiper switch. Consumption should be between 2.3 to 3.1 amps.

2. If no current is passing through the motor check that the switch is operating correctly.

3. If the wiper motor takes a very high current check the wiper blades for freedom of movement. If this is satisfactory check the gearbox cover and gear assembly for damage.

4. If the motor takes a very low current ensure that the battery is fully charged. Check the brush gear and ensure the brushes are bearing on the commutator. If not, check the brushes for freedom of movement and, if necessary, renew the tension springs. If the brushes are very worn they should be replaced with new ones. Check the armature by substitution if this unit is suspect.

31. WINDSCREEN WIPER SWITCH & WASHER ASSEMBLY - REMOVAL & REPLACEMENT

1. With a piece of thick wire push the pin on the underside of the switch knob upwards until it clears the hole in the knob and then pull off the knob.

2. Unscrew the chrome bezel and remove it together with the offset plastic distance piece.

3. Allow the switch assembly to drop below the fascia level and carefully note the positions of the three wires and two water pipes before removing them. NOTE: One of two types of switch may be fitted, one has a built in washer pump, while the second type has a detachable pump.

4. Replacement of the switch is a reversal of the above procedure but, before screwing in the bezel, ensure that the thickest part of the plastic distance piece, behind the bezel is uppermost, or the switch will not be at right angles to the fascia when tightened down.

32. WINDSCREEN WIPER MOTOR & LINKAGE - REMOVAL & REPLACEMENT

1. Disconnect the battery by removing the negative earth lead and then remove the wiper blades and arms as detailed in Sections 28 and 29 of this chapter.

2. In order to give enough room for manoeuvring the linkage, when disconnected, it is necessary to take out the glove compartment. This is done by drilling out the nine 'pop' rivets holding it in place.

3. Remove the demister flexible hoses and also the face level vent hoses as these will also get in the way if left in place.

4. Take out the three self tapping Phillips screws holding the heater trim panel in place and remove the trim panel.

5. The Author also found it necessary to remove his radio which was mounted in front of the heater trim panel, but this may not be necessary if the radio is mounted in alternative positions.

6. From outside the car remove the two large nuts holding the wiper spindles to the car bodywork.

7. Remove the wiper switch from the fascia as detailed in Section 31 and disconnect the wires from the switch to the wiper motor at their snap connectors.

8. Disconnect the black wire from its snap connector on the wiper motor.

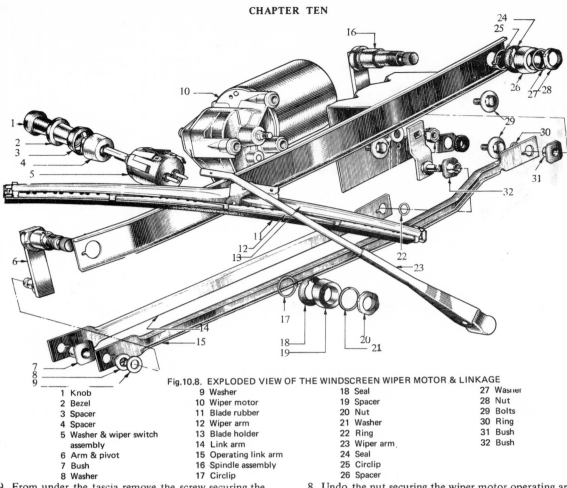

Fig.10.8. EXPLODED VIEW OF THE WINDSCREEN WIPER MOTOR & LINKAGE

1 Knob	9 Washer	18 Seal	27 Washer
2 Bezel	10 Wiper motor	19 Spacer	28 Nut
3 Spacer	11 Blade rubber	20 Nut	29 Bolts
4 Spacer	12 Wiper arm	21 Washer	30 Ring
5 Washer & wiper switch	13 Blade holder	22 Ring	31 Bush
assembly	14 Link arm	23 Wiper arm	32 Bush
6 Arm & pivot	15 Operating link arm	24 Seal	
7 Bush	16 Spindle assembly	25 Circlip	
8 Washer	17 Circlip	26 Spacer	

9. From under the fascia remove the screw securing the wiper motor bracket to the bodywork and then lower the motor and linkage out below the glove compartment hole.

10 Replacement is a straight forward reversal of the above procedure, but care must be taken to ensure that the spindles are properly located in their holes in the bodywork before tightening down the screw which holds the motor in place.

33. WINDSCREEN WIPER MOTOR - DISMANTLING, INSPECTION & REASSEMBLY

1. Start by removing the linkage mechanism from the motor. Carefully prise the short wiper link off the motor operating arm and remove the plastic pivot bush.

2. Undo the three screws which hold the linkage to the wiper motor and separate the two.

3. Unscrew the two bolts which hold the motor case to the gearbox housing and withdraw the motor case complete with the armature.

4. Take the brushes out of their holders and remove the brush springs.

5. Undo the three screws which hold the brush mounting plate to the wiper gearbox and remove the brush mounting plate.

6. Remove the earth contact on the gearbox cover plate by undoing the screw nearest the motor case. Undo the other screw on the gearbox cover plate and remove the cover plate and switch assembly.

7. Pull the spring steel armature stop out of the gearbox casing, then remove the spring clip and washer which retain the wiper pinion gear in place and withdraw the gear and washer.

8. Undo the nut securing the wiper motor operating arm and remove the lockwasher, arm, wave washer and flat washer in that order.

9. Having removed the operating arm withdraw the output gear, park switch assembly and washer from the gearbox casing.

10 Carefully examine all parts for signs of wear or damage and replace as necessary.

11 Reassembly is a direct reversal of the above procedure.

34. HORN - REMOVAL & REPLACEMENT

1. Disconnect the battery by removing the negative earth lead.

2. Remove both headlamp bezels by undoing the four retaining screws on each bezel.

3. Drill out the six 'pop' rivets and remove the two screws which hold the radiator grille to the car and remove the grille.

4. Make a careful note of the wires connected to the horn and disconnect them at their snap connectors.

5. Remove the two bolts securing the horn to the bodywork and lift out the horn. Replacement is a reversal of the above procedure.

35. HORN - FAULT TRACING & RECTIFICATION

1. If the horn works badly or fails to work altogether check all the wiring leading to the horn for cracks or breaks and also check that the snap connectors on the horn are clean and free from corrosion.

2. Check that the horn is secure on its mounting and that nothing is lying on the horn body.

3. If the fault is not an external one then the horn will have to be replaced as it is not possible to effect repairs.

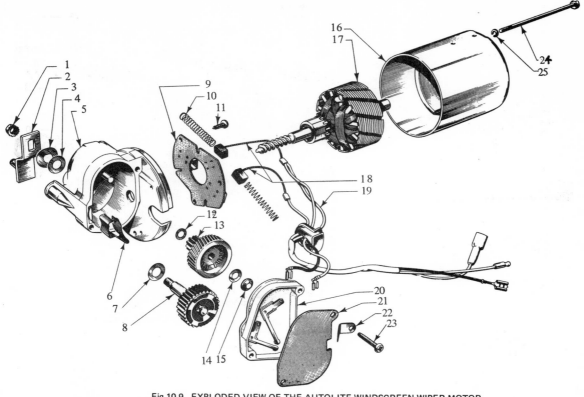

Fig.10.9. EXPLODED VIEW OF THE AUTOLITE WINDSCREEN WIPER MOTOR

1 Nut & shakeproof washer	8 Gear & shaft	15 Clip	21 Switch unit cover
2 Output arm	9 Brush holder plate	16 Wiper motor body & magnet	22 Terminal
3 Shim	10 Spring	assembly	23 Screw
4 Shim	11 Screw	17 Armature	24 Wiper motor through bolt
5 Gearbox casing	12 Shim	18 Brush assembly	25 Lockwasher
6 Stop	13 Gear & pinion	19 Wiper motor wiring loom	
7 Shim	14 Washer	20 Wiper parking switch body	

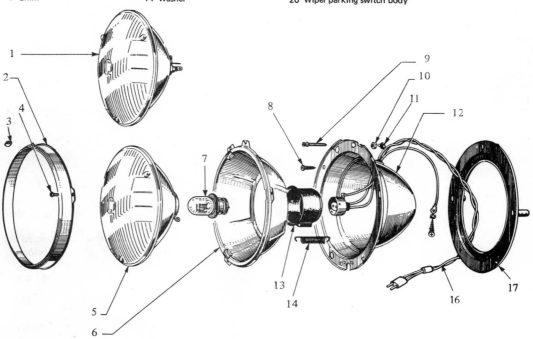

Fig.10.10. EXPLODED VIEW OF THE HEADLAMP UNIT

1 Sealed beam lamp unit	5 Semi-sealed beam lamp unit	9 Adjusting screw	13 Bulb & socket holder
2 Rim	6 Headlamp seating rim	10 Nut	14 Spring
3 Clip	7 Bulb	11 Screw housing	16 Wiring & adaptor assembly
4 Screw	8 Screw	12 Headlamp body assembly	17 Headlamp body gasket

36. SEALED BEAM HEADLAMP - REMOVAL & REPLACEMENT

1. Disconnect the battery by removing the negative earth lead.

2. Remove the four screws holding the head and sidelamp bezel in place and pull the bezel forward.

3. Undo the three screws holding the chrome headlamp bezel in place and remove the bezel.

4. Pull the sealed beam unit forward from its recess and disconnect the wiring plug at the back of the unit.

5. Replacement is a direct reversal of the above procedure, but it is always advisable to check the headlamps for correct alignment after replacing a unit. Headlamp alignment is dealt with in Section 37.

37. HEADLAMP ALIGNMENT

1. It is always advisable to have the headlamps aligned on proper optical beam setting equipment but if this is not available the following procedure may be used.

2. Position the car on level ground ten feet (3 metres) in front of a dark wall or board. The wall or board must be at right angles to the centre line of the car.

3. Draw a vertical line on the board in line with the centre line of the car.

4. Bounce the car on its suspension to ensure correct settlement and then measure the height between the ground and the centre of the headlamps.

5. Draw a horizontal line across the board at this measured height. On this horizontal line mark a cross 21.6 in. (54.85 cm) either side of the vertical centre line.

6. Remove the two head and sidelamp bezels by undoing the four screws on either side and switch the headlamps onto full beam;

7. By carefully adjusting the horizontal and vertical adjusting screws on each lamp, align the centres of each beam onto the crosses which you have previously marked on the horizontal line.

8. Bounce the car on its suspension again and check that the beams return to the correct positions. At the same time check the operation of the dip switch, replace the bezel.

38. FRONT SIDELAMP & INDICATOR LAMP - REMOVAL & REPLACEMENT

1. Disconnect the battery by removing the negative earth lead.

2. Remove the four screws holding the lead and sidelamp bezel in place and pull the bezel forward.

3. The side and indicator lamp assembly will come away with the bezel and can be removed by undoing the single retaining screw.

4. Pull the press fit bulb holders from their sockets and replace broken or damaged bulbs as necessary.

5. The lenses can be separated from the backplate by undoing the three retaining screws.

6. Reassembly and replacement is a reversal of the above procedure but, if the lenses have been removed, care must be taken to ensure that the sealing gasket is properly in place on reassembly or water will enter the lenses resulting in unnecessary damage.

39. TAIL, STOP & REAR INDICATOR LAMPS - BULB REMOVAL & REPLACEMENT

1. Open the boot lid or, in the case of estate cars, the tailgate and pull off the rear lamp cluster trim cover.

2. Pull the bulb holder which needs attention from its socket in the light cluster and remove the bulb by depressing it and rotating it in an anti-clockwise direction.

3. Replacement is a direct reversal of the removal procedure.

40. REAR NUMBER PLATE LAMP - BULB REMOVAL & REPLACEMENT

1. With a small screwdriver gently prise off the lamp cover from the top of the rear bumper.

2. The bulb which is a straight push fit is now exposed and can be replaced.

3. Push the lamp cover back into its retaining slots and check the operation of the new bulb.

41. INDICATOR, HEADLAMP FLASHER, DIPPER AND HORN SWITCH - REMOVAL & REPLACEMENT

1. Disconnect the battery by removing the negative earth lead.

2. Undo the four screws holding the steering column shrouds in place and remove the shrouds.

3. Remove the two screws retaining the switch assembly to the steering column.

4. Disconnect the switches multi-pin plug from the harness and remove the switch assembly.

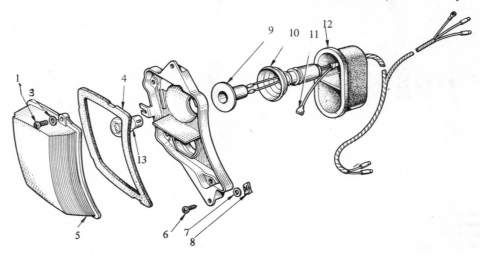

Fig.10.11. EXPLODED VIEW OF THE WING & FRONT FLASHER LAMPS (U.S.A.)

1 Screw	5 Lens	8 Clip	11 Lucar connector
3 Washer	6 Screw	9 Bulb holder	12 Grommet
4 Gasket	7 Washer	10 Bulb holder cover	13 Bulb

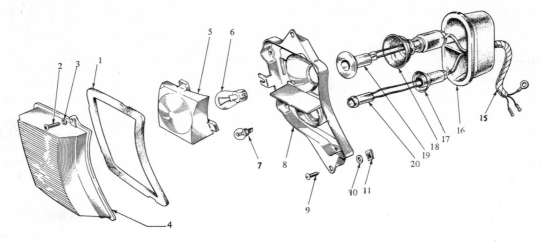

Fig.10.12. EXPLODED VIEW OF THE WING & FRONT FLASHER (NOT U.S.A.)

1 Gasket	6 Flasher bulb	11 Clip	19 Bulb holder-flasher
2 Screw	7 Sidelight bulb	15 Unit wiring loom	20 Bulb holder-sidelight
3 Washer	8 Unit body	16 Grommet	
4 Lens	9 Screw	17 Bulb holder cover-sidelight	
5 Flasher lens	10 Washer	18 Bulb holder cover-flasher	

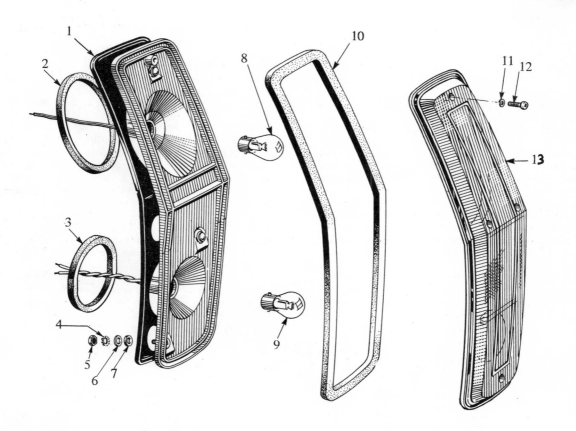

Fig.10.13. EXPLODED VIEW OF REAR LAMPS — ESTATE

1 Gasket	5 Nut	9 Bulb	13 Lens
2 Sealing ring	6 Washer	10 Gasket	
3 Sealing ring	7 Washer	11 Lockwasher	
4 Shakeproof washer	8 Bulb	12 Screw	

5. The switch unit is not repairable and, if defective, must be replaced. Reassembly is a direct reversal of the above procedure. Test the switch operations before taking the car on the road.

42. COMBINED FUEL GAUGE, TEMPERATURE GAUGE, OIL PRESSURE & IGNITION WARNING LIGHTS - REMOVAL & REPLACEMENT

1. The bulb illuminating the cluster and also the oil pressure warning light bulb and the ignition warning light bulb can be replaced without removal of the complete unit. The bulbs are located in push fit holders in the back of the instrument cluster and can be reached from under the fascia and replaced as necessary.

2. To completely remove the cluster press firmly with the tips of the fingers on the inner chrome ring surrounding the instruments. Then with the other, free, hand under the fascia rotate the whole instrument one third of a turn anti-clockwise.

3. This action will disengage the instrument and together with the outer bezel it can be pulled forward into the car.

4. Pull out the push fit bulb holders, making a careful note of their relative positions and disconnect the wiring to the two gauges, once again taking note of the wiring positions.

5. To remove the front glass turn the smaller chrome ring until it disengages from its slots and take out the glass and the inner panel.

6. The fuel and temperature gauges can now be removed by undoing the nuts on the back of the instrument and withdrawing the gauges through the front.

7. Reassembly of the complete unit and replacement is a direct reversal of the above procedure, but ensure that the outer large chrome bezel is located correctly with its two widest portions on either side of the instrument.

43. SPEEDOMETER HEAD & INSTRUMENT VOLTAGE REGULATOR - REMOVAL & REPLACEMENT

1. Working under the fascia undo the knurled nut on the end of the speedometer cable and withdraw the cable from the instrument.

2. Remove the instrument from the panel as described in Section 41 of this chapter.

3. Having pulled the speedometer forwards out of the fascia remove the illumination bulb and the main beam indicator bulb.

4. To remove the instrument voltage regulator, carefully note the relative position of the wires and pull them off. Then undo the single nut retaining the regulator to the back of the speedometer and remove the regulator.

5. Replacement is a straight forward reversal of the above procedure.

44. TACHOMETER (G.T. & 1600E) - REMOVAL & REPLACEMENT

1. The tachometer on G.T. and 1600E models is removed in the same way as described in Section 43 of this chapter.

2. Having pulled the instrument away from the fascia pull out the illumination bulb holder and disconnect the wiring making a careful note of their positions.

3. Replacement is a reversal of the removal sequence.

45. G.T. & 1600E FUEL GAUGE, OIL PRESSURE GAUGE, TEMPERATURE GAUGE & AMMETER - REMOVAL & REPLACEMENT

1. All the four small centrally mounted gauges on G.T. and 1600E models are removed in the same manner.

2. With the tips of the fingers push firmly on the instruments chrome ring and rotate the whole instrument approximately one third of a turn anti-clockwise until it disengages from its retaining lugs.

3. Pull the instrument out of the fascia and remove the illumination bulb holder. If the bulb is defective it can now be replaced.

4. Make a careful note of the wiring positions prior to taking off the wires and removing the instrument.

5. Replacement is a direct reversal of the removal instructions.

46. IGNITION SWITCH - REMOVAL & REPLACEMENT

1. Disconnect the battery by removing the negative earth lead.

2. Unscrew the ignition switch chrome bezel and push the switch through the fascia and allow it to drop below the facia.

3. After having made a careful note of the wiring positions disconnect the wires and remove the switch.

4. Replacement is a straight forward reversal of the removal procedure, but ensure that the key slot is in the vertical position before tightening down the chrome bezel.

47. LIGHT SWITCH & PANEL LIGHT SWITCH - REMOVAL & REPLACEMENT

1. Disconnect the battery by removing the negative earth lead.

2. Unscrew the small chrome bezel surrounding the switch and push the switch through the fascia.

3. Allow the switch to drop below the fascia, make a note of the wiring positions and disconnect the wires.

4. Replacement is a direct reversal of the removal instructions.

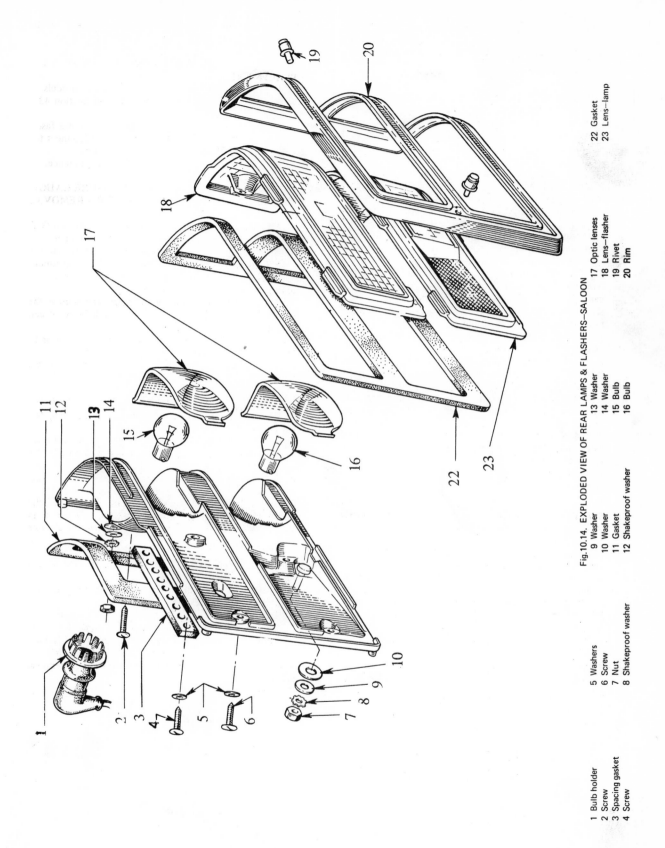

Fig.10.14. EXPLODED VIEW OF REAR LAMPS & FLASHERS—SALOON

1 Bulb holder	5 Washers	9 Washer	13 Washer	17 Optic lenses
2 Screw	6 Screw	10 Washer	14 Washer	18 Lens—flasher
3 Spacing gasket	7 Nut	11 Gasket	15 Bulb	19 Rivet
4 Screw	8 Shakeproof washer	12 Shakeproof washer	16 Bulb	20 Rim
				22 Gasket
				23 Lens—lamp

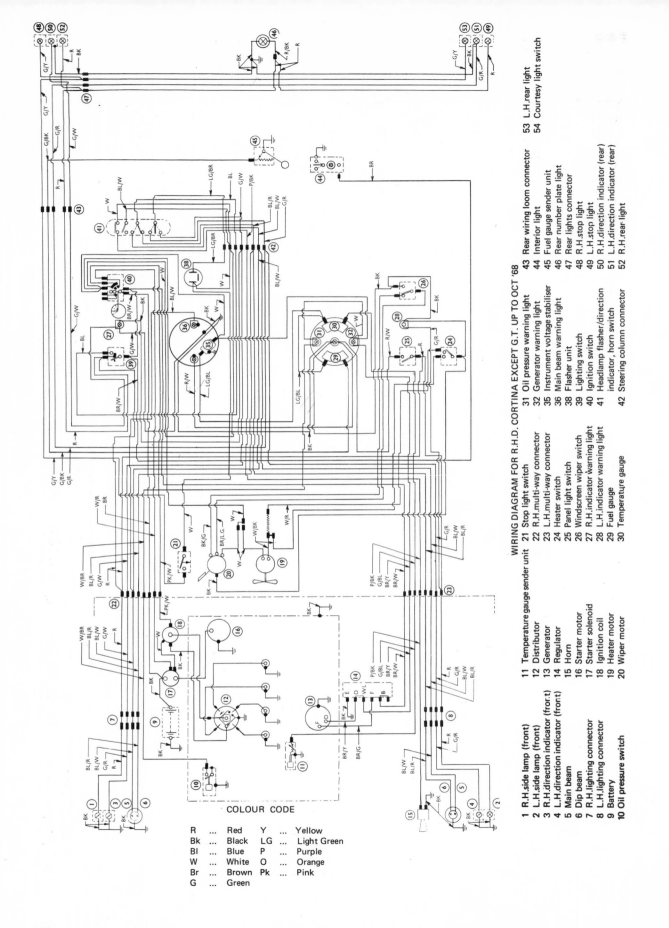

WIRING DIAGRAM FOR R.H.D. CORTINA EXCEPT G.T. UP TO OCT '68

1 R.H.side lamp (front)
2 L.H.side lamp (front)
3 R.H.direction indicator (fror.t)
4 L.H.direction indicator (front)
5 Main beam
6 Dip beam
7 R.H.lighting connector
8 L.H.lighting connector
9 Battery
10 Oil pressure switch

11 Temperature gauge sender unit
12 Distributor
13 Generator
14 Regulator
15 Horn
16 Starter motor
17 Starter solenoid
18 Ignition coil
19 Heater motor
20 Wiper motor

21 Stop light switch
22 R.H.multi-way connector
23 L.H.multi-way connector
24 Heater switch
25 Panel light switch
26 Windscreen wiper switch
27 R.H.indicator warning light
28 L.H.indicator warning light
29 Fuel gauge
30 Temperature gauge

31 Oil pressure warning light
32 Generator warning light
35 Instrument voltage stabiliser
36 Main beam warning light
38 Flasher unit
39 Lighting switch
40 Ignition switch
41 Headlamp flasher/direction
   indicator, horn switch
42 Steering column connector

43 Rear wiring loom connector
44 Interior light
45 Fuel gauge sender unit
46 Rear number plate light
47 Rear lights connector
48 R.H.stop light
49 L.H.stop light
50 R.H.direction indicator (rear)
51 L.H.direction indicator (rear)
52 R.H.rear light

53 L.H.rear light
54 Courtesy light switch

COLOUR CODE

R ...	Red	Y ...	Yellow
Bk ...	Black	LG ...	Light Green
Bl ...	Blue	P ...	Purple
W ...	White	O ...	Orange
Br ...	Brown	Pk ...	Pink
G ...	Green		

158

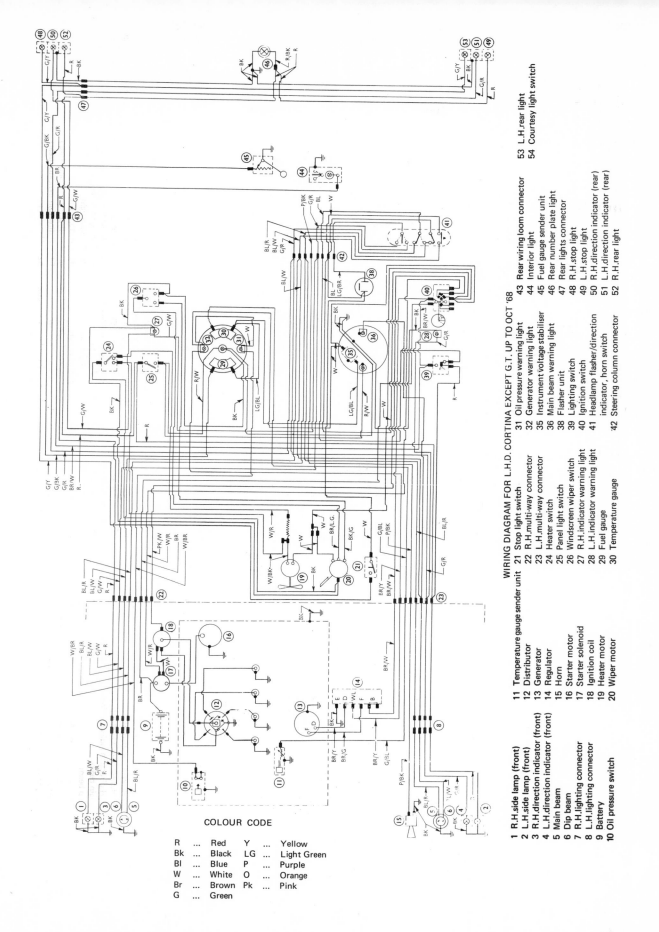

WIRING DIAGRAM FOR L.H.D. CORTINA EXCEPT G.T. UP TO OCT '68

1 R.H.side lamp (front)
2 L.H.side lamp (front)
3 R.H.direction indicator (front)
4 L.H.direction indicator (front)
5 Main beam
6 Dip beam
7 R.H.lighting connector
8 L.H.lighting connector
9 Battery
10 Oil pressure switch
11 Temperature gauge sender unit
12 Distributor
13 Generator
14 Regulator
15 Horn
16 Starter motor
17 Starter solenoid
18 Ignition coil
19 Heater motor
20 Wiper motor
21 Stop light switch
22 R.H.multi-way connector
23 L.H.multi-way connector
24 Heater switch
25 Panel light switch
26 Windscreen wiper switch
27 R.H.indicator warning light
28 L.H.indicator warning light
29 Fuel gauge
30 Temperature gauge
31 Oil pressure warning light
32 Generator warning light
35 Instrument voltage stabiliser
36 Main beam warning light
38 Flasher unit
39 Lighting switch
40 Ignition switch
41 Headlamp flasher/direction indicator, horn switch
42 Steering column connector
43 Rear wiring loom connector
44 Interior light
45 Fuel gauge sender unit
46 Rear number plate light
47 Rear lights connector
48 R.H.stop light
49 L.H.stop light
50 R.H.direction indicator (rear)
51 L.H.direction indicator (rear)
52 R.H.rear light
53 L.H.rear light
54 Courtesy light switch

COLOUR CODE

R	... Red	Y	... Yellow
Bk	... Black	LG	... Light Green
Bl	... Blue	P	... Purple
W	... White	O	... Orange
Br	... Brown	Pk	... Pink
G	... Green		

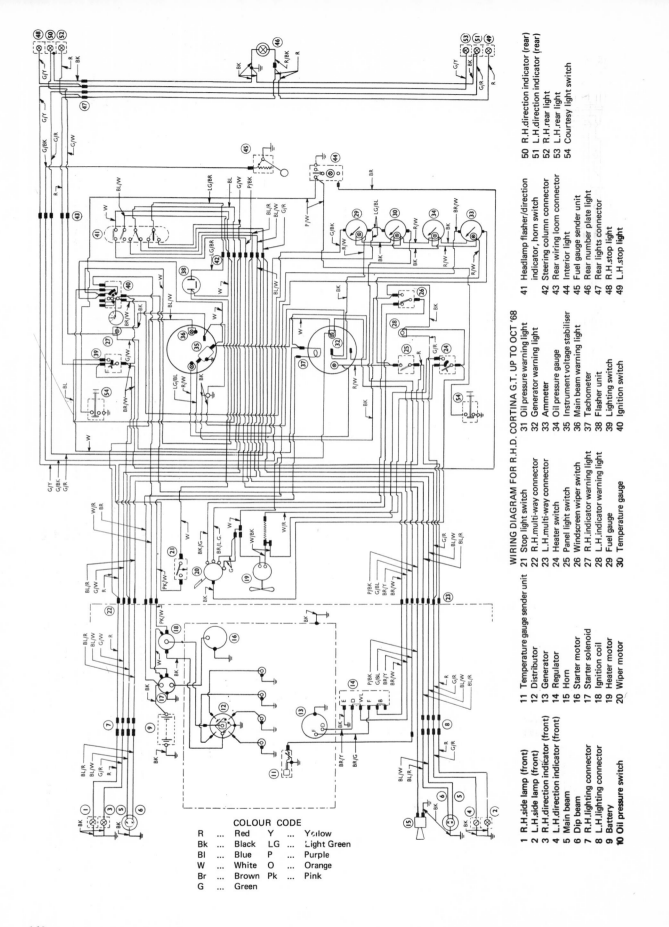

WIRING DIAGRAM FOR R.H.D. CORTINA G.T. UP TO OCT '68

1 R.H.side lamp (front)
2 L.H.side lamp (front)
3 R.H.direction indicator (front)
4 L.H.direction indicator (front)
5 Main beam
6 Dip beam
7 R.H.lighting connector
8 L.H.lighting connector
9 Battery
10 Oil pressure switch

11 Temperature gauge sender unit
12 Distributor
13 Generator
14 Regulator
15 Horn
16 Starter motor
17 Starter solenoid
18 Ignition coil
19 Heater motor
20 Wiper motor

21 Stop light switch
22 R.H.multi-way connector
23 L.H.multi-way connector
24 Heater switch
25 Panel light switch
26 Windscreen wiper switch
27 R.H.indicator warning light
28 L.H.indicator warning light
29 Fuel gauge
30 Temperature gauge

31 Oil pressure warning light
32 Generator warning light
33 Ammeter
34 Oil pressure gauge
35 Instrument voltage stabiliser
36 Main beam warning light
37 Tachometer
38 Flasher unit
39 Lighting switch
40 Ignition switch

41 Headlamp flasher/direction
   indicator, horn switch
42 Steering column connector
43 Rear wiring loom connector
44 Interior light
45 Fuel gauge sender unit
46 Rear number plate light
47 Rear lights connector
48 R.H.stop light
49 L.H.stop light

50 R.H.direction indicator (rear)
51 L.H.direction indicator (rear)
52 R.H.rear light
53 L.H.rear light
54 Courtesy light switch

COLOUR CODE

R ... Red   Y ... Yellow
Bk ... Black   LG ... Light Green
Bl ... Blue   P ... Purple
W ... White   O ... Orange
Br ... Brown   Pk ... Pink
G ... Green

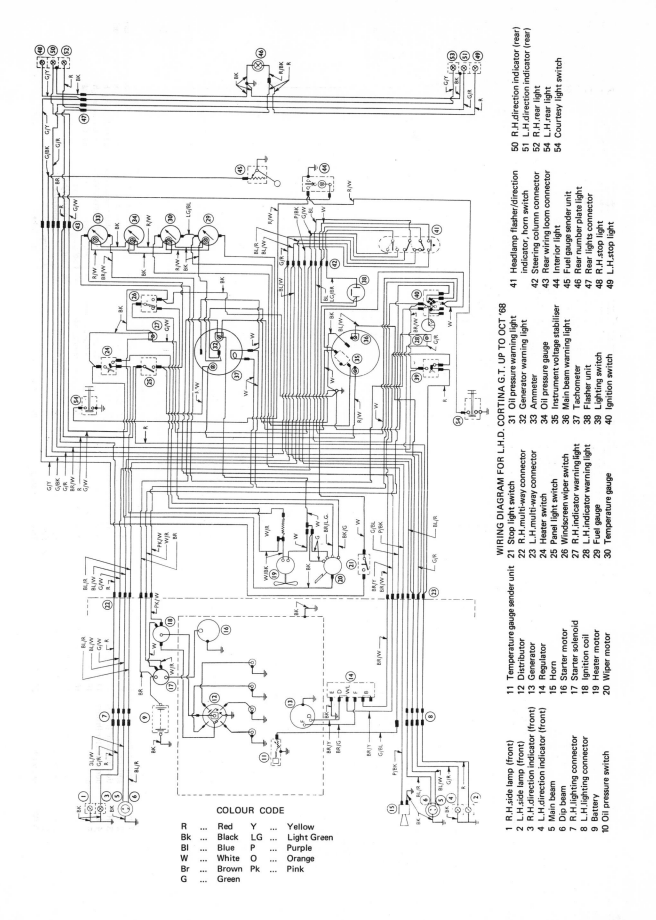

WIRING DIAGRAM FOR L.H.D. CORTINA G.T. UP TO OCT '68

1 R.H.side lamp (front)
2 L.H.side lamp (front)
3 R.H.direction indicator (front)
4 L.H.direction indicator (front)
5 Main beam
6 Dip beam
7 R.H.lighting connector
8 L.H.lighting connector
9 Battery
10 Oil pressure switch

11 Temperature gauge sender unit
12 Distributor
13 Generator
14 Regulator
15 Horn
16 Starter motor
17 Starter solenoid
18 Ignition coil
19 Heater motor
20 Wiper motor

21 Stop light switch
22 R.H.multi-way connector
23 L.H.multi-way connector
24 Heater switch
25 Panel light switch
26 Windscreen wiper switch
27 R.H.indicator warning light
28 L.H.indicator warning light
29 Fuel gauge
30 Temperature gauge

31 Oil pressure warning light
32 Generator warning light
33 Ammeter
34 Oil pressure gauge
35 Instrument voltage stabiliser
36 Main beam warning light
37 Tachometer
38 Flasher unit
39 Lighting switch
40 Ignition switch

41 Headlamp flasher/direction indicator, horn switch
42 Steering column connector
43 Rear wiring loom connector
44 Interior light
45 Fuel gauge sender unit
46 Rear number plate light
47 Rear lights connector
48 R.H.stop light
49 L.H.stop light

50 R.H.direction indicator (rear)
51 L.H.direction indicator (rear)
52 R.H.rear light
54 L.H.rear light
54 Courtesy light switch

COLOUR CODE

R	... Red	Y	... Yellow
Bk	... Black	LG	... Light Green
Bl	... Blue	P	... Purple
W	... White	O	... Orange
Br	... Brown	Pk	... Pink
G	... Green		

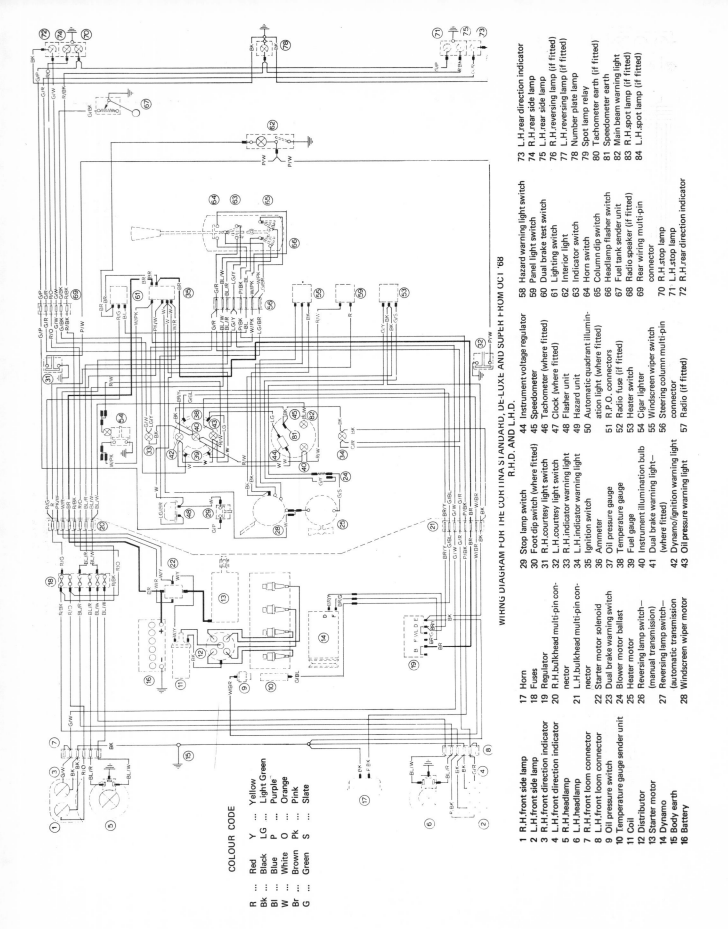

WIRING DIAGRAM FOR THE CORTINA STANDARD, DE-LUXE AND SUPER FROM OCT '68
R.H.D. AND L.H.D.

COLOUR CODE

R	...	Red	Y	...	Yellow
Bk	...	Black	LG	...	Light Green
Bl	...	Blue	P	...	Purple
W	...	White	O	...	Orange
Br	...	Brown	Pk	...	Pink
G	...	Green	S	...	Slate

1 R.H.front side lamp
2 L.H.front side lamp
3 R.H.front direction indicator
4 L.H.front direction indicator
5 R.H.headlamp
6 L.H.headlamp
7 R.H.front loom connector
8 L.H.front loom connector
9 Oil pressure switch
10 Temperature gauge sender unit
11 Coil
12 Distributor
13 Starter motor
14 Dynamo
15 Body earth
16 Battery

17 Horn
18 Fuses
19 Regulator
20 R.H.bulkhead multi-pin connector
21 L.H.bulkhead multi-pin connector
22 Starter motor solenoid
23 Dual brake warning switch
24 Blower motor ballast
25 Heater motor
26 Reversing lamp switch—(manual transmission)
27 Reversing lamp switch—(automatic transmission)
28 Windscreen wiper motor

29 Stop lamp switch
30 Foot dip switch (where fitted)
31 R.H.courtesy light switch
32 L.H.courtesy light switch
33 R.H.indicator warning light
34 L.H.indicator warning light
35 Ignition switch
36 Ammeter
37 Oil pressure gauge
38 Temperature gauge
39 Fuel gauge
40 Instrument illumination bulb
41 Dual brake warning light—(where fitted)
42 Dynamo/ignition warning light
43 Oil pressure warning light

44 Instrument voltage regulator
45 Speedometer
46 Tachometer (where fitted)
47 Clock (where fitted)
48 Flasher unit
49 Hazard unit
50 Automatic quadrant illumination light (where fitted)
51 R.P.O. connectors
52 Radio fuse (if fitted)
53 Heater switch
54 Cigar lighter
55 Windscreen wiper switch
56 Steering column multi-pin connector
57 Radio (if fitted)

58 Hazard warning light switch
59 Panel light switch
60 Dual brake test switch
61 Lighting switch
62 Interior light
63 Indicator switch
64 Horn switch
65 Column dip switch
66 Headlamp flasher switch
67 Fuel tank sender unit
68 Radio speaker (if fitted)
69 Rear wiring multi-pin connector
70 R.H.stop lamp
71 L.H.stop lamp
72 R.H.rear direction indicator

73 L.H.rear direction indicator
74 R.H.rear side lamp
75 L.H.rear side lamp
76 R.H.reversing lamp (if fitted)
77 L.H.reversing lamp (if fitted)
78 Number plate lamp
79 Spot lamp relay
80 Tachometer earth (if fitted)
81 Speedometer earth
82 Main beam warning light
83 R.H.spot lamp (if fitted)
84 L.H.spot lamp (if fitted)

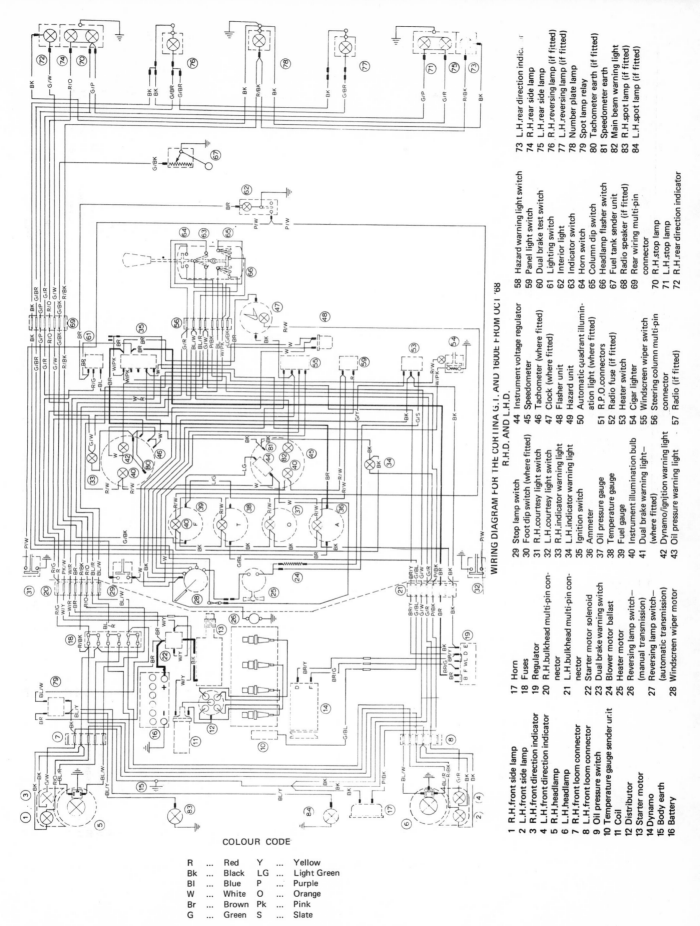

WIRING DIAGRAM FOR THE CORTINA G.T. AND 1600E FROM OCT '68
R.H.D. AND L.H.D.

1 R.H.front side lamp
2 L.H.front side lamp
3 R.H.front direction indicator
4 L.H.front direction indicator
5 R.H.headlamp
6 L.H.headlamp
7 R.H.front loom connector
8 L.H.front loom connector
9 Oil pressure switch
10 Temperature gauge sender unit
11 Coil
12 Distributor
13 Starter motor
14 Dynamo
15 Body earth
16 Battery
17 Horn
18 Fuses
19 Regulator
20 R.H.bulkhead multi-pin connector
21 L.H.bulkhead multi-pin connector
22 Starter motor solenoid
23 Dual brake warning switch
24 Blower motor ballast
25 Heater motor
26 Reversing lamp switch—
   (manual transmission)
27 Reversing lamp switch—
   (automatic transmission)
28 Windscreen wiper motor

29 Stop lamp switch
30 Foot dip switch (where fitted)
31 R.H.courtesy light switch
32 L.H.courtesy light switch
33 R.H.indicator warning light
34 L.H.indicator warning light
35 Ignition switch
36 Ammeter
37 Oil pressure gauge
38 Temperature gauge
39 Fuel gauge
40 Instrument illumination bulb
41 Dual brake warning light—
   (where fitted)
42 Dynamo/ignition warning light
43 Oil pressure warning light

44 Instrument voltage regulator
45 Speedometer
46 Tachometer (where fitted)
47 Clock (where fitted)
48 Flasher unit
49 Hazard unit
50 Automatic quadrant illumination light (where fitted)
51 R.P.O.connectors
52 Radio fuse (if fitted)
53 Heater switch
54 Cigar lighter
55 Windscreen wiper switch
56 Steering column multi-pin
   connector
57 Radio (if fitted)

58 Hazard warning light switch
59 Panel light switch
60 Dual brake test switch
61 Lighting switch
62 Interior light
63 Indicator switch
64 Horn switch
65 Column dip switch
66 Headlamp flasher switch
67 Fuel tank sender unit
68 Radio speaker (if fitted)
69 Rear wiring multi-pin
   connector
70 R.H.stop lamp
71 L.H.stop lamp
72 R.H.rear direction indicator

73 L.H.rear direction indic.
74 R.H.rear side lamp
75 L.H.rear side lamp
76 R.H.reversing lamp (if fitted)
77 L.H.reversing lamp (if fitted)
78 Number plate lamp
79 Spot lamp relay
80 Tachometer earth (if fitted)
81 Speedometer earth
82 Main beam warning light
83 R.H.spot lamp (if fitted)
84 L.H.spot lamp (if fitted)

COLOUR CODE

R	... Red	Y	... Yellow
Bk	... Black	LG	... Light Green
Bl	... Blue	P	... Purple
W	... White	O	... Orange
Br	... Brown	Pk	... Pink
G	... Green	S	... Slate

163

Cause	Trouble	Remedy
SYMPTOM:	**STARTER MOTOR FAILS TO TURN ENGINE**	
No electricity at starter motor	Battery discharged	Charge battery.
	Battery defective internally	Fit new battery.
	Battery terminal leads loose or earth lead not securely attached to body	Check and tighten leads.
	Loose or broken connections in starter motor circuit	Check all connections and tighten any that are loose.
	Starter motor switch or solenoid faulty	Test and replace faulty components with new.
Electricity at starter motor: faulty motor	Starter motor pinion jammed in mesh with flywheel gear ring	Disengage pinion by turning squared end of armature shaft.
	Starter brushes badly worn, sticking, or brush wires loose	Examine brushes, replace as necessary, tighten down brush wires.
	Commutator dirty, worn, or burnt	Clean commutator, recut if badly burnt.
	Starter motor armature faulty	Overhaul starter motor, fit new armature.
	Field coils earthed	Overhaul starter motor.
SYMPTOM:	**STARTER MOTOR TURNS ENGINE VERY SLOWLY**	
Electrical defects	Battery in discharged condition	Charge battery.
	Starter brushes badly worn, sticking, or brush wires loose	Examine brushes, replace as necessary, tighten down brush wires.
	Loose wires in starter motor circuit	Check wiring and tighten as necessary.
SYMPTOM:	**STARTER MOTOR OPERATES WITHOUT TURNING ENGINE**	
Dirt or oil on drive gear	Starter motor pinion sticking on the screwed sleeve	Remove starter motor, clean starter motor drive.
Mechanical damage	Pinion or flywheel gear teeth broken or worn	Fit new gear ring to flywheel, and new pinion to starter motor drive.
SYMPTOMS:	**STARTER MOTOR NOISY OR EXCESSIVELY ROUGH ENGAGEMENT**	
Lack of attention or mechanical damage	Pinion or flywheel gear teeth broken or worn	Fit new gear teeth to flywheel, or new pinion to starter motor drive.
	Starter drive main spring broken	Dismantle and fit new main spring
	Starter motor retaining bolts loose	Tighten starter motor securing bolts. Fit new spring washer if necessary.
SYMPTOM:	**BATTERY WILL NOT HOLD CHARGE FOR MORE THAN A FEW DAYS**	
Wear or damage	Battery defective internally	Remove and fit new battery.
	Electrolyte level too low or electrolyte too weak due to leakage	Top up electrolyte level to just above plates
	Plate separators no longer fully effective	Remove and fit new battery.
	Battery plates severely sulphated	Remove and fit new battery.
Insufficient current flow to keep battery charged	Fan/dynamo belt slipping	Check belt for wear, replace if necessary, and tighten.
	Battery terminal connections loose or corroded	Check terminals for tightness, and remove all corrosion.
	Dynamo not charging properly	Remove and overhaul dynamo.
	Short in lighting circuit causing continual battery drain	Trace and rectify.
	Regulator unit not working correctly	Check setting, clean, and replace if defective.
SYMPTOM:	**IGNITION LIGHT FAILS TO GO OUT, BATTERY RUNS FLAT IN A FEW DAYS**	
Dynamo not charging	Fan belt loose and slipping, or broken	Check, replace, and tighten as necessary.
	Brushes worn, sticking, broken, or dirty	Examine, clean, or replace brushes as necessary.
	Brush springs weak or broken	Examine and test. Replace as necessary.
	Commutator dirty, greasy, worn, or burnt	Clean commutator and undercut segment separators.

	Armature badly worn or armature shaft bent	Fit new or reconditioned armature.
	Commutator bars shorting	Undercut segment separations.
	Dynamo bearings badly worn	Overhaul dynamo, fit new bearings.
	Dynamo field coils burnt, open, or shorted.	Remove and fit rebuilt dynamo.
	Commutator no longer circular	Recut commutator and undercut segment separators.
	Pole pieces very loose	Strip and overhaul dynamo. Tighten pole pieces.
Regulator or cut-out fails to work correctly	Regulator incorrectly set	Adjust regulator correctly.
	Cut-out incorrectly set	Adjust cut-out correctly.
	Open circuit in wiring of cut-out and regulator unit	Remove, examine, and renew as necessary.

Failure of individual electrical equipment to function correctly is dealt with alphabetically, item by item, under the headings listed below:

FUEL GAUGE

Fuel gauge gives no reading	Fuel tank empty!	Fill fuel tank.
	Electric cable between tank sender unit and gauge earthed or loose	Check cable for earthing and joints for tightness.
	Fuel gauge case not earthed	Ensure case is well earthed.
	Fuel gauge supply cable interrupted	Check and replace cable if necessary.
	Fuel gauge unit broken	Replace fuel gauge.
Fuel gauge registers full all the time	Electric cable between tank unit and gauge broken or disconnected	Check over cable and repair as necessary.

HORN

Horn operates all the time	Horn push either earthed or stuck down	Disconnect battery earth. Check and rectify source of trouble.
	Horn cable to horn push earthed	Disconnect battery earth. Check and rectify source of trouble.
Horn fails to operate	Blown fuse	Check and renew if broken. Ascertain cause.
	Cable or cable connection loose, broken or disconnected	Check all connections for tightness and cables for breaks.
	Horn has an internal fault	Remove and overhaul horn.
Horn emits intermittent or unsatisfactory noise	Cable connections loose	Check and tighten all connections.
	Horn incorrectly adjusted	Adjust horn until best note obtained.

LIGHTS

Lights do not come on	If engine not running, battery discharged	Push-start car, charge battery.
	Light bulb filament burnt out or bulbs broken	Test bulbs in live bulb holder.
	Wire connections loose, disconnected or broken	Check all connections for tightness and wire cable for breaks.
	Light switch shorting or otherwise faulty	By-pass light switch to ascertain if fault is in switch and fit new switch as appropriate.
Lights come on but fade out	If engine not running battery discharged	Push-start car, and charge battery.
Lights give very poor illumination	Lamp glasses dirty	Clean glasses.
	Reflector tarnished or dirty	Fit new reflectors.
	Lamps badly out of adjustment	Adjust lamps correctly.
	Incorrect bulb with too low wattage fitted	Remove bulb and replace with correct grade
	Existing bulbs old and badly discoloured	Renew bulb units.
	Electrical wiring too thin not allowing full current to pass	Rewire lighting system.

ELECTRICAL SYSTEM

Cause	Trouble	Remedy
Lights work erratically – flashing on and off, especially over bumps	Battery terminals or earth connection loose Lights not earthing properly Contacts in light switch faulty	Tighten battery terminals and earth connection. Examine and rectify. By-pass light switch to ascertain if fault is in switch and fit new switch as appropriate.
WIPERS		
Wiper motor fails to work	Blown fuse Wire connections loose, disconnected, or broken Brushes badly worn Armature worn or faulty Field coils faulty	Check and replace fuse if necessary. Check wiper wiring. Tighten loose connections. Remove and fit new brushes. If electricity at wiper motor remove and overhaul and fit replacement armature. Purchase reconditioned wiper motor.
Wiper motor works very slowly and takes excessive current	Commutator dirty, greasy, or burnt Drive to wheelboxes too bent or un-lubricated Wheelbox spindle binding or damaged Armature bearings dry or unaligned Armature badly worn or faulty	Clean commutator thoroughly. Examine drive and straighten out severe curvature. Lubricate. Remove, overhaul, or fit replacement. Replace with new bearings correctly aligned. Remove, overhaul, or fit replacement armature.
Wiper motor works slowly and takes little current	Brushes badly worn Commutator dirty, greasy, or burnt Armature badly worn or faulty	Remove and fit new brushes. Clean commutator thoroughly. Remove and overhaul armature or fit replacement.
Wiper motor works but wiper blades remain static	Driving cable rack disengaged or faulty Wheelbox gear and spindle damaged or worn Wiper motor gearbox parts badly worn	Examine and if faulty, replace. Examine and if faulty, replace. Overhaul or fit new gearbox.

CHAPTER ELEVEN

SUSPENSION - DAMPERS - STEERING

CONTENTS

SPECIFICATIONS

Front Suspension	Independent MacPherson strut
Coil spring identification	
Standard...	Green
G.T.	Brown
Heavy duty	Yellow

Load	
Standard...	582 lb. (263.99 kg.)
G.T	599 lb. (271.70 kg.)
Heavy duty	582 lb. (263.99 kg.)
Mean diameter of coils	4.84 in. (12.29 cm)

Wire Diameter	
Standard...	.438 in. (11.13 mm)
G.T	.492 in. (12.50 mm)
Heavy duty	.460 in. (11.68 mm)

Shock absorber type	Telescopic direct double acting
Fluid capacity	350 c.c.
Bore diameter	1.25 in. (3.18 cm)
Stroke	8.16 in. (20.72 cm)
Castor	-0° 54' to +0° 36'
Camber	1°00' to 2° 30'
King pin inclination	6° 23' to 7° 53'
Toe-in..	.10 to .20 in. (2.8 to 5.2 mm)
Rear suspension..	Semi-elliptic leaf spring, radius arms on 1600E & early G.T models

Number of Spring Leaves:	
Standard up to Sept '67	4
Heavy duty up to Sept '67	5
Later saloons standard..	3
Later saloons heavy duty...	4
G.T Sept '67 on..	4
G.T heavy duty Sept '67 on	5
Estate Sept '67 on...	5
Estate heavy duty Sept '67 on	6
Spring length	47 in. (114.4 cm) between eye centres

Width of leaves...	2 in. (5,1 cm)
Shock absorber type (Saloons)	Telescopic double acting sealed
(Estate cars)	Twin cylinder lever arm
Steering type	Recirculating ball
Lubricant..	S.A.E.90 E.P.
Lubricant capacity... ... ... ?...	420 c.c.
Steering box ratio	16.4 to 1
Number of turns lock to lock	4½ approx.
Steering wheel diameter	15½ in. (40.4 cm)
Steering shaft bearing adjustment	Shims
Steering shaft bearing preload	.002 to .004 in. (.051 to .102 mm)
Steering shaft shims	.010 in. (.254 mm) paper 105E - 3592 - B
	.004 in. (.102 mm) steel 105E - 3595 - A
	.010 in. (.254 mm) steel 105E - 3595 - B
	.002 in. (.051 mm) steel 3014E - 3595 - A
Rocker shaft end float adjustment	Adjusting stud & locknut
Rocker shaft bush diameter	.8755 to .8765 in. (22.24 to 22.26 mm)
Number of balls in nut	13
Diameter...	5/16th in. (7.94 mm)
Number of balls in bearings (each)	12
Diameter...	7/32nd in. (5.56 mm)

Wheels & Tyres

Wheel sizes:-

All models up to Sept '67	4J x 13
DeLuxe saloons with crossply tyres..	4J x 13
Super saloons & estate with crossply tyres	4.5J x 13
With radial tyres	4.5J x 13
1600E..	5.5J x 13

Tyres		Normal pressure		Full load pressure	
		Front	Rear	Front	Rear
1300 saloon up to Sept '67	5.20 x 13 crossply...	24 (1.7)	24 (1.7)	24 (1.7)	26 (1.85)
	145 x 13 radial	24 (1.7)	24 (1.7)	24 (1.7)	30 (2.1)
1300 saloon from Sept '67	5.60 x 13 crossply...	24 (1.7)	24 (1.7)	24 (1.7)	28 (2.0)
	165 x 13 radial	24 (1.7)	28 (2.0)	24 (1.7)	28 (2.0)
1500 & GT up to Sept '67	5.60 x 13 crossply..	24 (1.7)	24 (1.7)	24 (1.7)	24 (1.7)
	155 x 13 radial	24 (1.7)	24 (1.7)	24 (1.7)	30 (2.1)
1600 c.c. Saloon	5.60 x 13 crossply..	24 (1.7)	24 (1.7)	24 (1.7)	28 (2.0)
	165 x 13 radial	24 (1.7)	28 (2.0)	24 (1.7)	28 (2.0)
Estate car	6.00 x 13 crossply..	24 (1.7)	24 (1.7)	24 (1.7)	33 (2.3)
	165 x 13 radial	24 (1.7)	30 (2.1)	24 (1.7)	30 (2.1)
1600 G.T.	165 x 13 radial	24 (1.7)	28 (2.0)	24 (1.7)	28 (2.0)
1600E	165 x 13 radial	24 (1.7)	24 (1.7)	24 (1.7)	30 (2.1)

Note:- The above tyre pressures are quoted in lb/sq.in. and in brackets kg/sq.cm. The above recommended pressures should be taken when the tyre is cold, as a hot tyre normally shows a higher pressure.

TORQUE WRENCH SETTINGS

Front suspension unit upper mounting bolts...	15 to 18 lb/ft. (2.07 to 2.49 kg.m)
Spindle to top mount assembly	28 to 32 lb/ft. (3.90 to 4.40 kg.m)
Track control arm ball stud nut...	30 to 35 lb/ft. (4.15 to 4.85 kg.m)
Stabiliser bar attachment clamps	15 to 18 lb/ft. (2.07 to 2.49 kg.m)
Stabiliser bar to track control arm nut...	25 to 30 lb/ft. (3.46 to 4.15 kg.m)
Crossmember to body sidemember...	25 to 30 lb/ft. (3.46 to 4.15 kg.m)
Radius arm to axle (1600E & G.T. only)	22 to 27 lb/ft. (3.04 to 3.73 kg.m)
Radius arm to body (1600E & G.T. only)..	45 to 50 lb/ft. (6.22 to 6.91 kg.m)
Shock absorber to body	15 to 20 lb/ft. (2.07 to 2.76 kg.m)
Shock absorber to axle	40 to 45 lb/ft. (5.54 to 6.22 kg.m)
Rear spring 'U' bolts	20 to 25 lb/ft. (2.76 to 3.46 kg.m)
Rear spring front hanger	25 to 30 lb/ft. (3.46 to 4.15 kg.m)
Rear spring axle shackle nuts..	12 to 15 lb/ft. (1.66 to 2.07 kg.m)
Steering idler arm bracket to body	25 to 30 lb/ft. (3.46 to 4.15 kg.m)
Drop arm nut	60 to 80 lb/ft. (8.2 to 11.0 kg.m)
Steering wheel nut...	20 to 25 lb/ft. (2.7 to 3.4 kg.m)
Spindle arm to front suspension unit	30 to 35 lb/ft. (4.15 to 4.85 kg.m)
Steering & idler arm joints	25 to 30 lb/ft. (3.46 to 4.15 kg.m)
Steering gear to body	25 to 30 lb/ft. (3.46 to 4.15 kg.m)
Steering gear top cover	18 to 20 lb/ft. (2.49 to 2.7 kg.m)
Brake calliper securing bolts...	45 to 50 lb/ft. (6.22 to 6.94 kg.m)

1. GENERAL DESCRIPTION

Each of the independent front suspension Macpherson Strut units consists of a vertical strut enclosing a double acting damper surrounded by a coil spring.

The upper end of each strut is secured to the front mudguard by rubber mountings, and the wheel spindle carrying the brake assembly and wheel hub is forged integrally with the suspension unit foot.

A track rod arm is connected to each unit, the inner end being mounted to the front crossmember in rubber bushes, while the outer end is connected to the steering arm.

A stabilising torsion bar is fitted between the outer ends of each track control arm and secured at the front to a mounting on the body sidemembers.

On all cars except G.T. and 1600E models, a rubber bump stop is fitted around the suspension unit piston rod. This comes into operation before the spring is fully compressed. As G.T. and 1600E models have harder springs the bump stop is not required.

When repairs are being carried out on any part of the front suspension unit it is essential that spring clips be fitted to the coil springs otherwise personal injury may result when dismantling the unit.

Whenever repairs have been carried out on a suspension unit it is essential to check the wheel alignment as the linkage could be altered which will affect the correct front wheel settings.

Every time the car goes over a bump vertical movement of a front wheel pushes the damper body upwards against the combined resistance of the coil spring and the damper piston.

Hydraulic fluid in the damper is displaced and it is then forced through the compression valve into the space between the inner and outer cylinder. On the downward movement of the suspension, the road spring forces the damper body downward against the pressure of the hydraulic fluid which is forced back again through the rebound valve. In this way the natural oscillations of the spring are damped out and a comfortable ride is obtained.

On the front uprights it is worth noting that there is a shroud inside the coil spring which protects the machined surface of the piston rod from road dirt.

The upper mounting assembly consists of a steel sleeve with a rubber bush bonded to it.

On models produced before August 1967 a thrust ball race is fitted in the rubber bush. This bearing can be renewed when necessary, but the mounting must be replaced as a complete assembly. On later models the bearing is replaced by a tapered rubber bush bonded to the top mounting.

The steering gear on the Cortina is of the worm and nut type with thirteen recirculatory balls running inside the nut. The steering box is attached to the right reinforced sidemember and an idler arm is fitted in a corresponding position on the opposite side of the engine compartment.

Inside the steering box a rocker shaft running in bushes has its splined bottom end fixed to the drop arm, and its top end connected to the nut.

Turning the steering wheel turns the shaft which, because the nut cannot turn screws it up or down. As the nut is connected to the rocker shaft this rotates so turning the drop arm.

Two adjustments are provided for the steering:-
a) Steering shaft bearing adjustment and
b) Rocker shaft end-float adjustment.

Only the rocker shaft end-float adjustment can be carried out with the steering box in position, and when it is evident that such adjustment is required, this will also indicate that the box needs a complete overhaul, and should be removed from the vehicle.

At the rear the axle is held by two inverted 'U' bolts at each end of the casing to underslung semi-elliptical leaf springs which provide both lateral and longitudinal location. On G.T. and 1600E models further stability is provided by addition of a radius arm on either side bolted to the front of the axle casing and to the bodyframe.

On saloon cars double acting telescopic dampers which work on the same principle as the front dampers are fitted.

On estate cars twin cylinder hydraulic dampers are fitted and work in principle in a similar way to those at the front but of course they are of a different design. On hitting a bump the damper arm moves the piston inside the larger cylinder so forcing hydraulic fluid past a valve to the second cylinder. As the wheel comes down bringing the arm with it the fluid is forced back into the first cylinder against the resistance of the valve so damping out the natural oscillation of the spring.

2. REAR SPRINGS - ROUTINE MAINTENANCE

Every 6,000 miles or sooner if the springs start to squeak, clean the dirt off the rear springs and spray them with penetrating oil. With a spanner check the inverted 'U' bolts for tightness. At the same time check the condition of the rubber bushes at either end of each spring.

3. STEERING GEAR - ROUTINE MAINTENANCE

Every 6,000 miles remove the plug on the top of the steering box and add Castrol Hypoy 90 Gear oil or any oil conforming to S.A.E.90 E.P. until the level reaches the filler plug hole. Then replace the filler plug.

3.0

4. FRONT HUB BEARINGS - MAINTENANCE, REMOVAL & REPLACEMENT

1. After jacking up the car and removing the front road wheel, disconnect the hydraulic brake pipe at the union on the suspension unit and either plug the open ends of the pipes, or have a jar handy to catch the escaping fluid.

2. Bend back the locking tabs on the two bolts holding the brake calliper to the suspension unit, undo the bolts and remove the calliper.

3. By judicious tapping and levering remove the dust cap from the centre of the hub.

4. Remove the split pin from the nut retainer and undo the larger adjusting nut from the stub axle.

5. Withdraw the thrust washer and the outer tapered bearing.

6. Pull off the complete hub and disc assembly from the stub axle.

7. From the back of the hub assembly carefully prise out the grease seal and remove the inner tapered bearing.

8. Carefully clean out the hub and wash the bearings with petrol making sure that no grease or oil is allowed to get onto the brake disc.

9. Working the grease well into the bearings fully pack the bearing cages and rollers with Castrolease LM or any suitable lithium based grease. NOTE Leave the hub and grease seal empty to allow for subsequent expansion of the grease.

10 To reassemble the hub assembly first fit the inner bearing and then gently tap the grease seal back into the hub. If the oil seal was at all damaged during removal a new one must be fitted.

11 Replace the hub and disc assembly on the stub axle and slide on the outer bearing and the thrust washer.

12 Tighten down the centre adjusting nut to a torque of 27 lb/ft. (3.73 kg.m) whilst rotating the hub and disc to ensure free movement then slacken the nut off 90° and hit the nut retainer and new split pin but at this stage do not bend back the split pin.

13 At this stage it is advisable, if a dial gauge is available to check the disc for run-out. The measurement should be taken as near to the edge of the worn, smooth part of

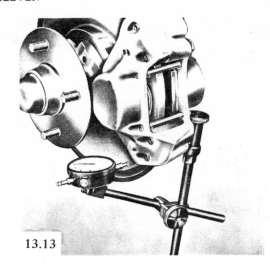

13.13

the disc as possible and must not exceed 0.004 in. (0.10 mm.). If this figure is found to be excessive check the mating surfaces of the disc and hub for dirt or damage and also check the bearings and cups for excessive wear or damage.

14 If a dial gauge is not available refit the calliper to the suspension unit, using new locking tabs, and tighten the securing bolts to a torque of 45 to 50 lb/ft. (6.22 to 6.94 kg.m.).

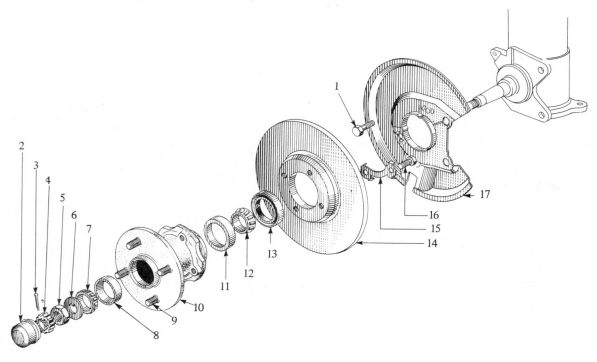

Fig.11.1 EXPLODED VIEW OF THE FRONT WHEEL DISC, HUB & BEARINGS

1 Bolt	6 Washer	11 Inner bearing race	16 Bolt
2 Dust cap	7 Outer bearing	12 Inner bearing	17 Brake lockplate
3 Split pin	8 Outer bearing race	13 Grease seal	
4 Castellated lock washer	9 Wheel stud	14 Brake disc	
5 Nut	10 Hub	15 Tab washer	

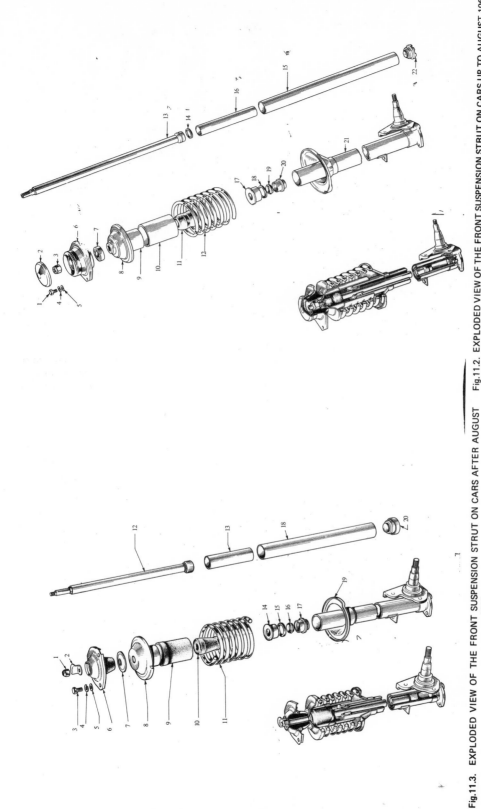

Fig. 11.3. EXPLODED VIEW OF THE FRONT SUSPENSION STRUT ON CARS AFTER AUGUST 1967

1 Nut
2 Rebound stop bracket
3 Bolt
4 Split washer
5 Washer
6 Upper mounting
7 Spring seat retainer

8 Upper spring seat
9 Spring seat extension
10 Bumper
11 Coil spring
12 Piston
13 Rebound stop tube
14 Piston rod gland cap

15 Outer tube oil seal ring
16 Piston rod gland
17 Piston rod bush & guide assembly
18 Cylinder
19 Tube & spindle assembly
20 Compression valve

Fig. 11.2. EXPLODED VIEW OF THE FRONT SUSPENSION STRUT ON CARS UP TO AUGUST 1967

1 Bolt
2 Dust cap
3 Nut
4 Split washer
5 Washer
6 Upper mounting
7 Bearing
8 Upper spring seat assembly

9 Upper spring seat assembly
10 Spring seat extension
11 Bumper
12 Coil spring
13 Piston
14 Piston ring
15 Cylinder
16 Rebound stop tube

17 Piston rod gland cap
18 Outer tube oil seal ring
19 Piston rod gland
20 Piston rod bush & guide assembly
21 Tube & spindle assembly
22 Compression valve

15 The brake disc run-out can now be checked by means of a feeler gauge or gauges between the casting of the calliper and the disc. Establish a reasonably tight fit with the gauges between the top of the casting and the disc (on the authors car it was found to be .041 in.) and rotate the disc and hub. Any high or low spot will immediately become obvious by the extra tightness or looseness of the fit of the gauges, and the amount of run-out can be checked by adding or subtracting gauges as necessary. It is only fair to point out that this method is not as accurate as when using a dial gauge owing to the rough nature of the calliper casting.

16 Once the disc run-out has been checked and found to be correct, bend the ends of the split pin back and replace the dust cap.

17 Reconnect the brake hydraulic pipe and bleed the brakes as described in Chapter 9, Section 3.

5.   FRONT HUB BEARINGS - ADJUSTMENT

1. To check the conditions of the hub bearings, jack up the front end of the car and grasp the road wheel at two opposite points to check for any rocking movement in the wheel hub. Watch carefully for any movement in the steering gear, which can easily be mistaken for hub movement.

2. If a front wheel hub has excessive movement, this is adjusted by removing the hub cap and then levering off the small dust cap. Remove the split pin through the stub axle and take off the adjusting nut retainer.

3. If a torque wrench is available tighten the centre adjusting nut down to a torque of 27 lb/ft. (3.73 kg.m) and then slacken it off 90° and replace the nut retainer and a new split pin.

4. Assuming a torque wrench is not available however, tighten up the centre nut until a slight drag is felt on rotating the wheel. Then loosen the nut very slowly until the wheel turns freely again and there is just a perceptible end-float.

5. Now replace the nut retainer, a new split pin and the dust cap.

6.   FRONT HUB - REMOVAL & REPLACEMENT

1. Follow the instructions given in Section 4 of this chapter up to and including paragraph 7.

2. Bend back the locking tabs and undo the four bolts holding the hub to the brake disc.

3. If a new hub assembly is being fitted it is supplied complete with new bearing cups and bearings. The bearing cups will already be fitted in the hub. It is essential to check that the cups and bearings are of the same manufacture; this can be done by reading the name on the bearings and by looking at the initial letter stamped on the hub. 'T' stands for Timken and 'S' for Skefco.

4. Clean with scrupulous care the mating surfaces of the hub and check for blemishes or damage. Any dirt or blemishes will almost certainly give rise to disc run-out. Using new locking tabs bolt the disc and the hub together and tighten the bolts to a torque or 30 to 34 lb/ft. (4.15 to 4.70 kg.m).

5. To grease and reassemble the hub assembly follow the instructions given in Section 4 paragraphs 9 on.

7.   FRONT SUSPENSION UNITS - REMOVAL & RE-PLACEMENT

1. It is difficult to work on the front suspension of the Cortina without one or two special tools, the most important of which are a set of spring clips which is Ford Tool No.P.5030. This tool is vital and no attempt should be made to remove or dismantle the units unless it is available.

2. Get someone to sit on the wing of the car and with the spring partially compressed in this way, fit the spring clips and secure them with the safety strap provided.

3. Jack up the car and remove the road wheel then disconnect the brake pipe at the bracket on the suspension leg and plug the pipes or have a jar handy to catch the escaping hydraulic fluid.

4. Working under the bonnet remove the upper bearing plastic dust cover if fitted, and then undo the three bolts securing the top end of the unit to the reinforced panel.

5. On earlier models disconnect the track rod from the steering arm by taking the split pin out of the castellated nut and undoing the nut. Then disconnect the track control arm at the base of the suspension by the same method.

6. On later models all that is required is to undo the three bolts attaching the lower end of the suspension unit to the steering and track control arms, having first knocked up the tab washers.

7. The suspension unit together with the hub can now be lowered from the car.

8. Using Ford tool No.P.5025 the upper bearing retaining nut can now be removed. The upper bearing, spring seat and the coil spring can then be lifted off.

9. Replacement is a reversal of the removal sequence but remember to use new locking tabs and split pins where these have been removed.

10 On later models the three bolts holding the steering and track control arms to the bottom of the suspension unit must be tightened down to a torque of 30 to 35 lb.ft. (4.15 to 4.84 kg.m).

8.   FRONT COIL SPRING - REMOVAL & REPLACEMENT

1. Get someone to sit on the front wing of the car and with the spring partially compressed in this way, fit the spring clips, Tool No.P.5030, and secure them with the safety strap.

2. Jack up the front of the car and remove the road wheel.

3. Working under the bonnet remove the upper bearing plastic dust cover, if fitted, and by using Tool No.P.5025 unscrew the upper bearing retaining nut and push the piston rod down as far as possible.

4. From under the car continue to push the piston down as far as it will go by which time it will be possible to remove the upper spring seat and also to manoeuvre the spring off its lower seat and out of the car.

5. If a new spring is being fitted check extremely carefully that it is of the same rating as the spring on the other side of the car. The springs are colour coded as follows:-

Green - standard.

Brown - G.T.

Yellow - heavy duty

6. Before fitting a new spring it must be compressed and the clips placed on the same number of coils as on the spring that has just been removed. A suitable spring compressor is Ford Tool No.P.5027.

7. Place the new spring over the piston and locate it on its bottom seat, then pull the piston rod upwards and fit the upper spring seat to it making sure that the 'D' shaped hole in the spring seat locates correctly with the flat on the piston rod.

8. From this point on, reassembly is a direct reversal of the removal sequence but when using Tool No.P.5025 and P.5026 to replace and tighten the upper bearing retaining nut it must be tightened to a torque of 45 to 55 lb/ft. (6.22 to 7.6 kg.m) on later cars with no bearing

or 28 to 32 lb/ft. (3.9 to 4.4 kg.m) on earlier cars with a bearing.

9. TORSION BAR - REMOVAL & REPLACEMENT

1. By getting someone to sit on each front wing in turn, compress each spring as much as possible and fit spring clips P.5030 to both springs and secure them with their safety straps.

2. Jack up the front of the car and remove both road wheels.

3. Working under the car at the front, knock back the locking tabs on the four bolts securing the two front clamps that hold the torsion bar to the frame and then undo the four bolts and remove the clamps and rubber insulators.

4. Remove the split pins from the castellated nuts retaining the torsion bar to the track control arms then undo the nuts and pull off the large washers and the plastic bushes, noting the way in which they are fitted.

5. Pull the torsion bar forwards out of the two track control rods and remove it from the car.

6. With the torsion bar out of the car remove the second plastic bush, the sleeve and large washer from each end of the bar making a careful note of the way in which they are fitted.

7. Reassembly is a reversal of the above procedure, but the castellated nuts on the ends of the torsion bar, and the four nuts on the front clamps, must not be fully tightened down until the spring clips have been removed and the car is resting on its wheels.

8. Once the car is on its wheels the castellated nuts on the end of the torsion bar should be tightened down to a torque of 25 to 30 lb/ft. (3.46 to 4.15 kg.m) and a new split pin used to secure the nut. The four clamp bolts on the front must also be tightened down to a torque of

15 to 18 lb/ft. (2.07 to 2.47 kg.m) and the locking tabs knocked up.

10. STEERING GEAR - REMOVAL & REPLACEMENT

1. To remove the steering gear from the car, first disconnect the battery by removing the negative earth lead.

2. Working inside the car carefully prise off the Cortina emblem from the centre of the steering wheel, bend back the locking tab on the steering wheel retaining nut and remove the nut. The steering wheel can now be pulled off its splines.

3. Remove the shrouds surrounding the upper end of the steering column by undoing the four recessed screws on the underside of the shrouds.

4. Unplug the wires to the combined indicator, dip and headlamp switch at the multi-pin connector and then remove the switch from its bracket on the column by undoing the two retaining screws.

5. If the car has a full width parcel shelf fitted this must also be removed by undoing the two screws at either end of the shelf.

6. By rolling back the carpet from round the pedals expose the floor plate and remove it by undoing the two securing screws.

7. Detach the brake pedal return spring from the bracket on the steering column and then undo the single bolt securing the steering column to the pedal bracket.

8. At the top of the column remove the two bolts securing the steering column to the fascia and remove the 'U' bracket.

9. Now jack up the complete front of the car and release the lower end of the drop arm from the drop arm to idler arm rod by removing the split pin and undoing the castellated nut.

10 Undo the three self locking nuts holding the steering box to the side of the car and push the bolts through

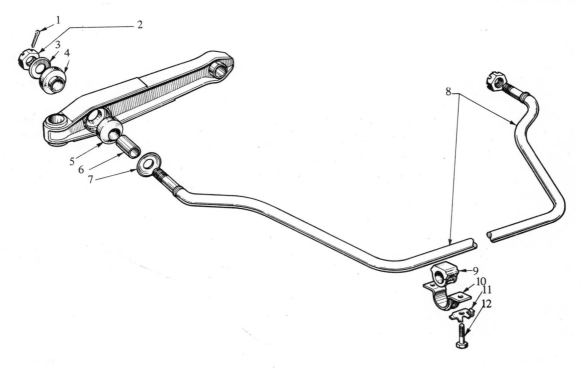

Fig. 11.4. EXPLODED VIEW OF THE STABILISER BAR

1 Split pin	4 Insulator	7 Stop washer	10 Clamp
2 Castellated nut	5 Insulator	8 Stabiliser bar	11 Tab washer
3 Washer	6 Sleeve	9 Bush	12 Bolt

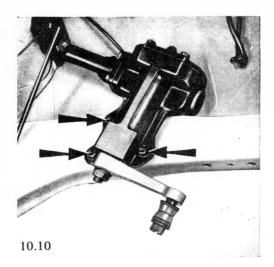

10.10

the wing and remove them from under the car. Note that there is a flat washer under each bolt head and also under each nut.

11 On all right-hand drive cars and all left-hand drive cars except the left-hand drive 1600E and G.T. the steering box complete with the steering.column can now be removed by withdrawing them from under the car.

12 On left-hand drive 1600E and G.T. cars the steering box and column must be removed through the top of the engine compartment. To do this it is necessary to remove the clutch slave cylinder and also the air cleaner. Details of these operations can be found in Chapter 5, Section 9, and Chapter 3, Section 2, respectively.

13 If it is required to remove the indicator cancelling cam this can be done by rotating the drop arm until the steering is in the straight ahead position and then making a careful note of the position of the cam on the splines at the top of the column before gently tapping it off.

14 When replacing the cam make absolutely sure it is located in exactly the same position as it was prior to removal.

15 Replacement of the steering assembly is a direct reversal of the above procedure but various points must be noted.

16 When refitting the steering box to the side of the car make certain that a flat washer is placed under each bolt head and nut and ensure that the self locking nuts are tightened down to a torque of 25 to 30 lb/ft. (3.4 to 4.1 kg.m.)

17 Before reassembling the drop arm to the idler arm rod the bores only of the conical rubber bushes should be lightly lubricated with hydraulic fluid. On reassembly the castellated nut should be tightened to a torque or 25 to 30 lb/ft. (3.4 to 4.1 kg.m) and always use a new split pin to lock the nut.

18 Before refitting the steering wheel onto its splines make sure that the drop arm is in the straight ahead position then push the wheel onto its splines and tighten the centre retaining nut to a torque of 20 to 25 lb/ft. (2.8 to 3.4 kg.m) before bending up the locking tab.

19 Finally after reassembly check the level of oil in the steering box by removing the plug and top up as necessary with Castrol Hypoy 90 gear oil or any oil conforming to S.A.E.90 E.P.

11. STEERING GEAR ROCKER SHAFT ENDFLOAT-ADJUSTMENT

1. Release the lower end of the drop arm from the drop arm to idler arm rod by removing the split pin and undoing the castellated nut.

2. Undo the adjusting stud and its locknut from the top of the steering box and clean all traces of sealing compound and dirt from the threads.

3. Centralise the steering gear so that it is in the straight ahead position. In this position the drop arm will be exactly parallel with the steering shaft.

4. Coat the adjusting stud with a suitable sealer and refit it to the steering box then loosely refit its locknut.

5. Attach a spring balance to the extreme edge of the steering wheel at its junction with one of the spokes.

6. By careful movement of the adjusting stud on the steering box establish a point where it requires a pull of 1.75 to 2 lbs on the spring balance to move the steering wheel.

7. Tighten down the locknut on the adjusting stud and check that the tension required at the steering wheel is still correct.

8. Once adjustment has been completed reconnect the lower end of the drop arm to the drop arm to idler arm rod by replacing the washer and castellated nut, tightening the nut to a torque of 25 to 30 lb/ft. (3.4 to 4.1 kg.m) Secure the nut with a new split pin.

12. REAR DAMPERS, TELESCOPIC TYPE - REMOVAL & REPLACEMENT

1. Chock the front wheels to prevent the car moving, then jack up the rear of the car and for convenience sake remove the road wheels.

2. Working inside the boot, hold the top of the piston and prevent it turning by holding a small spanner (¼ in.

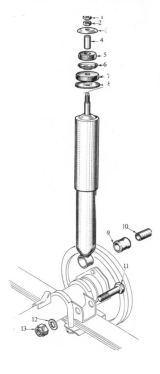

Fig.11.5. EXPLODED VIEW OF THE REAR DAMPER — SALOON
1 Locknut. 2 Nut. 3 Retaining washer. 4 Sleeve. 5 Rubber. 6 Retaining washer. 7 Rubber. 8 Washer. 9 Rubber bush. 10 Sleeve. 11 Through bolt. 12 Shakeproof washer. 13 Nut.

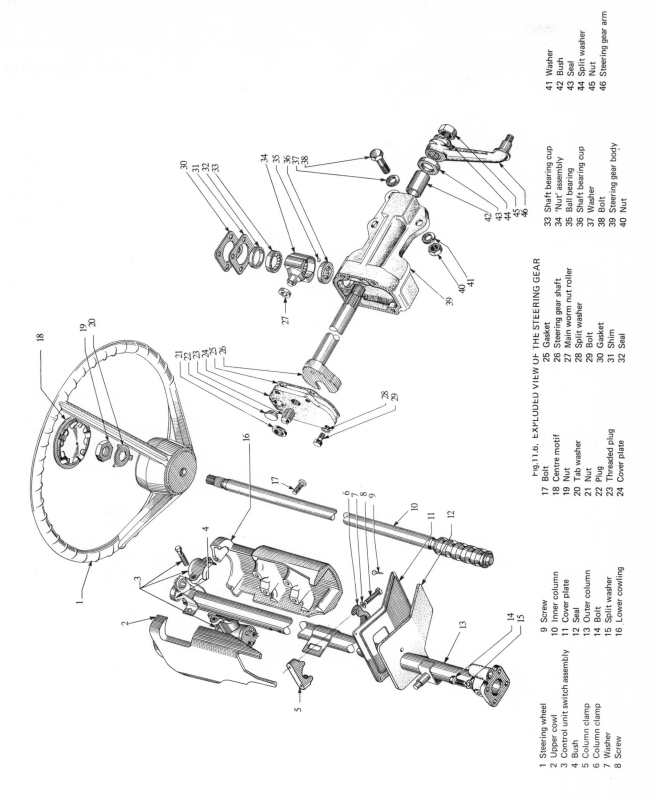

Fig. 11.6. EXPLODED VIEW OF THE STEERING GEAR

1 Steering wheel
2 Upper cowl
3 Control unit switch assembly
4 Bush
5 Column clamp
6 Column clamp
7 Washer
8 Screw
9 Screw
10 Inner column
11 Cover plate
12 Seal
13 Outer column
14 Bolt
15 Split washer
16 Lower cowling

17 Bolt
18 Centre motif
19 Nut
20 Tab washer
21 Nut
22 Plug
23 Threaded plug
24 Cover plate
25 Gasket
26 Steering gear shaft
27 Main worm nut roller
28 Split washer
29 Bolt
30 Gasket
31 Shim
32 Seal

33 Shaft bearing cup
34 'Nut' assembly
35 Ball bearing
36 Shaft bearing cup
37 Washer
38 Bolt
39 Steering gear body
40 Nut
41 Washer
42 Bush
43 Seal
44 Split washer
45 Nut
46 Steering gear arm

A/F across the flats provided and then with an open ended spanner remove the locknut and main nut from the piston rod.

3. Lift off the large dished steel washer, the rubber bush and where fitted the second dished washer.

4. Working under the car remove the nut, lockwasher and bolt that retain the lower end of the damper to the axle casing.

5. Lower the damper from the car then remove the further rubber bush and steel washer from the top of the piston rod.

6. Replacement is a reversal of the above procedure, but care must be taken to ensure that the dished steel washers are all fitted with their lips towards the adjacent rubber bushes.

7. The nut on the bolt securing the lower end of the damper must be tightened down to a torque of 40 to 45 lb.ft. (5.54 to 6.22 kg.m).

8. The main nut on the top mounting must be tightened to a torque of 15 to 20 lb/ft. (2.07 to 2.76 kg.m) but the piston must be prevented from rotating during this operation. Most torque wrenches will not allow the flats on the piston rod to be held to prevent turning so it is better to get an assistant to hold the upper half of the damper from under the car.

13. REAR DAMPERS, DROP ARM TYPE - REMOVAL & REPLACEMENT

1. This type of damper is only fitted to Cortina Estate cars and is removed in the following way.

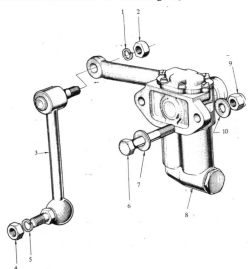

Fig.11.7. EXPLODED VIEW OF THE REAR DAMPER — ESTATE
1 Split washer. 2 Nut. 3 Swivel arm. 4 Nut. 5 Split washer. 6 Bolt. 7 Washer. 8 Damper body. 9 Nut. 10 Washer.

2. Chock the front wheels to prevent the car moving then jack up the rear of the car and for convenience sake remove the road wheels.

3. Undo the two self locking nuts and spring washers which retain the damper to the body side panel and then undo the nut and spring washer holding the link arm to the axle casing.

4. The damper can now be removed from the car, and the link arm removed from the damper by undoing the single retaining nut and spring washer.

5. Replacement of the unit is a direct reversal of the above instructions.

14. REAR SPRINGS - REMOVAL & REPLACEMENT

1. Chock the front wheels to prevent the car moving, then jack up the rear of the car and support it on suitable stands. To make the springs more accessible remove the road wheels.

2. Then place a further jack underneath the differential to give support to the rear axle when the springs are removed. Do not raise the jack under the differential so that the springs are flattened, but raise it just enough to take the full weight of the axle with the spring fully extended.

3. Undo the rear shackle nuts and remove the combined shackle bolt and plate assemblies. Then remove the four rubber bushes. When working on the rear of the left-hand spring it is necessary to remove the spare wheel from the boot and take out the rubber grommet in the side of the spare wheel well.

4. Undo the nut from the front mounting bracket and take out the bolt running through the mounting.

5. Undo the nuts on the ends of the four 'U' bolts and remove the 'U' bolts together with the attachment plates under the nuts. The spring can now be removed from the car.

7. Replacement is a direct reversal of the above procedure. The nuts on the spring 'U' bolts, spring front mounting and spring rear mounting shackles must be torqued down to the figures given in the specifications at the beginning of this chapter only AFTER the car has been lowered onto its wheels.

14.7

15. G.T. & 1600E RADIUS ARMS - REMOVAL & REPLACEMENT

1. Chock the front wheels to prevent the car moving, then jack up the rear of the car and support it on suitable stands.

2. Undo the nut and remove the bolt holding the rear end of the radius arm to the axle casing.

3. Repeat this procedure on the front mounting nut and bolt and remove the radius arm from the car.

4. Replacement is a reversal of the above procedure but the nuts should be torqued down to the figures given in the specifications at the beginning of this chapter AFTER the car has been lowered onto its wheels.

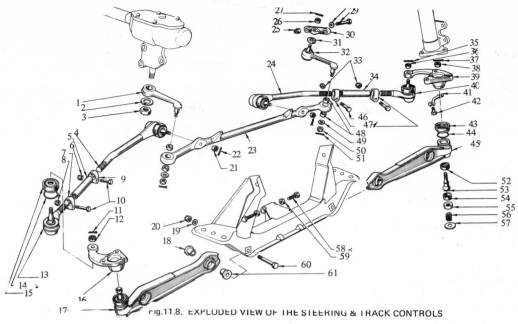

Fig.11.8. EXPLODED VIEW OF THE STEERING & TRACK CONTROLS

1	Steering gear arm	17	Track control arm	33	Nuts
2	Split washer	18	Bush	34	Drag link adjusting sleeve
3	Nut	19	Washer	35	Split pin
4	Spindle arm connectin rod	20	Nut	36	Castellated nut
5	Drag link adjusting sleeve	21	Castellated nut	37	Split pin
6	Nut	22	Split pin	38	Castellated nut
7	Sleeve clamp	23	Drop arm to idler arm rod	39	Steering spindle arm
8	Nut	24	Spindle arm connecting rod	40	Ball joint assembly
9	Sleeve clamp	25	Nut	41	Tab washer
10	Clamp bolts	26	Castellated nut	42	Bolt
11	Split pin	27	Split pin	43	Ball stud seal
12	Castellated nut	28	Washer	44	Seal retaining ring
13	Ball joint assembly	29	Bolt	45	Track control arm
14	Dust seal retaining ring	30	Idler arm mounting bracket	46	Clamp bolt
15	Ball joint dust seal	31	Washer	47	Sleeve clamps
16	Steering spindle arm	32	Idler cam	48	Bushes

49	Washer		
50	Castellated nut		
51	Split pin		
52	Seal		
53	Ball & stud assembly		
54	Seal		
55	Spacer		
56	Spring		
57	Cap		
58	Bolt		
59	Nut		
60	Bolt		
61	Bush		

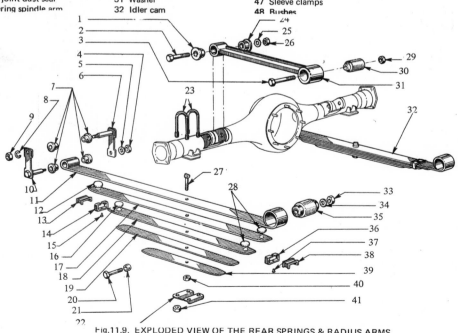

Fig.11.9. EXPLODED VIEW OF THE REAR SPRINGS & RADIUS ARMS

1	Bush	12	Insert	23	'U' bolts
2	Through bolt	13	Clamp insulator	24	Bush
3	Through bolt	14	Leaf clamp	25	Washer
4	Nut	15	Pin	26	Nut
5	Washer	16	Insert	27	Special bolt
6	Shackle bar & stud	17	No.2 leaf spring	28	Inserts
7	Shackle bushes	18	No.3 leaf spring	29	Nut
8	Split washer	19	No.4 leaf spring	30	Bush
9	Nut	20	Bolt	31	Radius arm
10	Shackle bar & stud	21	Spacer	32	Leaf spring assembly
11	No.1 leaf spring	22	'U' bolt plate	33	Nut

34	Washer
35	Bush
36	Leaf clamp
37	Pin
38	Clamp insulator
39	No.5 leaf spring
40	Nut
41	Nut

SUSPENSION – DAMPERS – STEERING

FAULT FINDING CHART

Cause	Trouble	Remedy
SYMPTOM:	STEERING FEELS VAGUE, CAR WANDERS AND FLOATS AT SPEED	
General wear or damage	Tyre pressures uneven Dampers worn or require topping up Spring clips broken Steering gear ball joints badly worn Suspension geometry incorrect Steering mechanism free play excessive Front suspension and rear axle pick-up points out of alignment	Check pressures and adjust as necessary. Top up dampers, test, and replace if worn. Renew spring clips. Fit new ball joints. Check and rectify. Adjust or overhaul steering mechanism. Normally caused by poor repair work after a serious accident. Extensive rebuilding necessary.
SYMPTOM:	STIFF & HEAVY STEERING	
Lack of maintenance or accident damage	Tyre pressures too low No grease in king pins No oil in steering gear No grease in steering and suspension ball joints Front wheel toe-in incorrect Suspension geometry incorrect Steering gear incorrectly adjusted too tightly Steering column badly misaligned	Check pressures and inflate tyres. Clean king pin nipples and grease thoroughly. Top up steering gear. Clean nipples and grease thoroughly. Check and reset toe-in. Check and rectify. Check and readjust steering gear. Determine cause and rectify (Usually due to bad repair after severe accident damage and difficult to correct).
SYMPTOM:	WHEEL WOBBLE & VIBRATION	
General wear or damage	Wheel nuts loose Front wheels and tyres out of balance Steering ball joints badly worn Hub bearings badly worn Steering gear free play excessive Front springs loose, weak or broken	Check and tighten as necessary. Balance wheels and tyres and add weights as necessary. Replace steering gear ball joints. Remove and fit new hub bearings. Adjust and overhaul steering gear. Inspect and overhaul as necessary.

CHAPTER TWELVE

BODYWORK AND UNDERFRAME

CONTENTS

1. GENERAL DESCRIPTION

The combined body and underframe is of an all steel welded construction. This makes a very strong and torsionally rigid shell.

The Cortina is available in either two door or four door form. The door hinges are securely bolted to both the doors and the body. The driver's door is locked from the outside by means of the key, all other doors being locked from the inside. Due to the efficiency of the 'Airoflow' type of ventilation system non opening front door quarter lights are fitted as standard equipment, but the opening type are available as an optional extra.

Toughened safety glass is fitted to all windows; as an additional safety precaution the windscreen glass has a specially toughened 'zone' in front of the driver. In the event of the windscreen shattering this 'Zone' breaks into much larger pieces than the rest of the screen thus giving the driver much better vision than would otherwise be possible.

The interior of all models is basically the same except that the G.T. and 1600E models have a more comprehensive range of instruments including separate ammeter, oil pressure gauge, fuel gauge and water temperature gauge all mounted centrally high up on the fascia. The normal combined instrument on the fascia being replaced by a tachometer.

All models have bucket type front seats but bench type front seating is available as an optional extra on cars with remote control gearchange or automatic transmission.

2. MAINTENANCE - BODYWORK & UNDERFRAME

1. The condition of your car's bodywork is of consider-able importance as it is on this that the second-hand value of the car will mainly depend. It is very much more difficult to repair neglected bodywork than to renew mechanical assemblies. The hidden portions of the body, such as the wheel arches and the underframe and the engine compartment are equally important, though obviously not requiring such frequent attention as the immediately visible paintwork.

2. Once a year or every 12,000 miles, it is a sound scheme to visit your local main agent and have the underside of the body steam cleaned. This will take about 1½ hours and cost about £4. All traces of dirt and oil will be removed and the underside can then be inspected carefully for rust, damaged hydraulic pipes, frayed electrical wiring and similar maladies. The car should be greased on completion of this job.

3. At the same time the engine compartment should be cleaned in the same manner. If steam cleaning facilities are not available then brush 'Gunk' or a similar cleanser over the whole engine and engine compartment with a stiff paint brush, working it well in where there is an accumulation of oil and dirt. Do not paint the ignition system but protect it with oily rags when the Gunk is washed off. As the Gunk is washed away it will take with it all traces of oil and dirt, leaving the engine looking clean and bright.

4. The wheel arches should be given particular attention as undersealing can easily come away here and stones and dirt thrown up from the road wheels can soon cause the paint to chip and flake, and so allow rust to set in. If rust is found, clean down the bare metal with wet and dry paper, paint on an anti-corrosive coating such as Kurust, or if preferred, red lead, and renew the paintwork and undercoating.

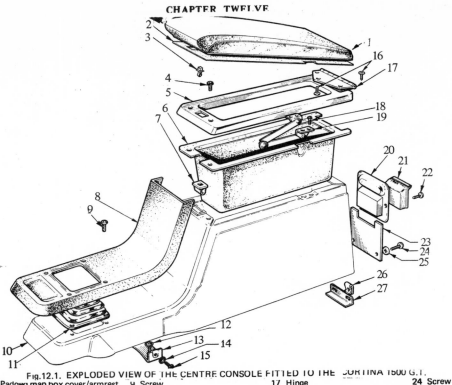

Fig.12.1. EXPLODED VIEW OF THE CENTRE CONSOLE FITTED TO THE CORTINA 1500 G.T.

1	Padded map box cover/armrest	9	Screw	17	Hinge
2	Cover base plate	10	Console body	18	Screw
3	Catch	11	Gearlever gaiter	19	Mapbox lid stay
4	Screw	12	Screw	20	Ash tray holder
5	Map box surround trim	13	Bracket	21	Ash tray
6	Map box	14	Washer	22	Screw
7	Lower half of catch	15	Screw	23	Ashtray assembly retaining plate
8	Trim panel	16	Screws		

24	Screw
25	Washer
26	Screw clip
27	Bracket-rear

5. The bodywork should be washed once a week or when dirty. Thoroughly wet the car to soften the dirt and then wash the car down with a soft sponge and plenty of clean water. If the surplus dirt is not washed off very gently, in time it will wear the paint down as surely as wet and dry paper. It is best to use a hose if this is available. Give the car a final washdown and then dry with a soft chamois leather to prevent the formation of spots.

6. Spots of tar and grease thrown up from the road can be removed with a rag dampened with petrol.

7. Once every six months, or every three months if wished, give the bodywork and chromium trim a thoroughly good wax polish. If a chromium cleaner is used to remove rust on any of the car's plated parts remember that the cleaner also removes part of the chromium so use sparingly.

3.   MAINTENANCE - UPHOLSTERY & CARPETS

1. Remove the carpets and thoroughly vacuum clean the interior of the car every three months or more frequently if necessary.

2. Beat out the carpets and vacuum clean them if they are very dirty. If the headlining or upholstery is soiled apply an upholstery cleaner with a damp sponge and wipe off with a clean dry cloth.

4.   MINOR BODY REPAIRS

1. At some time during your ownership of your car it is likely that it will be bumped or scraped in a mild way, causing some slight damage to the body.

2. Major damage must be repaired by your local Ford agent, but there is no reason why you cannot successfully beat out, repair, and respray minor damage your-

self. The essential items which the owner should gather together to ensure a really professional job are:-

a) A plastic filler such as Holts 'Cataloy'.

b) Paint whose colour matches exactly that of the bodywork, either in a can for application by a spray gun, or in an aerosol can.

c) Fine cutting paste.

d) Medium and fine grade wet and dry paper.

3. Never use a metal hammer to knock out small dents as the blows tend to scratch and distort the metal. Knock out the dent with a mallet or rawhide hammer and press on the underside of the dented surface a metal dolly or smooth wooden block roughly contoured to the normal shape of the damaged area.

4. After the worst of the damaged area has been knocked out, rub down the dent and surrounding area with medium wet and dry paper and thoroughly clean away all traces of dirt.

5. The plastic filler comprises a paste and a hardener which must be thoroughly mixed together. Mix only a small portion at a time as the paste sets hard within five to fifteen minutes depending on the amount of hardener used.

6. Smooth on the filler with a knife or stiff plastic to the shape of the damaged portion and allow to thoroughly dry - a process which takes about six hours. After the filler has dried it is likely that it will have contracted slightly so spread on a second layer of filler if necessary.

7. Smooth down the filler with fine wet and dry paper wrapped round a suitable block of wood and continue until the whole area is perfectly smooth and it is impossible to feel where the filler joins the rest of the paintwork.

8. Spray on from an aerosol can, or with a spray gun, an anti-rust undercoat, smooth down with wet and dry

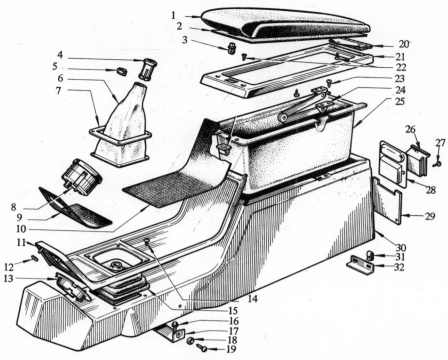

Fig.12.2. EXPLODED VIEW OF THE CENTRE CONSOLE UNIT FITTED TO EARLY
1600 G.T. & 1600E CORTINAS

1 Padded arm rest	9 Finish panel	17 Bracket	25 Map box
2 Map box cover	10 Finish panel	18 Washer	26 Ash tray
3 Catch	11 Trim panel	19 Screw	27 Screw
4 Gaiter cap	12 Clip	20 Hinge	28 Ash tray retainer
5 Clip	13 Clock holder	21 Map box trim	29 Ash tray backplate
6 Gearlever gaiter	14 Screw	22 Screws	30 Console body moulding
7 Gaiter retaining rim	15 Rubber gaiter	23 Screw	31 Clip
8 Clock	16 Bolt	24 Map box lid stay	32 Bracket

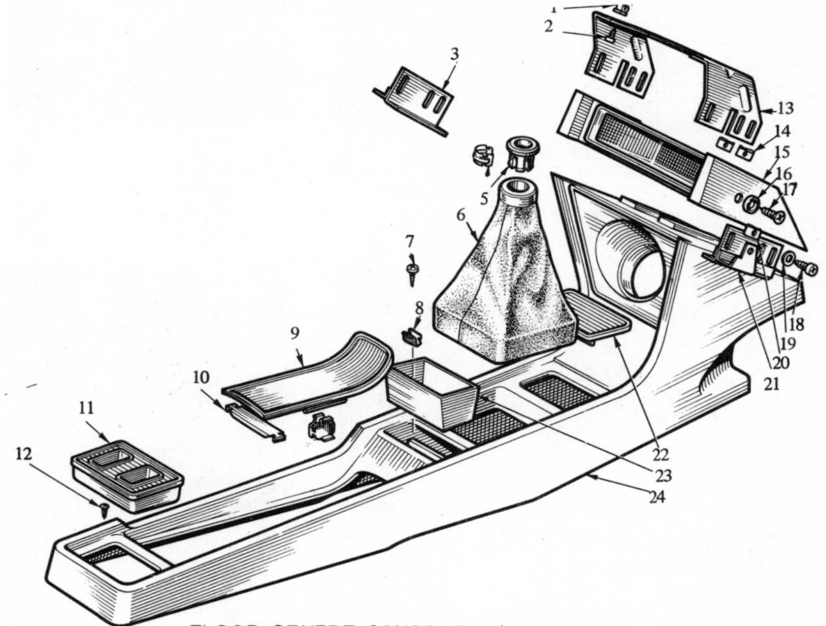

FLOOR CENTRE CONSOLE-10/68/-

Fig.12.3. EXPLODED VIEW OF THE CENTRE CONSOLE UNIT FITTED TO LATER
1600 G.T. & 1600E CORTINAS

1 Clip	7 Screw	13 Console/instrument panel	19 Washer
2 Screw	8 Clip	bracket	20 Screw plates
3 Bracket	9 Finish panel	14 Screw plates	21 Bracket
4 Clip	10 Brace	15 Glove/radio compartment	22 Finish panel
5 Gaiter cap	11 Seat belt buckle retainer	16 Spacer	23 Ash tray/receptacle
6 Gear lever gaiter	12 Screw	17 Screw	24 Console body moulding

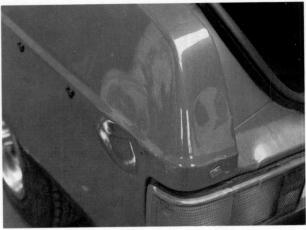

This sequence of photographs deals with the repair of the dent and scratch (above rear lamp) shown in this photo. The procedure will be similar for the repair of a hole. It should be noted that the procedures given here are simplified - more explicit instructions will be found in the text

In the case of a dent the first job - after removing surrounding trim - is to hammer out the dent where access is possible. This will minimise filling. Here, the large dent having been hammered out, the damaged area is being made slightly concave

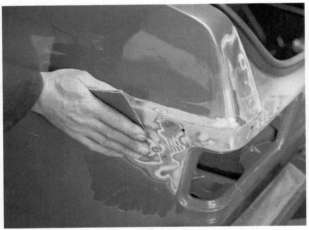

Now all paint must be removed from the damaged area, by rubbing with coarse abrasive paper. Alternatively, a wire brush or abrasive pad can be used in a power drill. Where the repair area meets good paintwork, the edge pf the paintwork should be 'feathered', using a finer grade of abrasive paper

In the case of a hole caused by rusting, all damaged sheet-metal should be cut away before proceeding to this stage. Here, the damaged area is being treated with rust remover and inhibitor before being filled

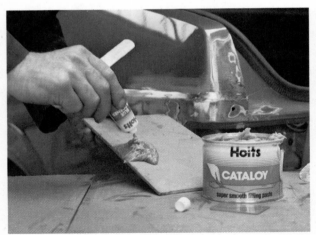

Mix the body filler according to its manufacturer's instructions. In the case of corrosion damage, it will be necessary to block off any large holes before filling - this can be done with zinc gauze or aluminium tape. Make sure the area is absolutely clean before ...

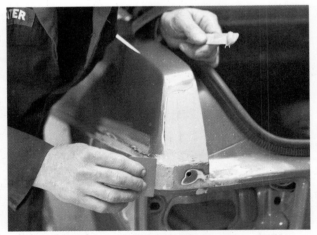

... applying the filler. Filler should be applied with a flexible applicator, as shown, for best results: the wooden spatula being used for confined areas. Apply thin layers of filler at 20-minute intervals, until the surface of the filler is slightly proud of the surrounding bodywork

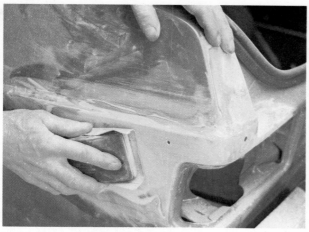

Initial shaping can be done with a Surform plane or Dreadnought file. Then, using progressively finer grades of wet-and-dry paper, wrapped around a sanding block, and copious amounts of clean water, rub-down the filler until really smooth and flat. Again, feather the edges of adjoining paintwork

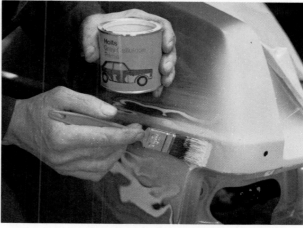

The whole repair area can now be sprayed or brush-painted with primer. If spraying, ensure adjoining areas are protected from over-spray. Note that at least one-inch of the surrounding sound paintwork should be coated with primer. Primer has a 'thick' consistency, so will fill small imperfections

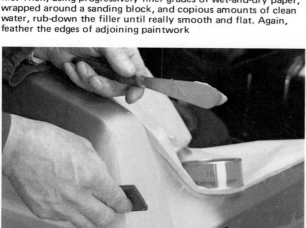

Again, using plenty of water, rub down the primer with a fine grade of wet-and-dry paper (400 grade is probably best) until it is really smooth and well blended into the surrounding paint-work. Any remaining imperfections can now be filled by carefully applied knifing stopper paste

When the stopper has hardened, rub-down the repair area again before applying the final coat of primer. Before rubbing-down this last coat of primer, ensure the repair area is blemish-free - use more stopper if necessary. To ensure that the surface of the primer is really smooth use some finishing compound

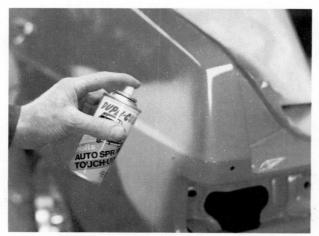

The top coat can now be applied. When working out of doors, pick a dry, warm and wind-free day. Ensure surrounding areas are protected from over-spray. Agitate the aerosol thoroughly, then spray the centre of the repair area, working outwards with a circular motion. Apply the paint as several thin coats.

After a period of about two-weeks, which the paint needs to harden fully, the surface of the repaired area can be 'cut' with a mild cutting compound prior to wax polishing. When carrying out bodywork repairs, remember that the quality of the finished job is proportional to the time and effort expended paper, and then spray on two coats of the final finishing using a circular motion.

9. When thoroughly dry polish the whole area with a fine cutting paste to smooth the resprayed area into the remainder of the wing and to remove the small particles of spray paint which will have settled round the area.

10 This will leave the wing looking perfect with not a trace of the previous unsightly dent.

5. MAJOR BODY REPAIRS

1. Because the body is built on the monocoque principle and is integral with the underframe, major damage must be repaired by competent mechanics with the necessary welding and hydraulic straightening equipment.

2. If the damage has been serious it is vital that the body is checked for correct alignment, as otherwise the handling of the car will suffer and many other faults such as excessive tyre wear and wear in the transmission and steering may occur. Fords produce a special alignment jig and to ensure that all is correct a repaired car should always be checked on this jig.

6. MAINTENANCE - HINGES & LOCKS

Once every six months or 6,000 miles the door, bonnet and boot hinges should be oiled with a few drops of engine oil from an oil can. The door striker plates can be given a thin smear of grease to reduce wear and ensure free movement.

7. FRONT BUMPER - REMOVAL & REPLACEMENT

1. Undo the single retaining bolt on either end of the bumper from inside the front wings of the car.

2. Working under the bumper remove the nuts from the two chrome headed bolts, remove the bolts and lift off the bumper.

3. Replacement is a reversal of the above procedure, but before replacing the two bolts from insdie the wings ensure that the bumper is straight and firm. To make sure this is correct it is advisable not to tighten the centre bolts fully down until the end bolts have been located.

8. REAR BUMPER - REMOVAL & REPLACEMENT

1. Remove the rear number plate illumination light as detailed in Chapter 10, Section 40.

2. Working under the bumper, remove the nuts from the four chrome headed bolts, take out the bolts and lift off the bumper.

3. Replacement is a direct reversal of the above procedure, but ensure the bumper is straight and properly located before finally tightening down the bolts.

9. WINDSCREEN GLASS - REMOVAL & REPLACEMENT

1. If you are unfortunate enough to have a windscreen shatter, or should you wish to renew your present windscreen, fitting a replacement is one of the few jobs which the average owner is advised to leave to a professional. For the owner who wishes to attempt the job himself the following instructions are given.

2. Cover the bonnet with a blanket or cloth to prevent accidental damage and remove the windscreen wiper blades and arms as detailed in Chapter 10, Sections 28 and 29.

3. Put on a pair of lightweight shoes and get into one of the front seats. With a piece of soft cloth between the soles of your shoes and the windscreen glass, place both feet in one top corner of the windscreen and push firmly.

4. When the weatherstrip has freed itself from the body flange in that area repeat the process at frequent intervals along the top edge of the windscreen until, from outside

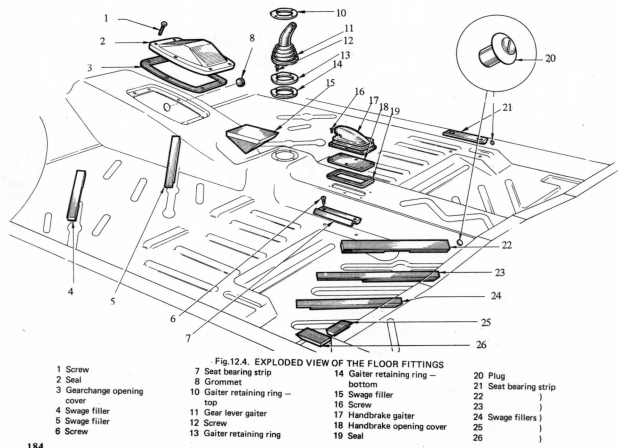

Fig.12.4. EXPLODED VIEW OF THE FLOOR FITTINGS

1 Screw	7 Seat bearing strip	14 Gaiter retaining ring — bottom	20 Plug
2 Seal	8 Grommet	15 Swage filler	21 Seat bearing strip
3 Gearchange opening cover	10 Gaiter retaining ring — top	16 Screw	22)
4 Swage filler	11 Gear lever gaiter	17 Handbrake gaiter	23)
5 Swage fiiler	12 Screw	18 Handbrake opening cover	24 Swage fillers)
6 Screw	13 Gaiter retaining ring	19 Seal	25)
			26)

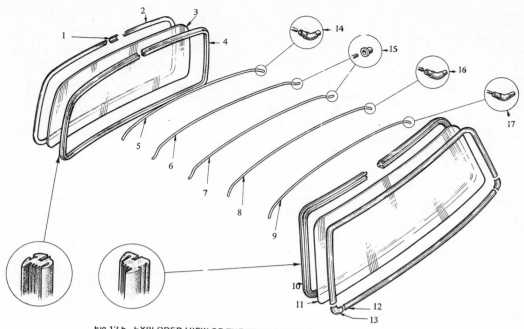

Fig.12.5. EXPLODED VIEW OF THE WINDSCREEN & REAR WINDOW LAYOUT

1 Clip
2 Chrome windowsurround
3 Glass
4 Window retaining rubber channel
5 Headlining support
6 Headlining support (Saloon and Estate)
7 Headlining support (Saloon and Estate)
8 Headlining support (Saloon and Estate)
9 Headlining support
10 Glass retaining rubber channel
11 Glass
12 Chrome window surround
13 Chrome surround corner piece
14)
15 Headlining support)
16 extensions)
17)

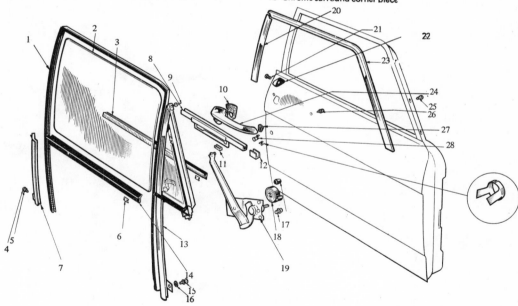

Fig.12.6. EXPLODED VIEW OF THE FRONT DOOR — EXTERIOR

1 Rubber channeling
2 Glass
3 Interior window seal
4 Screw
5 Washer
6 Clip
7 Window guide
8 Glass holder window actuating mechanism
9 Pin
10 Gasket
11 Slide
12 Channel piece
13 Window guide
14 Exterior sealing rubber
15 Screw
16 Washer
17 Screw
18 Spring
19 Window actuating mechanism
20 Chrome window trim
21 Screw
22 Plate
23 Chrome window trim
24 Exterior door handle
25 Screw
26 Screw
27 Gasket
28 Pin

the car the glass and weatherstrip can be removed together.

5. If you are having to replace your windscreen due to a shattered screen, remove all traces of sealing compound and broken glass from the weatherstrip and body flange.

6. Gently prise out the clip which covers the joint of the chromium finisher strip and pull the finisher strip out of the weatherstrip. Then remove the weatherstrip from the glass or if it is still on the car, as in the case of a shattered screen, remove it from the body flange.

7. To fit a new windscreen start by fitting the weatherstrip around the new windscreen glass.

8. Apply a suitable sealer such as Expandite SR-51-B to the weatherstrip to body groove. In this groove then fit a fine but strong piece of cord right the way round the groove allowing an overlap of about six inches at the joint.

9. From outside the car place the windscreen in its correct position making sure that the loose end of the cord is inside the car.

10 With an assistant pressing firmly on the outside of the windscreen get into the car and slowly pull out the cord thus drawing the weatherstrip over the body flange.

11 Apply a further layer of sealer to the underside of rubber to glass groove from outside the car.

12 Replace the chromium finisher strip into its groove in the weatherstrip and replace the clip which covers its joint.

13 Carefully clean off any surplus sealer from the windscreen glass before it has a chance to harden and then replace the windscreen wiper arms and blades.

10. DOOR RATTLES - TRACING & RECTIFICATION

1. The most common cause of door rattles is a mis-aligned, loose, or worn striker plate but other causes may be:-

a) Loose door handles or window winder handles.
b) Loose or misaligned door lock components.
c) Loose or worn remote control mechanism.

2. It is quite possible for door rattles to be the result of a combination of the above faults so a careful examination must be made to determine the causes of the fault.

3. If the nose of the striker plate is worn and as a result the door rattles, renew and then adjust the plate as described in Section 11.

4. Should the inner door handle or window winder rattle this is easily cured by putting a rubber washer between the escutcheon and the handle.

5. If the door lock is found to be worn and rattles as a consequence, then fit a new lock as described in Section 12.

11. DOOR STRIKER PLATE - REMOVAL, REPLACEMENT & ADJUSTMENT

1. If it is wished to renew a worn striker plate mark its position on the door pillar with a pencil so that a new plate can be fitted in the same position.

2. To remove the plate simply undo the three Phillips screws which hold the plate and anti-slip shim in position. Replacement is equally straight forward.

3. To adjust the striker plate, slightly loosen the three retaining screws and, with the outside door push button depressed, close the door and release the button.

4. Move the door in and out until it is flush with the surrounding bodywork then depress the button and open the door being careful not to disturb the striker plate.

5. Check that the striker plate is vertical and tighten down the three screws. Adjustment is now complete.

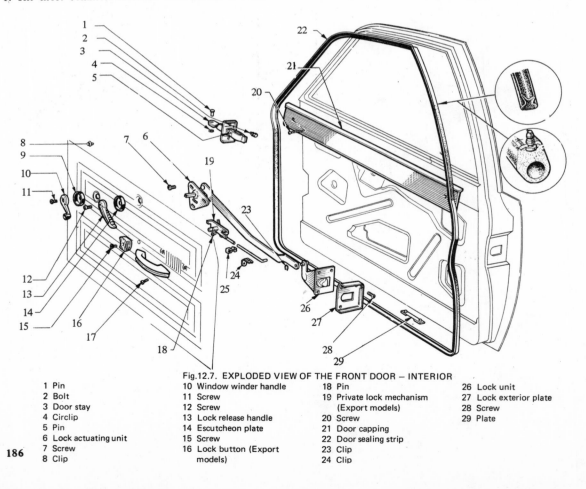

Fig.12.7. EXPLODED VIEW OF THE FRONT DOOR — INTERIOR

1 Pin	10 Window winder handle	18 Pin	26 Lock unit
2 Bolt	11 Screw	19 Private lock mechanism	27 Lock exterior plate
3 Door stay	12 Screw	(Export models)	28 Screw
4 Circlip	13 Lock release handle	20 Screw	29 Plate
5 Pin	14 Escutcheon plate	21 Door capping	
6 Lock actuating unit	15 Screw	22 Door sealing strip	
7 Screw	16 Lock button (Export	23 Clip	
8 Clip	models)	24 Clip	

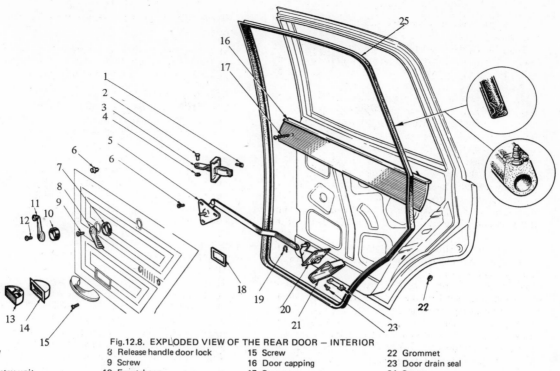

Fig.12.8. EXPLODED VIEW OF THE REAR DOOR — INTERIOR

1 Screw	8 Release handle door lock	15 Screw	22 Grommet
2 Pin	9 Screw	16 Door capping	23 Door drain seal
3 Door stay unit	10 Escutcheon	17 Screw	24 Screw
4 Clip	11 Window winder handle	18 Clip	25 Door sealing rubber
5 Window actuating mechanism	12 Screw	19 Clip	
6 Clip	13 Ash tray	20 Door catch mechanism	
7 Escutcheon	14 Ash tray holder	21 Door catch exterior plate	

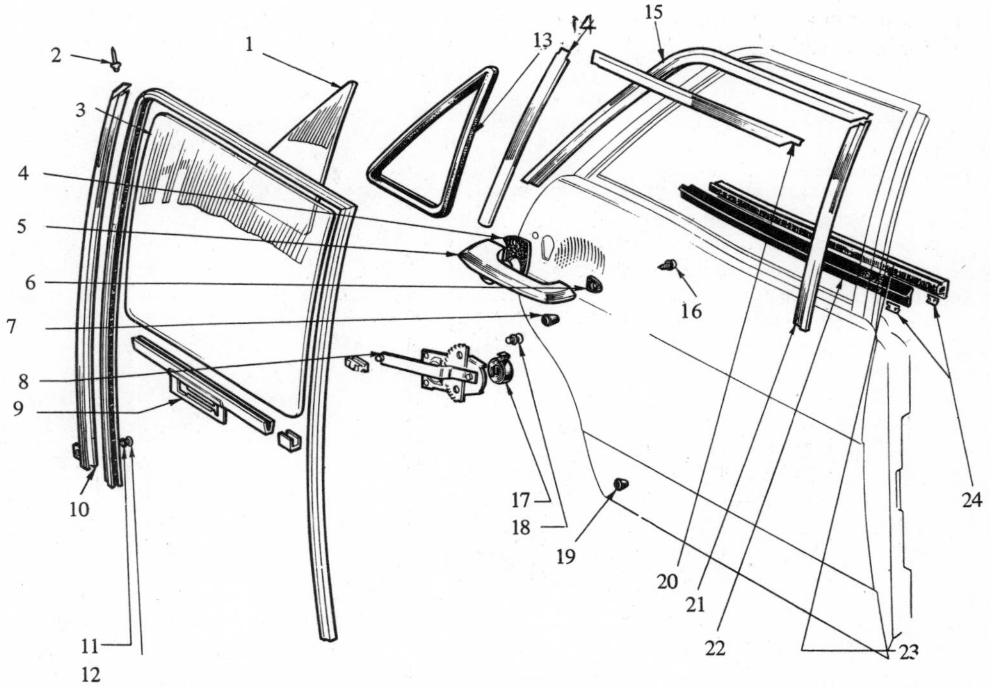

Fig.12.9. EXPLODED VIEW OF THE REAR DOOR — EXTERIOR

1 Glass	7 Bumper	13 Glass retaining rubber channel	19 Bumper
2 'pop' rivet	8 Window actuating mechanism	14 Chrome window trim	20 Chrome window trim
3 Glass	9 Glass holder	15 Chrome window trim	21 Chrome window trim
4 Gasket	10 Window guide	16 Screw	22 Exterior window sealing rubber
5 Exterior door handle	11 Washer	17 Spring	23 Interior window sealing strip
6 Gasket	12 Screw	18 Screw & shakeproof washer	24 Clips

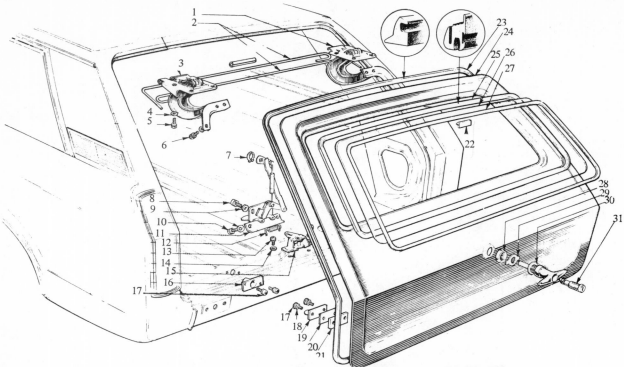

Fig.12.10. EXPLODED VIEW OF THE TAILGATE ASSEMBLY ON ESTATE CARS

1 Hinge unit	9 Washer	17 Screw	25 Weatherstrip
2 Torsion bars	10 Screw	18 Shakeproof washer	26 Glass
3 Hinge unit	11 Door lock unit	19 Striker	27 Chrome weatherstrip
4 Washer	12 Spring	20 Striker pad	surround
5 Screw	13 Screw	21 Striker plate	28 Escutcheon
6 Screw	14 Washer	22 Window trim finish cover	29 Ring
7 Circlip	15 Body lock unit	23 Tailgate seal	30 Washer
8 Screw	16 Striker dovetail	24 Tailgate	31 Lock barrel

12. DOOR LOCKS & REMOTE CONTROL - REMOVAL & REPLACEMENT

1. Wind up the window and remove the door remote control handle and the window regulator handle by undoing their centre screws and lifting off the washer, handles and escutcheon plates in that order.

2. Remove the combined arm rest and door pull by undoing its two retaining screws.

3. Insert a thin strip of metal with all the sharp edges removed between the recessed trim panel and the door. This will release one or two of the trim panel clips without damaging the trim. A short metal ruler is ideal for this job. The trim panel can then be eased off by hand and the polythene waterproof sheet removed.

4. Take off the spring clip which secures the door remote control operating arm to the lock mechanism and disconnect the operating arm.

5. To remove the outside door handle; from inside the door panel remove the screw and washer holding the rear of the handle to the door, then, through the door access hole, undo and remove the screw and washer securing the front of the handle. The handle and sealing gasket can now be withdrawn.

6. From the rear end of the door remove the single screw and washer which secure the bottom of the door window glass rear lower run in position. Pull the run downwards to free the metal backing channel from the window frame.

7. Undo the three screws which hold the lock to the door and having moved the rear lower run to one side, withdraw the door lock assembly through the door access hole.

8. The door remote control assembly can now be simply removed by undoing its three retaining screws.

9. Reassembly is a straight forward reversal of the above procedure.

13. BONNET ASSEMBLY - REMOVAL & REPLACEMENT

1. Open the bonnet lid and prop it open with the strut provided.

2. With a pencil draw a line round the hinge plates on the bonnet lid to ensure correct alignment when replacing.

3. Remove the two bolts and washers from either side of the bonnet lid and carefully lift the bonnet from the car.

4. When replacing the bonnet, loosely retain it with the the bolts and then carefully line up the hinge plates with the pencil marks before finally tightening down the bolts.

14. BOOT LID - REMOVAL & REPLACEMENT

1. Open the boot lid and, with a pencil, draw a line round the hinge plates on the boot lid to ensure correct alignment when replacing.

2. Remove the two bolts and washers on either side of the boot lid and lift the lid from the car.

3. When replacing the boot lid, loosely retain it with the bolts and then carefully line up the hinge plates with the pencil lines before finally tightening down the bolts.

15. RADIATOR GRILLE - REMOVAL & REPLACEMENT

1. Remove the four screws retaining each headlamp bezel in place and move the bezels clear of the grille.

2. Undo the two screws securing the bottom edge of the radiator grille and then drill out the six 'pop' rivets securing the top edge and lift the grille from the car.

3. Replacement is a direct reversal of the above procedure.

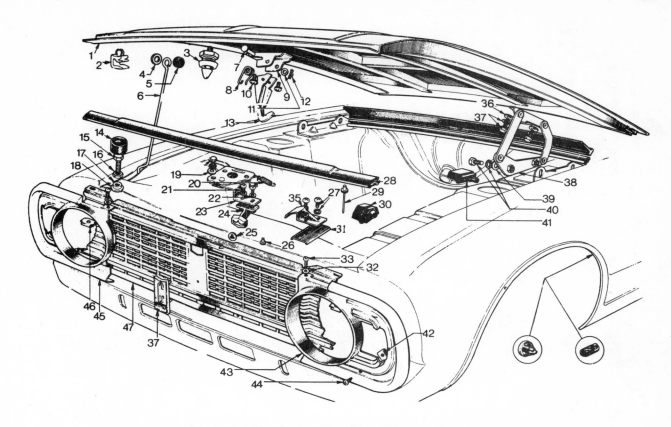

Fig. 12.11. EXPLODED VIEW OF THE BONNET ASSEMBLY

1	Bonnet moulding	13	Bonnet safety catch	25	Clip	37	Bolt and lockwasher
2	Stay clip	14	Rubber stop	26	Pin	38	Bonnet hinge assembly
3	Bonnet catch male piece	15	Adjusting bolt	27	Screw and washer	39	Washer
4	Washer	16	Nut	28	Chromed trim	40	Bolt and lockwasher
5	Grommet	17	Spacer	29	'Pop' rivet	41	Rubber stop
6	Bonnet stay	18	Spacer	30	Bonnet stop	42	Clip
7	Swivel pin	19	Bolt and washer	31	Plate	43	Headlamp trim unit LH
8	Spring	20	Spring	32	Washer	44	Screw
9	Bracket	21	Screw	33	Screw	45	Headlamp trim unit RH
10	Screw	22	Washer	34	Badge	46	Screw clip
11	Washer	23	Bracket	35	Safety catch latch	47	Grille trim unit
12	Pin clip	24	Bonnet	36	Washer		

16. WINDOW REGULATOR - REMOVAL & REPLACEMENT

1. Lower the window and remove the door remote control handle, the window regulator handle and the door trim panel as described in Section 12.

2. Support the window glass by means of a block of wood or similar object and undo the four screws holding the window regulator assembly to the door.

3. Disconnect the window regulator operating arm from the window glass lower run and then withdraw the regulator assembly through the door access hole.

4. Replacement is a reversal of the removal sequence.

17. WEATHERSTRIPS - GENERAL

1. The rubber weatherstrips fitted round all doors, and also on the boot surround, should be examined at regular intervals for signs of damage or rotting or in the event of water appearing inside a door or in the boot.

2. Should it be found necessary to replace a weatherstrip this is a very simple matter as they are just a push fit into the grooves provided.

3. It is not advisable to use any sealing compound when fitting a weatherstrip as this could make it extremely difficult to remove the weatherstrip again at a later date should it prove necessary.

18. HEATER ASSEMBLY - REMOVAL & REPLACEMENT

1. Disconnect the battery by removing the negative earth lead.

2. Remove the parcel shelf and the heater trim panel by undoing the retaining screws.

3. Working under the bonnet slacken off the two wire clips on the heater pipes and then pull the pipes off the bulkhead.

4. Remove the heater pipe plate and sealing gasket from the bulkhead by undoing the two retaining screws.

5. Release the two spring clips securing the two heater control cables to the heater operating arms and pull the cables out of operating arms.

6. Make a careful note of wiring positions and disconnect the wires from the heater blower motor.

7. Pull off the face level vent pipes and the demister pipes from the heater assembly.

8. Undo the four bolts securing the heater to the bulkhead and withdraw the complete heater assembly. Replacement is a reversal of the above procedure.

19. HEATER MOTOR - REMOVAL & REPLACEMENT

1. Undo the thirteen small screws securing the blower motor to the heater and remove the blower motor and mounting plate as an assembly from the heater.

2. Remove the sealing gasket from the mounting plate then remove the rubber gasket and pull the motor wires through the mounting plate.

3. Remove the spring clip holding the blower motor fan in place and withdraw the fan.

4. Undo the three screws holding the blower motor to the mounting plate and remove the motor.

5. Replacement is a straightforward reversal of the above procedure.

20. HEATER RADIATOR - REMOVAL & REPLACEMENT

1. Remove the heater blower motor and mounting plate as an assembly as described in Section 19 above.

2. Pull off the rear lower panel covering the radiator and remove the foam packing that will be found behind the panel.

3. Carefully slide the heater radiator out of its recess and examine it for signs of leaks or damage.

4. Replacement is a straightforward reversal of the above procedure.

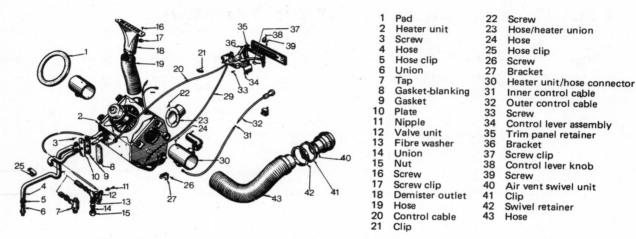

1	Pad	22	Screw
2	Heater unit	23	Hose/heater union
3	Screw	24	Hose
4	Hose	25	Hose clip
5	Hose clip	26	Screw
6	Union	27	Bracket
7	Tap	30	Heater unit/hose connector
8	Gasket-blanking	31	Inner control cable
9	Gasket	32	Outer control cable
10	Plate	33	Screw
11	Nipple	34	Control lever assembly
12	Valve unit	35	Trim panel retainer
13	Fibre washer	36	Bracket
14	Union	37	Screw clip
15	Nut	38	Control lever knob
16	Screw	39	Screw
17	Screw clip	40	Air vent swivel unit
18	Demister outlet	41	Clip
19	Hose	42	Swivel retainer
20	Control cable	43	Hose
21	Clip		

Fig. 12.12. EXPLODED VIEW OF THE HEATER ASSEMBLY FITTED UP TO SEPTEMBER 1967

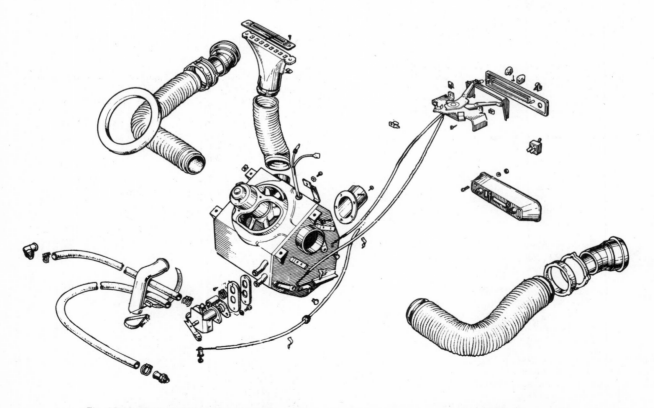

Fig. 12.13. EXPLODED VIEW OF THE HEATER ASSEMBLY FITTED FROM SEPTEMBER 1967

Chapter 13 Supplementary information

Contents

1 Specifications

Engine

Idling speed, automatic transmission in 'D' ... ... 615 rev/min

Torque wrench setting	**lb ft**	**kg m**
Flywheel bolts	50 to 55	6.9 to 7.6

Fuel system and carburation

1300 cc carburettor, type C7BHC (automatic transmission)

Idle channel restrictor ... ... 0.043 in. (1.10 mm)

1600 cc carburettor (with exhaust emission control)

Type	Ford single venturi, downdraught with accelerator pump and power valve and automatic choke	
Number:	C9BH-A (manual)	C9BH-B (automatic)
Idling speed	580 - 620 rev/min	
Fast idle	1100 - 1300 rev/min	2200 - 2400 rev/min
Float setting (up)	1.07 to 1.09 in. (27.2 to 27.6 mm)	
(down)	1.33 to 1.35 in. (33.8 to 34.3 mm)	
Choke pull-down	0.15 to 0.16 in. (3.8 to 4.1 mm)	
De-choke	—	0.200/0.240 in. (5.1/6.1 mm)
Accelerator pump stroke	0.135 to 0.145 in. (3.43 to 3.68 mm)	
Throttle barrel diameter	1.34 in. (34 mm)	
Venturi diameter	1.02 in. (26 mm)	
Main jet	0.056 in. (1.42 mm)	0.054 in. (1.37 mm)
Air correction jet	0.057 in. (1.45 mm)	0.051 in. (1.39 mm)
Idling jet	0.024 in. (0.60 mm)	
Idling air bleed (first)	0.041 in. (1.05 mm)	
(second)	0.024 in. (0.60 mm)	
Power jet	0.033 in. (0.85 mm)	0.024 in. (0.60 mm)
Pump jet	0.022 in. (0.55 mm)	
Pump spring	Red	
Vacuum piston link hole	Inner	
Thermostatic spring slot	Centre	

Exhaust emission control

Air pump pressure relief	13 in. (330.2 mm) Hg
Air pump driving belt free movement	½ in. (12.5 mm)
Pulley identification	1600 cc unmarked, GT white
Backfire suppressor valve identification	1600 cc unmarked, GT blue

Torque wrench settings

	lb ft	kg m
Air cleaner bolts (not GT)	5	0.7
Air cleaner (GT)	7	0.97
Air cleaner cover (GT)	7	0.97
Fuel tank securing bolts	5	0.7
Air pump adjuster strap bolts	18	2.5
Air pump mounting bolts	42	5.8
Air pump pulley bolts	7	0.97
Exhaust non-return valve	23	3.18
Air manifold union nuts	9	1.24
Backfire suppressor valve bolts	7	0.97

Automatic transmission

Type	3 speed, epicyclic with 3 element hydro-kinetic torque converter
Fluid capacity (including converter)	11¼ Imp. pints (6.39 litres), 13.5 U.S. pints

Speed ratios:
- 1st ... ...   2.393 : 1
- 2nd ... ...   1.450 : 1
- 3rd ... ...   1.000 : 1
- Reverse ... ...   2.094 : 1

Torque converter diameter	9.5 in. (241.3 mm)
Operating temperature	100 to 115° C (212 to 236° F)

Approximate shift speeds:

	Light throttle	Full throttle	Kick-down
1300 cc - 1 to 2	7 - 10 mph (11 - 16 kph)	23 - 32 mph (37 - 51 kph)	29 - 39 mph (47 - 63 kph)
- 2 to 3	9 - 14 mph (14 - 22 kph)	36 - 50 mph (58 - 80 kph)	51 - 61 mph (80 - 98 kph)
- 3 to 2			43 - 58 mph (69 - 93 kph)
- 2 to 1			20 - 34 mph (32 - 55 kph)
1600 cc - 1 to 2	4 - 8 mph (6 - 13 kph)	23 - 32 mph (37 - 51 kph)	31 - 40 mph (50 - 64 kph)
- 2 to 3	8 - 12 mph (13 - 19 kph)	39 - 50 mph (63 - 80 kph)	53 - 63 mph (85 - 101 kph)
- 3 to 2			47 - 59 mph (76 - 95 kph)
- 2 to 1			22 - 34 mph (35 - 55 kph)

Engine maximum shift speed	5000 rev/min
Speedometer driving gear. - 1300 cc	6 teeth
- 1600 cc	7 teeth

Torque wrench settings

	lb ft	kg m
Transmission case to converter housing	13	1.80
Extension housing bolts	13	1.80
Oil pan bolts	13	1.80
Drive plate to torque converter	45	6.91

Electrical system
Alternator

Type	Lucas 15 ACR
Rotational direction	Clockwise
Nominal rated output at 14V/6000 rev/min	34 amps
Number of poles	12
Stator phases	3
Max. continuous speed	12500 rev/min
Stator winding resistance (ohms per phase)	0.133
Rotor winding resistance (ohms at 20° C)	4.33 ± 5%
Slip ring end brush length (new)	0.5 in. (13 mm)
Regulating voltage	14.0 to 14.4 volts

Bulbs

Side marker lights	2.2 watts

Braking system

Rear wheel cylinder diameter (automatic transmission) ...	0.87 in. (22.1 mm)

Ford Cortina Mk II 1600 Estate for the North American market

2 Introduction

This supplementary chapter is provided to cover various modifications which have been carried out to the Cortina Mk 2 since its inception in 1966. Only the changes have been described in this chapter. In addition, servicing details are included in respect of special equipment and components fitted to North American versions in order to comply with safety and anti-pollution regulations. Owners of vehicles fitted with automatic transmission will find all necessary information within this supplement.

3 Routine maintenance

Every 6000 miles (9600 km)
Automatic transmission

Top up the level of fluid in the automatic transmission. This should be done with the unit at normal operating temperature, the speed selector in 'P' and the engine idling. Withdraw dipstick, wipe, insert, withdraw and read off level. Do not overfill above HIGH mark.

Air pump (exhaust emission control)

Check the tension of the driving belt. There should be a total deflection of the belt at the centre of its top run of ½ in (12.5 mm).

Check the tightening torque of the air pump mounting bolts (correct tightening torque 15 to 18 lb/ft (2.1 to 2.5 kg/m). Remove the filter element from the air pump air intake (not GT) and wash it in clean fuel and allow to dry before refitting.

Every 24000 miles (38600 km)
Air pump filter element (not GT) - renew.

4 Engine

Valves

1 The inlet valves are coated with aluminium alloy and cannot be ground in or replaced without destroying the coating. Where the valve seat is pitted or burned, use an old valve for grinding-in purposes. Where the valve itself is pitted, then a new valve must be installed.

2 The valve stem oil seals fitted to vehicles having exhaust emission control are retained by spring clips. These should be renewed whenever the oil seals are changed at time of overhaul or decarbonising.

3 Valve guides may be of integral or renewable type. Oversize stemmed valves are available so that the integral type guides can be drilled and reamed out if wear requires it. With either type of valve guide it is perferable to leave this work to your Ford dealer.

Sump

1 Improved access to the two rear sump retaining bolts will be attained if the crankshaft is rotated to position the flywheel so that its recesses are adjusted to the bolts.

2 Before fitting the front and rear semi-circular sump seals, apply jointing compound to the grooves of the carriers and at their points of contact with the side gaskets. Tighten side bolts first, followed by the rear and then front.

Crankcase ventilation system

Vehicles fitted with full exhaust emission control systems have a sealed type oil filter cap located on the top of the rocker cover with an interconnecting tube to the air cleaner body for the purpose of engine fume extraction. The other components used in the semi-sealed type crankcase ventilation system are deleted.

5 Cooling system

Fan belt adjustment

Where an alternator is fitted instead of a dynamo, the adjustment of the belt tension is precisely the same except that the adjustment should be carried out with the engine cold. Take greater care when prising the alternator away from the engine as the alloy body and plastic end cover can be easily damaged.

6 Fuel system and carburation

Description

Vehicles (not GT) which are fitted with full exhaust emission control system have an Autolite carburettor with automatic choke. Vehicles with automatic transmission have a similar carburettor. GT models which have a full exhaust emission control system are fitted with a model 32DFD Weber carburettor which has a manually operated choke.

The servicing, dismantling and reassembly instructions given in Chapter 3 of this manual for non-emission control carburettors will generally apply but reference must be made to the following sections for detail changes in construction and adjustment procedures.

The Autolite carburettors used in conjunction with 1600 cc engines are specially calibrated for compatibility with exhaust emission control systems and incorporate a smaller throttle barrel and venturi and modified float.

The Weber carburettors are specially calibrated for use with exhaust emission control systems and the full load enrichment system operates in the primary barrel instead of the secondary one.

Autolite (emission control type) carburettor - float level adjustment

1 This type of carburettor incorporates a modified float with a detachable top cover gasket which can be removed without disturbing the float assembly.

2 In consequence, the dimensions for setting the float (Chapter 3, Figs 3.9 amd 3.10) must be taken from the face of the top cover and not the face of the gasket.

Autolite (emission control type) carburettor - idling and slow-running adjustment

1 Ensure that all emission control connections are secure.

2 Run the engine to full operating temperature and check that the automatic choke is fully open.

3 Connect a vacuum gauge to the drilling in the inlet manifold and adjust the throttle stop screw until the specified idling speed is obtained. Now adjust the volume control screw until the highest reading is obtained on the vacuum gauge. Re-adjust the idling speed if necessary.

4 If an exhaust gas analyser is used (preferable for vehicles equipped with IMCO exhaust emission control system) the air/fuel ratio should be within the limits 13.4 to 13.9:1.

5 On certain carburettors, a limiter is fitted to the volume control screw to prevent excessively rich adjustment.

Weber (emission control type) carburettor - idling and slow-running adjustment

1 Ensure that all emission control connections are secure.

2 Run the engine to full operating temperature and check that the manually operated choke is pushed fully in.

3 Connect a vacuum gauge to the drilling in the inlet manifold and adjust the throttle stop screw until the specified idling speed is obtained. Now adjust the volume control screw until the highest reading is obtained on the vacuum gauge. Re-adjust the idling speed if necessary.

4 If an exhaust gas analyser is used, the air/fuel ratio should be within the limits 13.8 to 14.1:1.

Exhaust emission control system - general description

One of two types of system may be encountered, the 'Imco'

FIG. 13.1. AUTOMATIC CHOKE TYPE CARBURETTOR ADJUSTING SCREWS

1 Idling speed 2 Volume control (mixture)

FIG. 13.2. WEBER CARBURETTOR ADJUSTING SCREWS

1 Idling speed 2 Volume control (mixture)

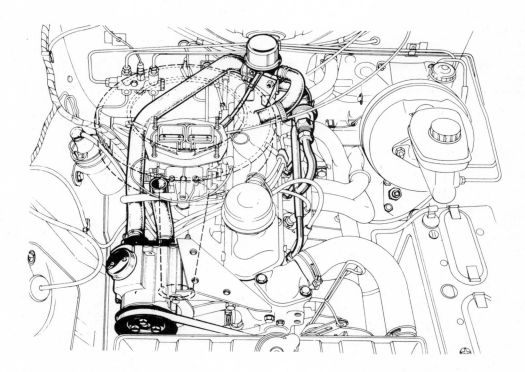

Fig. 13.3. Exhaust emission control system (air pump type) fitted to a GT

system fitted only to standard models and the 'Thermactor' air pump system always fitted to GT models but may be found on standard versions as well.

The 'Imco' system comprises a dual diaphragm vacuum capsule attached to the ignition distributor, a deceleration valve and a specially calibrated carburettor. The object of the second capsule diaphragm is to sense manifold vacuum (which is highest when the engine is decelerating or idling) and to retard the ignition spark under these conditions and so reduce exhaust emissions.

The deceleration valve is spring actuated and connected on one side to inlet manifold vacuum and on the other to atmospheric pressure. When inlet vacuum is very high during deceleration, the valve opens to admit more air/fuel mixture to improve combustion.

The 'Thermactor' air pump emission control system comprises a belt driven air pump and filter (no filter on GT models) an air manifold, a backfire suppressor valve, an exhaust non-return valve and various nozzles and hoses.

The principle of this system is to provide extra air in the vicinity of the exhaust valves to oxidise the exhaust gases before they are ejected to atmosphere. The backfire suppressor valve (air by-pass valve) diverts the extra air to the inlet manifold during conditions when an extremely rich mixture is required and an explosion (backfire) could occur in the exhaust manifold. The valve operates whenever there are sudden increases in the inlet vacuum pressure. The exhaust non-return valve is incorporated in the air injection line just before the nozzles to prevent any possibility of reverse flow of the exhaust gases to the air pump.

It should be noted that with both types of emission control systems, the timing specifications for the ignition system are revised as described later in this Chapter.

'Imco' emission control system - servicing
1 This is limited to examining the vacuum connecting tubes periodically for security of connections and deterioration. Renew as required.
2 The valve itself is pre-set during manufacture and adjustment of the nylon screw on the top cover should not be altered.

'Thermactor' emission control system - fault diagnosis and servicing
1 **Air supply hose to manifold baked or burned.** This condition will be caused by a defective exhaust non-return valve.
2 Check the operation of the valve by warming the engine to normal operating temperature and disconnecting the flexible air hose from the non-return valve. Increase the engine speed to 1500 rev/min and check the valve for leakage of exhaust gas. If there is any, renew the valve. Any fluttering or vibration of the valve should be ignored.
3 **Surging of engine speed at all throttle settings,** due to leaking or disconnected valve hoses.
4 **Rough engine idling** is probably caused by a defective backfire suppressor valve, a damaged hose or a faulty air pump or leaking air supply hoses. The backfire suppressor valve can only be tested by using a pressure gauge or by substitution of a new unit. Where a pressure gauge is available, disconnect the by-pass hose from the air cleaner and secure the gauge in the open end of the hose. Run the engine at 1500 rev/min when no pressure should be indicated on the gauge. If a pressure is recorded, renew the valve. Open and close the throttle rapidly when the pressure gauge needle should swing rapidly and slowly settle back to zero. If the gauge does not respond in this way, renew the valve.
5 **Backfiring in the exhaust system** will probably be caused by a faulty backfire-suppressor valve or leaking or damaged connecting hoses. Test and renew the valve, if necessary, as described in the preceding paragraph.
6 **Difficult starting** may be due to a faulty backfire suppressor valve or leaking or disconnected hoses or a faulty air pump or slipping or broken drive belt. Test and renew the backfire-suppressor valve as described in paragraph 4. On models other than GT check the condition of the air pump filter and renew if clogged.
7 Check the tension of the drive belt. There should be a maximum deflection of ½ in (12.7 mm) at the centre of the top run of the belt. To adjust the tension, loosen the air pump mounting bolt and strap-adjuster bolt and move the pump in towards or away from the engine until the correct tension is obtained. Re-tighten both bolts.

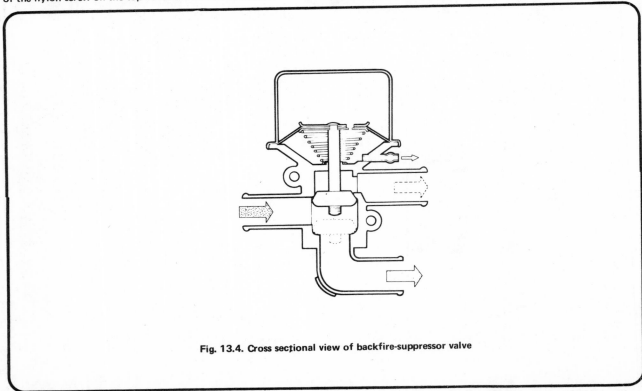

Fig. 13.4. Cross sectional view of backfire-suppressor valve

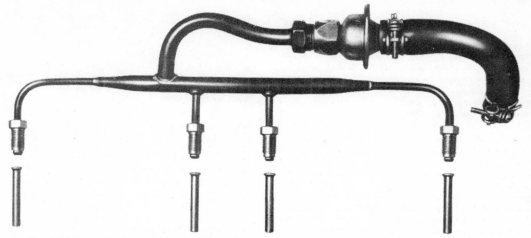

Fig. 13.5. Components of exhaust emission control air injection system and exhaust non-return valve

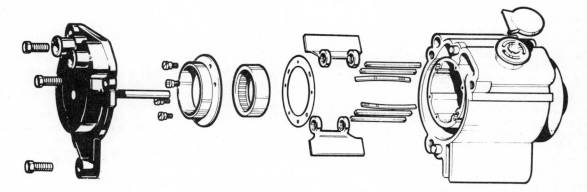

Fig. 13.6. Exploded view of exhaust emission control air pump

Fig. 13.7. Exhaust emission control air pump filter

Fig. 13.8. Exhaust emission control air pump drive belt tension diagram

8 Renewal of the drive belt is carried out in a similar manner by pushing the air pump as far as it will go towards the engine.
9 Operation of the air pump can be checked by disconnecting the outlet hose and placing a finger over the end of the pump nozzle and feeling the air pressure. Do not completely obstruct the opening as a pressure relief valve operates at a pre-set valve.
10 Cleaning of components is not required other than at times of major overhaul. The air nozzles should be cleaned and if renewal is required, they can be extracted from the cylinder head (without removing the head) by using a piece of hooked rod.

7 Ignition system

Initial advance settings for exhaust emission control vehicles.
The initial or static ignition advance for vehicles fitted with an exhaust emission control system is less than for vehicles without such a system.
The respective markings on the crankshaft pulley and the timing chain cover are shown.

Ignition timing - vehicles fitted with IMCO emission control
Before carrying out ignition timing with a stroboscope it is essential that both vacuum pipes are disconnected from the distributor vacuum capsule.

8 Automatic transmission

General description
The system comprises two main components:
1 A three element hydrokinetic torque convertor coupling, capable of torque multiplication at an infinitely variable ratio between 1.91 : 1 and 1 : 1.
2 A torque/speed responsive and hydraulically operated epicyclic gearbox comprising a planetary gearset providing three forward ratios and one reverse ratio.
Due to the complexity of the automatic transmission unit if performance is not up to standard, or overhaul is necessary, it is imperative that this be left to a main agent who will have the special equipment and knowledge for fault diagnosis and rectification.
The contents of the following Sections are therefore confined to supplying general information and any service information and instruction than can be used by the owner.

Fluid level
It is important that transmission fluid manufactured only to the correct specification such as Castrol TQF is used. The capacity of the complete unit is 11.25 pints (6.4 litres). Drain and refill capacity will be less as the torque converter cannot be completely drained, but this operation should not be neccessary except for repairs.

Maintenance
1 Ensure that the exterior of the converter housing and gearbox is always kept clean of dust or mud, otherwise overheating will occur.
2 Every 6,000 miles (10,000 km) or more frequently, check the automatic transmission fluid level. With the engine at its normal operating temperature move the selector to the 'P' position and allow the engine to idle for two minutes. With the engine still idling in the 'P' position withdraw the dipstick, wipe it clean and replace it. Quickly withdraw it again and if necessary top up with Castrol TQF automatic transmission fluid. The difference between the 'LOW and 'FULL' marks on the dipstick is 1 pint (0.50 litre).
3 If the unit has been drained, it is recommended that only new fluid is used. Fill up to the correct 'HIGH' level gradually

refilling the unit, the exact amount will depend on how much was left in the converter after draining.

Removal and replacement
Any suspected faults must be referred to the main agent before unit removal, as with this type of transmission the fault must be confirmed, using specialist equipment, before it has been removed from the car.
1 Open the engine compartment lid and place old blankets over the wings to prevent accidental scratching of the paintwork.
2 Undo and remove the battery earth connection nut and bolt from the battery terminal.
3 The air cleaner should next be removed. Full information will be found in Chapter 3.
4 Refer to Chapter 10, Section 18 and remove the starter motor.
5 Jack up the front of the car and place on firmly based axle stands. Alternatively place the car on a ramp or over a pit.
6 Undo and remove the upper bolts that secure the torque converter housing to the engine. One of these bolts also secures the dipstick tube support bracket and earth strap.
7 Place a clean container having a capacity of at least 10 pints (5.58 litres) under the automatic transmission unit reservoir. Remove the drain plug and allow the fluid to run out into the container. Refit the drain plug, Take extreme care if the car has just been driven as this oil can be very hot.
8 Disconnect the exhaust down pipe at the exhaust manifold.
9 Slacken the locknut which secures the downshift outer cable to its bracket, remove the inner cable clevis pin and withdraw the cable assembly from its engine rear bulkhead bracket.
10 Disconnect the leads from the inhibitor/reversing light switch noting that the wider terminals are the reverse light connections.
11 Mark the edges of the propeller shaft and rear axle pinion mating flanges and then remove the four connecting bolts. Push the propeller shaft fractionally forward to disconnect the drive flanges and then lower and withdraw the propeller shaft and its splined sliding sleeve from the transmission rear extension housing.
12 Unhook the handbrake secondary cable from its relay lever and disengage it from the eye on the rear supporting crossmember.
13 Refer to Fig. 13.12 and peel back the rubber boot which covers the selector cross shaft universal joint. Remove a split pin and one of the clevis pins and disconnect the cross shaft coupling.
14 Unbolt the speedometer drive cable from the transmission housing extension.
15 Undo and remove the set bolts and spring washers that secure the torque converter housing cover plate and lift away the cover plate.
16 The torque converter should next be disconnected from the crankshaft driving plate. Rotate the crankshaft until each bolt may be seen through the starter motor aperture. Undo each bolt a turn at a time until the bolts are free.
17 Place a piece of soft wood on the saddle of a jack and support the weight across the rear of the engine. Take care to position the jack securely so that it cannot fly out when the automatic transmission unit is being disconnected or reconnected to the rear of the engine.
18 Place an additional jack under the automatic transmission unit and remove the two bolts and spring washers that secure the unit to the crossmember. Also remove the four bolts that locate the crossmember to the underside of the floor panel.
Slowly lower the transmission unit and engine jacks until there is sufficent clearance for the dipstick to be removed.
Withdraw the dipstick and pull the oil filler tube (dipstick tube) sharply from the side of the transmission unit. Remove the 'O' ring.
19 Undo and remove the remaining bolts and spring washers that secure the converter housing to the engine.

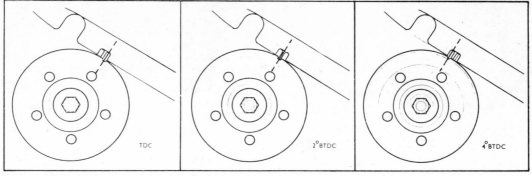

Fig. 13.9. Ignition timing marks — 1600 cc and GT engines fitted with exhaust emission control system

TDC   2° BTDC   4° BTDC

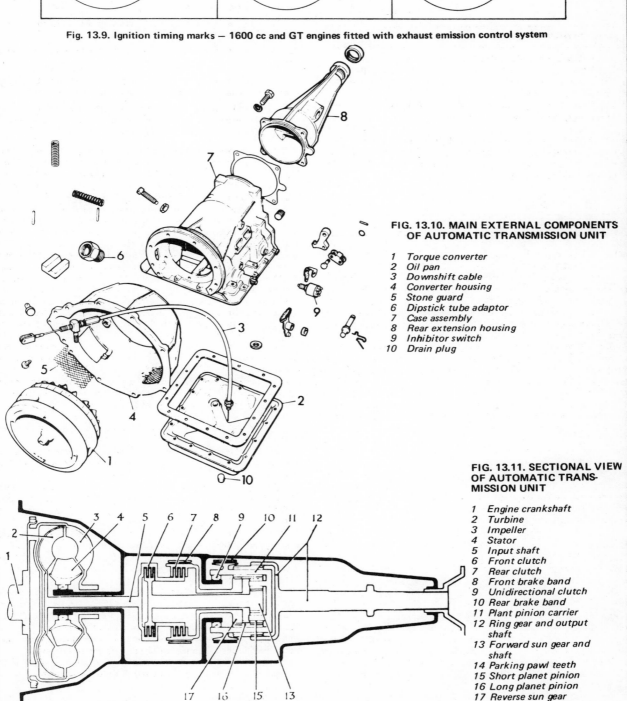

FIG. 13.10. MAIN EXTERNAL COMPONENTS OF AUTOMATIC TRANSMISSION UNIT

1 Torque converter
2 Oil pan
3 Downshift cable
4 Converter housing
5 Stone guard
6 Dipstick tube adaptor
7 Case assembly
8 Rear extension housing
9 Inhibitor switch
10 Drain plug

FIG. 13.11. SECTIONAL VIEW OF AUTOMATIC TRANS-MISSION UNIT

1 Engine crankshaft
2 Turbine
3 Impeller
4 Stator
5 Input shaft
6 Front clutch
7 Rear clutch
8 Front brake band
9 Unidirectional clutch
10 Rear brake band
11 Plant pinion carrier
12 Ring gear and output shaft
13 Forward sun gear and shaft
14 Parking pawl teeth
15 Short planet pinion
16 Long planet pinion
17 Reverse sun gear

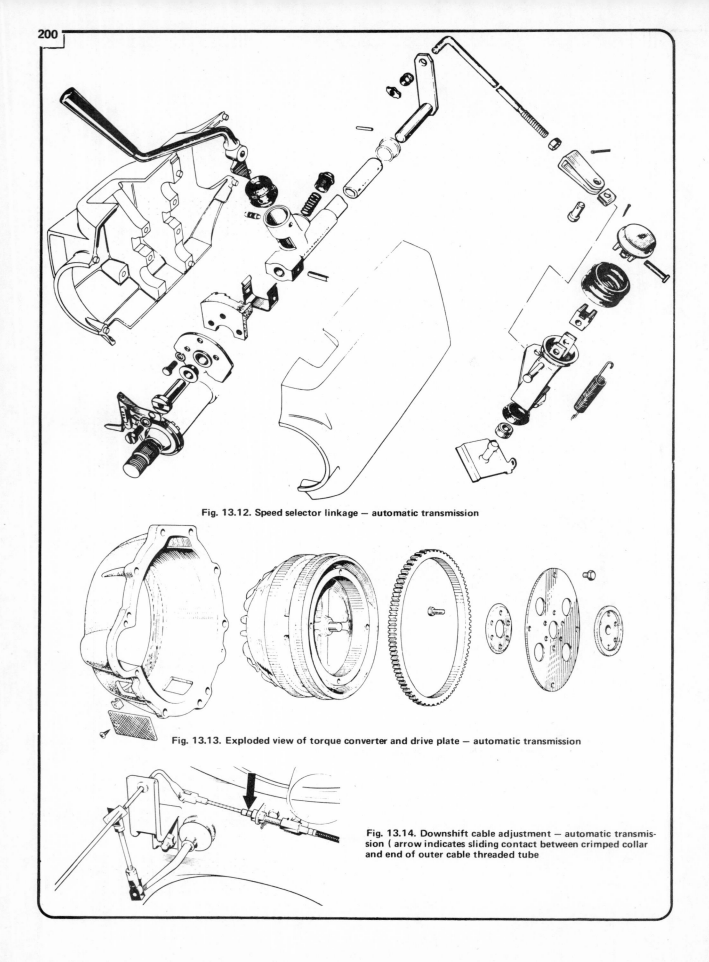

Fig. 13.12. Speed selector linkage — automatic transmission

Fig. 13.13. Exploded view of torque converter and drive plate — automatic transmission

Fig. 13.14. Downshift cable adjustment — automatic transmission (arrow indicates sliding contact between crimped collar and end of outer cable threaded tube

Continue to lower the jacks until there is sufficient clearance between the top of the converter housing and underside of the floor for the transmission unit to satisfactorily withdraw.

Check that no cable or securing bolts have been left in position and tuck the speedometer cable out of the way.

The assistance of at least one person is now required because of the weight of the complete unit.

20 Carefully pull the unit rearwards and, when possible, hold the converter in place in the housing as it will still be full of hydraulic fluid.

Finally withdraw the unit from under the car and place on wooden blocks so that the selector lever is not damaged or bent.

21 The engine rear plate is sandwiched between the converter housing and the engine cylinder block and as the transmission unit is removed, the plate will fall from its locating dowels.

22 To separate the converter housing from the transmission case first lift off the converter from the transmission unit, taking suitable precautions to catch the fluid upon separation. Undo and remove the six bolts and spring washers that secure the converter housing to the transmission case. Lift away the converter housing.

23 Refitting the automatic transmission unit is the reverse sequence to removal, but there are several additional points which will assist:

24 If the torque converter has been removed, before refitting the transmission unit it will be necessary to align the front drive tangs with the slots in the inner gear and then carefully replace the torque converter. Take extreme precautions not to damage the oil seal.

25 Adjust the selector cable and inhibitor switch as described later in this Chapter.

Refill the transmission unit with Castrol TQF before starting the engine and check the oil level as described previously.

Downshift cable - adjustment

Before the cable is adjusted, it is necessary to confirm that it is the cable that needs adjustment and not some other fault. Generally, if difficulty is experienced in obtaining downshift from 2 to 1 in the 'kickdown' position at just below 31 mph it is an indication that the outer cable is too long.

During production of the car, the adjustment is set by a crimped stop on the carburettor end of the inner cable and it is unusual for this setting to change except at high mileages when the inner cable can stretch. To adjust proceed as follows:

1 Apply the handbrake firmly and chock the front wheels for safety reasons.

2 Run the engine until it reaches normal operating temperature, adjust the engine idle speed to approximately 500 rpm with the selector in the 'D' position.

3 Stop the engine and, with an open ended spanner slacken the locknut and adjust the outer cable so that the crimped stop on the inner is almost making contact with the end of the outer cable adjuster sleeve (0.030 to 0.060 in gap).

4 Should the crimped stop have become loose or the inner cable have broken then the transmission sump will have to be removed.

5 Wipe the area around the drain plug and sump. Place a clean container of at least 10 pints (5.58 litres) capacity under the pan drain plug. Undo the plug and allow the oil to drain into the container.

6 Undo and remove the fifteen sump pan retaining bolts and spring washers. Take care not to damage the joint between the transmission casing and sump pan.

7 With the accelerator pedal in the 'kick-down' position check that the downshift valve cam is in the position shown in Fig. 13.15. Adjust the outer cable until the position is correct.

8 With the accelerator pedal released and the carburettor throttle stop correctly set the cam within the transmission unit should appear as shown in Fig. 13.16. If necessary pull the cable to achieve this setting and then securely crimp the stop collar to

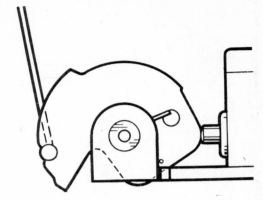

Fig. 13.15. Downshift cable cam 'kick-down' position in interior of automatic transmission unit

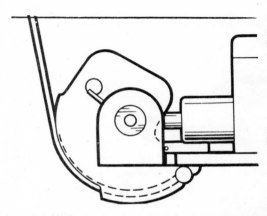

Fig. 13.16. Downshift cable cam 'idling' position in interior of automatic transmission unit

the inner cable so that it just contacts the outer cable adjuster set to the centre of its threaded length. New cables are supplied with the stop collar a loose fit on the cable for individual setting.

9 Refit the sump pan joint, sump pan and retaining bolts with spring washers. Tighten the bolts in a diagonal manner.

10 Refill the transmission with correct hydraulic fluid or use the fluid that was drained originally if it is clean with no streaks showing signs of contamination.

Selector linkage - adjustment

1 Jack up the front of the vehicle and support on axle stands.

2 Disconnect the short operating rod clevis fork from the cross shaft block.

3 Place the steering column selector lever in 'R'.

4 Pull the cross shaft block operating arm pulley towards the rear of the vehicle. Now push it forward to the fifth position. Count the clicks carefully to establish that it is in the 'R' detent.

5 Exert a slight forward pressure on the cross shaft operating arm to remove any slackness and then adjust the forked clevis on the short operating arm so that its clevis pin hole will line up perfectly with the hole in the cross shaft block operating arm. The help of an assistant to hold the steering column lever in 'R' during this operation is advisable.

6 Move the selector lever to all speed positions and check that the operating arm on the cross shaft is not under any tension. This can be checked by removing and inserting the clevis pin at all selector positions when the pin should be a sliding fit within the clevis fork and operating arm holes.

7 Check particularly the engagement of the transmission

parking brake (with the selector lever in 'P'). Push the vehicle in both directions to ensure that the locking pawl within the transmission is fully engaged.

8   Finally check that the selector lever indicator pointer follows accurately the speed selection. If this is not the case, remove the steering column shroud by unscrewing the four retaining screws from below it.

9   Place the selector lever in 'N' and then using a small screw-driver turn the pointer adjusting screw until it indicates the selected speed accurately.

Starter inhibitor/reverse light switch - adjustment

1   Place the speed selector lever in 'D' 'I' or '2' position.

2   Disconnect the cables from the switch which is screwed into the side of the transmission unit. Note that the two larger terminals on the switch are for the reversing lights, the smaller ones for the starter/inhibitor.

3   Loosen the switch locknut and unscrew the switch approximately two turns.

4   Connect a test lamp across the two smaller terminals and switch on the ignition. Screw in the switch until the test lamp just goes out. Mark the position of the switch body in relation to the transmission housing.

5   Now connect the test lamp across the two larger terminals (reversing lights) when the test lamp should not illuminate. Screw in the switch until the test lamp just lights. Make a second mark on the switch body opposite to the one previously made on the transmission housing.

6   Unscrew the switch until the mark on the transmission housing is mid-way between the two switch body marks.

7   Tighten the switch locknut just enough to retain the switch in position, overtightening will shear the alloy switch threaded stem.

8   Reconnect the cables and check that the starter motor operates only with the selector lever in P or N also that the reversing lights only operate with the lever in the 'R' position.

Front and rear bands - adjustment

1   It is unlikely that this adjustment will be required unless the unit has undergone a major overhaul or the following symptoms occur in the transmission, in which case such adjustment may provide a cure.

   Adjust front band when:
       Delayed or no 1-2 speed shift.
       Slip on 1-2 speed shift.
       Delayed or no 2-3 shift.
       Slip or engine speed up on 2-3 shift.
       Drag on 2-3 speed shift.
       No 3-2 downshift or noticeable engine braking.

Adjust rear band when:
       Drag in 'D' and '2'.
       No 2-1 downshift or engine braking.
       Slip in 'R' or no drive.
       No engine braking in 1.

2   To adjust the front band, drain the transmission fluid and remove the sump as previously described.

3   Slacken the front band adjusting screw locknut and move the servo lever outwards and place a ¼ in (6.35 mm) thick flat bar between the piston pin and the adjusting screw. Tighten the adjusting screw to a torque of only 10 lb/in (0.14 kg/m) the use of s spring balance will probably be the easiest method of achieving this. Tighten the locknut to between 15 and 20 lb/ft (2.1 to 2.8 kg/m).

4   Remove the flat bar, refit the sump using a new gasket and refill the transmission unit.

5   To adjust the rear band, remove the rubber plug from the floor inside the vehicle and slacken the locknut from the adjuster screw on the right hand top surface of the transmission unit.

6   Tighten the adjuster screw to a torque of 10 lb/ft (1.4 kg/m) and then unscrew it one full turn and retighten the locknut.

Fig. 13.17. Automatic transmission front band adjustment

Fig. 13.18. Automatic transmission rear band adjustment

Perfomance testing

The following procedure is given to enable the owner to satisfy himself that the automatic transmission is operating correctly. It is not intended that he should diagnose or rectify any faults but a detailed report of the exact nature of the malfunction will enable your Ford dealer to quickly ascertain the trouble with reduced cost to himself. Before carrying out the tests, ensure that the transmission fluid level is correct and all adjustments as previously described in this Section are correct.

Stall test procedure:

The function of a stall test is to determine that the torque converter and gearbox are operating satisfactory.

1 Check the condition of the engine. An engine which is not developing full power will affect the stall test readings.
2 Allow the engine and transmission to reach correct working temperatures.
3 Connect a tachometer to the vehicle.
4 Chock the wheels and apply the handbrake and footbrake.
5 Select '1' or 'R' and depress the throttle to the 'kick down' position. Note the reading on the tachometer which should be 1,800 rpm. If the reading is below 1,000 rpm suspect the converter for stator slip. If the reading is down to 1,200 rpm the engine is not developing full power. If the reading is in excess of 2,000 rpm suspect the gearbox for brake bind or clutch slip. NOTE: Do not carry out a stall test for a longer period than 10 seconds, otherwise the transmission will become overheated.

Transmission unit and torque converter - testing

1 Inability to start on steep gradients, combined with poor acceleration from rest and low stall speed (1,000 rpm) indicate that the converter stator uni-directional clutch is slipping. This condition permits the stator to rotate in an opposite direction to the impeller and turbine, and torque multiplication cannot occur.
2 Poor acceleration in third gear above 30 mph (48.3 kpm) and reduced maximum speed indicates that the stator uni-directional clutch has seized. The stator will not rotate with the turbine and impeller and the 'fluid flywheel' phase cannot occur. This condition will also be indicated by excessive overheating of the transmission although the stall speed will be correct.

Road test procedure

1 Check that the engine will only start with the selector lever in the 'P' or 'N' position and that the reverse light operates only in 'R'.
2 Apply the handbrake and with the engine idling select 'N' - 'D', 'N' - 'R' and 'N' - 'I'. Engagement should be positive.
3 With the transmission at normal running temperature 'select' 'D', release the brakes and accelerator with minimum throttle. Check 1-2 and 2-3 shift speeds and quality of change.
4 At a minimum road speed of 30 mph (48.3 kpm) select 'N' and switch off ignition. Allow the road speed to drop to approximately 28 mph (45.1 kpm) switch on the ignition, select 'D' and the engine should start.
5 Stop the vehicle, select 'D' and re-start, using 'full throttle'. Check 1-2 and 2-3 shift speeds and quality of change.
6 At 25 mph (40.3 kpm) apply 'full throttle'. The vehicle should accelerate in third gear and should not downshift to second.
7 At a maximum of 45 mph (72.42 kpm) 'kick down' fully, the transmission should downshift to second.
8 At a maximum of 31 mph (49.89 kpm) in third gear 'kick down' fully. The transmission should downshift to first gear.
9 Stop the vehicle, select 'D' and re-starting using 'kick-down' check the 1-2 and 2-3 shift speeds.
10 At 40 mph (64.4 kpm) in third gear, select '1' and release the throttle. Check 2-3 downshift and engine braking.
11 With '1' still engaged stop the vehicle and accelerate to over 25 mph (40.3 kpm) using 'kick down'. Check for slip, 'squawk'

and absence of upshifts.
12 Stop the vehicle and select 'R'. Reverse using 'full throttle' if possible. Check for slip and clutch 'squawk'.
13 Stop the vehicle on a gradient. Apply the handbrake and select 'P'. Check the parking pawl hold when the handbrake is released. Turn the vehicle around and repeat the procedure. Check that the selector lever is held firmly in the gate in 'P'.

9 Electrical system

Alternator - general description

Later models in the Cortina range are fitted with a Lucas type 15 ACR alternator.

The main advantage of the alternator lies in its ability to provide a high charge at low revolutions. Driving slowly in heavy traffic with a dynamo invariably means no charge is reaching the battery. In similar conditions even with the wipers, heater, lights and perhaps radio switched on, the Lucas alternator will ensure a charge reaches the battery.

An important feature of the alternator is a built in output control regulator, based on 'thick film' hybrid integrated micro-circuit technique, which results in this alternator being a self contained generating and control unit.

The system provides for direct connection of a charge light, and eliminates the need for a field switching relay and warning light control unit, necessary with former systems.

The alternator is of the rotating field ventilated design and comprises principally a laminated stator on which is wound a star connected 3 phase output winding, a twelve pole rotor carrying the field windings - each end of the rotor shaft runs in ball race bearings which are lubricated for life, natural finish aluminium die-cast end brackets, incorporating the mounting lugs, a rectifier pack for converting the AC output of the machine to DC for battery charging, and an output control regulator.

The rotor is belt driven from the engine through a pulley keyed to the rotor shaft. A pressed steel fan adjacent to the pulley draws cooling air through the alternator. This fan forms an integral part of the alternator specification. It has been designed to provide adequate air flow with a minimum of noise, and to withstand the high stresses associated with maximum speed. Rotation is clockwise viewed on the drive end.

Rectification of alternator output is achieved by six silicone diodes housed in a rectifier pack and connected as a 3 phase full wave bridge. The rectifier pack is attached to the outer face of the slip ring end bracket and contains also three 'field' diodes, at normal operating speeds, rectified current from the stator output windings flows through these diodes to provide self excitation of the rotor field, via brushes bearing on face type slip rings.

The slip rings are carried on a small diameter moulded drum attached to the rotor shaft outboard of the rotor shaft axle, while the outer ring has a mean diameter of ¾ in. By keeping the mean diameter of the slip ring to a minimum, relative speeds between brushes and rings, and hence wear, are also minimal. The slip rings are connected to the rotor field winding by wires carried in grooves in the rotor shaft.

The brush gear is housed in a moulding screwed to the outside of the slip ring end bracket. This moulding thus encloses the slip ring and brush gear assembly, and together with the shielded bearing, protects the assembly against the entry of dust and moisture.

The regulator is set during manufacture and requires no further attention. Briefly the 'thick film' regulator comprises resistors and conductors screen printed onto a 1 in square aluminium substrate. Mounted on the substrate are Lucas semi--conductors consisting of three transistors, a voltage reference diode and a field recirculation diode, and two capacitors. The internal connections between these components and the substrate are made by Lucas patented connectors. The whole assembly is 1/16 in thick and is housed in a recess in an

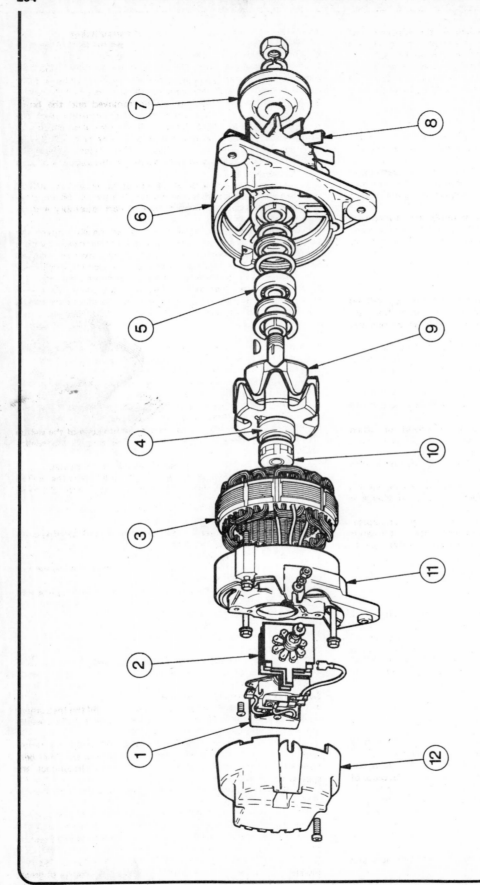

FIG. 13.19. EXPLODED VIEW OF ALTERNATOR

1 Brush gear and
   regulator assembly
2 Rectifier pack
3 Stator
4 Ball race
   bearing
5 Ball race bearing

6 Drive end bracket
7 Pulley
8 Fan
9 12 pole rotor
10 Slip ring
11 Slip ring end bracket
12 Cover

aluminium heat sink, which is attached to the slip ring end bracket. Complete hermetic sealing is achieved by a silicone rubber encapsulant to provide environmental protection.

Electrical connections to external circuits are brought out to Lucar connector blades, these being grouped to accept a moulded connector socket which ensures correct connections.

Alternator - routine maintenance —

1 The equipment has been designed for the minimum amount of maintenance in service. The only items subject to wear being the brushes and bearings.
2 Brushes should be examined after about 75,000 miles (120,000 km) and renewed if necessary. The bearings are pre-packed with grease for life, and should not require further attention.
3 Check the fan belt every 3,000 miles (5,000 km) for correct adjustment which should be 0.5 in (12.70 mm) total movement at the centre of the run between the alternator and water pump pulleys.

Alternator - special procedures

Whenever the electrical system of the car is being attended to, or external means of starting the engine are used, there are certain precautions that must be taken otherwise serious and expensive damage can result.
1 Always make sure that the negative terminal of the battery is earthed. If the terminal connections are accidentally reversed or if the battery has been reverse charged the alternator diodes will burn out.
2 The output terminal on the alternator marked 'BAT' or B+ must never be earthed but should always be connected directly to the positive terminal of the battery.
3 Whenever the alternator is to be removed or when disconnecting the terminals of the alternator circuit always disconnect the battery earth terminal first.
4 The alternator must never be operated without the battery to alternator cable connected.
5 If the battery is to be charged by external means always disconnect both battery cables before the external charge is connected.
6 Should it be necessary to use a booster charger or booster battery to start the engine always double check that the negative cable is connected to negative terminal and the positive cable to positive terminal.

Alternator - removal and refitting

1 Disconnect the battery leads.
2 Note the terminal connections at the rear of the alternator and disconnect the plug or multi pin connector.
3 Undo and remove the alternator adjustment arm bolt, slacken the alternator mounting bolts and push the alternator inwards towards the engine. Lift away the fan belt from the pulley.
4 Remove the remaining two mounting bolts and carefully lift the alternator away from the car.
5 Take care not to knock or drop the alternator.

Alternator - fault finding and repair

Due to the specialist knowledge and equipment required to test or service an alternator it is recommended that if the performance is suspect, the car be taken to an automobile electrician who will have the facilities for such work. Because of this recommendation, information is limited to the inspection and renewal of the brushes. Should the alternator not charge or the system be suspect the following points may be checked before seeking further assistance:
1 Check the fan belt tension.
2 Check the battery.
3 Check all electrical cable connections for cleanliness and security.

Alternator brushes - inspection, removal and refitting

1 Refer to Fig. 13.19 and undo and remove the two screws that hold on the end cover. Lift away the end cover.
2 To inspect the brushes correctly the brush holder moulding should be removed by undoing the two securing bolts and disconnecting the 'Lucar' connector to the diode plates.
3 With the brush holder moulding removed and the brush assemblies still in position check that they protrude from the face of the moulding by at least 0.2 in (5 mm). Also check that when depressed, the spring pressure is 7-10 oz (198 - 283 gms) when the end of the brush is flush with the face of the brush moulding. To be done with any accuracy this requires a push type spring scale.
4 Should either of the foregoing requirements not be fulfilled the spring assemblies must be renewed. This can be done by simply removing the holding screws of each assembly and replacing them.
5 With the brush holder moulding removed the slip rings on the face end of the rotor are exposed. These can be cleaned with a petrol soaked cloth and any signs of burning may be removed very carefully with fine glass paper. On no account should any other abrasive be used or any attempt at machining be made.
6 Reassemble in the reverse order of dismantling. Make sure that leads which may have been connected to any of the screws are reconnected correctly.

Combined light switch, panel switch, dual brake test switch and hazard light switch assembly - removal and refitting

1 From under the instrument panel, disconnect the wiring plugs from the light switch and the combined panel and dual brake test switch.
2 Disconnect the wires from the hazard warning light switch after making a careful note of their locations.
3 Depress the two lugs which secure the top edge of the switch assembly to the facia panel and pull the top of the switch assembly from the panel.
4 Depress the bottom two lugs and withdraw the switch.
5 Refitting is a reversal of removal. Simply press the switch into position so that the securing lugs engage with the facia panel.

Combined parking, direction indicator and hazard warning lamp assembly - removal and refitting

1 Disconnect the battery.
2 Disconnect the lamp leads by unplugging the connector within the engine compartment.
3 From under the front wing remove the two nuts which secure the lamp assembly and withdraw it.
4 Refitting is a reversal of removal.

Fuses

The separate fuse used for the reversing light circuit is now housed within the engine compartment.

Speedometer drive cable - renewal

1 On 1300 cc and 1600 cc models, reach behind the instrument panel and unscrew the knurled nut which secures the speedometer cable to the speedometer head.
2 On GT models, remove either the combined fuel/water temperature gauge or the tachometer as previously described. Reach through the instrument aperture and disconnect the speedometer cable from the head.
3 Withdraw the inner drive cable from the speedometer outer cable.
4 If the cable has broken, then its attachment to the gearbox extension housing will have to be disconnected (one bolt) and the complete cable assembly removed so that the broken section of inner cable may be removed.
5 When refitting a speedometer inner cable, ensure that it is inserted the correct way round and apply multi-purpose grease

to the bottom half of the cable. Insert the cable with a twisting motion and when it is fully in engagement with the gearbox drive it will lock and cannot be rotated by the fingers any more.
6   Tighten the knurled nut to the speedometer head ensuring that it is not cross threaded.

10 Suspension - dampers - steering

Front suspension units - refitting
On later model vehicles fitted with rebound stop brackets, these must be located so that they point inwards when the suspension units are installed in the vehicle. On the very latest models, the brackets have two lugs in which case the wider of

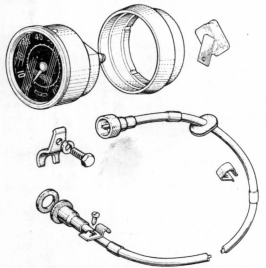

Fig. 13.20. Speedometer and drive cable components

the lugs should point inwards.

Steering gear - general description
Very late model vehicles incorporate a double row of recirculating balls within the steering nut instead of the single row used in earlier models.

11 Bodywork

General description
Outward appearance of late models is similar to earlier versions of the range. Vehicles built for the North American market however, incorporate side marker lights and over-riders and opening ventilators (quarter lights) are fitted as standard.

Laminated windscreens are installed on all North American models in the interest of road safety due to road conditions and regulations.

Bucket type seats are available with manual or automatic versions destined for the North American market.

Ventilator (quarter light) - removal and refitting
1   Remove the door interior panel, window regulator handle and interior door lock handle as described in Chapter 12, Section 12. Vehicles designed for overseas markets are fitted with a separate door interior lock knob instead of the standard two position remote control handle.
2   Temporarily refit the window regulator handle and wind the window fully down.
3   Unscrew and remove the screw which secures the lower end of the ventilator dividing channel.
4   Carefully drill out the two 'pop' rivets which secure the top of the dividing channel and then remove the three screws which secure the front edge of the ventilator to the door frame.
5   Pull the ventilator assembly rearwards and draw it out of the door cavity.
6   Installation is a reverse of removal.

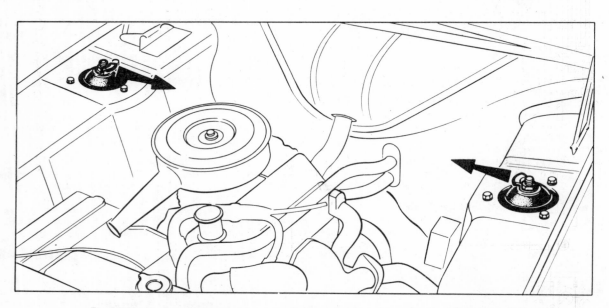

Fig. 13.21. Correct alignment of front suspension unit rebound stop brackets (single lug type)

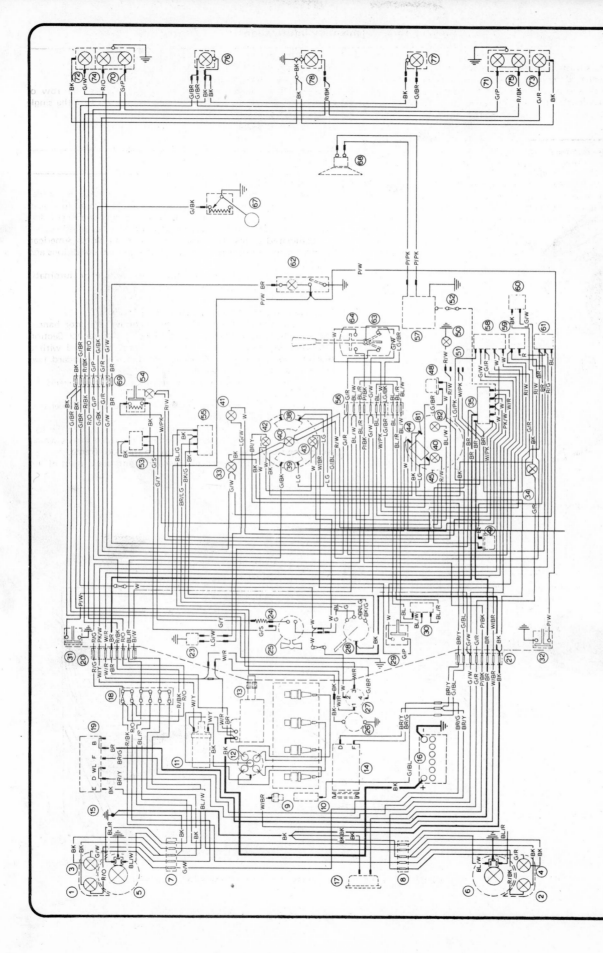

Fig. 13.22. Wiring diagram 1969 1300 cc and 1600 cc de-luxe models (North America) (See page 208 for coding)

CODING FOR WIRING DIAGRAMS 1969 – 1300 cc AND 1600 cc DE-LUXE AND GT (NORTH AMERICA)

Code	Wire Colour
R	Red
Bk	Black
Bi	Blue

Code	Item
1	RH parking lamp (front)
2	LH parking lamp (front)
3	RH turn indicator (front)
4	LH turn indicator (front)
5	RH headlamp
6	LH headlamp
7	RH front loom connector
8	LH front loom connector
9	Oil pressure switch
10	Temperature sender unit
11	Coil
12	Distributor
13	Starter motor
14	Generator
15	Body earth
16	Battery
17	Horn
18	Fuses
19	Regulator
20	RH bulkhead multi-way connector

Code	Wire Colour
W	White
Br	Brown
G	Green

Code	Item
21	LH bulkhead multi-way connector
22	Starter motor solenoid
23	Dual brake warning switch
24	Blower motor resistance
25	Heater motor
26	Back-up lamp switch (Manual trans.)
27	Back-up lamp switch (Automatic)
28	Windscreen wiper motor
29	Stop lamp switch
30	Dip switch
31	RH courtesy light switch
32	LH courtesy light switch
33	RH indicator warning light
34	LH indicator warning light
35	Ignition switch
36	Ammeter
37	Oil pressure gauge
38	Temperature gauge
39	Fuel gauge
40	Instrument illumination bulb

Code	Wire Colour
Y	Yellow
LG	Light Green
P	Purple

Code	Item
41	Dual brake warning light
42	Generator warning light
43	Oil pressure warning light
44	Instrument voltage stabiliser
45	Speedometer
46	Tachometer
47	Clock
48	Turn signal unit
49	Hazard unit
50	Automatic quadrant illumination lamp
51	R.P.O. connectors
52	Radio fuse
53	Heater switch
54	Cigar lighter
55	Windscreen wiper switch
56	Steering column connector
57	Radio
58	Hazard warning light switch
59	Panel light switch

Code	Wire Colour
O	Orange
Pk	Pink

Code	Item
60	Dual brake test switch
61	Lighting switch
62	Interior light
63	Turn signal switch
64	Horn switch
67	Fuel tank sender unit
68	Radio speaker
69	Rear wiring connector
70	RH stop lamp
71	LH stop lamp
72	RH turn indicator (rear)
73	LH turn indicator (rear)
74	RH parking lamp (rear)
75	LH parking lamp (rear)
76	RH back-up lamp
77	LH back-up lamp
78	License plate lamp
80	Tachometer earth
81	Speedometer earth
82	Main beam warning light

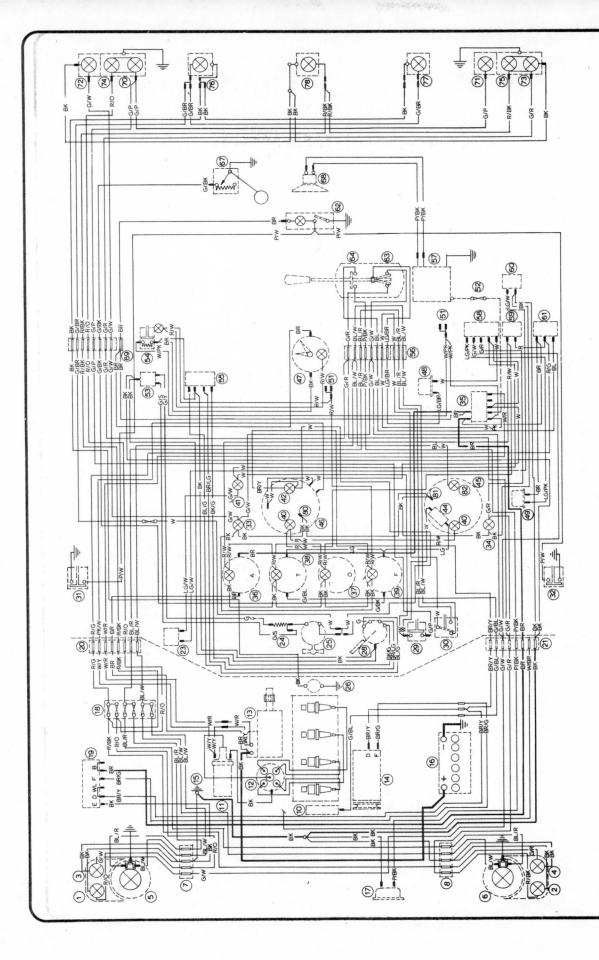

Fig. 13.23. Wiring diagram 1969 GT (North America)

Index

Metric conversion tables

Inches	Decimals	Millimetres	Millimetres to Inches		Inches to Millimetres	
			mm	Inches	Inches	mm
1/64	0.015625	0.3969	0.01	0.00039	0.001	0.0254
1/32	0.03125	0.7937	0.02	0.00079	0.002	0.0508
3/64	0.046875	1.1906	0.03	0.00118	0.003	0.0762
1/16	0.0625	1.5875	0.04	0.00157	0.004	0.1016
5/64	0.078125	1.9844	0.05	0.00197	0.005	0.1270
3/32	0.09375	2.3812	0.06	0.00236	0.006	0.1524
7/64	0.109375	2.7781	0.07	0.00276	0.007	0.1778
1/8	0.125	3.1750	0.08	0.00315	0.008	0.2032
9/64	0.140625	3.5719	0.09	0.00354	0.009	0.2286
5/32	0.15625	3.9687	0.1	0.00394	0.01	0.254
11/64	0.171875	4.3656	0.2	0.00787	0.02	0.508
3/16	0.1875	4.7625	0.3	0.01181	0.03	0.762
13/64	0.203125	5.1594	0.4	0.01575	0.04	1.016
7/32	0.21875	5.5562	0.5	0.01969	0.05	1.270
15/64	0.234375	5.9531	0.6	0.02362	0.06	1.524
1/4	0.25	6.3500	0.7	0.02756	0.07	1.778
17/64	0.265625	6.7469	0.8	0.03150	0.08	2.032
9/32	0.28125	7.1437	0.9	0.03543	0.09	2.286
19/64	0.296875	7.5406	1	0.03937	0.1	2.54
5/16	0.3125	7.9375	2	0.07874	0.2	5.08
21/64	0.328125	8.3344	3	0.11811	0.3	7.62
11/32	0.34375	8.7312	4	0.15748	0.4	10.16
23/64	0.359375	9.1281	5	0.19685	0.5	12.70
3/8	0.375	9.5250	6	0.23622	0.6	15.24
25/64	0.390625	9.9219	7	0.27559	0.7	17.78
13/32	0.40625	10.3187	8	0.31496	0.8	20.32
27/64	0.421875	10.7156	9	0.35433	0.9	22.86
7/16	0.4375	11.1125	10	0.39370	1	25.4
29/64	0.453125	11.5094	11	0.43307	2	50.8
15/32	0.46875	11.9062	12	0.47244	3	76.2
31/64	0.484375	12.3031	13	0.51181	4	101.6
1/2	0.5	12.7000	14	0.55118	5	127.0
33/64	0.515625	13.0969	15	0.59055	6	152.4
17/32	0.53125	13.4937	16	0.62992	7	177.8
35/64	0.546875	13.8906	17	0.66929	8	203.2
9/16	0.5625	14.2875	18	0.70866	9	228.6
37/64	0.578125	14.6844	19	0.74803	10	254.0
19/32	0.59375	15.0812	20	0.78740	11	279.4
39/64	0.609375	15.4781	21	0.82677	12	304.8
5/8	0.625	15.8750	22	0.86614	13	330.2
41/64	0.640625	16.2719	23	0.90551	14	355.6
21/32	0.65625	16.6687	24	0.94488	15	381.0
43/64	0.671875	17.0656	25	0.98425	16	406.4
11/16	0.6875	17.4625	26	1.02362	17	431.8
45/64	0.703125	17.8594	27	1.06299	18	457.2
23/32	0.71875	18.2562	28	1.10236	19	482.6
47/64	0.734375	18.6531	29	1.14173	20	508.0
3/4	0.75	19.0500	30	1.18110	21	533.4
49/64	0.765625	19.4469	31	1.22047	22	558.8
25/32	0.78125	19.8437	32	1.25984	23	584.2
51/64	0.796875	20.2406	33	1.29921	24	609.6
13/16	0.8125	20.6375	34	1.33858	25	635.0
53/64	0.828125	21.0344	35	1.37795	26	660.4
27/32	0.84375	21.4312	36	1.41732	27	685.8
55/64	0.859375	21.8281	37	1.4567	28	711.2
7/8	0.875	22.2250	38	1.4961	29	736.6
57/64	0.890625	22.6219	39	1.5354	30	762.0
29/32	0.90625	23.0187	40	1.5748	31	787.4
59/64	0.921875	23.4156	41	1.6142	32	812.8
15/16	0.9375	23.8125	42	1.6535	33	838.2
61/64	0.953125	24.2094	43	1.6929	34	863.6
31/32	0.96875	24.6062	44	1.7323	35	889.0
63/64	0.984375	25.0031	45	1.7717	36	914.4

Castrol GRADES

Castrol Engine Oils

Castrol GTX

An ultra high performance SAE 20W/50 motor oil which exceeds the latest API MS requirements and manufacturers' specifications. Castrol GTX with liquid tungsten† generously protects engines at the extreme limits of performance, and combines both good cold starting with oil consumption control. Approved by leading car makers.

Castrol XL 20/50

Contains liquid tungsten†; well suited to the majority of conditions giving good oil consumption control in both new and old cars.

Castrolite (Multi-grade)

This is the lightest multi-grade oil of the Castrol motor oil family containing liquid tungsten†. It is best suited to ensure easy winter starting and for those car models whose manufacturers specify lighter weight oils.

Castrol Grand Prix

An SAE 50 engine oil for use where a heavy, full-bodied lubricant is required.

Castrol Two-Stroke-Four

A premium SAE 30 motor oil possessing good detergency characteristics and corrosion inhibitors, coupled with low ash forming tendency and excellent anti-scuff properties. It is suitable for all two-stroke motor-cycles, and for two-stroke and small four-stroke horticultural machines.

Castrol CR (Multi-grade)

A high quality engine oil of the SAE-20W/30 multi-grade type, suited to mixed fleet operations.

Castrol CRI 10, 20, 30

Primarily for diesel engines, a range of heavily fortified, fully detergent oils, covering the requirements of DEF 2101-D and Supplement 1 specifications.

Castrol CRB 20, 30

Primarily for diesel engines, heavily fortified, fully detergent oils, covering the requirements of MIL-L-2104B.

Castrol R 40

Primarily designed and developed for highly stressed racing engines. Castrol 'R' should not be mixed with any other oil nor with any grade of Castrol.
†*Liquid Tungsten is an oil soluble long chain tertiary alkyl primary amine tungstate covered by British Patent No. 882,295.*

Castrol Gear Oils

Castrol Hypoy (90 EP)

A light-bodied powerful extreme pressure gear oil for use in hypoid rear axles and in some gearboxes.

Castrol Gear Oils (continued)

Castrol Hypoy Light (80 EP)

A very light-bodied powerful extreme pressure gear oil for use in hypoid rear axles in cold climates and in some gearboxes.

Castrol Hypoy B (90 EP)

A light-bodied powerful extreme pressure gear oil that complies with the requirements of the MIL-L-2105B specification, for use in certain gearboxes and rear axles.

Castrol Hi-Press (140 EP)

A heavy-bodied extreme pressure gear oil for use in spiral bevel rear axles and some gearboxes.

Castrol ST (90)

A light-bodied gear oil with fortifying additives

Castrol D (140)

A heavy full-bodied gear oil with fortifying additives.

Castrol Thio-Hypoy FD (90 EP)

A light-bodied powerful extreme pressure gear oil. This is a special oil for running-in certain hypoid gears.

Automatic Transmission Fluids

Castrol TQF
(Automatic Transmission Fluid)

Approved for use in all Borg-Warner Automatic Transmission Units. Castrol TQF also meets Ford specification M2C 33F.

Castrol TQ Dexron®
(Automatic Transmission Fluid)

Complies with the requirements of Dexron® Automatic Transmission Fluids as laid down by General Motors Corporation.

Castrol Greases

Castrol LM

A multi-purpose high melting point lithium based grease approved for most automotive applications including chassis and wheel bearing lubrication.

Castrol MS3

A high melting point lithium based grease containing molybdenum disulphide.

Castrol BNS

A high melting point grease for use where recommended by certain manufacturers in front wheel bearings when disc brakes are fitted.

Castrol Greases (continued)

Castrol CL

A semi-fluid calcium based grease, which is both waterproof and adhesive, intended for chassis lubrication.

Castrol Medium

A medium consistency calcium based grease.

Castrol Heavy

A heavy consistency calcium based grease.

Castrol PH

A white grease for plunger housings and other moving parts on brake mechanisms. *It must NOT be allowed to come into contact with brake fluid when applied to the moving parts of hydraulic brakes.*

Castrol Graphited Grease

A graphited grease for the lubrication of transmission chains.

Castrol Under-Water Grease

A grease for the under-water gears of outboard motors.

Anti-Freeze

Castrol Anti-Freeze

Contains anti-corrosion additives with ethylene glycol. Recommended for the cooling systems of all petrol and diesel engines.

Speciality Products

Castrol Girling Damper Oil Thin

The oil for Girling piston type hydraulic dampers.

Castrol Shockol

A light viscosity oil for use in some piston type shock absorbers and in some hydraulic systems employing synthetic rubber seals. It must not be used in braking systems.

Castrol Penetrating Oil

A leaf spring lubricant possessing a high degree of penetration and providing protection against rust.

Castrol Solvent Flushing Oil

A light-bodied solvent oil, designed for flushing engines, rear axles, gearboxes and gearcasings.

Castrollo

An upper cylinder lubricant for use in the proportion of 1 fluid ounce to two gallons of fuel.

Everyman Oil

A light-bodied machine oil containing anti-corrosion additives for both general use and cycle lubrication.

Printed by
J. H. HAYNES & Co. Ltd
Sparkford Yeovil Somerset
ENGLAND